WHERE
THE
ROAD
AND
THE
SKY
COLLIDE

ALSO BY K. T. BERGER

Zen Driving

WHERE THE ROAD AND THE SKY COLLIDE

America Through the Eyes of Its Drivers

K. T. BERGER

HENRY HOLT AND COMPANY
NEW YORK

Henry Holt and Company, Inc.
Publishers since 1866
115 West 18th Street
New York, New York 10011

Henry Holt® is a registered
trademark of Henry Holt and Company, Inc.

Published in Canada by Fitzhenry & Whiteside Ltd.,
91 Granton Drive, Richmond Hill, Ontario L4B 2N5.

Library of Congress Cataloging-in-Publication Data
Berger, K. T.
Where the road and the sky collide: America through the eyes of
its drivers/K. T. Berger.—1st ed.
p.   cm.
1. Automobile drivers—United States—Psychology.   2. Automobiles—
Social aspects—United States.   3. Automobile driving—United
States—Social aspects.   I. Title.
TL152.3.B48   1993   92-47047
303.48'32—dc20   CIP

ISBN 0-8050-1488-8

First Edition—1993

Designed by Brian Mulligan

Printed in the United States of America
All first editions are printed on acid-free paper. ∞

1   3   5   7   9   10   8   6   4   2

Due to limitations of space, permissions appear on page 415.

For
Parker Gerald Berger,
in hopes he'll drive in a more harmonious future.

Contents

Acknowledgments

Our deepest thanks are scarcely enough, but they wholeheartedly go to Leslie Franklin for her loving support and incredible patience and to Teresa Cirolia, whose love, insight, and endless research kept the book on track. Talk about crazy, she even clocked a good many unforgettable miles with us on the road.

We'd also like to offer a very special thanks to William Berger and Gerald Franklin.

The journey would have been tough without many people, but those who made it considerably easier were Carter Brooks, our computer whiz and eco-cheerleader; Robert Stricker, our agent; and Alison Juram, our editor.

Thanks to Tom Roberts for getting the book out of the starting gate and to Linda Hirneise at J. D. Power and Associates for showing us how to launch our questionnaire into the great beyond. Thanks to Sam Fejes for the snappy design and to David Hughes for the keen comments on the opening chapters. A hearty thanks to our sister Susan Stoltze, our "inside source" at Power and Associates.

Finally, we can hardly express our gratitude to all those across the country who offered their time, thoughts, and feelings. Their kindness in meeting with us and putting up with our endless questions is something we'll always remember.

PART I

OUT
OF
ALIGNMENT

One

S a v e
t h e
C a r

Nobody with a good car needs to be justified.
—Flannery O'Connor, *Wise Blood*

The Biscayne smoked. I mean it seriously coughed out killer smoke: a white billowing contrail as I tooled down the freeway. I didn't care. I bought the thing for $200 during the time I was living in a dingy flat in San Francisco, a white Chevy beast simply known as the Biscayne. It always ran and got nothing for its trouble but gas. The driver's side window was a piece of clear plastic held in place with duct tape. And it was big; people got out of your way, you didn't need to worry about keeping it between the lines on the road. It never had any insurance—you could wreck it and not give a damn. You could Steve McQueen it down the steep San Francisco hills, bottom out its suspension, and launch it off the lip of the next hill. It felt great! My friend Leslie got a ticket on I-80 for its assault on the environment. She said it was my fault. I never paid any attention to the ticket.

Then one sad day I had it on the sidewalk, hood up, peering inside. I called my dad, an unfathomably patient mechanic who always fixed our family cars, and told him: "I took the air cleaner off to adjust the carburetor and accidentally dropped the little nut into the carburetor intake. What should I do?" "No problem," he said, "just so you don't start the engine." Ooops. No wonder the engine had sounded like a dryer with a dime in it.

3

My dad said that was the little nut, spinning madly around inside one of the cylinder chambers. Soon tiny bits of finely shredded metal would cause the poor Biscayne's engine to seize. I called ABC Wreckers and they came and towed it to the scrap yard. I used the $35 to take myself to dinner and see Pink Floyd's *The Wall*. (It was a ghastly film.)

Now, a decade later, I was sitting comfortably in a new Dodge Caravan, complete with windows, insurance, and—of course—a catalytic converter. I was under an aching blue sky in Miami, Florida, 3,000 miles from my San Francisco home, idling in bumper-to-bumper traffic on I-95 ("Jive-95" to the local commuters), heading toward my next interview. I was embarking on a sort of field study. A car biologist, you could call me. I was out here in the Wild Kingdom, taking notes, exploring what even the most casual observer would notice as the dominant life-form roaming the countryside. I had been on the road for over a month, studying this particular organism—part human, part machine—trying to make sense of its role in a vast, complex ecosystem. Could this organism evolve, or would it continue on its apparent course of destruction, thereby assuring its extinction?

I was raised in Los Angeles, where you might say I was naturally trained as a car biologist. Just as many wildlife biologists grew up in the outbacks of Idaho and Montana, I grew up in the urban wilds and freeway wilderness of L.A., home of wide snaking rivers of cement, teeming machines, and legless car-conditioned inhabitants swarming beneath a nimbus of dirty yellow haze, a mixture of nitrous oxides, hydrocarbons, and sunshine. "I mean no one," exclaimed ecologist Paul Ehrlich, "in their right mind can justify Los Angeles." But I liked it. To me it was a happy motorhead way of life. I prayed like a monk for the day I turned sixteen and could get my driver's license. Thereafter I went nowhere without a car. Need a quart of milk? No problem, I'd take Dad's MG to the corner store and see who I could race along the way. Walk to school, take a bus to a concert? You've got to be kidding. I loved the freedom and romance of driving, and was well aware that having a car could rapidly up your social fortunes. I remember when the nerdiest loner in my high school bought a lime green Plymouth Road Runner. It was a shameless attempt to boost his self-esteem and win friends, but it worked wonderfully, and everyone seemed to accept it as a natural transformation. Cars never ceased to excite my imagination. *Hot Rod* magazine was practically my introduction to the written word, *Bullitt* was my favorite movie, and "Little Deuce Coupe" was the first Beach Boys song with which I could honestly identify (I didn't surf).

But as I got older, my perception reluctantly began to shift. After countless years of idling on the freeway in Los Angeles, and now in the San Francisco Bay Area, with little to do but inhale exhaust fumes and think about why it took over an hour to go twenty miles, I began to see that the ecosystem was in serious trouble. I began to realize that the cultural mindset that had turned America into a gridlocked, car-dependent society now seemed dangerously outmoded, incapable of addressing the mire of ecological problems the automobile had left in its wake.

FROM THE POORHOUSE TO THE GREENHOUSE

Recently the car celebrated its hundredth birthday. At practically the same time the great Interstate Highway System, 42,500 miles of superhighway connecting our cities, begun thirty-five years ago during the Eisenhower administration, saw its last stretch of pavement laid. America is now linked by 3.9 million miles of highways and streets, which translates to about forty yards for every car. Ten percent of our arable land and 50 percent of our urban areas are paved over with parking lots and roads. Our cities are immense, the latest census showing that people are streaming into them from rural America in greater numbers every day. In fact, our definition of a city is no longer adequate. Who can distinguish what is Phoenix and what is Tempe; what is Los Angeles and what is Long Beach; what is Baltimore and what is Washington, D.C.; what is Atlanta and what is Cobb County? These massive urban regions and the infrastructures that keep them functioning—namely, the great swaths of asphalt that serve the car—are beginning to buckle under their own weight. In California the number of registered vehicles has more than doubled in the last two decades—in Los Angeles, where they're tearing their hair out wondering what to do, there are 10,000 autos per mile of freeway. Everywhere you turn it's sprawl and gridlock, with little relief in sight. Nevertheless, our nation's population continues to grow, and the number of cars grows three times faster than the population. So if you think the traffic is bad now, you'd better start saving up for a helicopter. Using advanced computer modeling, the United States General Accounting Office predicted that by 2005 traffic delay ("the additional time experienced by a driver beyond what would reasonably be desired for a given trip") in cities across the country will have increased 452 percent!

One hundred years after its invention the car is in big trouble. Traffic and its attendant emotional stress (six-shooters and Valium in the glove compartment) rank as the most dramatic problem of driving today, but no less consequential is the economic stress—the ever-increasing expense of owning and operating an automobile. Simply keeping the thing on the road, with gas, oil, repairs, and insanely expensive insurance, drains a good 20 percent off our annual incomes. Cars are also absurdly subsidized. Factoring in the hidden costs of paving roads, parking, street maintenance, police, and municipal medical aid, we pay, through taxes, another $2,400 per car annually. (If we added these subsidies to the price of gasoline, we'd be shelling out $4.50 per gallon.) Yet these taxes hardly keep our city governments solvent. The Worldwatch Institute reports that driving alone costs our city governments $60 billion a year, exacerbating already horrendous regional deficits. Then there's the $55 billion we spend on imported oil every year and the billions of dollars our economy loses as our nation's employees sit in traffic producing nothing but anxiety. Will Rogers could hardly have known how prescient he was when he remarked in 1930: "We are the first nation in the history of the world to go to the poorhouse in an automobile."

The car could be said to be teetering on the slippery edge of extinction. "Whether by force or choice," declared Andrew Kimbrell, policy director for the Foundation on Economic Trends, in Washington, D.C., "the days of the automobile are numbered." Other experts say it has already doomed itself: having completely ruined its environment, the poor creature will go the way of those organisms that outstrip their habitat and destroy their own sustainability. Like the famous deer herd of Arizona's Kaibab National Forest, autos are eating themselves out of a home and out of existence. The ultimate problem, of course, is overpopulation—188 million vehicles, each one being driven farther and farther each year (a total of 2 trillion miles in 1990). Another problem is downdraw: cars depleting their own food supply (fossil fuel) beyond what the environment can replace (in one hundred years we've gobbled up 80 percent of what has taken 100 million years to deposit). Then there is the destruction of the car's symbiotic relationship with humans—poisoning us with smog, or killing us outright (45,000 deaths a year). Forests and lakes are also falling prey to the car, by dint of the sulfur and nitrous oxides pouring out of its tailpipe, causing acid rain. In fact, the car is mounting an assault on the planet itself: the chlorofluorocarbons escaping from its air conditioners are responsible for 50 percent of the damage to the ozone layer; the carbon dioxide and other offending vapors it sends snaking into the atmosphere are trapping the earth's warmth and causing the much-ballyhooed Greenhouse Effect. You won't have to worry about traffic congestion in L.A., Houston, or New York after the planet warms up and the polar ice melts—they'll be under water.

CAR WARS

The car as Grim Reaper is certainly not a specter that has appeared on the American scene overnight. Even in the heady postwar days, when President Eisenhower declared, "Automobiles mean progress for our country, greater happiness, and greater standards of living," social critics began uncovering the dark side of progress in the unceasing rise of auto fatalities, culturally barren suburbs, uniform houses seemingly built in deference to the garage, and gawdy roadside strips—motels, restaurants, and gas stations bound together in a veritable hodgepodge of architectural styles—that diverted travelers and robbed many rural communities of their livelihood. Taking his cue from the 1930s' regional planner and author Lewis Mumford, who once sarcastically remarked that America's national flower should be the highway cloverleaf, John Keats (not the poet, mind you, but the American social critic) in 1958 was the first to pull no punches in his assessment of the "insolent chariot." In his rather heated view, cars were "overblown, overpriced monstrosities built by oafs for thieves to sell to mental defectives."

As Detroit continued to produce bigger, faster, and more dangerous gas-guzzlers into the seventies, and Americans continued to buy them at an ever more rapid pace (from 1955 to 1974 the number of cars on U.S. highways doubled, totaling 105 million), critics lined up to take their shots. The loudest rounds were fired by *Car and Driver* magazine defector John Jerome and sociologist and city planner Kenneth Schneider. In *The Death of the Automobile*, Jerome canvassed the auto's history and concluded, "The men who perpetuated the golden era of runaway automobile merchandising will join those other American rogue-villains, who, in the pursuit of their niches, managed to wreak visible destruction on a land ever so large as this. The buffalo hunters fit the category. The exterminators of the Indians. The lumber barons, strip miners, railroad magnates; the professional rapists of land, water, air, souls. The competition is keen for the dubious honor, but we are beginning to see that perhaps the car-makers are the ones who have destroyed the most of all. The car is a bad machine— and the solution is not to build a better bad machine, but rather not to build bad machines. The auto must go." Schneider, meanwhile, was less obsessed with the car's destruction of the American landscape than with its assault on our psyche. "It's tyranny!" he bellowed in *Autokind vs. Mankind*. "*Tyrannus mobilitis* is a social malignancy that draws men into inescapable dependence and makes a tragicomedy of the human struggle for worthiness." In his view, the car has reduced humans to some new aberrant form of being, "a society of invertebrates as clumsy as a convention of turtles. The way we honor our new shells makes one wonder whether we have an atavistic urge to junk our whole mammalian inheritance."

Today, though, the doomsayers and neo-Luddites may as well retire their bullhorns, for the flagrant problems of driving have become lodged like a bad horror movie in mainstream culture. And nothing has slammed home this point more than our precarious dependence on Middle Eastern oil. Although we didn't sit like perfect fools in long gas lines—as we did in 1973, when Saudi Arabia cut off our oil supply to punish us for our support of Israel in the Yom Kippur War, and in 1979, when the disintegration of the Shah's government led to Iran's freeze on oil exports—the 1991 crisis in the Persian Gulf publicized like never before our cars' starring role in U.S. economy, foreign policy, and ultimately, war.

As Iraq invaded Kuwait, President Bush summed up the dangers: "Our jobs, our way of life, our own freedom and the freedom of friendly countries around the world would all suffer if control of the world's great oil reserves fell into the hands of Saddam Hussein." It wasn't difficult to read between the lines, and Russell Baker, the *New York Times's* widely syndicated columnist, sardonically echoed what many Americans believed to be the real reason for our military presence in the Middle East: "President Bush says the American way of life is threatened. He apparently means our ability to pick up the carry-out fried chicken in the drive-by lane at the fast-food shop, as well as our power to sit one-commuter-per-car for 45 minutes every day on the way home from work." During the crisis, millions of TV viewers tuned in to "Primetime Live" to learn that if the 13 percent of

Americans who drive less than twenty-one miles a day switched to electric cars, the nation would not need to import another drop of oil from the Middle East. Practically every other day metropolitan newspapers offered readers stories on alternative modes of transportation and feasible alternative fuels such as methanol and natural gas. An event in the Bay Area provided one of the most lasting images. As the war erupted, thousands of protesters formed a human wall to block cars from crossing the Bay Bridge at rush hour. Carrying signs that read "No Blood for Oil," the protesters' message was clear: sit there, alone, in your two tons of steel belching noxious gases, and think about it for a while. Accumulate a little guilt.

And I did. For I was one of the thousands of drivers tied up in the monstrous traffic jam. I kept my window rolled down, thinking I would hear some colorful curses from people berating the protesters for causing the traffic mess. Strangely enough, drivers seemed to be bearing it all with silent dignity. Or maybe it was just weary resignation.

Automobile industry watchdog David Abrahamson recently issued the storm warning that we have entered a "time when the social costs of the automobile will be accorded far more attention than its social benefits." It is the environmentalists who have taken up the cudgels to make sure that attention never lags. "Blight, Smog, Gridlock, Sprawl, and Death" reads the headline of the Sierra Club's 1990 Green State of the Nation Report, devoted entirely to the automobile and its attendant horrors. Joined by the Worldwatch Institute, the Environmental Defense Fund, and others, such powerful conservation outfits have begun rallying a significant part of their work forces, from regional volunteers to national lawyers, behind automobile and transportation issues. They have begun challenging Washington and state legislatures over the incessant spread of highways, which add more cars emitting more pollutants to an area; the lack of funds for mass transportation; and the failure to develop alternative fuels. They have also stepped up their lobbying efforts against Detroit and the oil companies, striving for less-polluting cars and cleaner-burning gasoline.

As these influential environmentalists gear up for the attack, today's auto manufacturers, the largest corporations in America, are trembling in their proverbial boots. Traffic congestion, stricter safety standards, urban air pollution, and global warming are causing panic in Detroit because they are bringing the Big Three car companies, already reeling from the loss of billions of dollars in sales over the last decade, face-to-face with their

greatest enemy: government regulation. They're trembling over Los Angeles smog crusaders like James Lents, of the South Coast Air Quality
Management District, who makes no secret of his intention to single-
handedly bend the will of the car companies to his design. They're worried
about urban areas like Minneapolis, whose city fathers, taking their cue
from Tokyo, are considering banning cars entirely from a whole section of
downtown. They're worried about Democrats like California senator Barbara Boxer, who is restlessly pursuing legislation to force them to build cars
that get 39 miles to the gallon instead of today's 27.5. "This one step," said
Boxer, "would eliminate Persian Gulf imports, eliminate the need to make
the air cleaner, save the consumer money, and lower the trade deficit." To
which the auto industry replied that it can't make cars get better mileage
because it can't make them any lighter. "You can't downsize anymore,"
groaned Chrysler chairman Lee Iacocca in a 1990 *Playboy* interview.
"That's like going on a diet and losing 40 pounds, then the doctor says,
'Lose 40 more, then 40 more.' Then you're dead."

REVOLUTION

The heated battle over the car is clearly rocking American society. Our
increasing awareness of the car's wicked ways is forcing us to question our
way of life. In national surveys over the last decade, Americans have ranked
transportation among the top three problems. In my own Bay Area, a
region of nine counties with a population of 6.2 million people, residents
have ranked transportation as the worst problem—above drugs, homeless-
ness, and crime—for the last eight years in a row.

In Richmond, just northeast of San Francisco, Ken Ryan, transportation chair of the Sierra Club, sat back with his hands folded over his
stomach like the Buddha. "We can either modify the transportation system
or throw up our hands and let it get worse," he said. He told me without
reservation that transportation is the predominant social issue into the next
century: "We had the segregation issue in the sixties; we had the abortion
issue in the seventies and eighties; and we're seeing the dust settle on both of
those. But I think this thing with highways and automobiles is going to be
every bit as big. It's a revolution." In other words, something has to give.
Finding out *what* was the inspiration for my expedition.

I initiated my journey with a random mailing of a couple of thousand questionnaires to drivers from all walks of life from all over the country. I wasn't trying to produce a scientific survey; mainly I wanted to introduce myself and ask people if they'd like to talk in person about living and driving in the land of the automobile. A good portion said, Yes, give me a call when you get to town. I guess they were intrigued by questions such as:

- When I sell, trade in, have stolen, or smash beyond repair my car, I feel like I've lost a close friend. True? False?
- If I had to pick one trait, I'd say most other drivers on the road in my area are: (a) inconsiderate numbskulls; (b) well-mannered and sensible; (c) just parts of the road environment.
- I would enjoy a more pastoral world, free of the gizmos and machines humans have created. True? False?
- I would be willing to change my driving habits to improve the environment. True? False?
- Which is more true? (a) While driving I feel connected with the environment around me; or (b) While driving I feel separate from my surroundings.

Essentially I wanted to uncover as many facets as possible of drivers' changing attitudes, especially their thoughts about driving's impact on the environment. I certainly wasn't trying to make anyone feel guilty about the hydrocarbons their cars were pumping into the atmosphere. But that didn't stop people from mistaking me for an environmentalist, another crazy Californian on a quest. Again and again I had to assure them that I was merely studying the ecology of driving. Only once did I make the mistake of actually referring to myself as a "car biologist." That was while chatting with a guy who worked in a Texaco station in Amarillo. "Whad'ya doin'?" he said. "Studyin' how Buicks mate?"

EVOLUTION OF THE SPECIES

No, I was attempting to get a reading on the degree of responsibility people felt for the machine that was such a crucial part of us. For driving and cars are synonymous with American life. And whether or not we wish to admit it, one of the most important and emotional relationships in our adult lives is the one we have with the automobile. Ruth Hall, of Hamden, Connecticut, told me she had a "particularly affectionate relationship" with her VW Rabbit and during a recent trip to Europe made a point of visiting its "birthplace" in Wolfsburg, Germany.

One evening, in the neon desert oasis that is Las Vegas, I sat and talked with Mary Jamison about dream cars. Mary, fifty-six, had recently moved to Las Vegas from Florida; up and left a good-paying job and crossed the country in her blue Toyota truck. But things had not worked out all that well and Mary had been struggling. She lived alone and barely made ends meet by working part-time at a dry cleaner's and doing some house cleaning.

At first she had her famous blue truck to protect her. She often dreamt of the truck. The two of them would travel surrealistic highways and be approached by danger—something sinister or strange and unknown; once it was a bright red car racing at them—but the danger always evaporated. Mary said she'd be behind the wheel of her truck in her dreams and look out the window at "all the garbage stuff in my life." Then she'd gaze at the steering wheel and watch it become luminous, growing brighter and brighter while she herself became more self-assured. In their waking relationship it was the same. She would think nothing of driving alone to California to visit friends. "I had a very personal attachment to the car," she said. "I took as good a care of that car as you would your own body."

Mary lost her ally the summer after she arrived in Las Vegas. She was coming out of a parking lot and a cab ran a stop sign. The Toyota was totaled. When she recovered physically she went down to the dealership to look at her truck. But the guy at Toyota said, "No, you don't wanna see it." He had kindly put all of Mary's possessions in a cardboard box. "I never dreamt of it again," Mary told me.

"I feel now something is missing," she said. She was lonely. She no longer felt confident enough to visit her friends in California. Her new car was an eighty-six Ford Tempo, but Mary didn't like it. She felt that because of its automatic transmission she had less control over the car. Perhaps over everything. The color of the car, she was told, was silver. But Mary said it was gray.

The automobile has become for people, in the words of the late French critic Roland Barthes, "a purely magical object." An emotional passage. Me and my car. It's certainly a special sort of relationship. More attention goes into selecting a car than a pet. "They satisfy some of our basic needs," said veterinarian and author Dr. Bruce Fogle about pets, but I personally don't see cars as much different. "Through talking with them, touching them, or just looking at them, we fulfill our instinctive need for attachment." Through my questionnaire, I learned that nearly half of the drivers gave their cars names, such as Honey, Old Bitch, the Zephyr, Patty Wagon, Hank the Tank, Gray Ghost, and LeMans from Hell. That same percentage also admitted to talking to their cars, whether to offer them encouragement and a pat on the dashboard to start in cold weather, or to cuss them out for breaking down in traffic. One young driver from Minneapolis wrote me that her sometimes "obnoxious" Olds Cutlass, Boris, literally talked back to her, if only to say: "A door is ajar." "We have been together for a lot of miles," wrote a retired Kansas City man of his 1962 Ford. No wonder "Knight Rider" was such a popular TV show. It was easy to relate to Michael walking down the sidewalk in a pensive, contemplative mood while KITT, his jet black computer-controlled sedan, followed respectfully on the street behind him.

Quickly imagine everything you know about a particular person and I bet you will include his or her car. It's who we are; it's how we function; it's more than a convenience, a mere possession, or a symbol of social status or identity. A car is a close friend, a family member, part of the family home. It even has its own room in the house—the garage.

From the car's cozy, freewheeling interior ("a living room on wheels," read an old Ford advertisement) we directly perceive our world. In our car we come into contact with every level and aspect of life in this country; there's no place we can't drive to, very little we can't see, or do, from within our automobile. In fact, as we know, the very way America physically looks, the shape and feel of our cities, the layout of our rural communities, the very look and behavior of a neighborhood, is shaped by the car. Pass through any typical suburban area and you'll see very few people in their front yards, no one on the sidewalks; they stay behind quiet facades, going nowhere, even a few blocks, except in their cars, as though walking was a vile habit and the air was poisoned (which, of course, in many cities it is). Everywhere we go we want to go with our cars.

Living in America without a car is worse than being single. At this point in our history, the car is practically braided into our genetic code.

Indeed, the car is part of us; there is more to this relationship than a statement of exaggerated life-style and mechanical fascination. To sound the obvious, we are not sedentary creatures. Our need to move over good distances is part of our innate makeup. British author J. G. Ballard, who has often placed cars center stage in his novels, once wrote that "apart from its obvious role as a handy means of transport, the car satisfies one basic human requirement—our need to understand as much as possible of the world around us." Our instincts to hunt, to work, to forage, to shop, to explore, to vacation—all these instincts are incorporated in the basic impulse toward movement. In a classical biological sense, this impulse toward movement is a "force." It's a force that drives us, and in the natural course of human development, it has led to the car. Raised in a world of perpetual motion and gadgetry as we are, the desire to drive is no more unnatural to us than the desire to walk. We used to walk, now we drive. That's evolution.

In America, this *driving force* has created a deep and abiding sense of freedom, something we often take for granted nowadays. Martin Wachs, UCLA urban planning professor and a member of the board of directors of Commuter Computer, L.A.'s car pool organization, reminded me of this one hot smoggy morning in Los Angeles. "Taking away the car reduces people's freedom of choice in very rational and explicable ways," he said. "I tend to be relatively committed to a rational approach. You have an enormously larger range of choices if you have the automobile. I have a sixteen-year-old and a twenty-year-old. I've been through that part of the life cycle where as soon as they turn sixteen they want their license, and about a week later they demand their own car. Given the way things are so spread out in this metropolitan area, I don't blame them. If I were in their situation I would want the same thing, because with the car they can do so much more in a limited period of time than they can without one. A car increases our choices. We can go to more schools, more social events, more parks, more doctors' offices, more movie theaters if we have a car. And we want to do those things. It's certainly a contribution to freedom that people value highly."

Professor Wachs grew testy when I insisted that driving wasn't always such a rational act, that sometimes, no matter where we're going, it's simply fun or relaxing. Maybe he was reluctant to accept my view because it's impossible to qualify the driving force in a tidy academic survey. I didn't mind, though, for I remain convinced that driving for pleasure runs deep in the American character, and that people are still crazy about cars for many reasons other than their practical value. Specialty car clubs, touring groups, professional auto racing, joyriding on country roads, cruising the boulevard in Dad's Acura—all these things are alive and well and proof that cars continue to animate American culture. (Is there any greater expression of Americans' utterly mad love affair with cars than stadium Tractor Pulls?)

The driving force has helped foster our most endearing trait as Americans, that fierce independence and individualism we prize and protect above all other things. Although Jefferson didn't know it, Americans wouldn't truly declare their independence until they got cars. Stated David Halberstam, author of *The Reckoning*, the great contemporary tome on the auto industry, the car "fit the nature of the people—restless, independent, less rooted than other people." It didn't take long for the car to weave itself deep into the fabric of the American psyche. To Jungian psychologist James Hillman, the car embodies a "dominant fantasy of self-determination and goal-directedness which governs our notions of work, individuality, and dignity. We do believe we are more dignified and individualized behind the wheel of our own car in a stream of ten thousand other such cars than sitting in a bus or train." Dr. Hillman made his remarks in a speech sponsored by the Center for Civic Leadership in Dallas, in response to the area's transportation problems. He went on to say that the car is a part of our larger fantasy of individualism, of ego control, the "fantasy that identifies the control of motion with the control of individual fate," which he called an essential part of Western thought. "I, the modern secular ego, is the self-moved mover, which is precisely what the word *auto-mobile* means. As long as I am driving, the wheel is in my hands; no matter the facts of death on the road, my fantasy assures me I have death in my control."

Today, though, the products of the driving force—freedom of mobility, pleasure, and autonomy—are in serious danger: the agonies of driving have caught up with the ecstasies. Cars have reached a critical mass, their sheer numbers alone placing them in peril. Freedom of choice may be enhanced by being able to drive to twenty-five different restaurants, but we're seldom hungry after all that time fighting our way across town. It's certainly a blast to take off for the mountains in a Toyota 4×4 Ridgerunner, but the thrill is gone when we're the fifteenth person in line at a traffic light and the mountains are obscured by smog. The sense of autonomy, of being masters of our fate, seems somewhat beside the point when we're wedged in an amorphous mass of Monday morning rush-hour traffic, going nowhere.

The preeminent zoologist George Schaller once asked, Is a tiger in a zoo really a tiger? He asked not as a philosopher, but as a biologist. Removed from its natural setting, with which it has become interwoven over millions of years of evolutionary accommodation, is the tiger we are viewing the real tiger? Schaller emphatically said it is not. An integral part of the tiger's nature *is* its setting. So I ask, Is a car driven along at a stop-and-go crawl in crowded, smoggy, congested urban traffic really a car? Its own excesses seem to have warped its original nature. And without some resolution to its sad plight, it seems pretty much doomed.

But I wonder: Would we miss it? What would it be like to look across the vast expanse of some urban plain, such as Sacramento or Denver or Atlanta, and not see any cars? Nothing but empty asphalt, devoid of motion. Would we miss them like the great herds of buffalo?

I believe many of us would. Sherri Livingstone of Phoenix told me that she bought her sixty-nine Buick from a finicky couple back in Ohio and that when she moved west, the couple insisted she send pictures—of the car. (Sherri did.) I know my dad missed his truck. He had a seventy-three Toyota pickup with 400,000 miles on it. He loved that truck. It had been on scores of hunting and fishing trips, it had been to visit a thousand clients, and it had hauled his work, his dogs, and his sons' motorcycles. When it finally stopped running, it sat for years on the same spot in my parents' driveway, its tires sagging for want of air. My dad always intended to fix it, but his health prevented him from doing so. Then one day he made the fatal call. "It's gone," he said sadly. "They came and hauled it off. Hooked it up and dragged it away. It had great big teardrops rolling down its windshield."

We would miss the car because it is a part of ourselves—it is our legs, it shapes our sense of self. Arthur C. Clarke once remarked that the species to replace *Homo sapiens*, just as *Homo sapiens* replaced *Homo erectus* in the natural evolutionary process, would be something called *Homo machinis*—part human, part machine. Similar images are rife in popular culture, from the Arnold Schwarzenegger cyborg in *The Terminator* to the conscious robot Data in "Star Trek: The Next Generation" to the synthesized rhythms and machinelike movements of the dance-rap group C & C Music Factory to novelist William Gibson's cyberspace cowboys, characters who have "jacks" behind their ears into which they can plug various software programs that interface with their neurons and provide them with new skills and knowledge. Today we practically take this fusion of flesh and machine for granted.

We are creatures reliant on sophisticated electronic gadgetry—computers, stereos, telecommunications. But in this rush of new technology, we tend to forget that by far the most influential machine of all is the car. William Gibson said that the personal computer has helped him in writing his stories, but it hasn't affected his perception of reality as much as the car. "Having a car that works, that one can drive around, changes one's view of one's environment," he said. "I think things like that have a more direct impact on me."

Just as the early Native American Indians thought the first Spanish conquistadors and their horses were one being, persons and their cars are one being, a sort of new centaur. Cars have become a second skin. When we climb into our cars and cinch ourselves into the seat belts it's as though we're literally putting on our cars, as we would a suit of clothes. The car responds to our every move: its fenders, bumpers, and tires are extensions of our body; it brakes and accelerates and turns as a result of something *we* do, not on its own. Our awareness and experience of driving flow out of a place other than the one reserved for walking or running: we think and act as something different. We *are* different. Again, our symbiosis with the car is so complete we might as well be considered a single entity, a new species that inhabits its own fundamental niche (sans competition) in the American ecological community. Perhaps we should coin a new term for this species. How about *hucar* (half human, half car)?

If nothing else, this hucar species, this car/driver entity, is an actual psychological verity. In their psyches, most Americans are part human, part machine. The car exists as part of our image of ourselves; as the psychologist James Hillman might say, it's part of our soul-making process: the automobile and driving are images that we include in how we view ourselves and our relationship with the world, interwoven into the fabric of our mind and being. To this degree, this "species" is *alive*.

The most direct evidence of this is the role cars play in dreams. Dr. Sarah White, of Drawbridge Dream Consultants in Lancaster, Pennsylvania, told me that the constant recurrence of cars in people's dreams made her "wonder how people got around in dreams before the auto." As I crossed the country making my field observations, I made a few side trips into the

American unconscious, curious as to what the driving landscape looked like there. With the help of the Association for the Study of Dreams, I accumulated hundreds of dreams from people from Vermont to Oregon. I soon discovered that cars and driving are quite prominent images in the nightworld.

"Where the house is the common psychic image for the dreamer's felt sense of his or her existence," Dr. White said, "the car seems to embody the dreamer's sense of how he or she is currently functioning." Cars and driving in dreams are broad metaphors that display how life's going.

"I was driving upside down and backward," Lucy Moorman from St. Louis explained. "I was lying there and the car started without me. On the highway there were accidents that had happened everywhere, and I was trying to steer through this." Lucy said that this dream perfectly represented how she was traveling through her life at the time.

Audrey Wood, of Prescott, Arizona, told me that she had been under a great deal of stress. "I had a sense of being a failure and not knowing what to do. I owned a lovely little bookstore which I kept hoping would turn a profit, but instead drained away my money. My ex-husband lost his job and moved in with me, and his constant criticism and refusal to leave added to my frustration. In my dream I'm driving at night on an unfamiliar road in a heavy downpour. I was alone and felt compelled to keep going although I could not see a thing. But somehow I stayed on the road. This surprised me in the dream and I woke up thinking that somehow I would make it."

Often someone else is driving the dreamer's car. "I was sitting in the backseat of a car being driven by my father in a reckless manner, and we ultimately went off a cliff," Elaine Aberer, of Hollis Hills, New York, related, adding that the dream was symbolic of her childhood in general and that it helped her get on the road to recovery. Often, for women, their husband is driving, controlling their life. Karen Pierce, of Newtown, Connecticut, dreamed: "I got *really mad* and hit Dan across the chest with a crowbar. I pushed down the gas pedal and turned the steering wheel hard from the passenger's seat. We did a few 360s and almost went flying out the door, which was open. I got out and said, 'I'll walk home.' "

Dreamers get taken for a ride and head off on some foolish venture. They spin their wheels and drive in circles. Often it's a matter of how the car's being driven—with anger, haltingly, recklessly, too fast—that expresses how the person's functioning in his or her waking life. People often drive around in the nightworld with the car in reverse. Mechanical conditions are also a tip-off: the steering wheel won't turn or the brakes won't work, hinting at an inability to change course, losing control. Dreamers mindlessly follow dream highways and get (as in life) hopelessly lost, or, calling on a rare sense of faith, find themselves in some beautiful, unknown terrain. They're able to cross creaky bridges, making an important transition in life; or they get stuck in the middle of the bridge, too afraid or uncertain to initiate change. Even people who don't drive find themselves behind the wheel of a dream car, often to escape unsavory situations or help someone in an emergency. All these images are reflections of personal driving forces governing our waking lives. They're a dynamic expression of self.

Just as we can't separate ourselves from our cars, we can't separate our role as drivers from the larger picture—the processes that keep American society running. In fact, no aspect of our daily existence is as influential as driving. In our cars on the road we influence foreign policy, which is based on maintaining politic relations with Mideast countries whose oil keeps us nourished; we influence domestic economy, one out of every six jobs in which involves a car; we influence the shape of our cities, whose sprawling suburbs are built on the notion that we can drive wherever we need to go, no matter how far; we influence the very air we breathe, which is tainted daily by our emissions; we influence the state of legislation, which annually issues new laws and regulations that invariably tap our pocketbooks; and we influence the very well-being of our neighbors, millions of whom we injure every year.

Yet the view of the car as separate from its driver, and the car and driver as separate from society and all its surroundings, permeates our culture, and may indeed be what got us into all this trouble in the first place. To begin addressing the plight of the car, we need to consider its role in the entire American environment, perhaps even the whole earth.

SAVE THE CAR

The hills in Marin County were newly green and the sky hinted of a friendly drizzle. It was warm and humid, the perfect fertile spring setting for Earth Day, 1990. In a bower of fat lawns and pendulous trees, I walked amid a crowd of good-natured Northern Californians slowly shuffling by tables and booths and listening to earnest men and women talk about air pollution, the warming of the planet, oil spills, endangered species, and other manifestations of environmental degradation. In less than an hour I was laden down with brochures and pamphlets exhorting me to save the cougar, save the redwoods, save the wetlands, and save the ozone layer. In practically all of the literature the car was portrayed as a granddaddy of environmental evils. In *The Green Handbook*, Andrew Kimbrell branded the car an emotional addiction—a habit more dangerous than smoking or drugs. He believes we're literally "driving ourselves to death." (Kimbrell obviously has a different idea of the driving force.) David Brower, the first executive director of the Sierra Club and considered the godfather of the environmental movement, provided the best summary of many environmentalists' agenda for the car: "I think they should go back where they came from. Melt the steel down and put it back into the earth." Never mind that everyone had arrived at the Great Gaean festival by automobile (80 percent of all trips *anywhere* are made by car) and that cars surrounded the grounds like a coiled iron snake.

As I drove home, feeling dutifully guilty about owning a car, I wondered what I was supposed to do with my new "Save the Whales" bumper sticker. (Put it on my bicycle?) I also wondered what I was supposed to do with my, and everyone else's, newly acquired conflict. On the one hand we still love to drive, and depend upon cars as the sole means of transportation in this country; on the other hand, maybe even because of this very love and dependency, the car is being blamed for the destruction of its environment. In other words, we need and want it, but there are very serious ramifications. We've reached that horizon where the road and the sky collide.

Yet as I wound through the lush hills along the bay, through the picturesque town of Sausalito, over the Golden Gate Bridge, and into the architectural grandeur of San Francisco, I couldn't help but enjoy myself. Even though I'd made the trip hundreds of times, it was an exhilarating drive. Guilt notwithstanding, it sure would be a lesser world, I thought, without cars and our natural right to drive them.

Besides, getting rid of the car is not the solution.

The environmentalists' antipathy toward the car seems misdirected, their vision rather narrow. What's missing is a vision of, and a deep-seated concern for, our urban areas—which include highways and cars. (For what good is an Earth Day that doesn't account for the whole earth?) Nowhere on the Earth Day green did I come across a "Save the Car" booth; no earnest folks detailing the threat to driving as a result of overpopulation and the diminishing beauty of our cities due to poor transportation planning. The conservation community seems handicapped by an antiurban bias, a separatist attitude, a tendency to ignore our public spaces and not see that all of creation, including human-made organisms such as the car, happen to be part of our ecology, part of nature.

"Reiterating the approach of the 'take nothing but pictures, leave nothing but footprints' crowd," wrote architecture critic Jane Holtz Kay, "they are endorsing the pastoral myth and ignoring the real footprints that compose the so-called built environment, a.k.a. architecture." Kay laments that our cities have lost any semblance of community and wonders why they're not included in the agenda to save Mother Earth. We fail to appreciate our cities as living ecosystems in their own right and to see that if we are to address the havoc cars and driving have caused in modern times, we need to understand their role in their natural environment.

The principle of ecology, that life is an interrelated web of energy exchanges and interactions among and between organisms and their environment, applies to our cities as well. "The components of the urban ecosystem interact as do the elements of the biological system," wrote urban architecture professors Christopher Exline, Gary Peters, and Robert Larkin in their book *The City*. "The city is fundamentally a system that is the product of a series of interrelationships and interactions among a myriad of social, economic, political, historical and physical variables. The city is viewed as a living organism—as a dynamic place with a vitality that causes growth and allows decay—just as the forest is." Furthermore, they added, "the ecosystem approach can help make an observer aware that the beauty and harmony found in nature may also be found in the city."

That harmony is seriously out of whack. Yet by maintaining the ecosystem approach, we can say one thing for sure: the car *itself* is not the problem. As Jane Jacobs said in *The Death and Life of Great American Cities*, "automobiles are often conveniently tagged as the villains responsible for the ills of cities and the disappointments and futilities of city planning. But the destructive effects of automobiles are much less a cause than a symptom of our incompetence at city building."

Had we patterned our cities with sufficient housing densities and beauty in the first place, assuring attractive livability and easy means of transportation, people would not have fled en masse to the sterile suburbs, leaving the urban cores to deteriorate. While these ersatz communities grew in part as a result of their easy accessibility by car—leading to further cement, congestion, and horrid air quality—they are not solely the car's fault, but the consequence of a lack of comprehensive planning. To unravel the essential incompetence of our cities, and to employ wiser urban planning, we need to think in terms of processes: everything affecting everything else. We need to consider a holistic view.

An Ecological Reading

This was the perspective I wanted to keep on my expedition. As a good car biologist it was my job to poke around in the driving ecosystem, find out what was happening, and be on the lookout for potential seeds of change. Of course I knew the ecosystem was utterly complex, and that I could go crazy measuring its seemingly indeterminate number of interconnected factors. There were cars and drivers, highways and road engineers, traffic managers and law enforcement factors, all the many elements that constitute the road-car-driver ecosystem, which, in turn, is intertwined with the larger ecosystem of the urban city-region, which itself is part of the state and federal organizational levels, which, as we enter the twenty-first century, operate within an international community governed by such concerns as world politics, global warming, and the world economy. The only way to get a handle on such complexity and present a valid picture of the ecosystem was to follow the lead of such modern thinkers as Nobel Prize–winning physicist Ilya Prigogine and adopt a systems approach. Thanks to the car's techno-cousin the computer, in recent years this approach has been employed by scientists such as ecologists and transportation experts to evaluate complex systems.

Like most natural phenomena, a complex system is a fluctuating web of variables, components, and information constantly wound and fed back into itself. Such a system creates itself as it goes along by continually reabsorbing what has come before, thereby defying any neat attempt to capture it conceptually and predict what it will do next. Ultimately, it is unanalyzable; it cannot be understood by reducing it to individual parts.

What appears to be a discrete, autonomous part or process is, at a different organizational level, quite dependent on its surroundings. At five in the morning we can zip down the freeway and pretty much dictate our own speed and mobility, but by seven we're part of a mass of cars that moves according to principles dictated by the traffic as a whole. Now it's the massive freeway snake that's autonomous, not the individual driver (though, of course, we could put a serious damper on the snake's progress by slamming into the guy in front of us, causing a backed-up-for-miles snarl!). Prigogine stated that to understand a complex system we need to accept that no single level of the system is more fundamental than another.

To get a reading on the health of the driving ecosystem I wanted to examine the different (but equal) levels. I began by concentrating on the ecosystem's predominant organism, the individual driver, who affects and is affected by the various levels. In the evolution of a complex system, the individual is not an unimportant player. Prigogine liked to promote the notion of the reenchantment of nature, whereby individuals are not accidental by-products of a mechanical, reductionist universe but an integral part of the movement of nature, of a spontaneous reality constantly creating itself. "Once you see that the world is sufficiently complex, then the problem of value becomes different," he wrote. "What we are doing leads to one of the branches of [change]. Our action is constructing the future. . . . Since even small fluctuations may grow and change the overall structure, as a result, individual activity is not doomed to insignificance."

In a complex system, individuals not only make a difference, they have a responsibility to consider the ecosystem as a whole, because they are interwoven with, and reflective of, all other levels. This, ideally, parallels our democratic process. This wider vision is what environmental writer and activist Joanna Macy called "the greening of the self." Macy once asked John Seed, director of the Rainforest Information Center, how he managed to handle the frustration of taking on powerful lumber interests and politicians without blowing a gasket or dropping into despair. He replied, "I try to remember that it's not me, John Seed, trying to protect the rain forest. Rather I'm part of the rain forest protecting myself. I am that part of the rain forest recently emerged into human thinking."

By talking and riding with individual drivers, I hoped to get a reading of

Americans' sense of democracy, of their interrelatedness, of the country's ecological state of mind. Do we believe we can make a difference? Are we willing to take responsibility for our cars and the health of the environment? The rising awareness of the car's nasty effects may indeed be the key to change, but I wondered if American drivers were really ready to turn the lock.

To complete the picture of the driving ecosystem, I attempted to interview as many experts as I could—people in the government, auto industry, academic, urban planning, and environmental communities. Given their social and cultural influence, I wanted to provide insight into their mind-set. I also wanted to capture their own ecological perspectives as daily users of the nation's highways. In America, driving is the great equalizer.

All journeys are personal voyages, searches for a better world, and mine was no different. I was out to "look for America," but unlike a sensible person—who drives across America visiting Yosemite, the Florida Everglades, or Niagara Falls in their natural beauty—I drove across America to visit traffic in its rush-hour splendor. In a sense, I began my expedition in search of ways of preserving the pleasures of motoring in the modern world. For if we as a country express little concern for the car's natural ecosystem, if we allow traffic, pollution, and the sheer number of cars to grow considerably worse, we are bound to ensure the end of the car itself. If it vanishes, we will have poisoned its habitat, not to mention its better human half. Paul Ehrlich told me, "I think the biggest mistake we made is not using the automobile as a tool to make life better for human beings, but allowing the automobile to dominate our society." It doesn't take an expert to see that restoring the car to a vehicle of enhancement will take a radical reordering of our priorities. Given the widening public awareness of driving's assault on our lands, skies, and spirits, I could only believe that ecological change had begun taking root. So I hit the road, literally and figuratively, and headed into America's Wild Kingdom of driving with "The Great American Driving Survey" stenciled in fancy silver letters on both sides of the Caravan.

I began nowhere other than my own home state, car-crazy California, land of nearly 20 percent of the nation's drivers, and on whose roads drivers clock a cool 240 billion miles a year.

Two

Conflict

For all the shut-down strangers and hot rod angels,
Rumbling through this promised land
Tonight my baby and me, we're gonna ride to the sea
And wash these sins off our hands.
—Bruce Springsteen, "Racing in the Street"

I f you close your eyes the freeway sounds like the ocean." Tom Tompkins was standing on the front porch of his small house in Richmond, overlooking the I-80 freeway not far below. It was late in the evening. A stone's throw south sat Berkeley; beyond the busy freeway and dark waters of the bay glowed the lights of San Francisco. I was in the field, in the center of the fifth largest metropolitan area in the United States, taking notes.

Citizen Tom was giving me what might be called his rap on rolling. "Driving diverts the outer layer of my brain," he said, "so that the things that usually tie it up—petty bullshit, anxieties of the day, being tired—get diverted by the minimal attention it takes to drive. Consequently, a whole other part of me is free to feel and think." Tom said he loved to drive. "When I drive," he said, "I feel the quality of my life is enriched." But he was also conflicted by his love, as more and more Americans appear to be. He knew about the environmental consequences of driving, and he knew about congestion. Gazing down on the freeway he was thrilled at the traffic's brisk pace, but in the morning, every morning, he said, the freeway looks like a huge parking lot. "Sometimes I feel like American society is gonna gradually come to this gummed-up, utterly frustrated glob that's hopelessly stuck."

Tom, forty-three, was a tall man with long, rapidly receding hair and an eager, almost boyish face. He lived in blue-collar Richmond with his girlfriend and thirteen-year-old son. Born in Brooklyn, he had practically come of age with the white lines of America's highways running beneath him. He moved to the Bay Area in the late sixties to become a "rich and famous California writer," and supported himself by driving a cab. While the writing and editing assignments were plentiful, the checks didn't exactly break the bank, and Tom continued to pilot a hack intermittently for a decade.

Today, however, he routinely drives his seventy-four Dodge Slant-6, "your vintage poor-guy-from-Berkeley's car," to the suburb Walnut Creek to work as the senior editor of a slick life-style magazine. The magazine's audience is precisely the wealthy elite that Tom and his radical friends in the sixties regarded as "the enemy." After a year, he is still not quite comfortable with the way of the 'burbs. Last week he parked next to a Mercedes with a Princeton alumni sticker on the back windshield. "I'm also a Princeton alumnus," he related bemusedly, "and here I am driving up in my seventy-four Dodge, and this guy who looks like he's eleven years old and owns his own company jumps out of this Mercedes and gives me one of those looks." Tom said he felt "a little defensive" about his "station in life." But not about his car. "Hey," he assured me, "I have a really good rapport with it."

Tom paced around his living room, blossoming to life as we talked. Like most of the drivers I would interview, he was thrilled that I was asking him, a "nonexpert," to explain himself and put a portion of his life into perspective.

RHYTHM OF THE ROAD

Tom's relationship with the car was based on music. "Ever since I was a kid, I grew up glued to a radio. I would get in the car, sitting there pushing the buttons and driving my parents nuts looking for favorite songs. As soon as I was old enough to get a license it was the same thing, except I was more in charge. And then with the advent of FM radio, and radio really as a window onto a way of being—the sixties kind of thing—it even took on a new dimension. Between 1968 and 1972 I drove across the country about ten times, and every time the bottom, the bedrock, of every trip was: what tapes did you have—you know, eight-tracks, right? And what kind of system did you have. That slightly diverted state you get into while driving is really wonderful for listening to music. It allows me to really feel the music, to really immerse myself in it. Listening to music while driving a car to me is one of the most enjoyable things I do. I really love doing it. I have tons of tapes, and I never listen to music at home, or very rarely."

It seemed that driving was a means of escape to Tom. But not at all, he said. "I feel that what it does is allow me to really feel more at the center of myself, as opposed to diverting myself from what's important. As part of the writing I do, I actually go out in the car and turn on the music and just drive. Interstate 580 is a really nice freeway to drive on. Sometimes I go out as far as Livermore or Pleasanton and just think about or feel the story I'm writing. New ideas come. It isn't like flashes of insight, but driving removes an amount of tension from the conscious part of me. It takes the governor off the part of me that really feels. So when I think of a car, I think of music. The pleasure of driving is what I like—driving is not a chore for me. But it isn't just the act of driving. It's like the world around you. You go through neighborhoods, you're feeling different parts of the city, you're interacting with people. You're seeing life as it exists—the daily trivialities of people going about their business, and that kind of stuff. It's a mobile way of plugging into the world.

"If you drive a taxi and you're at all reflective, you start to think about what it is that you're doing and why it appeals to you. Driving was my way of getting a feel for the whole city of San Francisco. The driving thing was always connected with the people and the neighborhoods; it wasn't just like going through and having a movie run past you on the side. Wherever you were, you were part of what was going on. It's an extroverted way of driving. It's the way I am in life in general. People connecting up with each other— that's what life is all about. For me, driving is part and parcel of that."

But Tom realized the opposite experience was epitomized by those drivers who, feeling disconnected from everyone else, vented their prejudices and anger. "I feel there's this illusion of separation when you drive. It gives people the freedom to let ugliness come out. Gay bashing—a lot of that comes from people going by in cars and yelling stuff. It starts in this kind of unreal setting and then all of a sudden crosses a line into genuine terror and ugliness. I feel that this is related to cars and how they allow people to be."

Tom stayed cool behind the wheel by learning to tolerate all the drivers in his vicinity and by realizing there are different personalities out there— that sometimes you need to stop when you don't want to stop. "It's just like the weather—you know, sometimes it rains—and you have to really develop that sense of what driving entails. Some people think that the driving experience is being on a freeway with no other cars, and that's not what it is. A good driver almost forms an organic connection with the car. Like when you're driving a cab, you're looking in mirrors and checking out traffic, you got one hand on the wheel and you have one hand on the radio. You're listening to the dispatcher, you're talking to your passenger, and you're also dealing with driving. It's like that AA prayer that says, 'Give me the courage to change the things I can, the strength to accept the things I cannot, and the wisdom to know the difference.' You've got to have that if you're driving, and you can make it into a pleasurable experience by and large."

POETRY VERSUS PROFIT

With a Zen-like attitude, driving was a pleasurable experience; it had a musical quality. As for the negative effects of cars and driving, things like pollution and congestion, Tom wasn't quite sure what he could do personally—or, indeed, if anything was even possible. "I've always been relatively attuned to social winds," he said, "but I confess to having ignored this particular one. And willfully so. I think people's whole relationship with their cars is so deeply embedded in the American right to individuality and freedom that they aren't going to change. Cars are basically a form of getting from one place to another, but because there's the mythology around cars and the way they interpenetrate with people's lives in so many different ways, it's really difficult to shake them emotionally. Psychologically cars are much more than the way to get around, so the thought of not having a car is not having that experience that's fundamental to being an American in this century.

"I also feel that capital chases capital, profit chases profit. To do anything requires such a massive reorientation of how America has grown up. I mean, 54-40 or fight! Westward ho! There's no place to go, but it's so ingrained in the American sensibility that I really feel that the country's incapable of being different. Look what happened with the Bay Bridge. When it was closed after the earthquake, and even right after it reopened, things were better, and people took BART [Bay Area Rapid Transit] or rode the ferry. But little by little each of us snuck back into our cars and started driving again. And then we all got pissed off when everyone else started doing it. I really do feel it will only end when it physically ends, when you just can't get from point A to point B anymore without a disruption in daily life that's so massive that things don't work."

Tom was not pleased with his attitude; it made him feel "helpless and probably culpable in some way," he said. "Look, by the time the U.S. government was in Saudi Arabia it was too late to stop the war. It was gonna happen. That war was in the books. It was out of our hands. To some extent driving a car at this point is out of our hands. Everything is set up around the car." And pity those who don't have one. The deck is stacked against them. "When I drove a cab, on the first and fifteenth of the month the phones went wild. Because people in the housing projects and ghettos would always call cabs because they would do their shopping then. Why? 'Cause that's when their checks came out. It was really sad because here were these people paying quite a chunk of their income for taxi rides because they couldn't even afford a damn car.

"And yes, we do need to understand environmental stuff—consciousness is the bedrock of action. But it's not like the people who run society are out there just waiting for us to get our shit together so that we can transform society. People think that just because Jimmy Carter or someone gets on a grandstand and says something on Earth Day that that means we're evolving—I think that's naive. Old schools still run stuff. I don't want to paint it all bleak, but I do think that to get over the top means a lot of hard choices and probably a lot of hard fighting as well. I really don't know what it would take in this country to retool society, but it certainly wouldn't be as simple as just knowing that it needs to be.

"I can't exempt myself from this stuff. Damn. Even with my dire predictions the biggest part of me is quietly hoping that things won't get too much worse—knowing that they will—but it's kind of like what happened when people didn't really hate the Vietnam War until the draft started to be a big question. Suddenly things were a little different because your ass was on the line. The bottom line often is, How does it affect me?

"I listen to Bruce Springsteen sometimes when I'm thinking about cars, because I used to really like his music in the seventies. Now, though, I don't like much of his seventies stuff because there's a lot of indulgence in his view of cars and freedom. In a lot of ways it was the freedom of 'This is America, the American Century.' I grew up in the fifties and sixties and so I really know that feeling of anything's possible. Right or wrong wasn't even a question, it was just, What do you want to do? Even though that was an illusion fundamentally, it was so widely held that it made people approach life a certain way. Cars are part and parcel of that, and it hurts me to say that, because it makes me realize that in spite of what I know about the world, there's a lot of illusion in me that I cling to."

Tom looked as though he was in authentic pain. "I don't know if the individual can make a difference," he said. "I feel it's important to see the collective responsibility as a society, and that every individual plays a role in it, but if you ignore the power relationships then you really screw yourself. Yeah, people need to recycle, but you and I don't manufacture plastic bags. That's how power works. I think that power is why we're in cars as well. We have no alternatives.

"I'm not going to be so presumptuous to say I know how change takes place—and I do feel raising the consciousness of the majority of people is the key element—but you still have to attack power. I feel like as long as there's a market for cars, the manufacturers will do whatever they can the cheapest. Whatever they can get over with, that's what they'll do. Maybe all societies are dehumanizing, certainly the one we live in is. It's because the cultural bedrock isn't very deep. The poetry is robbed from people's lives on a regular basis. You make music and your band gets signed and the next thing you know you got some schmuck telling you how you got to dress and play. Suddenly the people who made the music are looking at strangers on television and it's them.

"We're stuck with cars right now. We have to have them to get around. They're a particular necessity and they offer certain possibilities. And everybody's poetry is different. Maybe it's having a big long white Cadillac with golf clubs in the back. Or look at how Asian kids expand the parameters of their cars; they put those pin things on their trucks and smoke the windows and widen the tires. Or low riders. The whole thing's incredible! What they do might look ludicrous to us, but what they're doing is really us without the trimmings. Driving and fixing up their cars is a way of fitting in, a way of adding poetry and grace to life. I'm very hesitant to slam down on driving because in a mass sense it's one of the ways that people add poetry to their lives.

"And you can only sacrifice the poetry in your life if you understand that there is a reason for it. Otherwise it's just sacrifice. And your mind will not let you sacrifice if it doesn't make any sense. You can tell yourself to do it, and then you'll wind up a twisted person. The thing is, you and I don't have power to help the environment. The worst thing in the world is feeling responsibility and not having power to change something. That's what drives people crazy. The average person tries his or her best to live a good life, to be honorable and just, and I think that's in people's hearts. But how much freedom do you really have to do anything else? It's important for people to lean into things, and a wider consciousness can create a warmth and a bond between people. But to fix the automobile problem in our life now is going to take a frontal assault on the very roots of power in this country, in the world.

"I don't really know how change happens, but I'm against changes that rob people of ways to express what's really important to them. I see slogans like 'Split wood, not atoms,' or hear things like 'Can we do without the car?' Those are the wrong questions to pose. Some of these environmentalists, you know, they gut the world of poetry. For these issue-oriented people, these crusaders, suddenly it's all just an issue and they forget all the human factors, the poetry involved. I suppose in the long run if we keep pouring crap into the air we'll be fighting ourselves and killing ourselves. It's hard to feel free in this society, it's hard to soar. But when you're driving you can feel like a bird. You have music going on, and your girlfriend next to you."

He laughed. "Corny as this is, the Springsteen lines that I'll never forget of any song are, 'What else can we do now except roll down the window and let the wind blow back your hair.' That is as powerful a line in rock and roll as I've heard. Man, what else *can* we do now?

"Or look at the end of *Huck Finn*, where Aunt Sally is crowding him, so he is going to 'light out for the territory.' That's my favorite line of

American literature because it's so purely American. I think there's a relation between that and how we feel when we're in our cars. Not why we drive cars. We drive cars because that's the only way you get around. But that's why driving has become so much a part of our culture. It's this thing of movement, lighting out for the territory, of feeling in transit. Look at me. I was born in Brooklyn, and I definitely moved west. That's another reason why 'lighting out for the territory' has always struck me. Not because I did it. But because I *felt* it. You know, if I ever manage to get a decent job, the very first thing I'm going to do is go out and buy a decent car. An Acura Legend."

I couldn't have asked for a better starting-off place than Tom. He was where Westward Ho ended and where it remained, wheels still spinning. An illusion of progress and freedom slowly winding down—in Tom's case, into awareness and recognition. Tom pried open the heart of America's driving conflict and captured its many sides. But what to do with the conflict? He loved his rolling jukebox/think tank, but felt our dependence on cars reinforced our social powerlessness, cars being an omnipresent indication that we have been severed by the powers that be from effectively shaping the course of our lives and country. We didn't build the vehicles that emit the toxins, we didn't build the cities that gave us congested roads, we didn't create the economy dependent on foreign oil. We have merely inherited this world and so must turn to something as mundane, and perhaps superficial, as the car to fashion poetry and meaning in our lives. Cars may provide only an illusion of freedom, but it's the only freedom we've got. Clinging to this illusion was, it seemed, how Tom came to accommodate his driving contradictions.

His resolution struck me as both sophisticated and a little sad. Sophisticated because he seemed to understand the workings of America's raging free enterprise system and was willing to confront its social and economic inequalities. No longer a good Berkeley radical, though, Tom seemed to have lost faith that individuals can transform the country into a socially equitable and spiritually rewarding place to live—and drive. The view outside his windshield was of a fragmented ecosystem, the forces of evolution lingering desperately out of balance, individuals left clinging to their own freedom devices, stereos blaring.

CHAOS

I was down the peninsula in Redwood City, twenty-five miles south of San Francisco. We were in the parking lot, in fourth gear, before we hit the streets. I was riding shotgun with Sher McGuire in her Nissan 240Z, leaving the software firm where she worked as a graphic designer. It's no wonder that whenever Sher and her colleagues went to lunch her colleagues were quick to suggest that *they* drive. We were on the freeway in no time, joining the hordes of commuters inching along Highway 101, the main artery of Silicon Valley.

Zigzagging through the evening snarl, Sher kept up a running commentary on the traffic. "I completely lose my mind. If I could just stay in first gear and coast and not have to clutch all the time and put on my brake that would be okay," she said as she downshifted to first. "It's almost like I wouldn't mind going twenty-five miles per hour! But this constant start and stop and start and stop and people not paying attention and people getting angry and people cutting people off—it's a big battle. One or two car lengths is a big deal to them. *Like they're gonna get home any faster.*"

Sher, twenty-eight, was slender, stylishly dressed, and had long natural red hair. She told me she wore a pacemaker. We were headed toward San Jose, where she grew up and still lived, now in an apartment with her boyfriend. Once a fairly sleepy midsize city devoted to manufacturing and agriculture, San Jose was transformed by the computer industry into a bustling metropolis—it is now California's third largest city behind Los Angeles and San Diego—and has inherited the problems of every sprawling urban area: skyrocketing housing prices, uprooted communities, violence, and, of course, traffic. As we drove, cars flooded onto the freeway from adjacent industrial parks, homes of microprocessor companies, software manufacturers, and computer magazines. The freeway of foreign-made cars was Lee Iacocca's worst nightmare, a veritable showroom of Hondas, Acuras, Toyotas, and BMWs. Looking out the Nissan's window at the well-dressed engineers and computer executives in their expensive but indistinguishable imports, I felt as if I were gliding through a glossy TV car commercial. Although riding with Sher was anything but a glide.

We switched lanes. "There's someone with a car phone. They're not as bad as people who drive with two feet in an automatic. People have that bonus-foot brake action going on. I just lose my mind when I see a brake light! People are writing on their notepads hanging from the windshield and talking on the phone and hitting the brake, just in case the traffic is slowing down. It's like the boy who cried wolf. You just want to ram into him! They're not driving. They're not even an obstacle. They're a threat! If for one second they decide not to stop, that's when they're gonna have to, and that's when you just want to get the hell around them. So if by chance you run into two people like that in the next ten minutes, then you're really having a bad day."

Luckily we didn't run into anybody like that in the next sixty minutes. Inside Sher's apartment she offered me a beer, which I gladly accepted. As we sat down at her dining room table, she said that sports cars represented her "independence as a woman." She'd had ten cars, including four 240Zs and two Mazda RX-7s, and considered herself something of an automotive expert. "I'm young and I drive a stick shift, which is more than most women do," she said. "They never take the time to learn what a car's about, the mechanical properties of the whole car, whereas I think I know all about cars as a person, not even as a woman. I like the idea of using all four of my appendages to drive a vehicle. If I had just an automatic transmission, I'd fall asleep. And if I had cruise control, it would be all over."

Sher had owned so many cars because, well, she'd had a few accidents. "My first one was in my first car, a Datsun B-210," she said matter-of-factly. "It was a very good car. I did believe in Datsuns. It was my mother's car. She was buying a new car so that was a graduation present. I was sandwiched from both sides. A person rear-ended me and smashed me into another car—a guy in a Volkswagen. He got out of the car and said, 'Well, my dad told me to fix the brakes.'

"The next one was in my Saab. I was driving to work in the slow lane, with the exiting lane on my right. And there was an Oriental gal driving a very large Continental. And I noticed her maneuvering a lot but never looking. She came to my left, came to my front, got back over to the lane, and as she merged into the far lane to get off, she decided it's not where she wanted to be because it was backed up. Then she swerved over to my lane, and to avoid her I had to swerve into the next lane. At that time I didn't know that Saabs were front-wheel drive, and so I just lost complete control. The woman saw what was happening and exited. That turned into a six-car accident where I was hit on every side, spun around in traffic, and facing oncoming traffic in the fast lane, until I was taken out by one driver and slammed into the guardrail. I definitely saw my life flash before my eyes, but luckily nothing really serious happened to me. But I was really, really upset, because I really loved my Saab. It was my little Saab baby."

To Sher, people drove as they lived, which more often than not meant working out their aggressions on the road. "Americans are at everyone's throat until they have to come together," she declared. "And unfortunately, everyone has their own life, and no one comes together until it becomes apparent. I have a revelation and I drive really cool for a long time. I get no tickets, I have a good credit record, and suddenly I start driving a little bit more aggressively. I notice I'm doing it, but I still do it. Then I have another car accident, and it was still my fault. Not in anyone else's eyes but mine. Even if the insurance company said it wasn't my fault, it still was, because I did hit a person.

"Everyone is just into their own stuff. People tend to think that the rest of the world is the way they are. They view the world through their own eyes and suspect that everyone is the way they are when they're driving. And not everyone is. People out there have children, or aren't good drivers, or come from a different world, like Japan or Vietnam. Or they really are good drivers and you're not patient enough with them."

"Are you patient with them?" I asked.

"No, I'm not. I'm probably like ninety percent of the people that get caught up in thinking about what went on at home, like I've got to get the screen door fixed, and not really take into account that freak that just cut me off with the child in the front seat. One thing that really freaks me out is children, and I can appreciate mothers driving very calmly."

Sher regarded traffic as the one test of patience that everybody failed. "It's just the stress of it all. When you know you have to sit in something like that, you're not thinking about the traffic. You're thinking about your day, or you're unwinding, or you're listening to music, just so you can go home and not want to rip your kid's head off. Sometimes when I get so pissed off in traffic, it makes me wonder if I'm really not content in my life because I just want to kill someone. When I'm happy and things are going great or I had a wonderful day, I sit in the middle lane and just go cruising and no one really pisses me off and it goes unrecognized, whereas if you have a bad day, it's like you're looking for something.

Somebody cuts you off and you take personal offense and you're going to get them!"

She was quick to point out, though, that not all of her accidents resulted from anger. "In my last one, I was totally content. I liked my job, I had a good boyfriend, I was going along, everything was paid off. Just cruising and everything was beautiful. Well, that's not completely true. I did feel I was getting to be more of a risky driver than usual. I was getting a little more reckless, and I suspect it was me taking it out on my car because I was angry that my starter stopped working. I was also getting angry that I had a small dent. It always looked very, very nice and now it was starting to get a little bit of rust, the starter stopped working, and it was my neglect, it all started and stopped with me, obviously, it wasn't the car's fault, but it was just that I wasn't really happy with the car. These things were actually going through my head while I saw this person careening up on me going at least seventy miles per hour while everyone else was going forty-five. I should have probably just jumped into the commuter lane and taken the risk of a forty-dollar ticket instead of sitting there and freaking out and getting hit."

In the long run, Sher felt drivers were locked in their own private worlds. "There's no bonding on the freeway," she asserted. "All you can do is stay out of their way or be in their way. There's only right or left. I feel like when I'm in harmony with myself and things I'm out of the way. And when I'm focusing on something that seems to be of major significance in my life, which may be something that doesn't even matter, and you know it's going to go away in two days or four days or a week—you're so involved in that immediate problem, and that's where the conflict begins. It always begins with someone looking at their immediate problems and not the overall picture.

"It's mandatory that you get put in a time frame of, you know, five-thirty to seven o'clock [commute times] and you have to deal with everyone's attitudes, including your own, and you have to be conscious of yours, and the only thing that's going to make life easier is for you to acknowledge yourself. *You just have to be a better person.* It has to start with you. Driving's a perfect example. Because you're forced to deal with it. It's just the situation—deal with it! It's like a bad boss. Just deal with it.

"Driving and traffic aren't a problem. It's just a way of life, a factor. Life/drive. It's just a way of life."

I rode the commuter train from San Jose to Redwood City to reclaim my car. With Sher's Me versus Them vision of the freeway as a battlefield of unstable personalities dancing in my head, I welcomed the safe and stream-lined ride on the rails. But a strange thing happened when I got back out on the freeway. Sher had utterly sensitized me to the driving environment. This charged awareness was accompanied by a sharp sense of fear, causing me to think that at any moment the seemingly harmonious flow of cars would devolve into total chaos.

Sher, it seemed, had uncovered a buried tension, something we trem-ble over but rarely articulate. For when we actually consider how many miles we drive every day, how many maneuvers we make inches away from tons of deadly steel, piloted by God knows who, what's most remarkable is how few accidents there actually are. In a long conversation one afternoon with William Garrison, head of the Department of Transportation at the University of California at Berkeley, during which we seemingly docu-mented every major trend in the history of transportation, Garrison paused and said that the most amazing development in driving in America is "the collective understanding of how things really work on the highway, where individuals and society as a whole have learned to operate their vehicles safely. That is a remarkable piece of social learning, and how it happens is beyond me."

It's even more remarkable when you consider the highways from an ecological perspective, as a complex system governed by a number of interdependent factors. One of the dominant factors is, no doubt, the driver's mood—or, as Sher saw it, his or her bad mood. But what are some of the other factors, both internal (personal) and external, that lead to this inexplicable piece of "social learning" and maintain roadway harmony—or, as the case may be, disharmony and chaos? As one who has received his fair share of tickets, I can vouch for one specific external force of control, if not actually visible in the rearview mirror, then hiding behind a billboard in our mind. Off to seek insight into the fragile harmony of the roads, I spent part of a day riding with someone who had spent his life on them.

DELICATE BALANCE

It was a fine Wednesday morning as I pulled out of the Golden Gate Division with California Highway Patrolman Don Gappa to patrol the San Francisco freeways. As we cruised down Highway 101, cars around and ahead of us quickly slowed down and peeled out of the way, wary and hypervigilant. What power! For once I was the cheetah and not one of the herd of antelope. A few cars, however, didn't notice us until we were right on top of them. Officer Gappa shook his head. These were the inattentive ones, the inexperienced and unaccomplished drivers. He was slightly peeved. "The bottom line on accidents," he offered, "is unaware- ness." But he didn't bother ticketing the daydreamers because they remained in the flow of traffic. It's the cars that shoot beyond the herd that he singles out as his main quarry. "If you're pulling away from the flow then you're mine," he said. A certain glee curled across his face.

Just south of San Francisco a large truck was stopped in the number three lane (the fast lane is number one) with the driver standing behind it and directing traffic to either side. We pulled next to him and stopped in the number four lane, causing a nasty traffic jam behind us. Officer Gappa got out and sternly instructed me to stay put. He walked around the truck and returned to the patrol car, noticeably anxious. The truck had stopped behind an elderly couple in a small car that had stopped running. Officer Gappa radioed a nearby Caltrans truck to push the stalled car to the side. "It's dangerous being out there for something like that," he admitted. "Two- thirds of the patrolmen killed in highway accidents are killed in traffic situations exactly like this."

After half an hour I was kind of disappointed we hadn't experienced any *real* action. This was not like TV at all. Nevertheless, Officer Gappa was a fine conversationalist and gracefully answered my questions. No, he didn't think that chaos was imminent. Most of the time the traffic flowed uni- formly, and while he was constantly on the lookout for speeders and other scofflaws, his primary task was to restore harmony when one element scooted out of balance. "My job is to see that traffic is continuously moving, *safely*," he said. "That includes everything we do out here, whether writing a ticket, removing a hazard, working an accident, aiding a motorist—anything that would impede the free movement of traffic."

Contrary to popular belief (and too many reruns of "CHiPs"), Califor- nia Highway Patrol officers do not use radar on the freeways, and only rarely do they sit and hide. "We want to be seen," he declared. "By being visible out here people are more aware that we're around and will pay a little closer attention to their driving." But too much visibility was counter- productive. Every couple of miles we exited and reentered the freeway. I wondered if this was a trick to catch the drivers who immediately sped up when we pulled off. No, he answered, it was to allow the freeway to return to a normal pace. If we stayed put the traffic would back up into congestion because everybody would drive too slowly.

Officer Gappa told me that after twenty-five years he still enjoyed his job, that he still liked being on the road as his own boss. "If you don't think of it as fun, you lose your whole sense of perspective. It's a job that has to be done, so why not enjoy it?" Stress, though, certainly took its toll. The patrolman must drive, gauge the flow of traffic, look for violators, and talk on the radio at the same time. In fact, Officer Gappa was doing all these things while carrying on a conversation with me. I wasn't exactly sure why he offered this bit of information, but he told me that on the average, patrolmen live only two years after retirement.

As we cruised by San Francisco International Airport, a Ford van went flying by us, doing at least seventy-five. The conversation stopped, and Officer Gappa gave chase. All right! He used the flashing red light but not the siren or loudspeaker. Finally the van saw us and pulled over. Officer Gappa put on his hat and stepped out of the car with his ticket book, dropping his truncheon into his belt loop. After a short conversation he let the driver off with a warning.

"Brazilians," he said, getting back into the car. Evidently they had just arrived in this country, a whole family. Officer Gappa told me he was lenient because he wanted them to enjoy America. He added that when he is on vacation in another country he hopes to receive equal treatment. As we reentered traffic, no longer a conspicuous predator crouched by the side of the freeway, I felt traffic give a sigh of relief and pick up its pace. "If I stop someone alongside the road," Officer Gappa told me, "I'm not affecting safety as much as the free movement of traffic. But I would hate to drive a car on the day they said there's no more rules and regulations on how to drive the car. The laws are in place so that we have uniformity on the way people drive. And that's what we're trying to do, enforce the laws so that everybody drives the same, uniform way. That's what helps the traffic flow."

But other than the well-documented foibles of inattention, mood and personality, and lack of experience leading to momentary lapses of driving skill (good for over a million tickets in California in 1989), what causes drivers to break out of the uniform flow and act in all manner of unruly antics? What inner forces of the psyche spawn disharmony and break the highway's continuity?

Perhaps Sher was onto something when she intimated that beneath the placid surface of daily traffic loomed real trouble. A famous study of drivers in the sixties seemed to confirm these subterranean dangers. Psychologist L. Black interviewed a cross section of drivers who agreed that safety should be the most important feature of cars, and that people should drive cautiously and conscientiously. Black then hypnotized the same drivers and discovered that they were all dying to own fast and sleek cars they could power with great authority through their neighborhoods. The usual interpretation of Black's study, one heavily influenced by the teachings of Freud, suggests that individuals' desire for power and mastery, enhanced by sitting like royalty on the throne of the driver's seat, is what causes reckless driving and accidents.

Novelist J. G. Ballard took the Freudian notion one step further, declaring that cars provided an outlet for repressed sexuality and aggression. He believed such an outlet represented the most liberating freedom of all: "When one is driving a car there exists, on a second-by-second basis, the absolute freedom to involve oneself in the most dramatic event of one's life, barring birth, which is death." This rather farfetched idea was tapped by Woody Allen for comic effect in *Annie Hall*. Sitting in his bedroom with a faraway look in his eyes, Annie Hall's brother Duane (Christopher Walken) confessed his innermost desire to Allen. "I tell you this because, as an artist, I think you'll understand. Sometimes when I'm driving, on the road at night, I see two headlights coming toward me. Fast. I have this sudden impulse to turn the wheel quickly, head-on into the oncoming car. I can anticipate the explosion. The sound of shattering glass. The flames rising out of the flowing gasoline." To which Woody Allen responded: "Right. Well, I have to go now, Duane, because I'm due back on planet earth." The next scene, of course, featured a petrified Allen riding with Duane as headlights from an oncoming car flashed in their windshield.

Back on planet earth, the serious point of this fusion between mind and machine is that we often fail to take responsibility for our 2,000-pound iron exteriors. Although he didn't put it in such terms, Officer Gappa did bring up one subject that stressed this breakdown of responsibility and caused an ugly ripple in the highway ecosystem—the curious ecological factor of ethanol alcohol (ETOH). Booze.

Through a Glass, Darkly

Driving while intoxicated is self-absorption turned monstrous. Having doused conscious control in alcohol, we completely blind ourselves to our surroundings. While the personal reasons for excessive drinking are many, drunk driving is not solely a personal problem but a social one, and we've made few significant strides toward preventing it. Drunk-driving citations and arrests have increased in the last few decades. (California alone issued 139,000 such citations in 1989.) It's been estimated that up to 50 percent of drivers on the road at any given time have had a drink or two or more. All of a sudden Sher sounds more prescient than paranoid.

Despite the noble efforts of grass roots groups such as Mothers Against Drunk Driving, driving while intoxicated remains a travesty of consumer culture. Beer and wine are a ticket to the good life in a never-ending merry-go-round of TV commercials, while sexy billboards for hard liquor line our city roadsides like neon strip joints. Worried about their tarnished image, a coalition of alcohol companies recently raised $40 million for an anti–drunk driving media campaign. Yet that is pocket change compared to the $2 billion annually spent by the liquor industry to promote consumption. To put it in higher relief, Americans watch an average of six hours a day of TV. Alcohol is featured in 80 percent of TV shows. On the other hand, TV public service messages against drinking appear about once in every sixteen hours of viewing.

Still, statistics are tiresome, and they never tell the real story. It's practically meaningless to say that there were over 2.3 million traffic accidents in 1990, and that alcohol was a factor in over 50 percent of them. Or that CHP officer Larry Hollingsworth, out of Sacramento, told me that in his experience eight out of ten accidents involved substance abuse, adding that every time he came upon a "really bad" accident, he always suspected and usually found evidence of drug or alcohol abuse. To understand fully the desperate consequences of alcohol abuse, we need to meet just *one person* who has suffered a serious accident at the hands of a drunk driver. After that, all the statistics, programs, education, and bolstering of law enforcement seem like shouts in the wind. Then we will really know that something is seriously and deeply wrong in American society.

In May 1988, Michael Poimboeuf was driving over a windy mountain road to his home in Half Moon Bay. He was leaving his job as an electrical engineer for a start-up computer company located on the eastern side of the Silicon Valley. As usual, he had been working late. He had a computer monitor in the backseat of his Volvo and was driving extra carefully. As he came around a curve a speeding Toyota Supra speared him head-on, actually going right under the Volvo and flipping it over the side of the mountain. The Toyota crashed into a tree, and the driver's friends, coming upon the accident a few minutes later in another car, called for help. A rescue team from the fire department arrived and went to work pulling the driver and his girlfriend from the Toyota. After the paramedics got the couple into ambulances, they walked around the vicinity, shining their flashlights for debris. It was then that they saw, lodged in a tree on the side of the mountain, a car bumper. They rushed down the mountain, where they found Michael crushed in his car.

Michael's voice was drilling a hole through me. As he recounted the accident, nearly three years later, he did so in utter seriousness, with at times unabashed bitterness. We were sitting in a funky diner near my house in San Francisco. A native of Madison, Wisconsin, Michael, thirty-three, now lives just south of San Francisco in San Mateo. He was in the city to see his doctor, who, he raved, had just given him cushions for his shoes to make walking easier. Along with his hip—he now had an artificial one—Michael's feet were crushed in the accident. He walked with a nifty ivory-handled cane. Between the time I had phoned him to the time we met, he had clearly made a decision to relate his accident to me in as much detail as possible. I sensed that documenting his accident was extremely important to him, as if doing so allowed him to give meaning to a cruel twist of fate.

"I'll describe what I remember, then what I reconstructed from my memory afterwards," Michael began. "I'm driving home along 92, which is a classic Hollywood-style coast highway. I crossed over Crystal Springs Reservoir, which was pretty low because of the drought. I was approaching a thirty-five-mile-an-hour curve, so I didn't speed up too fast. They had just done construction there so the pavement was a little uneven, and I didn't want to jostle the computer. I was rounding the curve, going about thirty-five, and then bright lights, just bright lights everywhere. I remember trying to avoid a car that was coming straight at me really fast. I remember a feeling of I couldn't get away from him. I couldn't swerve away from him, he was swerving with me. I decided to drive off the edge into the reservoir, into the trees. It was just the thought of I need to drive off the road now: *I need to get away from here even if I hit the trees.*

"The next memory I have is a firefighter trying to explain to me what's going on, and big bright spotlights coming into the car. The light of the car coming at me, and the rescue lights, and the light of the operating table afterwards—all that light is one memory.

"What was reconstructed was that I came around the curve going about thirty-five and this guy was coming down the hill going about eighty or eighty-five in a thirty-five-mile-an-hour zone in a brand-new sports car. He had just bought it and he was out celebrating in his brand-new Toyota Supra, a supercharged red sports car. He was out there with his girlfriend. Along with two friends, they had just downed six bottles of champagne up on Skyline Boulevard. He came around the curve and he was already burning rubber. He was in my lane and swerved to get back into his lane. But I had swerved to get out of the way into his lane, so he came back into my lane and we were tracking each other and just couldn't get out of sync. We were just locked in somehow. I later learned that it's classic for a drunk driver just to follow lights. It seemed like it lasted a thousand years, but it probably lasted thousands of milliseconds. When I try to reconstruct it in my head, time is not a continuum. It's just this general thing that happened. In fact, I couldn't remember any of this until six months after the accident when I started getting memories back.

"I was crushed in the car. I hadn't yet realized what was going on. I just remember motion and feeling incredible pain. This guy starts talking to me. I knew he was a firefighter. I knew I was in the car. I knew I was down an embankment. I knew things were really bad. He said, 'Don't worry, we're going to get you out of there, and you'll feel much better.' They brought down the jaws of life and fired it up. He kept talking to me. They put the jaws of life on the car and started pulling the metal off. The noise was just horrendous. The lieutenant said that I lifted my left arm up and put it out the window and almost caught it in the jaws of life. They said they had to grab my arm and keep putting it back in. Then the metal started to move, and it came off my chest. The overwhelming sensation I had up to that moment was not being able to breathe because my lungs were crushed by the metal on top of me. Suddenly I was able to breathe. As I was breathing my first breath the pain came. I had the oxygen, and suddenly my crushed hip, broken leg, and everything else just started screaming at me in incredible pain. I remember screaming really loud, saying, 'No— don't—stop! Just leave me here.' He told me he couldn't do that, that it was going to hurt, but they had to take the metal off me so I could breathe. Once the metal was off and I was able to breathe I passed out. The firefighters thought that they had lost me. They were expecting me to die any moment.

"They pulled me out. They put me into the basket. I don't remember that at all. They dragged me up. Part of what I had broken through as the car had gone down the hillside was poison oak. I've gone back since and looked at it, and it was the biggest grove of poison oak I've ever seen in my whole life. I was bleeding and partially naked because my jacket and shirt had been cut off with the trauma shears. I got poison oak all over me, mixed with my blood, right into me. The firefighters dragged me up through it and they got it too. The reason that's significant is that later on when I was in a semicomatose state, the poison oak is the thing that pulled me out of it. What pulled me out of being comatose were things that disturbed me and made me mad. People would make noise and that would disturb my nice peaceful sleep. People would make noise or they would poke me, and that would annoy me, and I would start to come to. This poison oak was just itching all over me for weeks. That's what really pulled me out of being out to lunch. I'd have to wake up all the time to scratch it. Even though I was in excruciating pain, it was the poison oak that bothered me.

"Anyway, they dragged me up through this poison oak to the ambulance. They've got me in these pressure pants that they inflate to get your blood back up into your vital organs. They put those on me and I came to at that point. I remember that the firefighter—I found out later he was a rookie—had my blood all over him. I was covered in blood. I had this vision. It was like I was in the movie *Platoon* and I was being taken into the helicopter and flown away from the firefight. That was the first moment I felt that I wasn't going to survive. I reached out and grabbed the firefighter's jacket. I looked into his eyes and said, 'Don't let me die.'

"They take me in and I'm in incredible pain. I was begging for morphine, for any narcotics—anything to knock the pain out. They gave me a little, but not nearly enough. I was in incredible agony just thrashing around. They detected that I had a C2 fracture, which is a very major thing. It's the hangman's fracture. It's what would kill you if you were hung by a rope. They very quickly put me into spinal traction. Crutchfield's tongs, they're called. Did you see the movie *Jacob's Ladder?* Crutchfield's tongs are those things they drill into his head when he's in that worst nightmare scene. That's exactly what they did to me. In fact, what I went through is worse than that scene. I was hallucinating; I saw all sorts of horrible deformed things and faceless people. It was uncanny how close to my experience that scene from the movie was. It wasn't overdone at all. It was really much worse in reality. I went through stages of not knowing if I was dead or not. I remember thinking, Well maybe I'm already dead and I'm just looking at myself.

"See, these tongs are squeezing into my head. They drill them into your skull with pressure. Then they put a weight on it to pull your neck straight so you're dangling from that. They put you on a bed and they strap you down. I did injury to myself at this point. They didn't strap me down well enough, according to my friends. I was strapped down and I was in incredible pain. I wanted to get up and out of there because they weren't getting rid of my pain. They were torturing me. At various times I thought that I was in a prison camp in Vietnam, that I was being tortured. All the nurses were Filipinos speaking Tagalog, and I thought they were speaking Vietnamese and that I was in a prison camp where they were torturing me. I wanted to get out of the torture room and call my friends to rescue me. I kept wanting to make a telephone call. They didn't give me pain medication. And then one day, I remember, they didn't strap me down and I planned my escape. I acted real good for a while and they didn't strap me down, they let me loose. Then I tried to get out of bed with these tongs attached to my head. I got halfway out of the bed and I fell and twisted my neck. I had all these shooting, electric shock feelings up and down. At that moment I did some pretty major damage to my spine. And I remember the nurse coming over to me, putting me back in bed, and saying, 'Don't do that. You'll hurt yourself; you've got a spinal injury.' Then my arm went dead. I couldn't move my arm and I still can barely tie my shoelaces.

"The moral of the story is that the physicians, because I was asking for drugs, thought I was a druggie. I had long hair at that point. I looked like a nightmare because I had long hair. They had shaved parts of it off to put the tongs in, so I was just this Frankenstein thing asking for morphine. The doctors labeled me as a heroin addict and they wouldn't give me morphine. They put me on a blacklist for narcotics. Part of the reason I was thrashing around and hurt myself and have this spinal injury is because they didn't give me the pain medication that I needed.

"The worst loss that I've had, what's caused me the most anguish, has been the loss of the full use of my left arm. As I lost that, I've lost my edge as a white-water kayaker. I'm much slower at building hardware prototypes at work. I haven't lost the ability, but I've lost the ability to be quick about it—soldering and cutting wires—things you do as a hardware engineer. But the most anguish is not being able to play a lot of the songs that I wrote on the guitar. I never wrote them down or recorded them and now they're lost forever. When my sister brought my guitar into the hospital room after a couple months of being there, I thought that I would be able to play a few simple chords to get my fingers working again. But I couldn't hold the guitar and tune the strings. I couldn't even grasp the head well enough to turn the nuts. That was a shattering blow. That was the first moment I cried."

As for the driver of the Supra and his girlfriend, they spent time in the hospital, he with fractured ribs and a punctured lung, she with a scar where her face smacked against the dashboard. There was a partial settlement with, amazingly, the girlfriend getting a chunk. Her attorney attached a suit to Michael's suit against the drunk-driver boyfriend and forced a cash compensation. Michael didn't know whether the two were still going out or living together, but the money went from the guy's insurance company, through Michael, back to the girlfriend, and maybe back to him. It made Michael furious. It was part of the story he was most hesitant to talk about. He quietly mentioned that the guy spent not one day in jail.

Interestingly, Michael said he now drives more than ever. And enjoys it more. With part of his settlement money he bought a four-wheel-drive Range Rover. He liked its stability and its size; it's a massive vehicle with a big heavy frame. "Also, I wanted to have a good boating car that I could drive long distances and carry lots of gear out into the woods. That's important because I need to get as far back in there as I can because I can't carry a pack anymore.

"It's kind of a paradox. I was injured because I was in a car accident. But now I'm much more dependent on a car to get around. I can't walk to the grocery store and carry the groceries back, even though it's only a few blocks. And I like my car more, and I think about it more because I need it. It's more an extension of me now. The way I look at it is, my hip is mechanical and so is my car, and I would rather wear out the wheel bearings in my car than wear out the bearings in my hip. I enjoy driving now more than I did before, which is hard to believe, but it's the truth. I've had to think about it a lot more. I've had to study it. I've had to think about safety in driving, and I've had to rationalize this aspect of my own body that's mechanical. I've become much more aware in general."

Physicist John Gofman once remarked: "Suppose the devil appeared to Americans a hundred years ago and said, 'I'll give you a wonderful new device that will take you where you want to go at great speed in great comfort. The price I demand is fifty thousand human sacrifices every year.'" Clearly, Michael was one of the sacrifices—it was only by the slightest of mercies that he made the return trip. Since 1899, 2.5 million Americans have not been so lucky; car accidents have claimed more fatalities than all our twentieth-century wars combined. And as we know, every time we slow down to get a glimpse of the wreckage on the side of the road, we may be next. Disinterested statisticians give us a one-in-sixty chance of being sacrificed to the devil in a lifetime of driving.

What can we do with a system that presents such dangers and causes such suffering? Michael's accident exposes a conflict in need of a wise resolution. We've made cars somewhat safer, but we're driving them farther, so the rate of deaths to miles driven has declined negligibly. All the potential solutions thus far—such as standard air bags or computer systems such as VORAD (vehicular on-board radar), which spots hazards and automatically applies the brakes, or drunk-driving laws such as those in Minnesota and Colorado, which revoke the offender's license within days of the arrest and mandate anti-alcohol education programs and have led to drops in traffic fatalities of, respectively, 31 and 50 percent in the last decade—all these seem rather meager in the face of our addicted society. Perhaps this is just one conflict we have to put up with. As individuals, we regard driving as what sociologists call an "acceptable risk": the benefits supposedly outweigh the costs. But I wonder about this type of bargaining with the devil. Is this the same attitude we should have about the environmental horrors caused by driving?

THE ENVIRONMENTAL DILEMMA

The trouble is, unlike highway accidents, which are there for us to see on the side of the road in horrid color, environmental destruction is often as invisible as the hydrocarbons pouring out of a Mercedes's tailpipe. It's hard to feel personally involved, and thus inspired to change, when we can't immediately see or feel the devastation.

Yet the truth seems to be that the car is choking the life out of the very planet, and the United States holds the biggest and tightest rope. We drive one-third of all the cars on earth and suck down most of the world's oil. Even after the war we just fought over the slimy stuff, our country's thirst for fuel shows no signs of being quenched: following the Western allies' successful banishment of Iraqi troops from Kuwait in March 1991, U.S. imports increased and gasoline prices plummeted. (Gasoline prices today are about 40 percent lower than they were a decade ago, after we factor in inflation.)

From 1973 to 1985, however, we made great strides in energy efficiency. In *The Prize: The Epic Quest for Oil, Money and Power,* Daniel Yergin explained that "the 1975 legislation that mandated a doubling of the average fuel efficiency of new automobile fleets by 1985 would reduce United States oil consumption by 2 million barrels per day from what it would otherwise have been—just about the equivalent of the 2 million barrels per day of additional oil production provided by Alaska. Altogether, by 1985, the United States was 25 percent more energy efficient and 32 percent more oil efficient than it had been in 1973."

Since then, though, conservation policy seems to have taken one step forward, two steps back. In 1986, for instance, the Reagan administration rolled back the fuel efficiency standard to 26 miles per gallon, and of the one hundred policy changes proposed in President Bush's 1991 energy plan, not one mentioned raising the fuel standard from 1990's 27.5. In 1985 we were using 5 million barrels of oil a day to run our vehicles; today we're using up to 9 million. We use twice as much oil per capita as the Europeans (who refer to us as "oil hogs") and four times as much as the Japanese. Our profligate ways have us eyeing hungrily the delicate and pristine lands of the Arctic National Wildlife Refuge in northern Alaska as a place to drill for more oil—even though experts speculate that, based on America's current needs, we would unearth only two years' worth of oil.

No matter where we get it, though, wide-ranging destruction results when all that oil meets the internal combustion engine. Ninety-six of our metropolitan areas violate the U.S. Environmental Protection Agency's ozone (smog) safety standard. And looking past our own borders, the most ominous threat appears to be the Greenhouse Effect and the destruction it promises. The Greenhouse Effect continues to be a subject of debate, with scientists giving it a 25 to 95 percent chance of actually occurring. Astutely, Paul Ehrlich, addressing a seminar audience in San Francisco, asked, "If you were told that there is a twenty-five to ninety-five percent chance of getting food poisoning at the restaurant you made reservations at tonight, wouldn't you change your plans?"

In the last decade, environmental awareness has received major boosts. The "nuclear accident" at Chernobyl. Exxon's 11-million-gallon oil "spill" in Alaska's Prince William Sound. The unwanted barge of household garbage afloat off the East Coast. Nuclear waste dumps in New Mexico. The death of thousands of dolphins in tuna fishermen's nets. Oil dumped into the Persian Gulf as a gambit of war. Endlessly burning oil wells in Kuwait. These events dramatically raised the national dudgeon and have brought individuals out on the side of the environment. The American Council on Education recently reported that six out of seven college students said the environment was their number one concern, and the Roper Institute released a poll in 1990 stating that three-fourths of the country believe "something should be done" to protect the environment.

Darby Watkins, thirty-six, had enjoyed a lifetime of political and environmental activism. He was, as a matter of fact, one of the protesters blocking rush-hour commuters from crossing the Bay Bridge at the out-break of the Gulf War. Yet every day he himself commuted, by car, sixty-five miles each way to and from work. He realized the "hypocrisy" of his commute and his environmental concerns (he even drove to the protest) but he knew no way to reconcile the matter.

I spoke with Darby one evening in Antioch at the All-Star Sports Bar, situated next to a Safeway, a Pizza Hut, a video store, and a Radio Shack— your basic all-American mini-mall (I could have been anywhere in the United States). Located sixty miles northeast of San Francisco on the Sacramento Delta, Antioch is a working-class community of 60,000. From the shore of the delta rise the belching smokestacks of Pacific Gas & Electric, Union Carbide, U.S. Steel, and Dow Chemical. Apparently

Darby's political views were well known in the confines of the bar. When I arrived a couple of his friends who worked in a nearby paper mill were kidding him about participating in the antiwar protest. At one point they taped business cards that read "Ban the Bridge Blockers" to Popsicle sticks and marched around our table. Darby laughed. "Ah, there's some good people here, I tell you." Darby agreed to meet them later at another bar down the street to throw darts.

Darby spoke with an almost disarming openness and sincerity. Raised in Cleveland, Mississippi (where "traffic jams were something that happened in the parking lot of a football game"), he had lived in Antioch for two years. He lived there not only because the cost of living was significantly less than in other parts of the Bay Area, but because it reminded him of the South, with a more "down-home" feeling of neighborhood. "It's got a touchstone," he said. He was currently buying a house with his girlfriend. For work, Darby managed a record store in Milpitas. One of the reasons he commuted so far was that he liked the company he worked for, a family-run business and one of the few independently owned record store chains in California. He underwent his daily 130-mile commute in a "nondisposable" Subaru Justy plastered with bumper stickers such as "Think Globally, Act Locally," "Walk Gently on Mother Earth," and "No Nukes." The bumper stickers were "like pelts on a trapper's belt," he said proudly.

FLAWED CRUSADER

"But driving does make me feel bad," he confessed. "I haven't really tried to carpool, but I don't guess there's anybody else stupid enough to drive to Milpitas from here. Maybe there are, I don't know. It's funny how I'll split hairs. I'll go into a grocery store and I'll even give a speech: 'Why are you still giving plastic bags?' I'll make a big deal about that. I'd ride mass transit if it came out to Antioch. I've been a good staunch Democrat all my life. I've never been one who's afraid of taxes. I would gladly fund mass transit. I think it's our folly that we're not doing that. By commuting I'm gone twenty extra hours a week. That could be a part-time job. Even with this car I'm spending a hundred and ten dollars a month on gas. I'm driving about twenty-eight hundred miles a month. I don't like that. There are times when I literally cannot remember the commute. I'm just there. I stop and I pass, but I don't remember. It's literally like putting on your socks in the morning, or taking a leak. You can't remember the exact time you did it or if you even did it. But your bladder's empty, and I know I'm there when I get there. I used to look at people all around me, look in the rearview mirror. Or look at the beautiful sky. Or I'd drive on Highway One and there'd be someone right on my ass, but I'd go, 'Wow, look down there. I don't want to speed through here, it's beautiful.' But people don't do that. I think there's a direct link between that and people's disregard for environmental issues.

"See, I'm not just blowing smoke, I'm a very environmentally conscious guy." He showed me a tattoo of a globe on his arm. "But commuting's corrupting me. I became like them. I didn't look anymore, I didn't smell the flowers with my eyes or anything. I just tunnel-visioned it to work. I lost everything that I was about. I've been a recycling fanatic for years. I coordinated citywide recycling in Colorado Springs. I was very active. And here I was using thirty percent more gas, going seventy-five, eighty miles an hour, cutting people off."

The situation was definitely getting to him. A week earlier an overly aggressive driver, wanting Darby to speed up, put his bright lights on behind him. Darby pulled back and put on his brights. When the guy finally slowed down, Darby flipped him off. "I felt real bad about it," he said. "It made me combative. Here I was, a person who marched in the last four days. I marched in San Jose at the big downtown antiwar thing. I marched in Palo Alto, and I marched in San Francisco. And here I flipped a guy off on the highway because he put his brights on me. Why would I do that? I've always been a pacifist, but there I was in a piece of metal rocketing down the road that could've killed somebody or myself. It made me feel horrible.

"My stress level was too high. Maybe subconsciously I've hated the commute. It's made me tired, it's made me irritable. When I come home, I want to be left alone, and it hurts my girlfriend's feelings. But since I got a ticket last week from the CHP for speeding, I'm better. Really! I'm more relaxed, and I'm looking around more. Thank God it didn't take a wreck. That's what I told my girlfriend. I called her right after I got the ticket and I said I could be dead, or I could have killed someone. I was a maniac out there.

"So yeah, I've felt hypocritical, very hypocritical. I honestly don't think I can reconcile the commute. I really don't. I think it's wrong. It's funny, I get out there on the road, and I think about this a lot. You're going to this town to work, and people are coming from that town toward you to the town you just left. Why can't you just swap houses with them? It's the funniest thing. I think the bottom line is: It's always tax-based and things are hodgepodge and thrown together. There's no planning."

Darby was worried about his spiritual well-being, his respect for life, the practice of nonviolence, the choices he made when he bought things. He said he turned his life around seven years ago when he became a vegetarian. "It's become a life-style for me," he said, "and I'm very conscious of that. I don't wear leather. See, I'm not wearing a belt. It's become my whole life. Respect for the planet and all. And I've got into a lot of sticky situations in bars because people say you're not American. I say, 'I'm a citizen of the earth first, and I'm an American second.' We're a very xenophobic nation."

Darby was always something of a rebel. After high school in Mississippi he was involved in the civil rights movement. He worked as a volunteer probation officer for juveniles in Memphis, tutored people who couldn't read, worked with the developmentally disabled, helped with a recycling program called Wecycle, and in Colorado Springs was on the executive committee of the county Democratic party. Then he experienced a lag of inactivity.

"I'm trying to get my life together ever since I moved to California," he said. "The war has helped me get my vertical wings again. Helped me get active again. But it has also pointed out my own falseness with the car. You know, it's funny, I remember riding the passenger train from Bald Knob to Beebe, Arkansas, when I was a little kid, and I remember when the train used to come into my hometown when I was in the third grade, the Illinois Central. And they're all gone. They're all beat-up, slow-rolling freight trains. And those old stations they used to go into, those big turn-of-the-century Greek things, half of them are boarded up, or they have a section cut out of them, and there's urine on the floor and all that. Now it's the freeway and the car. And they've made it impossible for us, at least in the foreseeable future, to give up our car, or want to give up our car. I will give up my car, and I won't feel bad about it. I'll adapt. I changed my life-style for vegetarianism. I buy unbleached coffee filters. I buy recycled napkins and toilet paper. I get bulk peanut butter. That's the thing about my driving. It got me away from my life. Getting that ticket was my savior. The cop was real nice. We talked for about twenty minutes. He told me he couldn't take the traffic anymore, that after ten years he was going to give up his job. It was the funniest thing. I was real tense. I was going to work. And after I got the ticket I felt so calm. It was so cool. I'm really glad about that ticket!"

THE TRAFFIC GAME

Not everyone is as environmentally conscientious as Darby, and maybe a lot of people would consider him tuned in to a different channel from the rest of the country. I didn't, though, and neither did Darby's Antioch friend and neighbor, Michael Evans, a financial controller for Joan Walters, a women's apparel manufacturer. "I would like to see us go to something that's less destructive to the environment than driving," said Michael, sitting in the dining room of his condominium one Saturday afternoon and assembling a propane barbecue. "I think there's enough people out there that are environmentally concerned—maybe they're not going to chain themselves to a redwood—but if there is something that they can do to prevent the destruction of earth, they are going to do it." Unlike Darby, though, Michael was not torn over the conflict between the car's environmental perils and his lengthy commute. "There is no way you can reconcile it," he said, "so I don't even try."

Michael, thirty-five, and his wife also live in Antioch for the affordable housing, forcing Michael to navigate the Bay Area's treacherous freeways. (In terms of time wasted per mile driven, the Bay Area has the worst congestion in the United States: 1,500 miles of highway and eight toll bridges of snarled, untoward traffic.) Yet to him the commute was no problem. He adopted a cavalier, cool attitude. "When I went to interview for the job I have now in south San Francisco, they said, 'We're concerned about how far away you live, because we have a senior person with the company who lives in Marin and has a thirty-five-mile commute and it's just killing her. She's done it for a few years and can't handle it.' I said, 'Well, it just depends on the personality. If I commuted thirty-five miles I would feel like I was going cold turkey.' "

Michael kept his head over his commute because, ultimately, he said, it was just a game. It began every weekday morning as he listened to traffic reports piped throughout his condo. "As I'm walking from room to room, getting my coffee or whatever, that's playing," he said. "I'm listening to what's going on and I'm formulating my plan for how I'm going to attack traffic. Literally it all starts there. Assuming that it's a typical day, I take Highway 4 to Highway 242. Then 242 to 24/680. If you listen to the traffic reports, you'll hear them mention Somerville Road, which is the exit you took to get here. That's typically where the Bay Area congestion starts. So I'm right at the starting line. As you travel up the hill by Pittsburg it gets heavy, and when you get to the 242/24 interchange there's a bottleneck. That one's the killer, but I've come up with a way to get on the frontage road and travel along the frontage road to Ignatio Valley Boulevard and get back on 24/680. Then I get off in Lafayette to pick up two people who ride with me three days a week. Then back on 24, through the tunnel, down to the Bay Bridge, across the Bay Bridge. Then I drop off one person in San Francisco. Get off at Fremont Street. Drop him off at Howard. Get back on freeway to 101 south. I'm typically at work between seven-thirty and seven-forty-five. So it's been an hour and a half since I left the house.

"A big part of it is that you're running strategies through your mind. It's like playing a video game. It's actually degenerated into that. Depending on the traffic pattern, I know which lane to be in at a certain point in time. For example, at the Walnut Creek section there are several dotted exit lanes. As the interchange goes over the freeway and onto the Gregory Lane exit, everybody immediately tries to merge into traffic. But if you don't immediately merge into traffic and wait till the last possible moment you can usually keep up to forty-five miles an hour. So it's that kind of game. And as you get to the next exit it's the same thing. So you play this game of trying to dart in and out without pissing anybody off too much.

"I never look at the commute as a chore, because I would probably go crazy if I did. It's a game; it's strategy. When I started riding with [car pool mate] Lynn, I knew about forty-eight ways to get to the Bay Bridge without using the freeway, and literally ending up right at the toll plaza, by cutting through Oakland. The second day I was riding with him we ran into this traffic on the maze [where Highways 980, 24, and 580 meet], and he showed me a way I didn't know. I was ecstatic. A new way! So in compensation for showing me a new way on the Oakland side, I showed him a new way on the San Francisco side, once it's clogged up, to get off the freeway and get on a surface street. He was doing this commute thirty-five years and he didn't know this street was there, and so he was ecstatic.

"I suppose the commute would really get to me if I had the type of job where I had to be there at a given time. But my hours are flexible enough to where I never feel like 'God, I've got to be there.' And I never schedule anything for eight o'clock in the morning, because if I did then I might get tensed up and get excited. This way it's just a game. The earlier I get there the more points I score in my mind. The only time I've recently felt any real stress is when I'm trying to get home at a reasonable hour, for going out to dinner. A truck caught on fire in the tunnel in front of me not long ago. You just sit there. There's nothing you can do, there's no place you can go. The traffic has come to a complete and total stop. If you're going to get upset about it, it's obviously not for you. You should move closer. I just don't let it upset me. I stop, get out, read the paper, do something, go shopping. I literally got off the freeway at Claremont Avenue, went to Rockridge and did a little window-shopping, picked up a newspaper and sat there and read it."

Michael sure is a well-adjusted commuter, I later mentioned to Darby. But Darby wasn't so sure. He's seen his friend at the end of the day, plopped on the living room sofa, unable or unwilling to talk to his wife, just sitting there in a white daze, a glazed look on his face. He remains like that, said Darby, a long time.

COMING INTO LOS ANGELES

"Chronic exposure to traffic congestion impairs health, psychological adjustment, and work performance," wrote Dr. Raymond Novaco, of the University of California at Irvine, one of the leading experts on highway stress and aggression. Traffic "impedance," he maintained in basic academic argot, also caused chest pain, elevated blood pressure, negative mood, frustration intolerance (these last two important in lowering the violence threshold), job change, and variations in job attitude and performance, residential attitude, and last but not least, overall life satisfaction.

Stress. It's the real reason cars are killing us. It's why we hate traffic. Congestion and overpopulation adversely affect creatures as diverse as lions, deer, lemmings, and crowded ducks on a pond; the physiological reactions are nearly identical. To the driver on the freeway, though, stress translates to boiling blood pressure ("Why is that idiot stopping to switch lanes?"), shortage of breath ("I'll never make it home in time for the concert"), chest pains ("Do they have to work on the road now!"), and great strains on the adrenocortex ("That inconsiderate jackass—I'm gonna kill

'im!"). But the absolute worst thing about it is that it seems so *unnecessary*.
There is something about being ensconced in our comfortable, modern,
high-performance cars (able to go in excess of one hundred miles per hour)
and going ten miles per hour in fits and starts that grates against our nature.
It's a physical and psychological anomaly. Our bodies and minds don't
know what to do in traffic other than rebel—against ourselves, against
society. One of the most common complaints I heard from drivers across
the country was, with slight variation, "If we can put a man on the moon,
why can't we design a transportation system that doesn't have traffic?" The
great paradox, though, is that while we can't accept traffic, like Michael
Evans, we keep adapting to it. Or at least trying to. Despite help from the
likes of San Diego morning deejay Mark Larson, who prescribes calming
freeway aerobics such as "ear wiggling" and "bun lifting," some of us,
obviously, are failing to cope. Who can forget the long hot summer of
1987, when the L.A. freeways became a jungle of Road Rambos, leading to
over one hundred incidents of highway shootings?

The individual in traffic—trapped in a perpetual cycle of anxiety and
adaptation—may be the best metaphor for the flux of the whole driving
ecosystem. How much longer can we take it before we short-circuit and life
in urban America comes grinding to a halt? There is, of course, only one
place to go to begin examining this situation. So I packed my bags and
headed down Highway 5, a pleasant if bland drive through the San Joaquin
Valley along mostly dry and fallow fields to visit the grand auto-hive of them
all. Lotusland. City of Lost Angels.

Ah, my old hometown. As I cruised through Simi Valley, the post–
Vietnam War model of suburban sprawl just west of the post–World War II
model, the San Fernando Valley, I conjured up the Van Morrison lyrics:
"This must be what paradise is about." For all the people who live in their
brand-new faux-Mediterranean tract houses jammed in this chaparral
valley, this is exactly what it is about. Here they are, far from the nasty inner
city, plunked down amid good law-abiding citizens just like themselves,
with plenty of safe, air-conditioned shopping malls to meet their daily
needs and a wide (and crowded) new freeway to link them to the adjacent
suburbs where the corporations they work for sit lodged behind acacia trees,
geometric lawns, and fountains.

I was back in the great exurban paradise. But there's trouble. Here, amid
too many people and too many cars, frustrations run high: constant immi-

gration, no water, crime, crowding, exorbitant housing prices, and, of course, horrid air quality, belying one of the main reasons people came to Los Angeles in the first place, the fantastic weather. Southern California's smog problem is easily the worst in the United States. In many areas children have 15 percent less lung capacity than normal. To all these frustrations add in the final ingredient of congestion, which, because of more and more people, more and more cars per family, and more and more trips and miles driven per car, is only getting worse. Endless workday hours are wasted on the freeways. Cars stream in from Thousand Oaks in Ventura County, sixty miles northwest of downtown; from Moreno Valley in Riverside County, seventy miles southeast. Many commuters leave for work at three in the morning to avoid traffic, then, in the parking lots of their places of employment, sleep in their cars till work begins.

The problems have something to do with the lay of the land. L.A. spills out haphazardly in all directions (author John Gregory Dunne called it "a city without a common character or a common narrative") as though some great god shook a bottle of instant city people and poured them out, seeing them fill every available nook and cranny. It's a city that was *designed* to spread out, not up. It was to be a "horizontal city." It was the great postwar Dream City, with enough land so that everyone could have their very own little ranch-style home under the perfect Pacific sun, with enough roads (two-thirds of L.A. is cement) so that everyone could drive wherever they wanted to go. Here real estate developers swarmed like gold prospectors. Aided by cut-rate property taxes and the use of regional sales tax for commercial development, money-mad builders transformed L.A. into one vast sprawling megalopolis, what urban critic Mike Davis called a "city without boundaries . . . a permanent boomtown."

The car propelled the boom the whole way. By 1925 L.A. had a car-per-person ratio (1 to 1.6) that the rest of the country wouldn't match for another thirty years. "The automobile created windfall-profit opportunities for the developers of the first suburban, auto-centered shopping complexes," wrote Davis in his book on the rise and fall of L.A., *City of Quartz*. Developers slapped up complexes on relatively inexpensive land far from the madding crowds and raked in the bucks as people flocked to them in their cars. Where there is open land in Southern California, there will soon be condominiums, mini-malls, and traffic. Land-rich Los Angeles was also a Valhalla for road architects, and the extraordinary freeway system they designed further engendered suburban sprawl, as businesses and communities sprang up in the freeways' proximity to capitalize on the easy access they afforded the area's swelling work force. The car, though, was the city's chief architect. As city planner David Brodsly said, the freeways were "an extension of the automobile, the radically new form of transportation which did revolutionize urban development." But the revolution was too successful, too many people came, and the freeways were no longer free, either of gridlock or of emotional stress. No city was raised in closer tandem with cars and driving than Los Angeles—and no city has suffered a more critical blow to its culture.

DOCTOR STRESS

It was six A.M. on the Ventura Freeway, the main thoroughfare of the San Fernando Valley, and the most crowded freeway in the United States. I had just begun an eighty-mile jaunt through mid-week Los Angeles traffic. The flow was sluggish but moving. I was headed to the University of California at Irvine in Orange County to talk to the Highway Stress Professor, Dr. Raymond Novaco. His pioneering studies on highway aggression (published mostly in academic journals) had become notorious—whenever the L.A. media needed a quote or two for a story on freeway shootings, they called him. I was especially interested in his notion that the actual physical sensation of driving was an important factor in drivers' flipping their lids—what I called the "jiggle effect." I took a quick survey of how many people there were in each car. A white Ford Aerostar van—one person; a burgundy Infiniti—one person; a blue Toyota Tercel—one person. The sun crept up through a brown shroud of smog that hung so low I felt I could reach up and touch it. As I transferred onto the San Diego Freeway, freedom of motion was soon rectified. The freeway stretched up the hill, over the Santa Monica Mountains, in five dead-full lanes at a dead stop. It was already hot and would get hotter, the temperature expected to reach, as it did yesterday, 112. I looked around. One person, one person, one person. Most had blank expressions; no one looked particularly happy. Some drank coffee; a fellow in a Ford pickup talked on his cellular phone; a guy in a brown Chevy sedan with an NRA sticker ate an Egg McMuffin. The hills around me mushroomed with new housing developments. I dropped into

West L.A. and picked up a little speed. A woman in a four-wheel-drive Mitsubishi passed me; she had a bumper sticker that said "Drive an Urban Gorilla and You'll Go Ape." I passed over the Santa Monica Freeway. One person, one person, one person. The sun spread a glaring, diffuse light. I passed over the Harbor Freeway, thick with stop-and-go traffic. The scenery now was mostly industrial, with a few scraggly eucalyptus trees adding a hint of green. As I neared the Long Beach Freeway interchange the traffic ground to a halt. I watched a few cars speed by in the car pool lane. They were going sixty miles per hour; me and everyone else, zero. I trudged through Anaheim and Santa Ana until, mercifully, I located my off ramp.

The Irvine campus, once isolated in beautiful rolling hills near the exclusive seaside town of Balboa, now blended into a nondescript sprawl of commercial development. I found Dr. Novaco in the Social Ecology Building in a neat, tiny office, busy at work in front of a computer. "Let's find a place to talk," he said by way of introduction. I followed him down the hallway. "I don't have much time, so let's get straight to it." Dr. Novaco was a relatively short man with sharp features and a dark complexion. He did not smile much. "Much of my work is on anger," he told me as I sat on the edge of my seat in a staff conference room. "Particularly in terms of the treatment of anger and aggressive behavior. My key research was on the development of treatment interventions for people with serious aggression problems. In fact, the procedures that I developed are pretty much the standard ones now in most facilities that are psychologically and behaviorally oriented in the United States and Europe." He asked me to ask a specific question, then glanced at his watch.

"What kind of car do you drive?"

He glowered, momentarily put off guard. "My car buying has very much been oriented toward performance cars. I've had a 1968 Charger. Did you see the movie *Bullitt*? Remember the green car that the hit men drove? That was my car. I'm presently driving more of a sports car, a Mitsubishi-made Chrysler Conquest."

"Do you think people have a bond with cars that goes deeper than their dependence on them for transportation?"

"That I really can't comment on. I have no information on that."

So much for small talk. Better get to the facts. Certainly the most compelling issue on which Dr. Novaco has written is Road Ramboism, which he has broken down into six categories: roadside confrontation;

shootings/throwings; assault with the vehicle itself; sniper/robber attacks; drive-by shootings; suicide/murder crashes. He has proven that combative driving ("annoyance-expressive behavior"), contrary to popular belief, is not limited to barroom brawlers and discontent teenagers in fuel-injected Camaros. In a survey of traffic school participants from all walks of life, he found that 31 percent have chased another driver, 12 percent have thrown an object at another car, and 5 percent have rammed someone. He discovered that 3 percent of drivers carry a gun in their car (which in L.A. translates to about 300,000 privately armed vehicles), that nearly 2 percent have brandished their guns at other drivers, and that a little less than 1 percent have actually pulled the trigger.

"People tend to think of roadway aggression in terms of these really simplistic ideas," he said. "It's not just freeway shootings—that's a very narrow perspective. You had the summer of contagion in 1987, this great media-generated phenomenon. But once the media gets tired of it and it gets off the air, people have the perception that it's no longer happening anymore. And newspaper reporters come into my office and say, 'Why did it stop?' What do you mean, why did it stop? What are you talking about? And I show them copies of articles in their own newspaper the week before—a woman getting shot in the head, et cetera, et cetera. And they're mystified. I mean, these people are clueless. My own personal observations are very distinctly that people, at least in this area, are becoming more antagonistic in their driving behaviors. More rushed, more hurried, more irritable. In terms of the Highway Patrol–monitored freeway violence reports, it is very distinctly on the upswing. For example, from July of 1987 through September of 1989, there were some three thousand, six hundred events of freeway violence."

Dr. Novaco explained that all forms of highway violence could be understood in terms of "disinhibitory influences on aggressive behavior." He continued. "Road violence is a product of weakened social and personal controls. Aspects of society have many disinhibitors or releasers that override the otherwise inculcated prohibitions against aggression. Cinematic portrayals, alcohol and drug use, violence-prone subcultures, the erosion of community values, the likelihood of making a good escape, carrying a firearm; all these lessen inhibitions. Driving an automobile involves many conditions of arousal activation and contributes to the override of inhibitory factors. Merely driving a car is arousing. Passing, braking, turning, attending to other cars, unexpected occurrences, et cetera, are even more potent activators of arousal."

The one external factor most likely to turn this generally benign arousal into anger and violence was, of course, traffic, which, Dr. Novaco pointed out, was getting worse. "It's very, very serious. The proportion of people commuting to work alone in their cars, which is about eighty-seven percent, has increased in Southern California rather than decreased, and that's been a national trend. Also, nationally, the largest increase in commuting has taken place between suburb to suburb, not suburb to city. And it's the afternoon commute times that are the ones that show the strongest effect in my studies, not only in increasing commute times, but in terms of stress and the effects that stress has on the quality of the home environment.

"But the curious thing is, I don't think traffic is bad enough. I think what people are doing is continually internalizing the costs associated with commuting. People continually adapt; we're very adaptive organisms. But every adaptation has its costs. And, you know, you see effects in terms of health at home and work. This isn't stupid stuff. I mean, I'm controlling for residential choice, residential satisfaction, job satisfaction, and work-social relationships. And looking at the effects of subjective abuse on mood at home in the evening. This is what's happening to us. I'm seeing powerful effects. Not to mention the effects on air quality."

Stress and violence will continue to increase on our highways—it is getting more crowded out there; people are getting more uptight. I asked the good doctor if he had some sort of prescription for highway stress. He answered by looking at his watch again. "Last question," he said, then explained that, at least for him, having a comfortable car with good insulation made an enormous difference. It was the only advice he could offer: buy as comfortable a car as you could afford; use your air-conditioner as much as possible; play music to facilitate the proper mood. "I've been a great fan of rock music for a long time, but I wouldn't play hard rock in conditions of traffic. I always look for selections that are serenity inducing and have a calming effect."

THE DEHUMANIZED CITY

Char Ghivaan didn't have enough time to relax to calming music; she was in her green Superbeetle but a few seconds, backing out of her driveway, when she completely lost it. "I panicked!" she said. Char lived in the inner city, near Baldwin Hills, a single mother whose children were now teenagers and in their early twenties. As she recounted it, there was already a lot of stress in her life, especially around her new job. "Oh, this is going to be painful," she said, forced to remember the incident. "I was sharing the car with my brother—which won't be happening again in my life. I had just gone through a bunch of stuff with my car; someone had stolen the license plate in broad daylight in Burbank. I couldn't go anywhere without being stopped every three seconds. So by the time I got my new license plate I taped it on the inside back window. They'd have to break the glass to get it this time. Anyhow, I guess my brother had driven it the night before. I got in the car that morning and it felt different. You know, wrong, like someone had been in your living space. The seat was adjusted wrong, the mirror was off, and I was backing out. I was already a bit upset; the seat, the tension in my life, the job; I guess all those things triggered it. As I'm looking in my rearview mirror, I see a space behind me and there's no license plate. It was gone! And I just lost control. I had a panic attack. I panicked and I guess I hit the accelerator instead of the brake. The car began spinning and spinning, careened off two parked cars, then another. In total, I jacked up three cars. Including my own."

Char's panic had been for nought. Her brother had screwed her new license plate back above the bumper where it belonged. But now the Superbeetle was gone, lost to a lien because Char didn't have insurance. "That was a very special car," she said pensively. "People were always trying to buy it off me. It just broke my heart. I loved that car. That car and I were inseparable. My car and I were like a relationship. You know, better than with men. Most of them, anyway. That *Fahrvergnügen* idea really worked with me. That idea that the car and I are one. And we're just moving with my energy."

Char was now in an unthinkable position. Horror of horrors—she was a person in Los Angeles without a car! I encountered her at her new job, working for Nolan, Norten & Co., an education and information technology firm located in the Citicorp Plaza Building in downtown Los Angeles. It was a typically hot winter day, the men in white shirts and short sleeves, the women in light, jaunty dresses. The Citicorp Building rose above the fashionable Seventh Street Market, one of those pits of descending, spiraling shops and restaurants, about half a city block from the roar of the

Harbor Freeway, about five blocks south of the establishing shot of the cityscape in the TV show "L.A. Law." The view from the twenty-ninth floor was exceptional, unseasonably clear. Char sat across her desk from me in her tiny office, the wall-size window at her back providing a wide view of the urban desert stretching west into the horizon, and out there somewhere the Pacific Ocean.

"I've lived in Los Angeles for twenty-five years and this is the first time I've been without a car," she said. "It's a lottery as to how I get back and forth to work now. Basically, my daughter and I commute together—till she moves out, which'll be shortly. Then I'll do Commuter Computer [L.A.'s car pool organization] or something. I'm thinking about taking a graduated approach and buying a mountain bike and biking in. It's six miles to work. In the evening if I work overtime I take a taxi home, or a bus if it's early enough. Or I get a ride with my sister.

"If I was a feeler extrovert, it'd be nice to have some company—a good reason to use Commuter Computer; that, and gas money. But I'm a thinker introvert, and I like quiet when I'm driving. I don't like chitchat. I do miss my car. As long as I've been driving, I've never been without a car.

"It makes a big difference. On the whim side, it just really deflates my fun quotient, because I just can't go anyplace on an impulse. Now I have to include other people—which is probably better for my mental health, but my temperament suffers. I don't like heavy-duty negotiations on spontaneous ideas. But one of the things that does help me tolerate being without my own transportation is that I know that by default, if nothing else, I'm contributing to the quality of life because I'm not taking up space, not burning up fuel. I'm not being selfish with my car space, just because I feel like going to do something.

"I'm concerned about the environment, but I can't honestly say I'm that concerned. I have an awareness of it, I'm sensitive to it, and I attend to it within my means, though I don't join organizations and get active, like I am with other issues."

Char was nevertheless concerned enough about her immediate environment to consider moving. She was raised in the Bavarian Alps, where there was little to compare to L.A. She wanted a place that wasn't so volatile—maybe Alaska?—a place like L.A. at seven on a Sunday morning when she could get in the car (if she had one) and just go and go, unimpeded.

"For me personally, what increasingly has concerned my thoughts was how long was it going to take me to get somewhere—against the sheer pleasure of getting there. Los Angeles is a multicommunity. There's many communities here; L.A. itself is not a community. It's a culture. There's a multiethnicity of drivers out there, all with different patterns of driving. I don't have this quasi-monocultural idea that we all know that the stop sign means stop. So I don't feel as safe driving in the sense that someone could be from China, or be Italian or something—that they have different ways of doing things there and they might bring it with them. And I don't know those rules."

But it wasn't merely the divergent drivers; there were also things like smog. "I would like to know what air is again, you know?" she said. "Not having to check, oh, is this a good day to breathe? I guess the automobile has decreased my sense, or my perception, of my quality of life because there's so many people here. I mean, I don't take the freeways, for example, unless it's late at night. And the wrecks. Everything is so packed! You have to consider the car with whatever you do. No, I'm not thinking of relocating, I'm *planning* on relocating. Kirkpatrick Sale in *Human Scale*—he talks about human beings having a topped-out population before the dehumanizing begins. This place here has long surpassed anything that resembles a human environment.

"Then there's the latent issue of racialism. During my orientation here they let me know of the benefits, one of them being the transportation network. But no arrangements were made for car pools to come into my part of town. They never sent me the information and no one ever called me back. When I started looking into it, I could see that if they were really going to set up a coordinated transportation service, it would take someone who is aggressive, aware of the city, whose top value is setting up the network and not servicing certain areas where they already have a clear bus path. I'm not saying someone looked at my file and said, 'Oh, she lives in the inner city, we can't service her.' I'm saying that there's a so-called vehicle for setting up a service and they have not responded to that."

Char was not sure she even wanted another car—a decision that to her was an ethical one. "Usually if something big happens in my life, I consider the larger picture, once I get over dealing with it. And it's like I look at all the things that're different since I don't have my beloved car. I have to talk with people more. I walk more; I see things I didn't see when I was driving. I see people, I see friends, I see vignettes I wouldn't have seen. I could get a bike. In Europe that's an accepted mode of transportation. Maybe I could even get some sort of subsidy for purchasing my bicycle? I'll check with the city and see." She laughed.

"I really do a lot more walking. I can't wait for these buses. If you're in New York you don't even need a car. Even San Francisco is decent. Here, they set up bus lines, try to be more responsive, but they're often in disrepair. And the buses that service where I live—there's another instance of the inner city being neglected. There're definite patterns there. Talk about seeing things.

"You see the people on the bus; you see the ethnic concentration sitting on the buses, where they go, where people are picked up, the quality of the service. The values are clear and evident. Like in my area, I've seen high-use avenues where you can't get a bus to come. But I've seen people from dominant-group environments have lines put in, added buses to the line. Wilshire Boulevard. Clean. A bus every ten minutes. I mean, it's beautiful, it's a dream, who wouldn't take the bus. I'd take it. But don't start going in a certain direction because you can only get so far and then it's a problem. Like I had to wait an hour in the dark on a corner, unprotected. So I can't work later hours, which is something I generally do. These are not startling things to me. They're just further evidence. But it was very interesting to see, because I'm coming from the perspective of a driver, not from the perspective of a person who takes the bus. I wasn't aware of the problem till I didn't have a car. It's a problem that requires the ACLU and group organization effort. I hear people complain on these lines as if they'd accepted that this's how the buses work. They didn't ride the plush lines, I guess. They hadn't any idea. I'd ask, 'Well, how long have you been taking this bus? 'Cause I've only been taking it a couple of times.' 'Oh, I've been taking this bus line for years.' And I'd go, 'And you tolerate this! If I thought I'd be doing this a lot, taking the bus, there'd have to be someone called to task somewhere. I couldn't pay for this kind of service.'

"It's a dynamic of racism. If the people are suppressed, you don't have any experience for self-care and empowerment. But I don't really like the term *racism*. I like *racialism, xenophobia*. I think Americans are really phobics. That's amazing to me, considering the origins of the country are made up of people from who knows where, catch-as-catch-can. But then that seems to be the paradox of humanity, isn't it? The very thing that you are, you can't stand to see or be around."

STREET RACER

Char's vision of L.A. as a quilt of unconnected and inequitable communities struck me as right on the money. Partly because of the spread of the city, Los Angelenos maintain their own life-styles in their own incorporated cities, sharing little more than the weather with their neighbors. But while L.A. itself is not a community, as Char said, its residents share an indigenous culture. And the symbol at the center of that culture, the one that literally and figuratively binds Los Angeles together, is the car and the freeway. As the city's literary anatomist, Joan Didion, wrote, the freeway experience "is the only secular communion Los Angeles has." The "mechanized rapture," as Didion called it, of cruising along the freeways is one thing that economically depressed residents of East L.A. barrios share with Westwood yuppies—just as they share the frustration of going nowhere in daily traffic.

L.A.'s car culture came to fruition with those who came of age with the horizontal city, mostly in the fifties and sixties. They lived through their cars, spawning a colorful autopia of mechanical baubles and fuel-injected characters, both real and mythic—low riders in their bouncing Impalas, hobbyists in their customized hot rods, hippies in their trashed VW buses, surfers in their creaking Woodies, moms in their lumbering station wagons, kids in their illegal go-carts, movie stars in their silver Ferraris, and 200-mph bonzai freeway racers in their Shelby Cobras.

I found one of the city's premier car-happy personalities living the quiet life in North Hollywood with his wife and eleven-year-old son. To me he seemed like the quintessential car culture elitist, Mr. L.A., who appeared to represent (at least from the predominantly white, upper-middle-class, Westside perspective) man and machine, past and present. Neal Meisenheimer, forty-four, worked as a creative jeweler ("By appointment only") in Beverly Hills. A former street racer, he now sedately motored to work every morning up Laurel Canyon, over Mulholland Drive (the road crossing the crest of the Hollywood Hills) to his office near Rodeo Drive. He was an extremely friendly man, warm, enthusiastic, with an almost theatrical sincerity. He was also a born storyteller. L. A.'s glory days, he said, are over.

"There's no pleasure in driving anymore because the streets are so overcrowded. It's just as fast to use the surface streets as it is to use the freeways, and in some cases it is faster. I drive over Mulholland because it isn't as crowded and it takes me forty-five minutes. You can't race and fool around like you used to be able to, but at least it's moving. But there's still a lot of traffic. You're in a group of fifteen cars. There's no reason to even try passing them.

"There's a section of Mulholland with no driveways coming in, a stretch of highway which you can easily pass on. Not long ago I was following five cars. The lead car was a group of foreigners that was going ten miles per hour. Whether they're from out of state or out of country, they're foreigners. They were gawking. Now they got four cars behind them and me, and one guy behind me. They're supposed to pull over when there's five cars behind them—there's turnouts—and so I know this place is coming up, and what are you going to do? Are you going to go ten miles an hour? You've had a tough day and you're tired, and you have all these considerations, and you just want to go around them. So I did. I passed them all. Well, when I did it, everybody did it. Because everybody that commutes up there knows exactly what the street is like. So we all passed him. At the end of the checkpoint, they had a radar setup. It's a thirty-mile-per-hour street, and so I got a ticket for going thirty-five and passing over the double yellow line. They got me for five miles per hour. They got everybody. They pulled over the guy we passed 'cause he was in the wrong for not pulling over. They pulled over all seven cars; everybody got a ticket."

To avoid an increase in his insurance rate, Neal went to traffic school to have the ticket expunged from his driving record. "Traffic school is so ridiculous. This guy that was teaching the class was from New York. He had never got his driver's license till he had got to California, and he couldn't figure out why he was getting so many tickets. It was really strange. This guy, can you believe this? He told us if you're going down the freeway at seventy miles per hour and you lose control you're going to flip." Neal laughed uproariously.

(I found out that no matter what speed you're going, if you start to spin you will not flip over—not unless you are "tripped," that is, your tires hit something that upends the car. This was amply demonstrated to me—*in a car*, a Mustang black-and-white—a few weeks after I talked to Neal. I was at the California Highway Patrol training grounds in Sacramento. Going around turn number two at over a hundred miles an hour into a wide cement area, Officer Bill Brooks said, "Here, I'll show you," and he cranked the wheel as hard as he could and stood on the brakes. We went spinning 'round and 'round—a huge blinding cloud of smoke from the tires engulfing us—eventually coming to a safe stop. "See?" he said, and slammed it back into first, burning yet more rubber as we raced back onto the track.)

Neal declared that cars "are not the answer" to L.A.'s traffic. "I don't care how clean they are. I don't care how great they are. There is not enough room." He would gladly give up driving for mass transit, and couldn't see why new technologies such as high-speed magnetic levitation trains weren't being developed for L.A. and other cities. "Maybe we should put some of our war technology toward our transportation. I mean, is it too much to ask Lockheed, or Northrop, to put together a mass transit program?"

For now, though, he was resigned to battling his way to work in his faded blue seventy-six Plymouth Duster, quite a change from the fast, high-performance cars he used to drive. He blamed the congestion and the crowding—he, in fact, felt so betrayed by his city that he was proud to report that he had recently found a new route over the hills to work—a dirt road.

"How's that for being environmentally conscious? I discovered it when they closed down Coldwater Canyon Road for construction. I got out my Thomas map and there it was. Franklin Drive—it goes through some sort of game preserve. Few people know about it. So I've been taking Franklin off Mulholland. It takes about thirty minutes. I can't go very fast, but there's no traffic. I see deer and rabbits and fox. How many people do you know that live and work in the middle of L.A. and drive to work on a dirt road?"

E-TICKET RIDES

Neal admitted that his desire to race through L.A. was long gone—"You'll end up hitting a whole station wagon full of somebody's family"—yet he clearly missed his days of street racing. He said he tried to explain street racing to the New York traffic school instructor, but "the guy kept saying that everybody that talked like me had a death wish. We were telling him stories about driving in the sixties. He said you all have death wishes; you all want to die. I said it had nothing to do with wanting to die. It had to do with mastering the automobile and the machinery."

Neal began mastering the automobile as a teenager. He built go-carts with lawnmower engines and completely dismantled and restored a Ford Model A to understand its mechanics. He received his initiation into road racing in 1963. "I grew up with a bunch of guys who were squirrelly road racers," he said. "Went to school with them. There was Frank with his Corvair. He had a Karmann Ghia with an air-blown Corvair engine in it. We used to go out and whistle at cops. I didn't know how to drive that well, but I could run the whistle. It was great! We had a road horn, too. They'd chase you every time, and they'd go through a corner as fast as you were going. I'll never forget that. You'd just see these lights go out in the mirror. And Frank would go, 'Are they with us?' And I'd go, 'Not that one!' In those days you couldn't correlate radios and other police cars fast enough to catch somebody. There weren't enough police around. Besides, you'd turn the lights off and you were gone. The streets weren't well lit. Everybody says you're crazy, you can't see where you're going. Yeah, but you can use the whole highway. Today if you drove that way you'd hit four joggers, two bikers, three or four cats and dogs. Because then there wasn't anybody on the highway and you could use the whole street and use other people's headlights to see if anybody's coming. Of course then you might hit another racer coming in the other direction with no lights on!

"It really was racing with Volkswagens and Karmann Ghias. I had that sixty-seven VW when I got out of the air force. It looked real stock. It was a brand-new sixty-seven Bug. I put a 912 Porsche engine in it. That thing was real quick. It was as fast as a 911. I put Koni shocks and sway bars on it. And the Volkswagen gearbox worked just fine. You would fry the wheels out of water. One tire would grab, and then the other tire would grab, and every time it did this it would fishtail one way, and then fishtail the other, and when it finally got to the dry street, if you're in first gear, it would end up on one wheel in a full wheelie. You could do wheelies in it.

"Then my dad had a 911 Porsche, which I was road racing to the grocery store and back. Finally there was no tires left on it. So I got together with him and we designed special steel-rim Goodyear blue-streak tires and

Konis and sway bars for his Porsche. You could drive into any corner at sixty miles an hour and crank the steering wheel and the car would go around the corner. No fishtail. No front end breaking loose. It was just perfect.

"And so Dad and I are driving home from his office one day from Beverly Hills. We're going out Sunset, and we're just driving, we're not racing. Then this police car pulls up behind us. Well, the tires were illegal. They were racing tires. You couldn't have them on the street. And now, he's frowning. He knows he's going to take two hundred and fifty dollars off his car, and what's two hundred and fifty dollars in '67? It's a lot of money. He was very upset. The police car stayed right on our tail. We went all the way home. We went up Will Rogers State Park to our house, into the cul-de-sac, pulled into our driveway, and the police car pulled up and stopped. I get out of the car, he gets out of the car, and the policeman gets out of the car. He walks over and goes, 'Those are the neatest tires I've ever seen on a Porsche.'

"He was Rod Simpson. So I took him, this L.A. policeman, for an E-ticket ride in the Porsche. So he came back the next weekend with his Porsche. He wanted to see how the tires and rims fit on his Porsche. So we jacked up my dad's car and took the tires and rims off and put them on Rod's car and Rod's tires on my dad's car. In the back of Rod's car was a 350-horsepower Corvette engine. Then he took *me* for an E-ticket ride.

"After that I sold the Bug and bought a theft-stripped 912 from an insurance company. And Jeff Cook and I took a summer and put the car together with a 375-horsepower fuel-injected Corvette engine in the back. It would go zero to sixty in three and a half seconds. It would go zero to a hundred and stop in thirteen seconds. It ran through the quarter mile in 11:50. It was built and designed for street racing. Amateur racing at its best is, I think, the only way you can put it. There was no protection, no roll cage; it was really just a stock Porsche that weighed in at twenty-three hundred pounds. Now, unfortunately, you're at the top of the class. There's no one out there to race, except Cobras and Ferraris. It looked stock. We started toying with a Cobra and they just wanted to get away from you and all of a sudden they found out they couldn't get away from this little 912, and that would really piss them off. You'd end up at a stop sign and get in a race with them, and the race would take you up to a hundred and fifty miles an hour on Sunset. Late at night. Literally you could pull alongside people and they'd race. People did that a lot."

Ultimately, people headed for Mulholland Drive. "You went to Mulholland for two reasons. You went up there with your girlfriend to neck, or you went up there to race. And at night nobody in their right mind would go up there for any other reason. The cops didn't even go up there. They couldn't catch anybody even if they were there." Neal often saw Paul Newman and Steve McQueen go flying by, but by the time he turned around to race them they were long gone. Neal savored one particular tale of the mythic Mulholland.

"There's a section I call Dead-man's. There's also a place called Grave-yard. And I think even today there's probably ninety cars at the bottom; they tried pulling them out but they can't. It's so steep and there's just car after car piled up on top of each other. They're just a blot on the environment. As you go through the race track, and I don't remember the street numbers anymore, but at this one place there are no streets coming in or exiting, there's no houses. It is a race track. You go into the side of the mountain and if you lose it you go over the edge. At the end of the race track, just before the streets start, there's a ninety-degree turn. There's a series of S turns before the ninety, and generally at the last S at a hundred and twenty miles an hour you got to stand on your brakes and it's an incredible g-force stop just before the ninety turn. The car's in a full drift and you keep it in your lane because any car coming in the other lane is a direct head-on. Get around the corner and stand on it and then you got to stop, because a quarter mile away starts another street and you're back in residential. So all the racers would make a U-turn at that street and go back, and then go back up to the race track to Grandstand.

"Now Grandstand is where a whole new housing development is. But it used to be the high point and you could watch them race from Coldwater to Laurel Canyon. Everybody would stand there and watch the race all the way from Graveyard to Dead-man's. This night I was racing, and I don't know where he came from, I'm in the Porsche and I'm just flying. There was nobody at Grandstand. There was nobody racing that night. It wasn't that everybody got their colors together and went up there. It would be gangs today. It was just a bunch of clubs then. And this guy in the Ferrari, we started dicing at the freeway, at 405 and Mulholland, and when we got to the race track I could tell he really didn't know it real well. I figured the Ferrari was a 275 LM, a V-12 roadster. There was another person in the car with him. Just before we got to Dead-man's I'm doing one-fifteen, I'm casual at one-fifteen, and stand on the brakes and start back down through the gears to set up for the turn and this guy passes me. Passes me! I don't know what he thinks he was doing. Because that was the last time he was going to pass anybody. He went straight off the mountain.

"I made the right turn. I went down to the first house. Banged on the door. And believe me, those people wouldn't open their doors to anybody. Even in those days, because they could hear all the racers. Banged on the door, said there's another accident, call the police, and left. I turned around and drove up to Grandstand. There's no way you can stick around. The police came. The ambulance came. The helicopter came.

"You don't race streets you don't know. You're taking a complete risk, like whether someone's automatic sprinklers are going to go on. That's what happened to Jeff in the Porsche. He was racing Beverly Glen. I don't know why he was racing Beverly Glen. It is just a complete death trap. All the houses are built right on the glen, and all the driveways and all the garages open right into traffic. It was one in the morning, and the street was dry and there was nobody around. He was coming downhill. And he came around a corner and some guy's sprinklers were on—you know, the Rain Birds that go *tch-tch-tch-tch-tch*—but of course they're not hitting this guy's property, they're watering this trench. Everything's soaking wet. They probably heard Jeff go up and said, 'We'll fix this guy's wagon.' He spun out and backed into a telephone pole. We rebuilt it but it was never the same car. It came back as the Road Warrior—four or five different colors but with a more powerful engine in it!"

END OF THE RACE

Neal credited his avoiding accidents to his driving skills and experience. He used to brag that he could drive after he had been drinking—but no longer. "I had a terrible accident leaving the Beach Club one night in the Porsche," he said. "I'd been out at Willow Springs racing all day long. Amateur racing. Went to the Beach Club and got stone drunk. No problem; I had been driving high-performance cars all day long, I could drive. I left the Beach Club, went through the tunnel going east on the Santa Monica Freeway to 405 north, and I'm in the fast lane doing seventy, and the turn comes up for 405. Vicki said, 'You're going to miss it.' I said, 'No I'm not.' I crank it around sideways to where I'm going to make it onto 405, and I'm going to cut the corner of the painted island. I said, 'I'll just race over the painted island.'

"I had to stab it to get around a few cars—there was a bus starting up the on ramp, which was two lanes wide, and about five cars. But when I got to the painted island, it wasn't a painted island at all. It was curbing! Well, you're committed at this point. You're not going to do anything but go into it. It blew all four tires and bent all four rims, and the car immediately swapped ends. Now we're going backwards. It looked like *Star Wars*. There are headlights going by, a bus goes by, and *bam*, into the railing and off the freeway backwards. So now the car's stopped, nobody's hurt. Vicki's sitting in the copilot seat and Tom Gordon's sitting in the backseat.

"Now, I've got a monk's outfit on because we had just come from a costume party. Vicki is dressed up like Dracula, she's got these teeth, and Tom Gordon is painted white on one side of his face and black on the other. We're off the freeway and down comes this huge black man that was driving the bus. The Porsche is just bent all to shit, and he pries the door open and says, 'Everybody OK in there?' 'Yeah, Jesus, we're OK, everybody's fine,' I said. And he goes, 'I just knew you were in trouble when you passed me backward!'

"Vicki now is in complete tears. Tom is screaming, 'Let me out before it explodes.' I said, 'Cars only explode in Hollywood.' He says, 'We're *in* Hollywood!' The guy in the bus says, 'I'll give you a ride and you can report this thing stolen.' I thought, This guy's together. I said, 'No, I'm gonna take the rap on this one. I just about killed my wife, my cousin, and myself, and my six-month-old boy would have had no parents. I've been drinking and driving and this is the end of that shit.'

"So by the time we get our fannies back up to the freeway the fire department is there, helicopters are flying around, and there are five or six black-and-white police cars. The cop that is there first, the arresting officer, looks like Peter O'Toole. I am sober now. He goes, 'Son, have you been drinking?' I said, 'Yeah.' I told him the whole story. That I was totally drunk, that the car had a 350-horsepower Corvette motor in it, that I was stupid to be driving anything, let alone that car, and it got away from me, and I just wanted to go to jail. He said, 'Sit in the back of the police car. I don't believe that thing's got a Corvette engine in it.' So I'm sitting in the back of the police car with Vicki and Tom and he goes over and he walks over to the Porsche, opens the engine compartment, sticks his head in there, pulls his head out, and slams the compartment shut. He's shaking his head all the way back to the police car. He opens the police car door and goes, 'You're nuts. I'm not taking you to jail. You sober up and call a friend.' So he took us to Ship's Restaurant in Westwood."

Neal insisted he was now the "most boring driver." Since L.A. had grown more crowded and impersonal, he made the extra effort to be courteous to drivers. Well, OK, he did flip people off once in a while. "But that has a direct correlation to what's going on in my life, not what happened on the road, really," he explained. "When I'm driving down the highway and everything's going good in my life and somebody comes barreling up behind me at five hundred miles an hour and wants to get by, my attitude is, let this guy go. If I'm in a rotten mood, it's the opposite: this son of a bitch is not getting past. The real problem is when you got two individuals who are in an angry mood and they run into each other. Then you got people with forty-fives shooting at each other, or people like me and guys in Mercedeses.

"I was on my motorcycle, going up Benedict Canyon. It's bumper-to-bumper traffic. All the bikes are going along, riding almost on the double yellow line, passing cars. And there's a lot of oncoming traffic the other way. And I'm going by this guy in a Mercedes, and he pulls to the left and cuts me into oncoming traffic. I stood on the back brake and grabbed the front brake, and fried them both right at this guy's door. That totally blew my mind! I couldn't believe anybody would do this on purpose. Two other bikes in front of me had passed him in the gutter lane on the right and he had swerved toward them. But he really did it to me. He pulled over to the double yellow line to where I had to go into oncoming traffic. He was pissed that I was passing him.

"So the traffic is now at a dead stop and I pull in front of him and park my bike in front of his car. I take my helmet off and start pounding dents in the top of this guy's Mercedes, screaming at him to get out of the car. I'm going to kill him. I was just going to kill him. That's what I felt like doing.

"Well, there was this guy behind me in a construction truck. I look at him and wonder if he's getting my license number. He comes toward me with a pickax in his hand and goes, 'Try this, kid!' I take the pickax and bury it in the back of this brand-new Mercedes. I bury it so hard I can't get it out. It is stuck in the Mercedes. Now this guy freaks out. He backs up and wheels to the left and cuts around the bike and tears into the oncoming traffic and just takes off. And the ax is still in his car. I walk back to the guy by the construction truck, finally beginning to cool down. The guy has tears running down his face, he's laughing so hard. 'Let me pay for the ax,' I say. He goes, 'No, that one was on me.'

"That's when I realized it was time to get rid of the bike. That kind of insanity I didn't ever need to see again."

BEYOND THE CAR

Reflecting on the driving ecosystem from a distance, thinking of the snarled traffic that Neal and Michael Evans face every day, of the chaos among drivers that Sher senses and Michael Poimboeuf nearly gave his life to, of the environmental degradation that haunts Darby, of Char's recognition of disparity and city conditions, and of Tom's deep sense that the problems are insurmountable, there's only one thing to say about the current state of driving in America: it stinks.

But it's a step in the right direction.

The conflicts of driving and its discontents highlighted by the seven Californians I spoke with signal an awareness and transformation in the fluctuating ecosystem. They reveal that today's driving conditions have quickened our perceptions and caused us to look on a world in desperate *need* of transformation. Dr. Novaco is certainly correct that drivers pathologically internalize today's driving nightmares, and my seven California drivers are no exception. But like most of us, Tom, Sher, Darby, Neal, and both Michaels *have* to drive; they are utterly dependent on their cars, so who can blame them for adapting? We all adapt the best we can. But as some evolutionary scientists have so kindly pointed out, a human's ability to adapt, once the species' greatest asset, may soon become our horrible downfall. Once awareness hits us, how long do we put up with things?

The most significant shift in perception caused by traffic, highway fatalities, and environmental degradation is of the car itself. My seven drivers, at one time or another, really do love to drive and can readily attest to the genuine pleasures of cars beyond their utilitarian qualities. Yet at the same time they have shown that they can look beyond their cars, beyond the thrills of driving, and see the deterioration in the quality of life for which their cars are in fact responsible.

No longer, it seems, are we blithely locking ourselves in our cars, for either a joyride or a trip to the supermarket, without considering the consequences. If I could isolate the dominant theme of the veritable library of automotive literature (and Lord, I've read it all), it would be that cars are a vehicle of separation, things that alienate us from our environment. I believe, though, with the justification of my California drivers, that cars are beginning to serve a different role in human consciousness, that of galvanizing awareness of the world around us, the world we're interchangeable with and that we are daily assaulting with our out-of-harmony technology. This shift of perception—heading toward the notion of the car as a "vehicle of integration"—may just be the beginning of what gets us back in balance with the whole ecosystem.

Unlike our paltry concerns for such things as the wolf, or old-growth timber, or whooping cranes, or saltwater marshes (yawn—who cares?—how's it help the economy?—see one yah seen 'em all . . .), the ecological and social problems of the car hit home like nothing before. Something is impinging on America's common, cherished, utilitarian, everyday device (for many of us, the single largest investment in our lives). Something is mucking with our freedom of motion. It's like we are being sold Nikes and Avias and Reeboks made of lead. How long do we put up with it?

Hobbled by congestion, maybe we begin to take a closer look at the problem of overpopulation? Beset by unending sprawl and cement and the get-rich-quick school of architecture, maybe we develop a finer-tuned appreciation of our urban surroundings? Having yellow shrouds of toxic smog and other fun effluvia hover over our cities and our planet, maybe we get a little more politically active? Who knows? As the comedian Judy Tenuta always accusingly shouts to her audiences after espousing one of her farfetched fantasies, *it could happen*.

Ultimately, a view beyond our cars could lead to greater responsibility for our actions in them. Saving the car may not be our highest priority as responsible citizens, but saving the global ecosystem is. They are intertwined goals. As we know, the fate of any beast rests on the conservancy of its habitat.

But can individual drivers really make a difference? Can we help steer the powerful socioeconomic system based on the car off its apparent road to ruin? I believe we can, and the most encouraging evidence lies in the history of the automobile itself. The saga of the car is a power play between individuals and daunting social and economic forces, with individuals coming out on top. While things today look pretty grim on the bottled-up freeway, while in fact we feel utterly powerless in an ever-widening sea of cars, history tells us we have a chance.

Three

Autopia

The only improvement in road transportation since Moses and the most
important influence on civilization of all time [is the car].
—James Rood Doolittle,
The Romance of the Automobile Industry, 1916

"Glorious, stirring sight!" blurted Mr. Toad of Kenneth Grahame's *The
Wind in the Willows* upon seeing his first automobile. "The poetry of
motion, the real way to travel! The only way to travel! Here today—in the
next week tomorrow! Villages skipped, towns and cities jumped—always
somebody else's horizon! O bliss! O poop poop! O my! O my!" It was the
machine to transport us to something better. Better times, better opportunities, wider and wilder adventures. In this century the car has become
synonymous with the American experience. Reminiscing in *Popular Mechanics* in 1989, David Halberstam said that for his grandfather the car
"had not merely transported him to different places, it had made him feel
more *American*, more a citizen of this land than a refugee from the old one.
It was in some way akin . . . to citizenship papers for a man of my
grandfather's generation." For his father's generation, the car meant that a
person was not bound to any particular part of the country where he or she
was doing poorly. They could move on, to some other place, and try their
luck again. "It changed the way we think of our lives. Here, because of the
car, we have grown up with the instinct for mobility and with a sense of
being less class dominated for the past 75 years."

Born in 1914, my dad came of age with the car as surely as any American. He was raised by his aunt and uncle on a small farm in Minersville, Ohio, a hamlet on the bank of the Ohio River. After serving in World War II and rising up the ranks as a commercial artist in Chicago, he moved west in 1954 during Los Angeles's heyday of promise and expansion. With his young family in his red Buick, he had shown up in L.A. to get his first taste of a new experience in automobility—which, for him, meant his first real driving commute. At first he was forced to drive from Pacific Palisades to downtown Los Angeles along city streets, but by the mid-sixties the freeway system was fully functional and driving became (for a while) a glide in heaven. One car was no longer enough. He soon traded in the Buick for a Ford station wagon and an English sports car called a Javelin Jupiter. And soon after that an MG coupe.

As more people cashed in on L.A.'s promise of the good life, the traffic grew heavier, and the freeways provided little relief. Eventually we moved northwest to Thousand Oaks in Ventura County, where people and businesses soon followed. What started out as another bedroom community of ranch tract homes tucked away in a picturesque valley of coastal mountains mushroomed into another massive suburban sprawl—or, as I like to say, another massive suburban *mall*. My dad drove eighty miles round-trip to work every day, watching the freeways soak up every car in sight.

Today my dad is semiretired. At age seventy-seven, he still sits in his studio to the side of the house and does his free-lance graphic art. On the wall to his back are various photographs of my brothers and sisters and me; his army buddies; and one particularly well-framed shot of him as a young man, his hair slicked back, standing proudly beside his white Javelin Jupiter. I once asked him what role driving played in his semi-retired life. He looked up over his drawing board, over his glasses, and in a disgruntled voice said, "I'd be completely retired if I couldn't drive. I'd be starved to death. You live in Southern California, what do you expect? The bus comes by every three days, and then it doesn't stop here. I don't see how you could possibly exist at all. You're absolutely dependent upon an automobile, for livelihood, for pleasure, for visiting, for anything there is—you can't go anyplace. There hasn't been a railroad train come through here in forty years. What else do you want to know?"

Pseudogrumpiness and Dissatisfaction

I remarked that in Los Angeles the traffic was only getting worse. In the *Times* it said that in the last year the average commute had gone up fifteen minutes and that commuting started earlier and ended later. The idea of a "rush hour" was passé. Dad merely grimaced. "I used to drive into the bowels of the city every day, but I can't do it anymore. Not at my age. Now, if I have to drive downtown I'll do anything to get out of going. It's a nightmare, it's a horror to drive all the way down there. It shoots the whole morning! You wasted all that time. Time is money. When I was your age, I used to sit for two hours every day in traffic and never thought a thing about it. I can't do it. I'm more impatient now as a driver. Because, you know, you get smarter. What am I doing sitting here? Just sitting there on the freeway. Here's the freeway: one person to a car; a 250-horsepower engine pulling a 150-pound body around. That's what it amounts to. Idling all its energy, all its fuel is being blown out of the exhaust pipe into the air."

When the family lived in Chicago, every morning my mom would drive him to the train station, and every evening, usually with my older brother and sister hiding in the backseat, would pick him up. I wondered if he missed mass transportation. "Oh, absolutely!" His face brightened. "When I lived in Chicago, you would *never* think of driving to the Loop. Mother drove me to the train station. Every morning I got on the train. I did it all my life when I lived in the East. You sit there in peace and let the engineer worry about it. You get to see and know the same people, the same conductors. I enjoyed living in the Palisades, but it was a big pain in the ass that there was no public transportation. And there still isn't. Fifty years later!

"I had the MG. That was my transportation. I got a ticket every time I was on that damn Sunset Boulevard. I got a ticket one morning and I'll be damned if I didn't get one the next morning. The cop said, 'Didn't I give you a ticket yesterday for doing this?' "

"You got thirty tickets in one year, as I recall," I said.

"They laid for sports cars. And then I had the Lincoln Continental. Remember? And the cop catches me, you know, going up there to Will Rogers Park where we lived. And he says, 'Boy, I just been waitin' to give someone who lives up here a ticket.' That's what the guy said. I had a light out or something.

"But no, I couldn't drive a sports car now like I did then. I could haul ass. I'm an old man now; you're talking to an old man, boy."

"But you don't often tell me that. You drive down the street and you say, 'Look at those old people, they don't know how to drive.' "

"I say that all the time because they don't. All the old people ought to be taken out to the freeway and taught to go on the ramp and told, 'Now, go!' They go peeking out, and looking . . . Mrs. Jenkins slows down. I say, 'You'll kill us, go, go!' Oh, I drive pretty well still; not as well as I did, of course. You know, when you get old you get doppy."

"How many times have you lost your driver's license?"

"It's been an ongoing fight with the law," he said. "The DMV is a foolish bureaucratic arrangement. I was never a friend of the DMV. I'm not a favorite of the Highway Patrol, either. It's an ongoing war with the DMV and the police that patrol the highways. They have my picture up on the wall." He laughed.

"I drove three years without a license. And you know what the guy at the DMV told me? He said, 'Mr. Berger, you are among the safest of our drivers, because those who do not have a driver's license are very, very careful.' But I finally got it back—I was in courtrooms a thousand times. They thought I was a lawyer. The judge nearly fell off the bench when I told my sad tale of not having a license.

"Once I went all the way to Sacramento on the bus in an attempt to get my license back. It'd work like this: You'd go into the Department of Motor Vehicles headquarters very bright and early, as soon as they opened, and sign in. I sat there an entire day. Finally the next day I saw this guy that worked there, and he was going to the john. So I follow him into the john, and while he's standing there at the urinal, I tell him, 'Listen, I been here two days, why in the hell can't I see somebody? This's ridiculous!' So he says, 'OK, I'll see you later at a certain hour.'

"You still manage to get into trouble, though, don't you? Didn't you get into it with a CHP officer not long ago?"

"It was over Malibu Canyon. I'll go that way sometimes to get to Brentwood. It's pretty and I enjoy going through the canyon and then looking at the ocean. I was going over the canyon going west and there's this old man in front of me doddering along. I had just had it, so I go zooming around him where that creek is, and there's this young highway patrolman. He pulls me over. The real young ones are the worst. They're cocky. They got the badge, the gun, the tinted glasses, and all that junk hanging from their belt. They're smart alecks.

"Well, we went 'round and 'round. I said, 'That old guy was bugging me, so I went around him.' 'No, you can't pass here.' This whole thing. 'Round and 'round. He's looking at my driver's license, and he says, 'How old are you?' And I say, 'Doesn't it say on the license? I was born in 1914, doesn't it say that there?' He couldn't figure my age from my birthdate. He really didn't know. Finally he says, 'Well, I hope when I get as old as you, I hope I'm a lot more mellow.' And then I said, 'I hope you're alive when you get to my age.' Then he wants the registration, and I say, 'It's in the glove compartment, go get it.' And he's rooting around in there, and he says, 'You know, you're a smart son of a bitch, I have a good notion to take you in.' I said, 'What are you gonna take me in for? You're just giving me a ticket, and for that you want to haul me all the way back to the station?' 'Well, I should.' 'What for?'

"I was giving him a hard time, but my attitude is, I won't take anything off them. If they're nice guys, well . . . but jerkin' off some old man. I don't know why they're like that. No respect. Let them take me to the station, I didn't care. I've listened to those guys so many times, I've been hauled in before, I don't care."

Through the doorway I caught a glimpse of my mom, who had been listening. She was shaking her head in resigned disbelief.

"Let's change the subject," I said. "You literally grew up with the automobile. Is there a change in how people sense the auto?"

"When I go back, and I lived in the country on the farm, on the Ohio River, I remember some of the neighbors had cars. Model T's. And I remember one family had a Dort, which was a forerunner of the Dodge. Mesher was their name. On a Saturday they'd go from Minersville down to Pomeroy, which is the county seat. Or they'd go to the county fair. It was a big deal. The car allowed them to go places they otherwise couldn't have gone. What are you gonna do, take the horse? When we wanted to go to Pomeroy we had to take the horse and wagon. It took a long time. The horse trots along . . .

"See, I remember the automobile when everybody didn't have one. Believe me. We never had any, we grew up poor. We always were. But I kinda reminisce about the car. The Parkers, I remember, they had a little car. And that was also a big deal. Now, of course, it's a huge pain in the ass.

Nothing but automobiles! But when I lived with my aunt and uncle, we never had a car. Nor did my mother, who lived in Cincinnati. When my mother lived with us on the farm she would take the steamboat, the paddle wheeler, downriver where she got a job. That's how you got around then.

"The first person in my family ever to have a car was me. A used 1929 Chevy. My Aunt Rose bought it for me. It cost about two hundred dollars. That was in 1931 or '32. By then we lived on Price Hill in Cincinnati. The house cost sixty-five hundred dollars. Three bedrooms and a garage and a yard in front and back. I go back, boy, remember, a long time. This's ancient stuff.

"The best thing about having a car was getting a date. I always had a girl. I remember driving a Nash Lafayette between Cincinnati and Columbus to see a girl I was going with. It was just a two-lane road. I took the four best-looking gals on Price Hill to work every day because I had a car. Now girls have their own cars and they take the guys. I'm old, old—"

"You keep saying that, Dad."

"Old age lives in the past, youth in the future. When I was a boy, it was a major trip to go from Pomeroy to Athens. It was a gravel road, about twenty-five miles. Now, people go to work every morning over the same distance. I think the biggest change wrought by the car is that—traveling greater distances with less trouble. No one thinks anything of traveling from here to Las Vegas. Two hundred and fifty miles.

"But the fun days of the automobile are over, mainly because of the horrible congestion. Maybe it'd still be fun if you lived way out in Wyoming and drove into Cheyenne. You think it's any fun driving an automobile down the Santa Monica or Ventura Freeway? You dread it. The car is a necessity, that's all it amounts to. You become dependent upon the car as soon as you get it."

I asked Dad if he ever considered moving out of L.A., away from all the people and traffic, back to the country. It was a question he'd been asked many times before and loved to consider. But his answer was always the same. "No," he said. "Your mom loves it here. She has all her friends here. I would consider leaving, but I'm forced into staying, even today. I have to work. I have to live in a metropolitan area. Sure, you can run up to Oregon and live in a pretty little town, but what are you gonna do? It's all right if you have a lot of money and are retired. I read an article recently about a big-shot advertising guy who thought, Ah, I'll just move to a small town and

raise cows. But it doesn't work out. He doesn't know a thing about cows—
he doesn't know a cow from a goat. A lot of people have had it here. They'd
love to go someplace else, but they simply can't because of their work."

TRAPPED

Many of the L.A. drivers I interviewed shared my dad's resignation to
the megalopolis. Most of them were younger, though, and had never
enjoyed the car's glory days. They had never seen the city as Autopia.
Their perennial fantasy in the Promised Land was: I'm going to move out
of here as soon as I can. This one's going to Oregon, this one to Idaho,
this one to some sleepy little town in the High Sierra. But, of course, they
never go.

Ellen Brouse, forty, a graphic artist who lived in Azusa, the smog
capital of Los Angeles, told me she felt she "had died and gone to heaven"
when she got a new job and no longer had to commute 150 miles. Although
she now worked ten minutes from her house, she still wanted to move to a
less populated area in New Mexico or Colorado. Los Angeles, she said, is
"a dying environment."

Gary Post, fifty-six, who had lived in L.A. his whole life, felt the same
way. He lived in Woodland Hills and worked for Citicorp's computer branch
in Santa Monica. Because he couldn't afford a second car, he drove one of
the company's van pools. Alone in his own car, he used to subscribe to the
obsessive-compulsive Michael Evans school of commuting. "I'd get out
there and I'd push—you know, God, I'm always late for something—I got
to get there. I actually came to the point where I timed myself." Now his
attitude was one of take-it-in-stride forbearance. Ho-hum, over Topanga
Canyon to the Santa Monica coast every morning; ah well, back to the
valley every evening. By "group rule" everyone in the van could talk on the
way to work; everyone remained silent on the way back.

"There's another issue for me," Gary said in his office one morning. "I
live in an area that's not far from the freeway and it's gotten to the point
where there's so many people using the area that traffic backs up for blocks. I
can't even turn into my own street. I have to go around the block to get into
my own house! It's one thing at work, and it's another when you get home
and you get the same problems."

Although he'd like to move, Gary admitted he wasn't going anyplace.

"I'd need a crowbar to get my wife out of this area," he offered plaintively. "I'm stuck. Economically stuck."

Driving every day in L.A., the vast urban monument to the car, it's hard not to feel that history has run its course. That the great freeway infrastructure that supports modern life no longer works enforces a sense of futility. And feeling trapped engenders a narrow vision. But perhaps evolution is on our side. For this is not the first time the transportation system has reached critical mass. In the science of ecology there is something called the Red Queen Hypothesis, which is adapted from Lewis Carroll's *Through the Looking Glass,* where to remain stationary the queen must, paradoxically, keep running. This hypothesis holds that for a population to prosper it must continue to evolve, otherwise changing environmental factors will force it into extinction. In other words, evolution is an indispensable mechanism of survival. So to widen our vision of the driving ecosystem, deepen our knowledge of its chief organism, and keep our sights open to change, a brief evolutionary sketch of the car is in order.

A CAR IS BORN

In the beginning, the whole thing stunk. Before the turn of the century, European gas-powered cars arrived in America as toys for the Donald Trumps of the day. For everyone else there were horses. Thirty million of them. Consuming 40 percent of the country's total grain crop. That's a lot of hay. And out the other end, each horse, each day, deposited forty-five pounds of dung in its path. (Statisticians of the day predicted that by 1940 New York City would be six feet deep in manure.) When it rained, the manure turned into an oozy yellow-green soup; when the sun beat down, it turned into a fine dust that filled the air. The smell was horrendous, and city dwellers sludged across streets with skirts or pant cuffs raised. Flies were everywhere. The root of disease and infection was no mystery to medical authorities.

Then there was the noise. It was often impossible to carry on a conversation outside because of the intolerable racket of steel-wheeled carriages and shod horses clattering over the crowded cobblestone streets. And it was dangerous. One historical study estimated that, per capita, serious-injury accidents were just as frequent then as now. The dumbest Ford had, by comparison, more traffic savvy than some poor drudge. But then the horses

were not as dumb as some of their owners. Overworked and often poorly
cared for, a draft animal's life was not a pleasant one. It was not uncommon
to come upon a dead, decomposing horse blocking the street. In the late
1800s New York City removed 15,000 dead horses from its streets each
year. Humane societies across America and Europe applauded the advent
of the automobile as the savior of the sad, beleaguered horse.

Saviors from the stench evolved in the form of engineers such as
Germany's Karl Benz and American bicycle designers Charles E. and
J. Frank Duryea. The public had read about their horseless carriages and
expected great things. As Julian Pettifer pointed out in *Automania: Man
and the Modern Car*, the man in the streets "was expecting it to provide a
cure for most of the ills for which the car is now blamed: air pollution,
congestion and death on the roads."

And it did, once Ranson Eli Olds got mass production under way in
1901. But the car provided not only healthy relief from the horse, it
delivered Americans unto themselves. Individual mobility put them in
control of their own time and fate. "The motor car has restored the romance
of travel," exulted American novelist Edith Wharton in 1904. "Freeing us
from all the compulsions and contacts of the railway, the bondage to fixed
hours and the beaten track, the approach to each town through the area of
ugliness created by the railway itself, it has given us back the wonder, the
adventure, and the novelty which enlivened the way of our posting grandparents." Furthermore, individual transport freed them from the robber
barons who ruled the railroads and steamship lines.

The auto's liberating powers motivated Henry Ford. He perfected the
assembly line, what he called the "new messiah." His Model T was the
realization of the egalitarian ideal, which he cemented in American society
by consistently dropping the car's price—from $780 in 1910 to $360 in
1914—so everyone from farmers to his own laborers could afford one. (For
transport only, mind you. Something of a Puritan, Ford designed the seats
to be so narrow that lovemaking was impossible. Or so he imagined.) An
early marketing genius as well as a populist, Ford hooked farmers on the
Model T by designing its wheelbase exactly as wide as that of horse-drawn
wagons so it would roll along nicely in the well-worn ruts in dirt roads.

The Model T literally transformed America's way of life, some histo-
rians going so far as to credit the "Tin Lizzy" with turning the tide of
"genetic degeneracy" by providing mountain folks a means of getting out

once in a while. The car's impact was felt from one coast to the other. People could now travel in relative comfort in any weather, and oil gushed from the ground to keep the creatures fed. Increased mobility meant an increase in marketplaces. Public and private monies formed safe roads that traversed mountains and crossed bodies of water, vacation touring became a phenomenon, and national parks came into being to preserve the land and enrich the visitors. Wrote David Halberstam: "With the Model T the modern industrial age—the industrial age that benefited rather than exploited the common man—began."

But where there are massive profits to be gained, exploitation is not far behind. Enter Alfred P. Sloan, Jr., the financial wizard who took over General Motors in the early twenties and didn't look back for forty years. He was all business and management, the man in the gray-flannel suit who, if truth be known, didn't even much like cars. As distinguished auto historian James Flink wrote, Sloan "abhorred 'personal' entrepreneurs such as Henry Ford. Under his leadership General Motors became the archetype of the depersonalized, decentralized corporation run by an anonymous technostructure." From the fourteenth floor of the GM headquarters in Detroit, Sloan ruled over his faceless executive committees with one goal: maximize profits. GM was driven by financial concerns—market first, consumer later. The corporation ushered big business into modern times.

Sloan introduced the "Drive Now, Pay Later" installment plan, a system that padded the company's coffers through interest on loans. He introduced *color*—multiple colors of the rainbow to attract buyers who wanted their cars to say more about them than was possible by driving a drab black Model T. "A car for every purse and purpose," stated GM's earliest ad. Sloan's brightest (and most sinister) idea was that each new model each new year should look different and cost more. For this purpose he drafted Harley Earl from a custom body shop in Hollywood, where Earl had been fashioning cars for the stars. The design changes were basically cosmetic, projecting an illusion of improvement—what Earl called "dynamic obsolescence"; a car was good for one year, then it looked old and out of place. Buying a new car every year allowed customers to broadcast to their neighbors: "I'm moving up the social ladder." All the car companies hawked the American dream like a carny (they still do) and advertised cars as an expression of America's triumphant life-style, but GM's 1924 ad entitled "The Psychology of the Automobile" took the cake: "How can

Bolshevism flourish in a motorized country having a standard of living and thinking too high to permit the existence of an ignorant, narrow, peasant majority? Is not the automobile entitled to the major credit in this elevation of our standard citizenship?"

By the late twenties, though, the nascent driving ecosystem experienced its first cycle of trouble. Bolshevik busters filled up the country so fast that there was literally no place for them to go. In ecological terms the auto population had reached its carrying capacity. It stopped expanding because it had consumed its main resource—namely, customers and roads. Yet manufacturers were building cars in such a fury that they neglected to notice that the market was saturated. In 1929 car salesmen sat in their jammed lots nervously twiddling their thumbs, expecting disaster. Which, of course, came when Black Friday called on October 29.

The car companies weathered the Great Depression without too much damage, if for no other reason than they had the product that no person wanted to do without. Still, they faced the problem of the freedom machines' running out of room. With all the farmers in cars, and many of them leaving the back forty for industrial jobs in the cities, the car companies, and especially GM, feared that people would park their cars for good and take the more convenient streetcar to work. Which they did. In 1937 some 7 billion passengers rode streetcars. Sloan couldn't have that, though, and so joined forces with Firestone Tires, Standard Oil, and Mack Machinery to buy up the nation's electric trolley and streetcar companies. Wrote Michael Renner of the Worldwatch Institute recently: "Beginning in the thirties, General Motors—together with counterparts in the oil, steel, and tire industries—acquired more than 100 electric rail systems in 45 cities, dismantled the electric lines, and paved over the tracks. By the late fifties, about 90 percent of the trolley network had been eliminated."

The auto industry was now gloating like the cat that had just swallowed the canary. While trumpeting cars as tickets to individual freedom, what in fact it was doing was methodically building a transportation oligopoly. After GM bought up the urban mass-transit companies, Sloan and his compatriots in the trucking union and tire and oil companies—dubbed "The Road Gang" by writer Helen Leavitt in *Superhighway—Super Hoax*—set their sights on providing more space for their products to roam. They rallied behind legislators with highway interests, legislators who eventually produced the 1956 Interstate Highway Act, which diverted funds from a special tax on cars, gasoline, and auto parts into highways and highways only. In the words of auto historian James Flink, the Interstate Highway Act "ensured the complete triumph of the automobile over mass-transit alternatives in the United States and killed off, except in a few large cities, the vestiges of balanced public transportation systems that remained in 1950s America."

Cars now proliferated like rabbits; highways and superhighways crisscrossed the nation. With the cities growing crowded, the generally affluent population fled to the newfangled suburbs and a dream home of their own—all made possible by the wondrous automobile. Manufacturers designed and promoted their cars with wild arrogance and glee. Car dealers were tripping over themselves to reel customers in for the kill. The cars themselves were symbols of jet stream progress and postwar confidence. Cadillacs featured tail fins that could impale a buffalo, while the GM Le Sabre offered the "Dagmar" dual-pointed bumper, named after a particularly well endowed Hollywood star. "We were putting on chrome with a trowel," remarked one of Harley Earl's protégés. As Jane and Michael Stern pointed out in *Auto Ads*, he wasn't kidding. "Presumably to keep it from taking off," they wrote, the 1958 Buick Airborne B-58 "featured an all-time record load of forty-four pounds of chrome-trim ballast." Autopia was in full bloom.

TROUBLE IN MOTOR CITY

Ecological wisdom tells us that when competition vanishes an ecosystem stagnates. The less diverse an ecosystem, the more unstable it becomes. By the early sixties competition had been squelched in the transportation ecosystem—you pretty much drove or you didn't get there—and the auto industry itself reflected this dominance. Basically it boiled down to when General Motors spoke, everybody listened. Lee Iacocca, who rose through the ranks at Ford (he developed the Mustang) before taking over at Chrysler, recently reflected: "We were controlled by General Motors." Chrysler was a "follow-GM group" that "marched lockstep to the big guy . . . I'm a student of this—I lived through it. GM was so powerful. They were the biggest bank in the world, the biggest everything. They had fifty percent of the market. They were so damned big, they could do anything they wanted. We were really in the ring with a thousand-pound gorilla."

Nevertheless, no one in Detroit in the early sixties was complaining about his place in the zoo. The manufacturers were annually earning billions without really trying. They had grown so smug that, as a 1982 National Research Council study put it, "innovation became increasingly incremental in nature and, in marketing terms, invisible." The study went on to note: "It may seem odd to think of manufacturing as anything other than a competitive weapon. . . . Yet the history of the automobile market in the United States suggests that by the late 1950s manufacturing had become a competitively neutral factor. . . . [N]one of the major producers sought to achieve a competitive advantage through superior manufacturing performance." Without diversity, choice was limited, and that meant one thing: individuals were at the mercy of the industry.

As the sixties unfolded, though, cracks in the monolith began appearing, with individuals exerting influence of their own. The safety issue provided the first breakthrough.

Automakers churned out cars for sixty-five years before introducing safety standards that prevented the steel-finned monsters from maiming and killing millions of people. The efforts of Connecticut senator Abraham Ribicoff and consumer crusader Ralph Nader turned the tables. Their research, and especially Nader's 1965 book on Chevy's misconceived Corvair, *Unsafe at Any Speed,* led to the National Traffic and Motor Vehicle Safety Act. (The poor Corvair. I had a black one in high school that I loved, even though it smoked so bad—inside the car!—that it made my Biscayne look like it was designed by Greenpeace.) Passed in 1966, the act mandated automakers to offer safety devices such as seat belts, padded dashes, impact-absorbing steering columns, dual braking systems, and standard bumper heights. From 1966 to 1979, the traffic death rate decreased by 39 percent.

Still, on the eve of the safety act's confirmation, GM vice president Harry Barr commented, "We feel that our cars are quite safe and quite reliable. . . . If the drivers do everything they should, there wouldn't be any accidents, would there?" Such tunnel vision defined the separatist attitude—the self-interest and shortsightedness—that remained entrenched in the industry and that American automakers would soon pay for in a big way.

The seventies signaled Detroit's lumbering out of step with the social and economic currents that guided the rest of the country. As for cultural savvy, it's doubtful Detroit ever had much to begin with. What can you say about an industry that attempted to reflect the psychedelic sixties by naming the color of a car AntiestablishMint? In fact, GM didn't initiate its own market-research division to determine what the public wanted or desired until 1980.

One of the most telling examples of Detroit's arrogance was its view of women. By 1970, women constituted 40 percent of the country's work force; by 1977 there were nearly 64 million licensed women drivers. That's quite a few women taking to the roads, women for whom driving itself represented independence and the liberty to live, work, and shop where they pleased. Nevertheless, Detroit and its Madison Avenue mouthpiece couldn't venture from the dark ages of sexual stereotyping. It's one thing for a 1959 Chevrolet ad targeted at women to read: "A busy homemaker . . . and how she travels! School in the morning, the store, luncheon with friends, the church guild, school again and, perhaps, tea. And what makes hers the best taxi service you ever saw? Her second love—a car of her own." But it's another thing entirely to come across a Dodge ad in 1978 that ends its sales pitch to women: "And bring Dad along. If things go the way they should, you and he will end up buying . . . the car." Heaven forbid, during the height of the women's movement, during the very year in which Janet Guthrie qualified for the Indianapolis 500, that a woman could buy a car by herself.

Even more revealing was a survey commissioned by *Woman's Day* magazine in 1979 to study the attitudes of, and interactions between, car dealers and consumers. The survey shot down the myth that women chose cars based on their comfort and style. "Being a woman, you'll appreciate De Soto interiors. They're as smartly styled as your own living room." Instead it proved that most women buyers were concerned with economy, reliability, durability, and handling. It also showed that most women couldn't care less about a car's brand; 90 percent said they would gladly replace an old car with a different make or model. These attitudes were shared by the suburbanites coming of age, a new generation of car buyers who not only didn't want to drive, but didn't want to be associated with their father's Oldsmobile. As Detroit slowly pulled its head out of its storied past, it was forced to see, with some chagrin, women and young adults behind the wheel of imports, notably the beetle-shaped one from Germany that got good gas mileage. In fact, Americans would buy more VW Bugs than any single make of car in history, including the Model T.

In the wake of the oil crises and overnight rises in gasoline prices in

1973 and 1979, Detroit rushed its small-car factories into overtime, pumping out Pintos, Vegas, Valiants, and Pacers. When gasoline prices stabilized, Americans returned to buying midsize and luxury cars, causing the small cars to languish on the lots like unwanted toasters. Free-market advocates have argued that had Congress lifted the price controls on oil, allowing gasoline prices to rise naturally, Americans would have continued to buy Detroit's small cars and would have conserved incalculable amounts of energy. Well, that may be so, but I think you'd have a tough time finding anyone who was genuinely pleased with his or her Vega, Pinto, or Pacer. They were proverbial buckets of bolts, hardly examples of the reliability, durability, and handling that a new generation of drivers demanded. At least when you were driving a Cadillac you didn't feel like the floorboard was going to fall out over the next bump.

Ralph Nader's efforts to improve auto safety spurred the consumer movement in the seventies. Drivers began complaining louder and longer about the quality of their cars, while independent investigators vindicated their complaints. (Over 50 million cars were recalled from 1966 to 1977.) The most widely publicized—and still disturbing—case revolved around the Pinto. As was uncovered by Mark Dowie of *Mother Jones* magazine in 1977, Ford manufactured Pintos for eight years with gas tanks that it knew were inclined to explode when impacted, even at speeds of less than ten miles per hour. While Ford lobbyists were busy battling the increasingly consumer-sensitive Washington over safety regulations, more than 5,000 people perished in fiery deaths in Pintos. As Dowie discovered, it would have cost Ford less than $11 a car to make the gas tanks safe.

Tantamount to the safety and consumer movements, environmental concerns rose in the seventies. As the nation mulled over the dying Great Lakes, birth defects from the toxic dump at Love Canal, grimy thick air over cities like Pittsburgh, and the escape of radioactive gases from the nuclear plant at Three Mile Island, big business looked more like what was bad than good for America. While Buckminster Fuller preached that Spaceship Earth was exhausting its natural resources, people fled in unprecedented numbers to national parks and wildlife refuges to enjoy the country's natural beauty. At the end of the decade, drivers didn't storm the dealers to trade in their gas-guzzlers for more fuel-efficient cars to preserve the earth, but at least now they were growing aware that the land and skies might be in serious trouble.

Meanwhile, Chevy Chevettes sat in greasy repair shops and expensive Chrysler LeBarons filled glistening new showrooms.

NATURAL SELECTION

One of the earmarks of evolution is "isolation"—which occurs in an insulated area where a new species develops, unencumbered, before expanding its range. This new species will survive on a wide scale if its attributes are favorable to, and therefore selected by, a new ecosystem. Natural selection is not just an "executioner of the unfit," as biologist Stephen Jay Gould puts it, but a creative force that actively adopts a new species and allows it to flourish. If a lack of competition has left an ecosystem stagnant and its organisms stumbling for health, and along comes a fit, strong, and durable new species, you can bet it will be welcomed with open arms, allowing the dance of evolution to continue on its merry way.

To the car biologist, this is precisely what happened in the eighties. On an isolated island in the Pacific, under protected conditions, a new species grew to maturity. When it arrived in the United States in full strength, it spread like kudzu.

The critical attribute of this new species was quality. Here were cars that ran smoothly with plenty of power, didn't hiss or rattle in the wind, turned and stopped with confidence and ease. Their appearance was simple and streamlined, not laden down with opulent features that implied obsolescence. In fact, they were painstakingly engineered to be anything but obsolescent. They were genuinely reliable and priced not to break anybody's bank. Naturally, Americans selected the new Hondas, Toyotas, and Datsuns with a fury.

Of course, the ecological rise of Japanese cars was spawned by material factors, namely economic nationalism. Like the early American auto industry, Japanese carmakers grew to maturity in their native land because they had no competition, neither from automakers abroad nor themselves— which is precisely how the Japanese government devised it. Under the motherly aegis of the Ministry of International Trade and Industry (MITI), Japan issued high tariffs and stringent inspections on imports to deter their arrival. MITI also dictated that all six major auto manufacturers remain wholly owned by the Japanese and be operated under national guidance.

That meant cooperation among the car companies, ancillary suppliers, and financial institutions. This relationship was managed by banking enterprises called *keiretsu*, which made sure that the car companies retained financial holdings in one another's companies—thus blocking foreign ownership—and maintained a high level of performance and quality.

How did American manufacturers feel about Japan's little arrangement? Lee Iacocca: "The Japanese market is rigged, I tell you. The son of a bitch is rigged! It's rigged! When I get up in the morning, I feel like I'm taking on Toyota, Honda, the Bank of Japan, and MITI."

Rigged or not, the high quality of Japan's cars ultimately stemmed from individual effort and efficient management that left American car companies laboring in the dark. Ironically, the Japanese system was based on the management philosophy of an American, W. Edwards Deming. During World War II, Deming worked in a Stanford think tank for the War Department, developing a statistical means of quality control that stressed the personal and social value of work. Following the war, American industries concentrated more on expanding production than improving quality, and Deming's philosophy fell on deaf ears. Disillusioned, he took a job at the U.S. Census Bureau, which sent him to Japan during the postwar American occupation to help the Japanese improve their census capabilities. In Japan Deming met a number of engineers who welcomed his quality-control philosophy, and in 1950 he hit the corporate lecture circuit. All of Japan's industry leaders attended.

As David Halberstam stated in *The Reckoning*, Deming's system for quality control provided the Japanese "with a manner of group participation that fitted well with the traditions of their culture. The Japanese workers were clearly a manager's dream—worthy, durable, industrious, unspoiled—and they were perfect for a system like Deming's, which required mathematical skill."

Hierarchy was nonexistent in the Japanese auto plants. The managers were not isolated in glass offices from the assembly workers but located in shouting distance on the factory floors. New models were not planned in isolated boardrooms but designed in meetings that combined financiers, engineers, and technicians. Nor were designs of any aspect of the cars etched in stone. If something went awry during the manufacturing process, workers were encouraged to speak up, and engineers would reconvene at the drawing board. It was a contributory process based on self-respect. In *Rude Awakening: The Rise, Fall, and Struggle for Recovery of General Motors*, Maryann Keller observed that "the Toyota secret was, finally, no secret at all, and it was as old as history: Treat both white- and blue-collar workers with respect, encourage them to think independently, allow them to make decisions, and make them feel connected to an important effort. Combine that culture with a good car and quality parts, and the results are obvious."

From 1977 to 1982, sales of Japanese cars rose from 12 percent of the American market to 22 percent. This ascension came at the same time that overall domestic car sales were taking a major plunge, from 9 million sold to 5.5 million. There was a recession on, but this only proved that when times were tough, the tough turned to the most economical and reliable cars. American car sales have picked up considerably since 1983, and to this day have experienced only small peaks and valleys in annual sales. Japanese cars, though, continue to rule the compact class. Especially on the West Coast. Tom Price, owner of eight Bay Area dealerships and eleven franchises, including GM, Ford, Nissan, and Lexus, told me that up to 80 percent of his sales are Japanese cars. "In fact," he said, "there's a great deal of peer pressure in the Bay Area *not* to buy an American car. People question other people's intelligence. They really do. Because the Japanese car is seen as a better quality, better price-value car."

Price, who bought his first dealership in 1976—selling Oldsmobiles—admitted that the Japanese did indeed produce a better quality car in the early eighties. Today, though, he believes that the only difference between American and Japanese compacts is one of perception. And that's because many of today's American compacts are, in reality, Japanese cars. How this union came about mirrors another ecological truth: when a new species flourishes in an ecosystem, it forces the prevailing and weakened species to comply or perish. Which, in essence, is what the American auto industry did. The Big Three manufacturers not only built cars in joint ventures with the Japanese—GM with Toyota (Geo Prizm); Ford with Mazda (Mercury Tracer); Chrysler with Mitsubishi (Plymouth Colt)—but introduced the Japanese management system in their plants. New cars were no longer planned by financial executives with an eye on the bottom line but by department members throughout the company working together in mutual respect. Maryann Keller concluded that the American auto industry's adaptation of Japan's successful methods represented "the most massive reorganization ever attempted in corporate America."

CONSUMER CHAMPION

The final upshot of the Japanese invasion is that it firmly placed the consumer in the driver's seat. Buyers can now venture into a showroom and choose from a wide range of cars that are actually (yes, it's true) designed to last. Not only that, it seems strange to walk into a modern car mart and see Hondas being sold alongside Chryslers and Pontiacs. Whatever happened to hot dogs, apple pie, and Chevrolet? Offering both Japanese and American makes is a matter of survival, said Price, and "is solely a function of the automobile market being consumer-driven instead of manufacturer-driven." And despite the contention of Tom and Ray Magliozzi (Click and Clack of the popular PBS radio show "Car Talk") that all cars look the same—"like jellybeans"—consumers actually have the greatest diversity of cars in history, a veritable candy store. Dealers, in fact, now fret that manufacturers are churning out more models than consumers can keep up with (the result being that showrooms are filling up with cars that nobody wants). And *too bad* that they no longer look like they belong on an aircraft carrier—or a 1959 Cadillac Sedan de Ville, which essayist P. J. O'Rourke once said looked like "the Batmobile after Robin wrecked it."

Today's mature market proves that true competition helps restore ecological balance and assures evolution (at least within the car sector of the transportation ecosystem). Japanese manufacturers have had no problem keeping pace with Washington's strict fuel-efficiency and air-quality regulations ("Tell us what the standard is, and we'll meet it," declared Nissan in the eighties), assuring an environment of clean-burning new cars. By choosing Japan's high-quality cars, consumers initiated one of the most progressive changes in the auto industry's history. But how far can consumers go? It's a tricky business talking about what people want and how they can affect an industry as complex as the automobile industry. But if anyone would have a handle on consumers' influence, it would be a man who has profited from exploring it for the past twenty years. Considering I was in Los Angeles, I paid a visit to J. D. Power.

Everyone who has glanced at a car ad in the past five years is probably

familiar with his name. As head of the respected independent consumer-
and market-research firm, his imprimatur on quality is blazoned across ads
as if it were an Olympic medal. Each year, based on over 2 million
questionnaires, his company produces hundreds of reports that measure car
owners' tastes and opinions, reports for which car companies shell out up to
$50,000. After working as a financial analyst for Ford, a market-research
consultant for GM, and director of corporate planning for McCulloch, the
chain saw people, Power went solo in 1968. His first big job was for Toyota,
who hired him to help plan its foray into the lucrative California market.
Today, said Joe Tetherow of Chrysler, "there isn't a car manufacturer
around that can ignore a J. D. Power report."

The company, J. D. Power and Associates, commands a modern two-
floor building in an office park in Agoura Hills, forty miles northwest of
Los Angeles. Power's personal conference room was a quiet refuge from the
frenetic office floor. We sat at a wide walnut table with a large crystal ball in
the middle. Power—his employees call him Dave—spoke softly and delib-
erately, resembling a New Englandish John Houseman. By the way, the
country's most influential consumer analyst drives a gray 1987 Oldsmobile.
"We test-drive all the new cars, but I do it more as a duty," he said. "I'm the
worst driver. I drive fast to get where I'm going as quickly as I can. So in the
gray Oldsmobile I'm able to avoid getting a ticket."

As we began discussing progressive changes in the auto industry, Power
agreed that the rise in quality of cars over the last two decades could be
traced to the consumer. By choosing Japan's reliable compacts in the
eighties, consumers sent a powerful message to the American auto industry
that said, You had better start meeting our desires. On the heels of technological improvements in fuel efficiency, brakes, and aerodynamics, domestic manufacturers were able to do just that. "Everything was then reduced
to a common denominator," said Power. "And when you have that kind of
situation, you have a lack of control by the manufacturer. General Motors
no longer controls the marketplace. The consumers do. And that's great for
the consumer."

What was great was that an improvement in the quality of cars ultimately meant an improvement in the quality of life. "I just know that we're
getting better personal transportation value than we were getting last year or
the year before," said Power. "Individuals today are under major pressures.
The pressure on time is worse than ever for the average commuter and car

owner. Therefore you start looking at what the passenger vehicle does for you today. And I think it's really improved life a lot. With all the labor-saving devices we have, and really a vehicle is a labor-saving device, I think we're reducing stress, and we should have more time available." As a result of feeling comfortable and safe in today's cars, Power believed, our relationship with cars was moving from simple status to something more lasting. "I don't think America's love affair with the automobile is over, but it's a different type of a love affair. More of a familial than a lover arrangement. It's like your sister rather than your wife or girlfriend."

Yet this relationship was under serious pressure from traffic and pollution, especially here in Southern California, where drivers lead the nation in the amount of time they spend in cars. Responding as a champion of both the consumer and the free market, Power asserted that the incentive to achieve clean air and excellent fuel efficiency must rest not with the industry but with consumers themselves. If people wanted less congestion and pollution they would have to pay for them. That was only fair. Federal regulations mandating automakers to produce fuel-efficient and clean-burning cars was, Power said, ultimately a blow against democracy and the individual consumer.

Consider safety regulations, he said. Did the consumer really want them? "That's what I don't think we understand in our society," said Power. "You might have a Ralph Nader, or people in the Department of Transportation, good engineers to a degree, looking out for the safety of the customer. In an elitist fashion they say, 'This should be done for the consumers.' OK, do it for the consumer, but who pays? The consumer pays. What I'm getting at is that people don't necessarily want what is being mandated across the board for everyone. You can have a professor of astrophysics who sides with Ralph Nader, who says we should have air bags across the board—this is all well and good. But does the consumer really want it? Anything that should be done should be put in terms of what the customer wants, and then let the market forces drive it."

Conserving energy and reducing pollution may be socially desirable, but Power didn't believe that car buyers were ready to foot the bill. "The consumer is smart. He says, 'Yeah, we want clean air and this and that, but when I go to buy a car, I'm going to get the best value I can for the three hundred and fifty dollars a month that I'm gonna have to pay for it. I don't really care about getting twenty-five miles per gallon versus thirty-two miles per gallon. There's a lot of other considerations. I want a big backseat because I might need to take my friends. Or I'm going to go camping so I'm going to get a sports-utility vehicle, and so what if it doesn't get the best gas mileage? It has a four-wheel drive, and I'm going to need it to go out and get away from the city and enjoy the green hills or the desert.' People want what's good for them in their own interests. They want everybody else to pay for clean air. There is a selfish motive and we're all that way—ninety-nine and forty-four one-hundredths percent of us."

Power speculated that if we as a society wanted to conserve energy, then the incentive to do so should come from government, not from the auto manufacturers. "If fuel efficiency is what we're striving for, then I would say through government policy you should tax to get that home," he said. "And the best way to do that is to put a tax on gasoline. If gasoline is a polluter and you think that alternative fuels are better, if you tax gas, alternative fuels become more competitive with gas. Electric vehicles then become more competitive. That will increase the development of those. If you put the gas tax on, you're going to reduce oil imports and make alternative means of transportation more competitive. And as part of the gas tax, you can dump that money back into rapid-transit development, and a third of it to improve the roads and the streets."

Power added that consumers today would never go for a gas tax in the voting booth, but perhaps as they better understood the personal consequences of the country's auto habit—namely, traffic congestion—their actions would change. In the meantime, though, "What we need is pressure from an economic standpoint to change behavior, to allocate resources in the direction of what the consumers want. And the consumers will begin to tell us what they want by their behavior."

OH, WHAT A FEELING

But will the automakers listen? Will they be responsive to new demands for clean and fuel-efficient cars or will they ignore them as they once ignored consumers' desires for a decent compact car? One real indication that consumers are wielding a bigger sword in the auto market is reflected in today's ads. The car commercials that dominate evening TV are more honest and credible: performance, quality, safety, and reliability now command more air time than status and the emphasis on new models, not to mention the outlandish claims the viewer was once subjected to between every segment of "The Andy Griffith Show" and "Happy Days." It may be hard, given advertising's track record of sorcery, to view ads that focus on air bags, safety cages, and antilock brakes ("For Once, a Pontiac Ad That Talks About Slowing Down") as little more than the emperor's new clothes, but at least they infer that buyers are concerned with a significant social issue. Similarly, using environmentalism as a selling point (Ford: "Today we're designing cars that are great looking and fit for the environment") may be no more than a ride on the green-marketing bandwagon, but it does help plant environmental issues in the mass media.

To me, the best new ads are TV commercials that express the joys of driving. Orchestrated with cinematic imagery, computer graphics, and quick-action editing, these ads suggest a modern fusion among driver, machine, and environment. When the man in the Acura puts his colleague on hold on his car phone, you sense he does so not only to enjoy the sensation of speeding along the winding country road ("Some things are too good to be interrupted") but to feel further in touch with the beauty outside his windshield. And even being mired in megalopolitan traffic is transformed into an enlightening experience as the fellow in his smooth, quiet Lexus climbs an on ramp to join the bumper-to-bumper grind. There's something inherently profound about the contemporary wave of commercials that stress the joys of driving. They don't play on fear or guilt. They seem downright respectful.

But let's not get carried away. Good old-fashioned deceit still abounds. In 1990 Volvo broadcast a TV commercial of a monster truck rolling over a bunch of Fords and a Volvo in a stadium. "There's only one car still standing out there," brags the PA announcer. "Apparently, not everyone appreciates the strength of a Volvo." Volvo was right about that. When Dan White, an auto mechanic in Austin, Texas, and his friend Pat Horne saw the commercial, they didn't appreciate the strength of Volvos at all. Before the commercial aired, they had been walking around a car show at the Texas Exposition and Heritage when they heard "the unmistakable noise of a saw cutting steel." They investigated and saw workers cutting roof-support pillars out of Ford Mavericks and Granadas. They also saw them reinforcing the inside of a Volvo with a wooden framework of two-by-fours. Civic-minded gents that they were, they reported their findings to the Texas district attorney's office after they saw the commercial. Following a brief investigation by the DA's office, Volvo confessed to the sham, issued a public apology, and reimbursed the DA's office $316,250 for investigative costs and legal fees.

But given that the temptation to manipulate powerful media images remains great, is it possible that the generally credible new car ads represent genuine respect for the consumer, perhaps even bear a social conscience? I took the question to Jack Palmer, senior vice president at Hill, Holiday and Connors, one of the nation's largest advertising agencies. Palmer supervised the initial ads for Nissan's Infiniti, surely the most notorious series of auto ads in recent history. The ads, which preceded the cars' arrival in showrooms by a couple of months, tossed current wisdom to the wind, mentioning neither engineering, safety, reliability, nor style. They didn't even show the car! Instead they featured images of a Japanese rock garden, the ocean, or a waterfall in the mountains. The radical ads were an immediate sensation in the media, where they were commonly ridiculed. Most of the jokes were variations on Jay Leno's remark that the $40,000 Infinitis might not be selling well, but, hey, sales of rocks and trees were going through the roof.

I met Palmer in chic Marina Del Rey, where the agency's offices, located in a high rise, overlooked a harbor of sailboats and glistening wood yachts. Your classic casual executive, he was dressed in Levi's, a pullover shirt, loafers, and no socks. He was personable, articulate, and unhurried. It seemed like he had come into the office for no other reason than to be interviewed. Curiously, we didn't conduct the interview in a gilded executive office or conference room, but in a small, vacant, data-entry office in a corner of the building.

Palmer explained that the Infiniti ads reflected "one of the cores of Japanese culture, which is respect for other individuals. One of the things I learned very quickly was how much stock Infiniti put in this respect for the customer—from the way the cars were designed to the way the showrooms were designed to the way the sales consultants were taught to interact with customers. It seemed as if a very low-key, a little bit cerebral, cool advertising approach would go hand-in-glove with that respect for people. By happy coincidence, the kind of people Infiniti wanted to talk to are presumably those most receptive to, and appreciative of, not having one more talking head scream at them out of the television set. Or some huge shot of the car with some snappy, semisnide headline and a couple paragraphs of

body copy in a magazine. That's been done to death. We had an opportunity to do something different, and I was absolutely delighted because it
was perceived not just as being different, but being respectful to people.
Long before I got into the advertising business I learned that you're more
likely to convince somebody of something by talking to them than screaming at them."

Palmer's agency sent its art director and copywriter to Japan, where they
were exposed to a Japanese rock garden. "The point of the Japanese rock
garden is that you don't look at any one thing that is there, so you fold in on
yourself," said Palmer. "It's the sense of looking at something that provides a
space in your mind. That was the genesis of the ad campaign. Everybody
has had the experience of confronting a picture or vista that causes you to
become more contemplative than your day-to-day business. So our point
was to give people in the course of their media consumption this breathing
space. What we were going to do with this space is drop in some pearls of
wisdom, something of the philosophy of Infiniti. We needed to generate
credibility. We recognized that the world was probably not breathlessly
awaiting another car, let alone another Japanese car, let alone a Japanese
luxury car, which is for most people a wonderful oxymoron. We wanted to
build awareness for Nissan's Infiniti division even before the cars were
available for sale."

Palmer stressed that advertising achieved its aims not by persuasion but
by capturing a spirit of the times. "The spoils of the game go to the people
who are quickest and most astute at meeting what's going on in the population," he said. He regarded the 1960s Volkswagen ad that consisted of a
picture of a lemon as the classic example. "People thought of VW in the
sixties, in the heyday of the Beetle, as being for people who marched to the
sound of a different drummer, or were iconoclastic or hip. Volkswagen did
not create a bunch of people who looked at the lemon ad and smiled and
said, 'Oh, I get it.' Those people were there, but nobody before had the wit
and the insight to write advertising that spoke to them in that fashion."

Palmer admitted that while there may be "certain people in advertising
playing fast and loose," advertising today had moved beyond "hype and
bombast" and become "more honest." Instead of making outlandish claims
for a product, advertising allowed consumers to make up their own minds.
At least that was the kind of advertising he sought to practice. "Nobody

ought to be in a position to say to the marketplace, 'This is good for you,' "
he said. "The role of advertising, in my mind, ought to be to modestly
convey the information about a product or service that will help the
consumer make a decision, preferably positive, with regard to that product
or service. In the long run, nothing else will work. Nobody knows how to
sell a car off a television screen or off a printed page—it doesn't work. It's
often stated, and it's absolutely true, that with the exception of former wives
and houses, the car is the most expensive thing you own. There is nothing I
can say to you, or hope to say to you, that is going to convince you to part
with twelve thousand dollars—never mind forty thousand—because I say
so. Well, who the fuck am I? What's it look like? What's it do? What's gonna
happen the first time it breaks?"

When I mentioned that the Infiniti ads seemed to validate his beliefs
that advertising was successful when it treated consumers with respect and
intelligence, Palmer smiled. "In a perverse way, the ad campaign could be
called too successful. One of the problems that dealers encountered was
this tidal wave of humanity that was storming the dealership. And the poor
sales consultants didn't know what to do. Because there were a whole lot of
people who came in because they were intrigued by the advertising but
simply weren't in the market for a thirty-eight-thousand-dollar car."

Alas, although they won prestigious advertising awards, the Japanese
rock garden ads may have been a step ahead of their time. Consumers—the
media, anyway—were not quite ready to accept a new car without first
taking its measurements. The ads lasted less than a month before giving
way, as Palmer said, "to what might uncharitably be called more traditional
car advertising." Uncharitable, indeed. The day after I interviewed Palmer,
he was fired from the agency.

Nevertheless, even if their subtlety bordered on the extreme, the Infiniti
ads signaled the auto industry's growing respect for the consumer. Clearly
the industry is no longer dictating consumers' needs, but responding to
them. As one industry wag put it, cars today have air bags not "because
Detroit got warmhearted all of a sudden" but because consumers grew
more sophisticated about safety and demanded them. What can consumers
demand next? Less congested roads? Cleaner skies? Alternative forms of
energy? If we can go from the Chevy Corvair to the Honda Accord in
twenty years, anything seems possible.

AT THE CROSSROADS

Change is spawned in areas of crisis, so as I left California to make my field observations around the country, I would concentrate my search on the most stressed ecosystems, the regions where the most cars were registered: Phoenix, Dallas and Houston, south Florida, Atlanta, and New York City. Yet as I traveled between the crisis points, I would encounter a range of individuals in the Southwest, South, Midwest, and East Coast who, when not pulling their hair out in traffic and smog, would contribute a unique and important voice to my overall ecological portrait.

Right now America's driving ecosystem stands at a crossroads, and every driver has a stake in mapping its future. Here we sit in traffic and pollution, turning our land into ugly cement roads, and fighting wars over oil. At the same time we have more power than ever to inaugurate change. The goals of preservation and healthy evolution are within reach. But which way will we turn?

Headed into the new realm of ecological possibility, I light out for the territory.

Eastward ho!

PART II

FIELD
OBSERVATIONS

Four

My
Car,
My
Kingdom

Everything that's happened in this goddamn country in the last fifty years
has happened in, on, around, with, or near a car.
—Harry Crews, *Car*

O ut of your car, off your horse," urged naturalist writer Wendell Berry,
"if you truly want to appreciate where you live. On foot, you can
discover that the earth is still "full of beguiling nooks and crannies" and feel
an active part of the landscape.

But then Mr. Berry probably didn't venture off his Kentucky farm
much. What did he know about the western cowboy consciousness of
cars? What did he know about freewheeling individualism and riding
across wild, wide-open spaces? I was driving with John Scott through the
Carson Valley on the eastern slope of the Sierra Nevada in his VW
Camper, one of four cars that had been sitting in the driveway of his
spacious Spanish-style home in the tiny town of Minden (we left behind a
Toyota 4×4 pickup, a Lincoln Town Car, and a new Mercedes). We
traveled along what was once the Overland Trail, past cattle grazing on
lush bottomland pasture, past Genoa (once called Mormon Station, the
first white settlement in the territory), through high-country sage and
stands of pine. Above us—and I mean directly above us, rising straight
into the air like skyscrapers—were the craggy, sheer mountains. Dark
thunderclouds, interspersed with blue sky, moved down over the valley.

"People say, 'Well, why did you come to Nevada?' " John said. He didn't feel he needed to finish the statement.

Like other drivers I would meet on the first western leg of my expedition, John gave the impression of a person born into the wrong century— or, rather, a person who carried many of the ideals of the last century into the present one. John still carried a gun now and then (he was a crack shot); in his wallet was the gold badge of a volunteer deputy sheriff; he rode his motorcycle cross-country whether or not there were trails or roads; and he talked of individual responsibility and community with passion. At age forty-seven, John ran a very successful insurance brokerage.

The car, naturally, played a big role in John's life—50 percent of his income was generated from the sale of auto insurance. He started with 135 files and went to his present clientele of 3,000 policyholders. "The car has impacted me considerably," he said.

The car has also impacted his area. When John arrived twenty years ago, Minden was not much more than a bedroom community for the casino workers at Lake Tahoe. But that changed as the roads got better; many people now commute to Reno, and the eastern slope has opened up to development. Reno has grown into Sparks, and Carson City has expanded into Dayton. Even his own little community of Gardnerville and Minden experienced a traffic bottleneck. The surrounding Carson City valley has grown to 28,000 people, with subdivisions approved to add another 25,000.

John said people's feelings about growth have shifted. "I would say the sentiment's now more, Let's protect the valley. Growth is important, but you don't want to have it rampant. In my own business, I feel that without people I probably would have starved to death. But I've reached a plateau where the amount of business I have is such that I would rather do with less population and keep the rural life-style than try to squeeze out more money and lose some of the benefits that we have here in the community.

"We don't have pollution. Reno has pollution, they have an inversion there, but the valley doesn't. Not yet. That's the reason I left Los Angeles, and to me, it was unhealthy. It was terrible, so I got the hell out of there. I came here for the blue skies. My motivation was clean air, believe it or not."

John got into the deputy sheriff business because it was just plain interesting. He was a friend of the sheriff; they were shooting buddies. "He had seen me handle myself," John said, "and I think in all fairness he didn't feel I would be a liability to him." Being a businessman, John also wanted to know what was actually going on in his community, and what better way than to be a cop. "In this community, people don't look at police officers as pigs, you know. They look at them as being people that are a helpful part of the community. I was what they called a special deputy. I only worked weekends. Most of the time you're just stopping civilians that had a little problem that could be straightened out. The people that we did arrest were really bad hombres."

Mainly, John helped out on patrol. "It was not a lot of showboating and taking out your weapon and, you know, spinning the cylinder." He liked his part-time job and felt it helped link him with the community. "You should be your brother's keeper," he said. "You should be involved to the point where you can do something positive." But eventually John began to worry about his dual roles: being a deputy sheriff and an insurance businessman could lead to conflict. Investigating a car accident, for instance, might prove to be a bit sticky. John stopped his patrol duties, but he kept his badge and got a permit to carry a concealed weapon. He was now a free-lance deputy—which had its own dangers.

"You have to be careful about free-lancing because you can get in a whole lot of trouble," he said. "Once I was driving my dad back to his residence in Carson City. I also had my little boy with us. We are coming down Highway 395 and my headlights catch this gal that is to the side of the road, just leaning there up against the barbed-wire fence. No car, nothing there.

"So I turn around and come back. I get out of the vehicle and she says, 'Can you help me? I think my leg's broken.' And she's bleeding, has facial injuries and so on. She tells me that her boyfriend has hit her with his car. Came by and sideswiped her with the open door. And she's in bad shape. She can hardly move.

"So I kinda prop her up and start to move her to my car, and she's crying, she's in a lot of pain. She's saying, 'We've gotta get outta here because he's gonna come back and get me.'

"Well, things get real bizarre real quick because just then someone runs up behind me, and of course I spin around and I tell him, 'Stop right there!' He is on foot. And he says the same thing: 'We've gotta get out of here.' I don't know where he came from. I say, 'You stay on the other side of my vehicle. I'm gonna get this gal in here. Do not come around to this side.'

"And so I get her loaded in the backseat of my car and I tell my dad to open the glove compartment and hand me my revolver. I put it in my belt in my back. And meantime I'm telling this guy to stay on the other side. I ask him who he is, what he has to do with all this. He explains that they were all three out at a bar and the girl's boyfriend got jealous of the attention he was paying her, and so he threw him out of the car and then he threw her out of the car and then he tried to run her over. This's how she got injured.

"All of a sudden this other vehicle comes roaring around the corner and piles up next to us. The guy gets out. He is definitely drunk. I mean, he could barely drive the automobile. He says he wants to take her. And I say, 'No problem. We would like to take her to the emergency room, and if you like you can come along, though I don't think it's a good idea to get her out of the car at this point.' He starts to get real belligerent. He's getting real upset. Real upset.

"And I got my little boy in the car, I got my dad in the car. He's white as a sheet. I got this bleeding lady in the car, and I got this other guy on the other side. The boyfriend's glaring at him, and he's real whipped up. I don't know what he's gonna do. So I'm just talking to him real nice and explaining that she needs medical help. And he's getting more belligerent and saying she deserved what she got. And I say, 'I don't really know, maybe she did, maybe she didn't, but we should get her checked out.'

"So he continues getting real nasty. Well, with that, I take my identification and I throw my wallet to him and say, 'Open the wallet.' It lands in the dirt in front of the headlights because I don't want him too close to me. He's too big and he's a real problem and I've got another problem, now, too, because I've got this firearm on me. I don't want him to wrestle it away from me.

"He picks up the wallet and says, 'You're a police officer?' And I say, 'Yes, that's right.' And I say, 'You can handle this without any problem. There's no reason for everybody to get all excited now. She's hurt. I'll take her to the hospital. Just let it slide.' But he's not impressed and he starts to take another step toward me. 'Look,' I say, 'the situation's escalated a little beyond what everybody can handle!' I figure I'm gonna have to draw out the revolver and use it. 'I suggest you get in your vehicle and just take off.'

"We were right on the verge, it could've gotten completely out of control. But instead he lets out a bunch of profanity and gets in his car and takes off.

"Right. So I load the other guy in the car and we make a U-turn and take off to the emergency room. When we get there, the nurse is trying to handle everything routinely, she doesn't realize what is going on. I say, 'I need to use your phone. I don't want this guy showing up here at the emergency room.'

"She is a little slow to let me use the phone, so I just grab it and call the sheriff's department. I think it's Steve Powell. I tell him to get somebody over here at the hospital right away, and I give him the plate number on the boyfriend and tell him he's headed toward Carson City, and he's real intoxicated and real nasty. In about twenty minutes the highway patrol arrests him.

"Steve comes down to the emergency room and takes the police report from the lady, and everything gets handled. What I don't realize is that I have blood all over me, you know, quite a bit of blood from carrying her from one place to the next. Also, I don't realize I still have my firearm sticking out of my belt. No wonder the nurse and everybody else is looking at me so strange. When I walk out, someone says to Steve, 'Who is that guy?' Steve says, 'Don't you know? That's the Lone Ranger.' They still talk about that down at the station."

The Lone Ranger had fled L.A. long before the absolute auto infestation of smog, sprawl, and gridlock. He'd found a picturesque valley with enough room to roam, a solid community with clear boundaries where individualism and hard work paid off, where you could sit in your backyard at the end of the day and stare across open space and gaze up at the High Sierra. But the eastern slope, as John said, was "being discovered." Already the first hints of the Los Angelesization process were evident: smog to the north; better roads leading to a higher population; land subdivided for housing. Even Minden had two new mini-malls. But the infiltration, though evident, was still minuscule. Such was not the case farther south in Arizona. Arizona had more than been discovered.

DESERT SPRAWL

By the time I got to Phoenix, the monsoons had just ended. Stacks of sandbags still lined curbsides and many yards and vacant lots were still murky brown lakes. The temperature was 110, and the humidity wasn't much better. My first impression was that Phoenix was another American

Dream (à la L.A.) come true—ticky-tacky tract housing complexes and mini-malls stretching boundlessly into the flat desert horizon. On the radio they were boasting that the population had just exceeded Denver's; Phoenix was now number seven in the U.S. of A. The city was first formed around an irrigation system created by Native Americans, but now it seemed as if Phoenix was perpetually remaking itself in obeisance to the car; they were building freeways as fast as they could slap down the cement. I leaned into the windshield and looked around. They called this region a valley, but damned if I could see any mountains. The area seemed a dull patchwork of Spanish-style condos, town houses, and richer, more sequestered (they had walls) "planned urban developments" with desert xeriscaping and the highest per capita incidence of swimming pools on the planet.

To talk about Phoenix, or any large contemporary metropolitan area, as a city is to use a complete misnomer. By shared usage, Phoenix is the common name for a large, contiguous urban region that includes two-thirds of the population of Arizona, encompassing Tempe, Scottsdale, Glendale, Alhambra, and more, and is earmarked by several dozen urban villages, clusters of large modern buildings and mammoth malls, usually always constructed at freeway and major highway intersections. These rather impressive pagodas of the Information Age are *big*, constituting millions of square feet of office, retail, entertainment, and hotel space—spectacles of steel and glass and boutiques jutting out of an otherwise veritable sea of sprawl and people.

My first, rather reluctant, contact worked in one of the region's housing squares, this one a fancy single-story apartment complex that could just as well have been a convalescent home or a huge swanky motel. The young woman's name was Laura—she wouldn't give me her last name. Nor would she tell me where she lived (she said she lived here, but then talked about her commute to work). She'd brought along a woman friend and workmate to, I guess, oversee the interview process and maintain a fast eye. After all, they didn't know who I was. Maybe I was some sort of Car Moonie, a recruiter for some bizarre automotive cult.

We sat in the common room of the apartment complex. They gave me a Pepsi. Laura remained shy and hesitant, never quite loosening up; every time she verged on enthusiasm or self-disclosure, she caught herself. I learned that traffic in the Phoenix area was somewhat seasonal; during the winter the population swelled with snow birds feasting on the fine weather and adding to the congestion. I learned that Laura was environmentally conscious, though not to the same extent as people on the coast. "It's like you're in your own little world over there," her friend said. I learned that Laura drove a Mazda RX7 sports car, and drove it fast—according to "Laura's rules," her friend chimed in. But all in all, the whole process was like pulling teeth, and I felt like an imposition.

Downtown, or what there is of downtown—more or less a strip with a few tall buildings—I poured dimes into a pay phone to drum up my next . . . what? contact? convert? I was beginning to feel like a missionary on the prowl for disciples. I reached Bob Hoke. Sure, he'd talk to me tonight, and he immediately invited me to his house in Scottsdale. I thought, OK, this's either a very trustful soul or else he's strange. (Naturally he turned out to be something of the latter.)

OSTRICH EGGS FOR THE REPUBLIC

"He's here!" shouted a thin man with a kind of crudely chiseled face. Completely uninterested, he invited me into a paneled living room where two cute little girls were lying on the floor watching TV. Soon a stocky man with a round face and a bushy black mustache emerged and introduced himself as Bob. "This is my brother and his kids," he said. "I live in a room on the side of the house. Let's go out to the back patio and talk." Bob was wiping his hands with a towel, trying to get rid of the last bit of grease. Earlier he had installed a new starter in his Suzuki Samurai.

For the last four years Bob, thirty-nine, has delivered pizzas, driving up to two hundred miles a day. Before that he was a salesman for a solar heating company, but just "kind of dropped out of life." He grew up in Winslow, Arizona, sixty miles east of Flagstaff. He learned to drive on dirt roads when he was twelve, and insisted he had been clocking sixty thousand miles a year since his late teens. I asked him what it was like driving in Phoenix.

"It's like the Wild West," he said. "In this valley, the freeway system is sucko. That's what they're trying to improve now. Driving in the metropolitan Phoenix valley, depending on what time of year it is, is really bad. Just too much traffic, too much congestion. It's overdeveloped. And it's not like New York City, where you have taxis doing the majority of chauffeuring people around. Here, because of the sprawled-out development, everybody needs a car. Of course, a car is a kind of personal power trip. Where a hundred years ago you walked to wherever you wanted to go, now you drive and there's no limitations. You can drive one hundred miles or two hundred or a thousand, what you feel like. There's no mass transit other than buses. I've ridden the bus maybe four times in my entire life, and I hated it every time.

"I feel at peace in my car. Why, I don't know. Maybe I'm a space driver and I'm driving a spaceship. In essence, we are all space travelers. We travel through space-time in a forward motion. Every second that goes by, we're traveling in time, just in forward time. It's a time we have no control over, but we are each individual time machines. So, in essence, the car may be a way to control that time.

"Driving to me is very enjoyable. I enjoy it because I don't obey the traffic laws. I drive within my ability. I'm an excellent driver. I'm sure everybody will say they are an excellent driver, but I have the ability to prove it if I was ever put to the test. My ability to physically maneuver the car, my alertness, my reaction time, my understanding of people, my understanding of the car.

"You can drive down the freeway at any point in time and the majority of people go ten to fifteen miles an hour over the posted speed limit. That even holds true on the general streets. People, as a whole, will drive to their ability, which is the way it should be, and that's the way the stupid laws were written to begin with: 'reasonable and prudent.' Well, what's reasonable and prudent for an old lady at sixty and what's reasonable and prudent for a young man who has better reflexes is an entirely different story. So you can't make a mandatory thirty-five-miles-an-hour speed limit and expect it to hold true for everybody. People are going to drive to their ability. That's nature."

"And you think it's safe to drive like that?" I asked.

"Absolutely. People get into accidents because they're so worried about trying to obey rules and regulations that they aren't truly paying attention to what's going on around them. I'm not saying we don't need guidelines, but let's don't call them laws because they're not laws. They're rules and regulations. What a person does with those rules and regulations is answerable only to their consciences and God, whoever that may be. Because we supposedly live in a free country. We don't, but they tell us we do. We should be left up to our abilities to do whatever.

"For me, it's actually safer, yes. When I'm driving down an open road or highway I drive thirty to fifty miles an hour faster than the flow of traffic because it takes me seconds to get around a car, where if I were going the same speed it would take me four to five times as long to get around that car than it would to zip around them. It doesn't take that much more to slow down to what that car's doing. If he's doing fifty-five and I'm doing ninety-five, I can slow down forty miles an hour—it doesn't take that much to slow down forty miles an hour. Now, if I had to come to a complete stop, that's an entirely different story. That's where people have their misconceptions. They feel if they're going ninety, they have to slow down ninety miles an hour, but you don't. You slow down to what your surroundings are. So, in that circumstance, I'm driving forty miles per hour.

"I don't smoke. I don't drink. I don't do drugs. Driving to me is an extremely serious business. I value my life more than anybody else's out on the road so I damn well ain't going into a position where I'm going to injure my life just because I want to drive fast. Now, if I didn't have the ability to drive the way I do, I wouldn't do it. But I have that ability and I'll be damned if someone is going to tell me that I can't."

The police were telling Bob that he can't. At least they were trying: they'd given him ten tickets in the last five years. According to Bob, though, they had pretty much given up. They wouldn't even pull him over anymore because he had beaten all ten tickets in court. He had marched into court and told the judge that he didn't have any authority over him. Bob claimed the judge agreed with him—not explicitly, mind you, but by dismissing the tickets. I nodded, but was confused. "What do you mean he didn't have any authority over you?"

"It's very simple. They have what they call these traffic laws. But a law is not a law unless it's a constitutional law. I recognize no other laws except God's laws, and that's natural laws. They cannot fine me or imprison me because I break one of their rules. It only becomes a rule to me if I agree to it, if I enter into a valid contract—which I have not done. I've signed a driver's license form, but I signed that under duress because they told me I had to. Therefore that is not a valid contract. All three elements of a contract—the offer, the acceptance, and the results—aren't in play. Under the Constitution, that's the only way you can be forced to conform to a contract. So I have not entered into a contract, and therefore they have no authority to ticket me."

"And the judges accept that?"

"Absolutely. They have no choice. Basically, I asked them two simple questions. Under what authority or jurisdiction am I being charged, and where do you get your authority to do that? They can't answer that. If they answer 'the traffic laws,' then it falls back onto the contract, and there is no contractual agreement between me and the state. So, since they refuse to answer that on record, they'll dismiss the ticket. Therefore I'm never liable.

"Here's a story for you. The last ticket I got was here in Scottsdale. You've probably been pulled over by the cops, right? Well, they're hard-asses. That's their job, I guess. He asked me for a driver's license, registration, insurance, and all those things, and I gave it to him. He goes back to the car and calls it in, and I don't know what they told him, but he comes back with an entirely different attitude. He says, 'What do you do? Does it work in court?' I say, 'What do you mean, what do I do?' He lets it slip like he didn't want to go any further with it. I was going twenty-five miles over the posted speed limit. He says, 'Well, you should slow it down, and I'm going to write you a ticket.' I said, 'You can give me a copy of it, but I don't have to sign anything.' So he says, 'OK.' I signed: 'Received under duress.' They don't like that at all. He says, 'Well, good luck in court.' I don't know what they had on the computer on me, but I'm probably listed as a troublemaker, a constitutionalist. They hate constitutionalists. They ain't American."

Bob viewed driving as rebellion more than anything else. "It's a rebellion against what they say is true, and I know is not." Bob was a truth seeker, he explained, and had spent his whole life seeking out who we are and why we are here. There were no simple answers, but he figured it had something to do with God. (Uh-oh, I thought.) "How my idea of driving fits the big picture is, I don't know who God is. I don't even know if there's a God. I suspect there's a God. I hope there's a God, but I can't tell you there's a God out there and this is who it is. Basically it all boils down to, Who do you answer to? I'm damn sure not going to answer to a government. There isn't a government on earth, there isn't a person on this earth, who's ever going to tell me what to do as long as I'm not hurting another soul. That truly falls under our Constitution. The only time you can be jailed or fined is when you cause harm to another human being, which is fair. I can't forcibly impress my views upon you, and vice versa. So, the government damn sure ain't going to enforce their views upon me because it's just a body of idiots up there that don't have a clue of what's going on. They're going to tell me what to do? Not a chance.

"The international banks front the world, the insurance companies answer to them. Money is the glue, the fabric of the entire world. We're caught in a web, for lack of a better way to explain it. We have to exist in this web, and the only way we're going to exist in this web is with money. And guess who controls the money? The international banks do.

"So there's many different facets of what's going on. My explanation is there's definitely a good and dark force in the universe. You can call that God and Satan as most people do. However you define it, it's there. The dark force, to me, is what runs this world."

"What are you going to replace the bankers with?"

"The truth."

"Do you have any credit cards?"

"No. I used to. I used to have American Express, Visa, MasterCard, Diner's, all of those. When I finally got informed enough I sent them all back. I don't even have a checking account anymore. I haven't paid income tax for six years. Wait a minute, I want to show you something. I'm also an artist."

Bob rushed into the house through a side door and returned with a carrying case. He opened it, stripped back layers of velvet, and pulled out an intricately carved ostrich egg. The egg displayed an engraved image of a smiling man and a naked woman surrounded by lacelike filigree. Bob read the inscription: "On July 1, 1989, Playboy Hugh M. Hefner seals his love to 1989 Playmate Kimberly Conrad forever." Bob had sent color photographs of the egg to Hefner in hopes of selling it to him, but so far Hef hadn't called back. Bob had, however, sold eggs commemorating Super Bowl XXI and the 1987 America's Cup victory to Ripley's Believe It or Not museums in, respectively, Dallas and Prince Edward Island. He also sent an egg carved with images of the American eagle to former President Reagan, whose office responded with a brief note of thanks. Bob filigreed the eggs with dental equipment, working on some for up to four hundred hours apiece. He showed me his latest work, the World Peace Egg. Carved to replicate a globe, it also featured a Christ-like portrait and the phrase "A World in Dire Trouble." He hoped to sell the egg (asking price: $250,000) to a major American corporation whose CEO would then present it to

Mikhail Gorbachev. Impressed as I was by the filigree eggs, I seized the opportunity to return to the ostensible subject of driving.

Bob seemed to believe that cars were destroying the environment, but his views on what to do next were, well, quintessential Bob. "If I were to give up my car—which I'm not going to do—if God comes down in the next ten to twenty years—and I'll believe it when I see it—then it's his problem. I would like to be able to do something if He gives me the means and the ability to. That's one of the reasons I want to become wealthy. But the working man can't do a damn thing. He's got to exist and his car is part of that existence. So what the hell is the working man going to do? It's the oil and insurance companies and the banks. They don't want to do anything. So the working man can't do a damn thing about his existence but complain.

"The oil companies like those billions and trillions of dollars they're lining their pockets with. They don't want to do away with the gasoline engine and all the gas stations. That's why they want to make a rechargeable battery for electric cars that's only going to get you two hundred miles so that you'll have to stop at a recharging station. It boils down to they don't want a free, independent individual.

"There's a growing number of people like me that are very unhappy with what they tell us is the truth. We're trying to educate ourselves to the point of understanding how to change it. There's no organization because most of us are poor and fighting to stay alive in a system that we don't like. I think the world's love affair with the automobile is their ability to control something, to control what they do in a world they can't control. Driving is someplace to vent my frustration at our lack of control."

Bob strongly felt that the best thing the government could do was to get out of our lives. It was not up to the government to do anything, it was up to the people. With the government out of the picture, people would respond to truth and their own conscience once again. "Why do we need government? We don't. No one has respect for the government simply because it is stupid in its mandatory policing of people. People are going to do what they want anyway. I do anything I want. I don't worry about their laws because their laws don't apply to me. They don't apply to any American if they choose to educate themselves about how to act under the Constitution. I am a free preamble constitutional citizen until they declare me otherwise."

Hucar Rights

Novelist David Brin once coined the phrase "dogma of otherness" to describe the prototypical American trait of defending a contrary opinion. " 'There's always another way of looking at things' is a basic assumption of a great many Americans," he said. Dogma of otherness would be the polite way to describe Bob's constitutionalist views. (Conspiratorial ravings, I guess, might be another way.) But iconoclastic views invariably hold out value to others. Bob's belief that traffic laws are not rooted in the Constitution stokes the familiar debate of whether driving is a right or a privilege bestowed by government. It's a question I asked on my questionnaire. (Eighty-five percent answered that driving was a privilege.) Yet there is a ground swell of Constitution sticklers who insist that driving is indeed a natural right, and that driver's license fees and traffic fines do little to promote the general welfare of America's carbound citizenry.

Glenn Braunstein heads the brigade of right-to-drivers. The thirty-seven-year-old paralegal from Spokane, Washington, told me he was the "first one in the country to challenge the issue of whether driving was a right or privilege." He got on his high horse in 1982 when his wife got stopped and ticketed for driving without a license. Now he appears on national TV talk shows, does seminars around the country, and is about to serve a nine-month jail sentence.

Glenn began by dipping into early Washington State driving law, where, between 1917 and 1921, the courts clearly spelled out that the individual citizen, in the ordinary course of life and business, had every *right* to use the common roads. Since then, Glenn maintained, the license has been used solely as an illegal means of generating revenue. "Not one person in seventy years challenged that," he said.

Glenn lost both his wife's case and the appeal—the Court of Appeals did concede that driving was a "qualified right"—but drafted a series of law briefs detailing his arguments. These briefs have become something of a cause célèbre among constitutionalists (Glenn is one of Bob's gurus; it was Bob who directed me to him), and Glenn insisted they have led to numerous dismissals of citations and driving-without-a-license cases in courts around the country. He admitted, however, that the dismissals were due less to the briefs' persuasiveness than to the fact that prosecutors just didn't want to take the time and expense to battle them in court. But not so in his own particular case. After driving for six years without a license, Glenn got nailed, and even though it was only his first offense, he was sentenced to nine months in jail (now on appeal). "Most people after their *sixth* offense don't even spend *one day* in jail," he said. "I got railroaded big-time. You know why? Because my issues are so damn valid that I scare them to death. They know that I'm the one that started this driver's license movement all across the United States."

Despite his notoriety, Glenn does not want to be considered a fanatic. "I'm more reasonable than most people you find in this movement," he said. "What I teach people is that along with a right comes a responsibility. And if you don't responsibly exercise your right, it can be taken away. With due process, of course.

"Constitutionalists don't want to be controlled in any way, shape, or form. And they don't think the government has a right to control them unless they agree to it, because of so-called consent of the governed. But what they're not looking at is the social contract. When you live in a society you have to give up certain things to benefit society. One of the things which is a valid use of the police power is to protect us from one another, OK? For instance, the testing of individuals to operate a motor vehicle. Taxing, on the other hand, is *not* a valid use of police power."

Although Glenn's first brief has resulted in many dismissals, there are also hundreds of people doing jail time. "What's happening is that they are creating a new body of law, case after case after case. For example, the ruling against my wife was subsequently used in a decision against a guy in Oregon, and then so on and so on." Not to be foiled, Glenn wrote a new brief with a fresh approach. His latest evidence turned up research that license fees do not accomplish the task for which they were supposedly designed—"to protect the people and improve the safety on the highways"—but end up in general funds to help pay for things like new jails and courthouses. In lieu of passing an easy test and forking over ten bucks to the DMV, Glenn wants to initiate legislation that would require of drivers the same thing the FAA requires of pilots: a Certificate of Demonstrated Ability that never expires. This certificate would be based on the ability to drive competently and safely and would grant the state the power to retest drivers. "Look what really happens," he said. "In Washington, every four years on my birthday suddenly I'm incompetent again. My license expires.

But to be competent, to get my license renewed and not have to be tested, all I need to do is go in at least one day before my birthday and pay taxes." Braunstein plans to file lawsuits against driver's license fees wherever and whenever he can. "If you don't have to pay taxes there's no reason for the license to expire, right? Now we're back to a Certificate of Demonstrated Ability. And that's what we're after. I'm not after people to be able to get out there and drive without a competency test. I don't want five-year-olds on the road. I'm after the illegal taxation."

"What is the ultimate goal of all this?" I asked.

"Freedom," he said. "Along with competency tests to drive, the ability to exercise your right to drive without interference and unjust revenue generation."

It may be difficult to accord much legitimacy to Bob and Glenn's driving outlook, hard to imagine that drivers' rights will be as compelling a social issue as civil rights and animal rights. Nevertheless, I do kind of secretly identify with that Wild West "Don't tie me down, bucko" sort of approach to things. I also think that when you look at driving on the evolutionary scale, as our predominant means of getting around, it's every bit as natural a right as walking. Still, speeding along the freeway at ninety-five, as Bob was inclined to do, did not strike me as a particularly responsible way to exercise that right. I wouldn't be too anxious to share the Phoenix roads with him. To tell the truth, and with no offense to the sensible people who call it home, I was happy to steer clear of Phoenix altogether.

LIFE IN THE SLOW LANE

Driving across northern Arizona to New Mexico epitomized every great thing anyone ever said about cars and driving. Cruising through the red desert, with yucca, purple sage, and mesquite completing the painting out my window, I felt unbounded and part of the land. I thought of the radical environmentalists who'd told me that cars should be banned. They had lost faith. It was the car that had made the gorgeous vistas out my window accessible to everyone. The images of New Mexico supplied by Willa Cather, Georgia O'Keeffe, and Billy the Kid were all here. The sky above the reddish buttes was a dazzling blue.

Albuquerque straddles the Rio Grande along the extension of the old Sante Fe Trail. Coming in on Interstate 40 on the high plain I could look down on the city and see where it started and where it ended. So long to the reckless desert sprawl of Los Angeles and Phoenix; this was my idea of a real city.

I ended up at the Chamber of Commerce downtown, where I spent some time talking with Jim Gillogly. Jim settled in New Mexico "by mistake" in 1953 when stationed here after he returned from overseas in the air force. He owned an Oldsmobile dealership from 1957 to 1972 and now is the chamber's avuncular salesman who circulates through the city enlisting new businesses. I chatted with him in his office, admiring his gold-and-silver bolo tie shaped like a horseshoe and very nearly as big as the real thing.

"Number one," Jim started off saying, "New Mexico has more darned uninsured motorists than any place in the country. I definitely suggest you carry uninsured motorist insurance. You'll also notice that the biggest complaint that every driver has in town right now is the idiotic orange barrel situation. Our worst intersection in the state of New Mexico is the corner of Montgomery and San Mateo. They just finished doing a whole project, putting in a special turn base to alleviate the worst traffic. Three weeks ago here comes the orange barrels again. They had to dig up the damn thing for the sewage system. They finished that and everything was clear for about six days. And Monday morning the orange barrels were back up there again because the water department was coming in to do some work they should have done when the sewage department was there. It's down to one lane now. Construction's not seasonal here, it's daily, three hundred and sixty-five days a year. One of the top disc jockeys in town had a raffle and arranged for the winners to fly to Indiana to see the factory where the orange barrels were made. You're gonna be in Albuquerque long enough to see these damn orange barrels.

"And we have a little smog, but only during the winter months when everybody's using their fireplace. My brother, who lives in Southern California, was visiting one winter. He said, 'You complained about the smog out in California, how about this stuff?' I said, 'Do you see that snow peak out to the west? Can you see the snow there? That's Mount Taylor, and it's eighty-eight miles away!'"

Jim drove older cars, a seventy-nine Olds and a seventy-six Chevy pickup. He didn't think there was a decent car on the market today—what's worse, they were getting three times the price for the damn things as when he was selling them. Nor was he happy with all the complicated technology. "If something goes wrong you need a genius to fix it. I've got one of the last big Oldsmobiles, a Delta 88, and I love it. I'm gonna drive it until the wheels fall off."

However, Jim felt that people's romance with cars and driving persevered. "Oh, yeah, yeah. But buying a car, a new car, is the most ridiculous thing in the world for most people. Now, I had customers that were buying cars every year. That's stupid. But I'm not gonna tell them that. There were a lot of people that I'd sell a new car to; they'd get fifteen thousand miles on it and bring it in and trade it in. Think of all the money they're losing.

"I think some people're getting less excited about cars when they go down and look at the car and find out that the sticker price is more than they paid for their house. When I bought my first home in Albuquerque, I bought it for nine thousand, seven hundred dollars. It was a three-bedroom home with a refrigerator and a stove. On the GI Bill. For fifty dollars down.

"I myself enjoy driving. Though I get a little bit more nervous on the road these days than I used to. The other guy bothers me. I mean, when you find out that fifty percent of the people coming toward you are intoxicated, and fifty percent of the people behind you are intoxicated, if you don't get a little nervous then you're nuts. That's the way I look at it.

"When you pick up the paper, every so often they'll come out with at least two full pages of DWI [driving while intoxicated] charges. The print is a bit larger than the regular print, and the columns will be four-wide on the paper. You read in there where some of these guys have had as many as seventeen DWIs and they're still driving a damn automobile.

"Every accident I had was with a noninsured driver. And they were all their fault. The first one I had was up in the Pecos, and that old boy had been drinking.

"My kids bought me a new rod and reel for my birthday. And we decided to go to the Pecos to test it out. It was on a Saturday. And as we were coming down the Pecos I saw this truck. I was leery of it. He parked on the side. And sure as hell just as soon as I got up to him he decided to make a U-turn and come across that damn blacktop. And I hit him dead center. And there was a state cop behind me. And you know, by the time I opened the tailgate and got one of the kids out, that cop had another kid in his arms. We limped home. And about two weeks later I got a telephone call. It was the nephew of the guy that I had the accident with. And he wanted to know if I'd like to have three head of cattle. I said, 'Well, I hadn't even thought about it.' He said, 'Well, we were even thinking about an acre on the Pecos.' I said, 'I hadn't thought about that, either—what're you getting at?' He said, 'My uncle isn't allowed to drive a car until you get taken care of.' I said, 'Well, that ain't how to take care of me, friend.' I wanted my car fixed."

To Jim, there wasn't enough local pollution "to shake a stick at." But globally, with things like the Greenhouse Effect and acid rain—"there we have a problem." He would like to see more conclusive testing, but he said he'd be willing to cooperate with any proposed solutions. Even if that meant trading in his Oldsmobile? "Not for a Honda!" he exclaimed. What about an Olds that didn't have as big an engine and got better gas mileage? "Sure, sure, I would do that. If it came down to a necessity, yeah."

I asked Jim if the area was growing. "By leaps and bounds," he said, and shrugging off my next question ("Aren't you worried about the overpopulation?"), he led me to the Chamber of Commerce's reception desk, where "the gals handle these sorts of questions. OK, Marsha," he said. "You got me to talk to this guy, now you have to answer a couple of questions. He wants to know where the people are coming from."

Marsha told me that the area contained half a million people and was growing rapidly. The growth was good for the economy, but people were getting, well, "pushier." Most of the requests for information came from California: approximately three hundred calls a day inquiring about moving to Albuquerque. "Some of them have heard wonderful things so they want to move here lock, stock, and barrel," said Marsha. "Some have traveled through here and have fallen in love with it. Others have no inkling whatsoever. They ask: 'Where do you go when you want to go to the ocean?' 'How deep do you have to dig for water?' 'Where do you get a visa?' "

"You think those are weird questions?" Jim said to Marsha. "You ought to sit down with this writer guy for ten minutes."

I left downtown Albuquerque during evening rush hour, following Jim's directions to land me in the most congested area he could think of. I drove up Louisiana Avenue, adjacent to the city's three-block-long shopping mall, cut west, and headed north up Interstate 25. Oh, there was some traffic all right. I think I actually slowed down to fifty miles per hour for a few minutes. How strange, I thought.

From Albuquerque I made a short jaunt upcountry to quaint Santa Fe, so quaint and clean, in fact, with pueblo-style shops and restaurants fashioned in the same earth-brown adobe, it makes you suspicious the town was built last year by some tasteful and enterprising development company. (Actually, despite its Aspenized feel, it's the oldest capital in the United States, the seat of the region's government since 1609.) Here I sat in a nice brown adobe home and discussed driving affairs with eighty-six-year-old Eleanor von Erffa. Eleanor was a spry, animated woman, a Quaker who lived alone. She'd moved to Santa Fe from Connecticut in 1984 after her husband, a Rutgers art professor, died. She drove a Ryder truck across the country with an elderly friend ("When we stopped at coffee shops we told them we were truck drivers") and planted herself near her daughter and family, where she could write short stories and poems. She showed me several stories, plus her first published book, a thin 1928 treatise on angels titled *Heavenly History.* Santa Fe had changed a great deal in the short time she'd lived here, she explained; it had become a New Age psychic center— that, and host to a score of new restaurants. She said it was impossible to get around without a car.

Eleanor told me that her first driving lessons were provided by her aunt's chauffeur in an electric car that opened from the front and was steered by a stick. She never got the hang of it. Then, in 1927, while she was living in Tucson, a neighbor with two cars loaned her one to master the skill. "I finally put it in a ditch," Eleanor said. "Then he said to me, 'You now know all there is to know about driving.' " Eleanor claimed she was a good driver and always drove whenever she went anywhere with her husband. Her mother, she said, was the same way. Currently Eleanor drove an eighty-two Volvo, which she loved. She said that there was an unconscious bond between people and their cars that was often taken for granted. "I think our relationship with a car gets very intimate," she said. "You don't say, 'I need to get my car's engine repaired'; you say, 'I need to get *my* engine repaired.' 'There's something wrong with *my* clutch.' "

With the Sangre de Cristo Mountains fading in the background, I cut down the desolate (and beautiful) Route 285 and rejoined Interstate 40 and continued eastward, across the breadth of New Mexico, flying by sad old signs telling me that this was once part of the fabled Route 66, across the Texas panhandle, across the richest grasslands with the fattest beef cows in America, and on into Oklahoma City, where I made a beeline to the

National Cowboy Hall of Fame. The museum (which didn't have a damn thing to do with automobiles) was a rich banquet of C. M. Russells and Remingtons and Bierstadts and contemporary western art, in addition to James Earle Fraser's emotional eighteen-foot sculpture—a dejected Indian warrior slouched with a downward-pointing lance atop his tired pony— titled *End of the Trail*. Finished in 1915, this was the place where the Old West ended.

FROM OIL BARONS TO GREEN GARAGES

My interview in Oklahoma City turned out to be a whole family of car-niks. John Trigg lived with his wife, Barbara, and twenty-two-year-old step-daughter, Liz, in Nichols Hills, the "Beverly Hills" subdivision of the city. John and his partners own a small domestic oil company, and thanks to Iraq's Satan Saddam, business was booming. Sitting in the wide driveway was a Lincoln Town Car, an Avanti, and Liz's brand-new jet black Nissan Maxima. The housekeeper, Gracie, let me in.

I sat in the lush living room with the whole family and commented that one of the first things I noticed in the area was the number of big cars.

"I knew you were going to say that," exclaimed Liz. "They're every-where. Huge cars."

"*Big cars*," I said.

John, who began driving at age fourteen in west Kansas sitting on a Sears catalog, said he definitely preferred big, heavy cars. Basically, cars for him were just a mode of transportation. But he said Barbara, who drove the Avanti, one of the few independently designed sports cars still produced in America, looked upon the car as a thing of beauty. "Mom just likes to look good," Liz threw in. Liz said driving to her was still something she loved. "To me, it's therapy. When something is really bothering me I like to go get in my car, turn on the music, and just drive."

I asked if Oklahomans considered the car's increasingly bad reputation in terms of traffic and pollution. They considered the issues, John said, but they didn't worry about them. As for traffic, Oklahoma City's streets and interstates "have been improved so much in recent years that it's easier to get around." As for public transportation, John shrugged: "Public transporta-tion has been a problem for years. They're trying to improve it. The only thing we have are buses. The last time I rode a bus was in high school." He yelled to the kitchen. "Gracie! When was the last time you rode the bus?" Gracie stuck her head around the corner. "It's been years," she said, "probably twenty-three years. It could be longer than that, twenty-eight." "I don't even know where the nearest bus stop is," Liz said. "I don't even know how to find it."

As for the environment, Liz had little faith that anything could be done. "I don't trust the government to do anything because it's too radical," she said. "A lot of times in politics, they consider the environmentalists to be the radicals. There's definitely a stigma attached to it when you say that you're an environmentalist, or a feminist, or any of that kind of thing. I don't think the politicians really like to connect themselves with something like that. So, I don't trust the government to do anything."

"Politicians in Washington want three things," said John. "That's being reelected, reelected, and reelected. I agree with Elizabeth one hundred percent. I don't think there's enough movement to do anything, frankly."

An independent oil man through and through, John had few kind words for the bureaucratic grind of politics and big corporations. "When I started in the oil business in 1954, we were buying foreign oil at one dollar a barrel. We were importing about twenty percent. Today we are fifty-five percent dependent on foreign oil at thirty dollars a barrel. To me and my partners, we all think that by the year 2000 there won't be any companies like ours, small independents. The majors, they don't want us around. We're a thorn in their side. They think they ought to be the only people in the business. We compete because we drill seventy-five to eighty-five percent of the oil in Oklahoma. They're looking for big reserves, and they're not here. To me, the fun of it is dwindling down. You have to be big."

When I said it was time for me to hit the road again, everyone insisted that I had not yet met the family's true-blue "car buff," Liz's brother, Mike Muckleroy, who owned and ran his own auto shop on the north side of town.

The garage was a long metal shed still bristling with business even though it was well after five o'clock. Mike, a cheerful and congenial sort, had been working on and collecting cars for twenty years. He owned fifteen muscle cars from the sixties and seventies and several old Cadillac "floaters" of the fifties, which he kept parked on his "Cadillac Farm" near his home across town. By way of introduction, Mike dragged me to the back of the shop and showed me his latest acquisition, a sixty-six Olds 442, one of only

157 made. He also had a new "fun" car, a brand-new Ford Mustang. But not from the dealer. Mike wanted the same Mustang the Oklahoma State Police drove, so he had cast about till a judge friend in a nearby small town authorized an official order for one.

With the shop finally locked up, Mike's friend and fellow mechanic John Juarez joined us and we sat around and drank beer and talked about driving. Mike gloated as he recalled street racing in his "purple Road Runner with a 440 six-pack" during high school. He realized, though, that his love of muscle cars was anachronistic. "Now the cops are stricter, gas is high, insurance is high. And the attitude is different. Now the cool thing is to put pink wiper blades on, have a big boom stereo that you can hear six miles away, and have stereo wars. It's what all the girls go for. They don't go for fast cars; they go for the big killer stereos."

In a significant way, Mike, too, had changed. As he talked, it was apparent that he was not your average grease monkey who cared about little but supercharged engines. "Me, I'm big on emission controls," he stated. "I like the old cars, but they're really superpolluters. The new cars, they've got them with fuel injection and all the electronic engine controls; they've got it all so dialed in that they're much cleaner. If you take one fifteen-year-old car off the road and replace it with ten new ones you'll have the same emission levels. So that's important. When the wind is still and you drive toward downtown, there's a little brown haze. Of course, being from L.A. you'd know all about that."

Recently Oklahoma City was the target of an emissions study by the Environmental Protection Agency, which concluded that drivers had been tampering with the emissions-control devices on their cars. In some cases, emissions-control devices sap the power of engines, prompting some people to remove them. As Mike explained, the EPA told the city: " 'You are tampering with your emissions too much and you better stop or we're going to cut off your federal money for roads.' See, there was no official inspection before about 1985. Then they started clamping down on the emission controls. We're strict here in this shop. This is not the inspection station you want to come to if your car won't pass. We take it deadly serious. My old station wagon doesn't have to pass the emissions test, but it will. I've made sure it will pass. I think our state should copy California to the T. I think every state should be hard-core like California."

California places the most strict emissions regulations on cars of anywhere in the world. Automakers, in fact, build one set of engines for California and one set for everywhere else. I told Mike that in Los Angeles there was now an 800 number that people could call to report a polluter's license plate number. "I would love that," he said. "It makes me sick to see somebody driving an old heap down the road just boiling out smoke. I have to breathe that."

"I worry about it, too," chimed in John. "I've got a little girl. Kids have to live in this world, too."

Both mechanics would like to see cars redesigned to run on "alcohol" fuels such as methanol or ethanol, which emit less than half of the smog-forming pollutants of gasoline. "Methanol is the alcohol fuel they make from natural gas and coal," explained John. "Ethanol is the one they make from organic products like corn, which would be my fuel of choice. We grow a lot of crops here, so it would be super, fantastic." Mike added that cars actually gained power from running on alcohol, which includes a higher level of octane than gasoline. "But the main thing is that it's so clean. And not just with emissions. If you run an engine a hundred thousand miles on alcohol and another on gasoline, when you tear the two down, the gas motor is going to be all carbony, nasty, dirty, stinky. The alcohol motor is clean. They do have some problems with the fuel systems. Alcohol has a tendency to produce moisture and they have a problem with corrosion, but they can deal with that. That's no big deal."

Mike realized that "they," meaning automakers, legislators, and oil companies, were a long way from converting gas stations and cars to alternative fuels, but he was considering setting an example himself. "I would gladly turn this shop into Oklahoma City's alternative fuel conversion center," he declared, mentioning suppliers that provided kits to retrofit cars to run on alternative fuels. "I'd probably lose my ass for a while, but it would really be something to have someone pull in here and say, 'Switch me over to alcohol.' The point is that they are so much cleaner and you don't have to give up anything. You get to keep your car; you get to drive around. I'd like to see alternatives. I really don't think it would hurt our business. They will still have to require maintenance. They're machines, they're going to break down no matter what you do."

Mike explained that he had already taken the first step toward making his garage environmentally sound. "Every time you have to change one little ten-cent O-ring in a leaky air-conditioning system, you let three pounds of refrigerant into the atmosphere," he said. "It goes into the air, rises, and damages the ozone layer. Well, we bought a recovery system, a three-thousand-dollar machine to suck out the stuff, clean it up, and reuse it. I thought we were going to be one of the hordes of shops buying these things. But all the other shops are sending everybody over here because they hear we've got this. We're the only one around that's got one of these things. And the customers complain. They go, 'You're recycling this? What do you mean, you suck it out and sell it back to me?' I get on my soapbox when they do that!

"People don't think about the environment. I got really upset with somebody the other day. I failed him on the inspection test because his emission controls were tampered with and he started going off on a big tirade. Well, I followed up with a big tirade of my own, and I really turned the guy off. But I don't want that guy around here. We're booked up way in advance, I don't need him. Let him go somewhere else and get a bogus inspection. I really get some people mad when I raise the hood and say, 'I won't pass this.' I fail people and then they'll come back and show me their sticker. I'll write down the sticker number and turn them in."

I apologized for the stereotype, but told Mike that his attitude seemed like it would be more at home in Berkeley than Oklahoma City. Here was a guy raised in one of the oil capitals of the country who loved gas-guzzling muscle cars, yet advocated alternative fuels and strict emission controls. The next thing you know he'd probably want to see an increase in the price of gas to discourage people from driving.

"Bring it on!" he exclaimed. "Two-dollar gas, no problem. I love to drive, but it's a privilege. It's a lucky deal and we probably won't get to do it for very long anyway. When we get everything so screwed up, we'll probably have to quit driving. If I had a bus that would take me back and forth to work, I'd take it. I would be glad to take it. To save the money, save the environment, save the wear-and-tear on my car. I could keep my car for just when I really want to do something special. I'd go for an electric car. I think that would be neat, just to hum right along. I'm all for it. But one of the things I love about cars is the sound. That's what an electric car wouldn't have. That's the one thing that I'll miss about the internal combustion engine when it finally goes, is there won't be that tremendous sound when you step on the gas and hear that V-8 roar. Maybe they could have an electric car with a cassette of the sound."

Despite the customers who argued about emission controls, Mike believed that drivers' attitudes were shifting. Soon they would have no choice. "Wait until people start going out for a little jog and come back gasping for air," he said. "When everything is all ruined, when we got everything so screwed up, they're going to say, 'Wow, we're going to have to do something.' We just got back from Mexico. We went down there and rented a little Nissan Sentra. You raise the hood—no emission controls of any kind, and regular, high-lead gas. They don't have anything! Have you ever been to Mexico City? Unbelievable! And we're not far from there.

"Pollution's affecting the whole world. And it's not just smog. It's acid rain and carbon dioxide causing the Greenhouse Effect. People better be damn sure that it's real! All you have to do is lock yourself in a room with a running car to know that the thing is putting out stuff that can kill us. But things are better than even five years ago. I think there's an improvement. It's just a matter of time. I just hope the earth can hold up until everyone figures it out."

THE TEXAS WAY

The sign that frequently crops up along the Lone Star State highways—"Drive Friendly, The Texas Way"—is apparently a favorite bit of local irony. Going sixty-five miles per hour banishes you to the slow lane, while using a turn signal is a dead giveaway that you are a tourist. Mike said that during a recent trip down I-35 to attend a Rolling Stones concert in Dallas he had to go eighty-five just to keep up with the flow of traffic. "When you get to Dallas," he said, "there'll be someone to run you over if you get in their way. You have to be aggressive there because the drivers are ultra-cowboys."

Unfortunately, I didn't get to experience the wild highway rodeo because my schedule landed me in Dallas on an uneventful Saturday afternoon. My drive down I-35 was a leisurely cruise along the prairie, and the only thing that snapped me out of highway hypnosis as I arrived in town was the garish, gold Mary Kay Cosmetics Building. (I later learned that Mary Kay herself was easy to spot around town because she drove a boat-length, shocking pink Cadillac.)

I was headed to the *Dallas Times Herald* to meet general assignment reporter Sue Morrison. "I cover everything from murders to snakebites," she said. In the eerily vacant newsroom, we had the editors' conference room all to ourselves. She was congenial and at times wonderfully caustic. She spent a good two hours every day on the roads in the Dallas–Fort Worth area, known as the Metroplex. And yes, it was true, Texans loved their cars. 'My car, my kingdom,' was how she described it.

"My father, we kid him about it," Sue said, "but it's true just the same. I call home and say, 'Dad, I just broke my leg.' He'll say, 'Honey, that's too bad, how's your car running?' I have two sisters so there are three girls in the family, and a very protective daddy. We were taught at an early age how to change tires, oil, how to look under the hood and make sure everything was OK. Up until about two years ago, when I got my first new car, a Chevrolet Corsica with the big engine, my dad still did all the repair work on my cars. I'm thirty-two and have been supporting myself since I was eighteen. When I go home he feels somewhat guilty about it, but not guilty enough to stop going out and checking the oil. He has to make sure. But he can't fix it. That was my rule when I got the new car. My best friend is a service manager at the Chevy dealership where I bought the car. I take it to him for everything. That was my rule, that it was finally time, at the ripe old age of thirty, to cut the car apron strings with my dad.

"The car I learned to drive in was a 1957 Chevy. I learned to drive when I was eleven or twelve. My dad would take us out on old country roads and teach us to drive. His rule was you had to learn to drive a standard shift before you could ever drive an automatic because God knows when you might be in an emergency and have to drive a standard. One day I spent something like thirty or forty minutes trying to pull the car up into the driveway, and ended up in tears. But my dad said that was the proper lesson.

"I used the car all in high school. I hot-rodded it. He said he'd replace the clutch for each child he taught to drive in the car. Of course I never told him that I hot-rodded the car, but he was leaving a football stadium after a high school football game and somebody came up next to him and started yelling like they wanted to race. Then they realized it wasn't me driving the car. Dad laughed. He knew exactly what was going on. The worst thing that could happen was that I would wreck the car. I ran over a Fotomat in it. I was going to pick up photos. At that point in my life I never eased into any drive-up parking space. You just careened in and skidded out. I careened in too fast, and this is not power steering, and I misjudged it and ran into the booth. I knocked it off its foundation. The Fotomat mate comes running out of the booth with her eyes this big. And the first thought in my mind is not how is this woman, or did I hurt anybody, it was, Oh my God, the car! She came running out and I say, 'I'm really fine, I think the car's OK, see you later.' And I drove off. It was one of the most guilt-inducing things I've ever done. I never went back.

"Nowadays it's wild down here. It's fast. People in Dallas go through a personality change when they get behind the wheel. The nicest person in the world becomes an absolute demon behind the wheel of a car. The car becomes the ultimate weapon. There is the basic devil-may-care attitude about traffic laws. People in Dallas don't use turn indicators. I'm as guilty as the rest. That's how I grew up. Maybe that's just Texas, but basically using turn indicators is a matter if the mood really hits you: if it does, you use them; if it doesn't, you don't. Another problem is that if you drive slower than other people, and somebody speeding comes up behind you, they expect you to move out of the way. I covered a shooting about four years ago that was supposed to have been a random highway shooting. But when they found the guy who did it, he said the guy he shot had pulled in front of him.

"I drive on any of the highways in Dallas, with the exception of Central Expressway. I don't know if you've heard the horror stories about that expressway. It's the most crowded highway in the Southwest. At any given time, I don't care if it's two-thirty in the morning, the traffic will practically be bumper-to-bumper. It's being widened now, which is a big joke in Dallas because the thing is obsolete now. My guess is that after it's widened it will be obsolete then. That's the biggest problem in transportation: this area has been rapidly growing in the last decade to twenty years and the road systems are obsolete.

"We do have mass transit, supposedly. I've never ridden it. I've never ridden a public bus in my life. We have people on bicycles. That's growing. As the bicycle craze hits the country more people ride bicycles, you see them. An interesting sidebar to that is that there're four northern suburbs right now that have banned cycling on certain stretches of roads because motorists have complained.

"I guess my main concern is, I have my car and everybody on my block has their car, or two or three. And even if we keep those cars at the highest standards that the law tells us to, every time I turn that key something toxic is being released into the air. You think about an entire nation of people doing that, and you think about an entire world doing that, and there has to be an end somewhere. There has to be a point where it all catches up with us. I would endorse electric transportation systems. And I know there is the potential for alternative power sources we have not even tapped into. I think it's imperative upon leaders in large cities like Dallas to do something, because this is where it has to stop. They have the financial backing to do it, unlike a small town that's just trying to make ends meet.

"But I don't think the city leaders are ready right now. It's just an attitude. Dallas follows whatever is in vogue nationally. The environment, yes, we're concerned. People are aware of the problems. But I don't know that they're doing anything. There's a big difference between acquiring knowledge and changing behavior."

COWBOY COP

Practically everyone who travels around the country carries mental images of the denizens of different regions. It's the movies' fault. Of course we know that not every Texan wears a Stetson and has bull horns on the front of his Cadillac; that New York City cabdrivers aren't all cynical, cigar-chomping Jews from Brooklyn; that most Californians don't see a crystal healer once a week. But every once in a while we meet a native of an area who just seems, well, perfect.

Imagine the archetypal Dallas cop: a real cowboy who appears to bend the rules to fit his righteousness, rode a motorcycle and was an accident investigator for five years, worked the homicide beat for ten years, was stationed in the most crime-ridden areas of the city, and after twenty-eight years on the force now teaches at the police academy, instilling the Code of the West in anxious young rookies. Imagine his appearance—short, burly, wearing a crew cut—someone you absolutely would not want to mess with. In fact, he is a martial arts instructor. Finally, he speaks with an ingratiating Texan twang that could charm a bar full of lawyers.

Such a person, Lloyd Richey, lived thirty miles south of Dallas in Cedar Hill, a pristine subdivision of new homes and immaculate lawns. He grew up in Dallas but refused to live there because the city council was "insane." He referred to one member as "Big Al, the whore's pal." These days, when he wasn't teaching, he was assigned to property crimes, searching for thieves and stolen goods. I remarked that, from the lay of the land,

Dallas seemed like pure car country. Detective Richey enjoyed the understatement.

"To Texans, mass transit is a jet airplane," he said. "The reason mass transit has never been successful in Texas, and probably never will be, is not only because we're so spread out, but we still have a Wild West mentality around here. And I kinda like it. It's my wagon, and I'll get there with *my* wagon the very best way I can, the devil take the hindmost. I'm not gonna share my wagon with anybody. In fact, that attitude is reflected in the way people drive, the discourtesy on the roads. Of course, that's all over the United States. That's not particular to Texas.

"Not that discourtesy is a violation of the traffic law, but disregard for the other driver leads to most of the problems. I think you'll find that ninety-nine percent of the people who are killed in traffic accidents are killed by discourteous traffic violators of one form or another. It's the anonymity of motion. Which means, I'm passing through here, I will never see that person in that wagon again. So why do I need to be courteous to him? And besides that, I'm in a hurry. I have to be someplace. If anyone interferes with my rate of travel, then I have to take it personally. Because this wagon is just an extension of me.

"Discourtesy, the lack of caring about the other person, is definitely on the upswing. I remember as a kid that the thought of giving someone the finger was, I mean, you chased them down the street to fight them. I still feel that way. If somebody gives me an obscene gesture, that means fight."

I asked if he ever chased down a driver because of such a gesture. "One time," he said tersely. "Mm-hm. Knocked 'im on his ass. He was stopped by the side of the highway, putting gas in the back of his car. I stopped and walked up and said, 'Remember the finger you gave me a while back?' and decked him. And I enjoyed every second of it. I was off duty, of course. Oh, yes, goodness, yes."

Another factor, related to driving discourtesy, was the disregard for traffic laws. "And a lot of that is our fault," Richey said. "I'm talking about police officers, because we don't like to write tickets. No matter what you hear or what it appears to be, policemen do not like to write traffic tickets. When I worked radar, I allowed twelve miles over the speed limit before I'd stop somebody. I've probably let go thirty percent of the people I've stopped. Maybe more. I'm a sucker for a sad story.

"Once I stopped this person for speeding on Lemon Avenue, which is a very large street. As I'm trying to get this car stopped, I couldn't see anybody in the car. I could see enough motion up there to realize someone had to be in the car. I could see the motion of a head, but still, whoever they were, they were driving like a maniac. Finally the car pulled over, and I called for backup. I felt like what I had—the way the car handled, weaving in and out of traffic, moving quickly—I felt like I probably had an eleven-year-old auto thief. But when I got up to the car, here was the most beautiful ninety-year-old lady that I'd ever seen in my life. I got up there and the window came down and she said, 'I know it, honey, I know it. But I just *got* to be at Louella's.'

"And I don't know why, but I said, 'Get out of my sight and go away.' I didn't even look for a driver's license. It was the sight of that beautiful blue-haired face that she had, that didn't even come above the steering wheel, but just looked through it. She was driving like a maniac, and knew it. But she had to be at Louella's. And that just fascinated me, that just tickled me."

Little old ladies aside, Richey was adamant that tickets made for better drivers. "Oh, Good Lord, yes. Were it not for that, it would be absolute chaos. Absolute chaos. Fear of traffic citations is the only thing that makes it safe for you and I to drive anywhere. If we left it up to the individual to drive any way they bloody well cared to, *chaos* is not even a good word. It undermines the carnage that there would be on the streets. The anonymity of motion coupled with no fear of reprisal for anything you do? Lord."

Overall, Richey was convinced that driver behavior had deteriorated. But congestion—not that bad in Dallas—was not the cause. He pointed instead to an inexplicable anger. "I think we've got the best life-style that anybody's ever had in the history of the world, the United States. It is anger, but it's not justified. Maybe it's a lack of patience. I myself have no patience at all, but I don't express it when I'm driving. Maybe it has something to do with the term *machismo* that's become so important nowadays. You know, if I give a signal before I change a lane, am I a weenie? If I allow somebody to pull out in front of me, am I a whoosie? Nobody's going to pull in front of me and get away with it—that kind of attitude. Besides that, they're in a thirty-five-hundred-pound automobile. How could they possibly be injured? Once again, the anonymity in motion. Why should I worry about that guy? I'm protected; I'm just passing through."

As a civilian, Richey didn't really mind being considered a weenie behind the wheel. But when it came to running down crooks he was fanatical. He took it as a personal affront when a suspect tried to get away. "You betcha. I take it personal as hell. It's a crime against nature, God, and the great state of Texas. And it's also a flip of the finger to me. And I do take it personally. I hate a thief worse than anything in this world. And I'll go get them through anything it takes. Yeah, I take it personally, you bet.

"I feel the same way about speeders. It's a duty to chase fleeting vehicles. Not to do so would be catastrophic. Is a criminal gonna stop speeding because he has an unquenchable desire to do good and follow society's rules? No. It's ridiculous. High-speed chases are dangerous, I know, but at least one of the drivers is skilled. How much good does skill do you when you're driving a hundred miles per hour in a municipal area? Not a lot, but it's kinda like using a phone book instead of good-quality toilet paper. It's just gotta be done. It ain't fun, it's just gotta be done. Sometimes you have to brush your teeth with your finger."

As for the stress of driving, Richey didn't worry. "I never had a problem with that. I worked something called freeway patrol when I first got started years ago. It was fighting traffic every day, and I loved it. I rode a motorcycle, and I liked that, too. I enjoy driving, on duty and off. Yes, I love it. The day I got a license it was graduation day, it was fabulous, fascinating. It was bar mitzvah for a Christian. I am an adult now—today I am grown. I can drive now. Oh yeah, I loved it. It's no different now, it hasn't changed a bit. You don't see as many hot rods as in my day. I burned enough rubber. But in that respect it's probably a lot better. Nowadays it seems that what's popular is to have one of those music machines in there where they can inflict their taste in music on everyone in the county. And how good the vehicle looks, how shiny it is. Of course, that's always been important. But how fast they run doesn't seem to be as important as it was in 1959 when I graduated from high school, and that's a plus.

"Now drunk driving, there's a problem that's got worse. Terrible, terrible. Now we also have drugs involved. In 1963, when I first became a police officer, drugs were not that big a thing."

Concern about the environment was also not a big thing thirty years ago, but that too was changing. "I think people are concerned enough that they don't gripe about things that we started griping about when people started worrying about the environment: catalytic converters, unleaded gas, all those things we have to pay for. The environment's a real valid concern, valid as can be. My main worry is oxygen. Anything that affects the oxygen, and that's probably gonna take in nearly everything. 'Cause we gotta breathe. So I'm for anything that can be done, within reason, to solve gasoline-burning cars. And deforestation, that concerns me. We learn in our chemistry courses in college that the oxygen supplied by the forests is minute in comparison with sea algae. It's still a problem. Why take a chance? Carbon burning, gasoline, chemicals, coal—all that concerns me."

Richey felt there were answers to these problems—answers the oil companies were bound to fight tooth-and-nail. He said we were pretty much powerless in the face of the oil companies, evinced by their wanton "war profiteering" and their raising of oil prices during the Gulf War. Yet Richey had no complaints about the United States' presence in the Gulf to protect the oil. "That's our life-style. I mean, Hussein was trying to control my life from over there. And I don't want it done. There's nothing sacred about our life-style, but, you know, this is the way we live. And we live this way because of an awful lot of sacrifices. We have an unbelievably high standard of living compared to the rest of the world. But we've paid for it. We've paid our dues as a nation, as individuals. I served in the military, and would be glad to go back again. I just feel that strongly about it. Yeah, it's about oil, sure it is. Oil is as important to America as water. But I think we would have been there eventually anyway. Because a madman was taking over the world again. And people are not going to let that happen. Not anymore."

Richey didn't know how we could break our dependence on oil, but he did know one thing: "It's not mass transit. A bus is a damn good place to stay away from because it's too slow. Have you ever tried to go anywhere on a bus? When I was in the army I spent a lot of time on the bus and I said, 'This is not the way to go.' We have DART—Dallas Area Rapid Transit. That's the most ridiculous thing that anybody's ever come up with. They've got funny buses with rabbit ears on 'em. Hop-A-Bus with rabbit ears. They say, 'Hop this bus and ride to the end of town for ten cents.' They do wonderful things like that. And then they don't understand why DART isn't showing a profit."

Richey said he and his partner were carpooling to work, something he never thought he'd do, but he believed solving the environmental problems of transportation ultimately fell on the shoulders of government. "It has to do something, some regulation. We certainly can't leave it up to big business. Hell, we saw that back when, in the early 1900s, they were serving rat turds in steaks—until the government controlled it. So I think we're gonna absolutely have to control things. They can't allow big business to get away with it. There's got to be a way to control the big companies so they'd still be able to make a profit. Because we don't want to throw the baby out with the bathwater. I think the government has to be a lot more willing to point the finger. It's you guys, OK. We're gonna give you X number of days to do whatever you gotta do. We'll help get some technology, some people with technological knowledge to help you.

"It's true for the personal, the individual as well. Like obeying a traffic law. No policeman around, I don't see anybody, do I stop for that red light? What motivates us to do the right thing? I wish I had a good answer to what would make people actually take some action. Doing something now would be a darn good time. But talk is cheap. I'm gonna quit taking two magazines that I've taken for a long time because I'm tired of seeing the environmental stuff. I'm singing in the choir and they're still preaching to me. I want something done! So go out and get 'em! And if it takes more money out of my pocket, that's OK. I'll pay for it. I'd rather pay for it now than have to start buying oxygen balls later."

MACHINE DREAMS

Sunday morning landed me at the other end of the Metroplex. Fort Worth seemed more provincial than Dallas, less related to that city's glitzy makeover as the "Silicon Prairie" than to Texas's storied past of towering oil derricks and expansive cattle ranches. Known as "Where the West Begins," Fort Worth was a famous stopover for cattlemen on the Chisholm Trail. For me, 120 years later, it was a stopover in New Age Haven.

In their red-brick home in an old, tree-shaded suburb, Carole and Jim Russell seemed the quintessential Texas couple. A Chevy pickup and seventy-nine Cadillac were parked in the driveway. We sat in wicker chairs on their screened back porch sipping lemonade. Looking like no stranger to hard work, Jim was tall and lean with a deep, resonant, preacherlike voice and manner. Having worked his entire career for the air force, he was now retired. Carole, confined to a reclining lawn chair, had a thick syrupy accent and a jolly laugh. She hadn't driven a car in two years and found it difficult to move about because of a nerve disorder called fibromyalgia. She said the condition might be the result of too much lucid dreaming.

Jim sat placidly as Carole explained her pursuit of knowledge, plumbing such sources as the Human Potential Movement, the Inner Peace Movement, the Association of Research and Enlightenment (Edgar Cayce's group), the Silva Mind Control Method, and Mid-Cities Meditation. Carole had recently been in contact with the Lucidity Institute at Stanford University, a research group studying the phenomenon of lucid dreaming (that strangely acute sense of feeling as though you're awake while you're dreaming). An active lucid dreamer, Carole believed she was missing too much deep delta-stage sleep and this was perhaps interfering with her muscle-nerve coordination.

Carole's interest in dreams went way back. She had her first lucid dream when she was seven—then moved her dreaming skills up a notch. "When I was little," she said, "I desired to have prophetic dreams because I believed that if people could do it in biblical times, they certainly could do it in my time." She had her first precognitive (seeing into the future) dream in 1956, but really didn't take dream study seriously until 1968. Because some of the dreams augured frightening and tragic events, Carole learned a method of reimagining the dream and then re-creating it. In 1978, at the time she was working in the graphics department at the local community college, Carole dreamed that she was driving along Loop 820/I-20 when a trailer truck loaded with smashed cars loomed in front of her. For some reason, she was feeling very dizzy. And then, suddenly, a large piece of crumpled metal tore loose from the bed of the truck and whipped through the air as if it had been a piece of cardboard. The metal crashed through Carole's windshield on the driver's side, killing her. She awoke screaming.

"Three months later," Carole said, "I left work early because I had been stung by a fire ant. I was having difficulty breathing so I went to the campus nurse. The nurse told me I should go to the doctor because my blood pressure was dangerously high. I was very dizzy as I drove away. The venom in my blood made everything take on an unreal quality, which made concentration on driving difficult. My breathing became more labored as I drove along I-20.

"I thought the nurse should have called an ambulance for me because I wasn't sure I was going to get home in one piece. The cause and effect of my words were never closer, for a large tractor trailer full of smashed cars merged into my lane of traffic. My heart, which was already pounding crazily from the fire ant sting, leaped right into my throat.

"Then a strange thing happened. Every thought I had expressed while re-creating my dream went whizzing through my mind. I shouted to myself, 'I have to do something!' And with that I pulled up to the left of the truck. I looked into my rearview mirror and saw the piece of crumpled metal. It was sweeping along the highway in the strong air currents made by the truck and the car."

I asked Carole how she explained such a thing. "A theory," she said, "might be that my life at this time was pure hell. I won't bore you with the details, but this was a time of great upheaval in our family. My negative attitude may have been setting up my own destruction. But I learned that fate wasn't in charge of my life. I had free will."

Perhaps my face betrayed bewilderment because Jim felt inclined to add, "Carole's a highly sensitive person. She's able to focus on things the rest of us are too busy to notice. She's thin-skinned or her nerves are real close to the surface. She had several precognitive dreams prior to this one. She saved her grandmother's life twice through dreams. Any time she perceives danger to someone she loves, that feeling seems to open the door for her."

They told me that over the years they'd learned something that might help me understand what had happened. What they learned was the use of *imagination*. "When you recall something in your mind, you use imagination," Jim said. "But there's more to imagination than people believe. It's usually thought of as daydreaming or conjuring up stories or visions. But really imagination is what every person uses who has psychic abilities." If you grew up in church, Carole said, imagination could be called faith. "Imagination is an extension of all your physical senses where they do not have boundaries," Jim continued. "Fear and doubt are eliminated from the equation, and that's like opening the door a little wider and being able to understand more things that come in."

Imagination came in handy when turning around negative life scenarios (such as those in dreams). It was also useful in the realm of acquisitions. "You can project the things you want," Jim said. "In fact, it's what most people do all the time but don't realize it. If they have a deep desire to achieve something, that strong desire vibrates out from you into the world. And you attract the same type of energy." Once Jim and Carole wanted some land, just five acres or so. They knew exactly what they wanted—near a school, near a pond or creek—and they sat down and imagined it. "It's almost like placing an order and then sitting back and waiting for somebody to ring your doorbell and say, 'Here's the delivery,' " Jim said.

In the case of their land, the delivery arrived when Jim's mother unexpectedly gave them a good sum of money. Later, Jim decided he wanted a pickup truck. Their money was gone by then, but that hardly mattered. Using their imagination techniques, they projected what they wanted, and several months hence, through serendipity and complicated financing, they had their 1988 Chevy pickup. "That sucker runs every day," Jim said, "and is absolutely great."

Through the years Carole and Jim had found many unusual ways to assure a good relationship with their cars and driving. Imagination was involved, but so was attitude. They reminded me of what John Muir had written in my old, greasy, dog-eared copy of *How to Repair Your Volkswagen: A Manual for the Complete Idiot*: "A car is an extension of your own sensory equipment. Its karma depends on your desire to make and keep it alive." Carole revealed that two things happened to her recently that exemplified this heightened state of automotive mind.

"My mother and grandmother wanted to go to a shopping center on the northeast side of town. I had learned in the Inner Peace Movement that if your car or house is acting up in some way, it probably had ghosts. What you do is cleanse yourself. What you do is put your hands over your head, shake them, and say, 'I cleanse my mind, I cleanse my body, I cleanse my spirit.' So we got to the mall and I was very upset because I didn't like driving that far but my grandmother and mother wanted to buy some stupid little plant. It started raining and the windshield wipers stopped working. The car stalled and was doing all kinds of things. The car had been in an accident before I had bought it. So I thought, based on the Inner Peace thing, that it must be ghosts. So I stopped and did the cleansing. Then the windshield wipers started working, and it scared my grandmother. But I learned later that it was my own negative energy that made the car act up, not any ghosts.

"A couple years after that, in the same car, I was driving home from the college and I was on a road between two bridges, and the car started to go *chug-chug*. I thought, Oh, let me get to the median. So I pulled in there, and the car absolutely stopped. There was no sound, no motor, no nothing. I turned the key and it wouldn't work, and I couldn't get to the filling station because it was a very dangerous street. I'd have to go across a bridge either way. So first I cried. And then, I thought, Please, God, let me get to our service station. So I visualized how I would just drive up to it. Then I turned on the key and it worked, and I drove up to the filling station, just to the place I'd visualized. Right at the entrance it stopped again. I told the mechanic, and he said, 'Well, how did you get here?' I explained what I did and he said, 'Yeah, sure, if what you explained happened, you couldn't get here.' He got in the car and turned the ignition and it wouldn't budge. He told me the car wasn't supposed to start and run or go anywhere until it was fixed.

"So your energy does affect the car. If you have a certain problem, a lot of times your car will have a certain problem. Jim has arthritis and he's always having trouble with his cars leaking oil. I know it sounds weird. If you're in a bad mood, you're going to find that people cuss at you on the freeway. But then you get more positive, and you'll find that drivers on the freeway will let you go in front of them. All it takes is just a change in your own attitude."

"Love attracts love from all around you," Jim said. "And anger and hate attracts anger and hate. A loving attitude toward our car will create a vibrational harmony in that car where it will perform in a loving way for us."

"In Silva Mind Control," Carole explained, "they teach you a three-finger technique where you put your three fingers together, breathe in and breathe out, relax, and imagine you get to your place safely. If you try this, you'll find more green lights than red lights."

"I never get in a car and go anywhere without doing it," Jim said. "It's the first thing I do before cranking up that car and leaving the driveway. I say, 'Safely to arrive, safely to return.' I don't have any doubt before I leave the driveway that the way is clear for me. I have removed fear; I have removed doubt."

"He used to go out and say, 'Those crazy drivers are trying to kill me!' "

"They were! But now, after ten years of doing this, I've brought positive faith to the fore. I pull into a parking lot and visualize where I want the parking place. I want it up front, not back in the south forty somewhere. And I don't want to speed up and I don't want to slow down. As I drive up I know somebody has just pulled out or somebody is going to pull out as I get in place. Nine times out of ten I get exactly where I want to park."

"This positive energy affects everything else. It's like putting yourself in sync with everything that's going on instead of being the squeaky wheel. You're putting yourself in harmony with all that is."

"However you think and feel—it vibrates from you in all directions. Now I can't explain how far it reaches and how many people get affected, but I can think of at least fifteen different things I could've been involved in had I not extended my energies beyond the perimeter of the car. For instance, I had passed under the Campus Bridge on I-20 just before a water tank trailer broke loose from its truck and hit one of the bridge supports and the whole bridge fell across westbound traffic."

The couple explained that attitudes toward the environment were also important. "The reason I worry about the environment," Jim said, "is not so much what the cars and trucks actually do, but what the attitudes are." He maintained that while there was terrible congestion in Dallas, the local politicians did nothing but spend unbelievable amounts of money on fruitless programs (like promoting the DART bus system) only to find that people are not going to give up their cars. Carole thought we should experiment more with cleaner fuels. "I'm sure there's some way we can get around without having to use fossil fuels."

"If we can send men to the moon and bring them back," Jim said, "then there is nothing on this earth that we can't do if we set our minds to it, our money to it, our attitudes to it. All these kinds of impossible things were done in the United States because the attitude was: This is important and this is what we're going to do. I think if an all-out effort was put forth to use electricity to create a source of transportation for us, whether from a battery source or from the sun, or something we haven't figured out yet, we'd have the transportation problems solved. There'd be no environmental problems at all.

"Today we've got things we either take for granted or things we consider impossible. That's the two ends of the spectrum for us. But the fact is, nothing is impossible."

HOUSTON-PROUD

It's a long 250 miles from Dallas to Houston. Sagebrush and grassland, the occasional patch of bluebonnets, are the extent of the scenery. "Majestic monotony" is how Welsh travel writer Jan Morris described it. I kept thinking to myself, Am I still in Texas? It seemed like I had been tumbling down this same prairie road for days. To experience Texas is to understand wholeheartedly the importance of cars and driving. As a nomadic Texan in the late twentieth century you simply cannot picture yourself or the environment without including the car.

Arriving in Houston, the state's biggest city (six hundred square miles; two hundred miles of freeways) and the fourth largest city in the United States, there was no need to change my tune. Despite Houston's being rated by the General Accounting Office as the city with the most severe traffic congestion in the United States, Houstonians seldom seemed to have a disparaging word for life behind the wheel. Everyone seemed to accept blithely the driving conditions—no fear of Los Angelesization here. On the contrary, they seemed to covet it.

My first morning there I took a cab from my hotel across town. When I asked Charlie, who had driven his cab in the city for eleven years, if Houston was entirely car-dependent, he nearly snapped his neck in turning around to see if I was from planet earth. "Are you fucking kidding?" he said. "This is cowtown. The oil capital of the world." He swerved the cab quickly into another lane so as not to have to slow down. "You gotta have something to eat up the oil, and that's your car. Besides, we don't have any options here. I've lived in Boston and New York, where you can take the subway. Damn—" He braked and jerked the car into another lane. "Here, you have no choice." But Charlie didn't mind spending a good part of every day in traffic, he said after he thought about it for a moment or two. "It's not like in New York, where they shoot you the finger. At least here if you let them know what you're doing and try to communicate with them, it's no problem."

Charlie dropped me off at the American Automobile Association, on the southwest side of town, just inside the Highway 610 loop that drivers navigate around Houston. Cathy McDonnell, director of public and government affairs, was equally sanguine about the local state of driving. "You should tell people that the thoughts about driving in Houston are misconceptions," she chided me. "Look at the traffic right now on the freeway. These people are zipping right along." It was after ten in the morning, but I said nothing. "Look at Los Angeles or New York, where the people are jammed together. Our situation is nowhere near that. We have a good freeway system and have made a lot of strides and improvements."

The fact of the matter was that Cathy had rearranged her own schedule to avoid driving during rush hour and had recently moved fifteen minutes closer to work. But even when she was commuting at eight in the morning she didn't mind. "I guess if sitting in traffic is really going to bother you," she said, "then maybe you should be somewhere else. There is traffic, there's no denying that. There is congestion. It might take you longer to go fifteen miles than it might in some smaller town. But there are other benefits, it's all a trade-off. Do you want to live in a small town or a big city?"

Well, personally, I prefer the big city. Without the god-awful traffic.

I looked out over Houston and thought, I don't care what people say, it looks exactly like L.A. A young and dumb L.A. I discovered that was a rather common comparison. Back in 1980 the *New York Times* declared of the two cities, "With their freeways, their dispersed patterns, their open spaces, their outdoor styles of living, their gleaming buildings, their atmosphere of gung-ho vitality and their very newness, they are urban brothers. Probably no two major cities in the country look and feel more alike."

They're alike in congestion and, with slight variations, getting mighty close in aggression. L.A. has its wonderfully skilled drivers, but it also has its shooters. Houston has its high-speed cowboy drivers (half of whom, I was told, have a gun somewhere in the car). Ben Roth, transportation writer for the *Houston Chronicle*, described Houston drivers as "manic" and "reckless"—"slalom drivers," he called them—ever weaving in and out of traffic. He handed me a typical letter to the editor. "Houston's drivers are the most inconsiderate, rude and bold I have ever seen," wrote Mr. Henry Parson, Sr., of Dickinson, just south of the city. "They speed, change lanes and stop without a signal, exit the freeway at the last possible moment from the center lane—and on and on! Where are the police?" Well, Sergeant Garrett, of the Houston Police Department's traffic and accident division, told me that afternoon, "We've got a ten-man task force assigned to running radar-enforcing speed laws on our freeway system. But if you're gonna get on the roadway and drive fifty-five miles an hour in Houston, you're probably gonna get run over. If you're a fairly aggressive driver and can go with the flow, you'll be all right."

Later that day a secretary at the Commission of Highways and Public Transportation told me in a perfectly sunny voice, "You know, if it was only Texans on the roads, everything would be fine."

I had read that Houstonians were great civic boosters, but this was getting strange. Over breakfast the next morning at my hotel, Doug Milburn defended the city's self-infatuation, a quality he himself found attractive. "Houston's still in its adolescence, still trying things out," he said. "It doesn't have the maturity, the personality of some cities yet. I think unpredictability is its most salient characteristic."

Doug has lived in Houston for thirty-five years. Formerly he edited the city magazine, *Houston*, and today teaches English as a second language while contributing articles to *Texas Monthly*. He had made close to a lifetime of studying the city, and his office was his Toyota Corolla. In the last two years he had driven 70,000 miles without ever leaving the city. "Houston is still in the early stage of sprawl where it's just sprawl with a lot of space inside. And that doesn't even include the suburbs. So like many Houstonians I live in my car as a second home. I also do my best thinking while driving. When I'm working on a story I just get in the car and drive around."

Doug said his favorite statistic buttressing Houston's car culture was the omnipresence of convenience stores. "There are more convenience stores in greater Houston, a population of three and a half million people, than there are in all of Southern California. Convenience is a way of life here because it's such a car-centered culture. On any given day, half of Houston goes to a convenience store at least once." And the city was doing everything in its power to keep the cars rolling. "Last year alone the Houston Metro Board spent more on freeway building than the entire state of California," he said. "The city is making a legitimately massive effort to raise the level of freeway accessibility and usability a quantum leap."

The environmental consequences of all that driving, Doug believed, was a foreign concept to Texans. Getting them to consider alternative transportation was like asking cattle ranchers to raise bean sprouts. "Mass transit will never catch on," Doug declared. "No one's going to give up their car. It's like a variant on the bumper stickers you see around, you know: 'They'll have to pry my cold dead fingers off my gun.' They'll have to pry Houstonians' cold dead fingers off their steering wheels." Doug admitted that he had ridden a bus only once since he'd lived in Houston: "I took my two boys on one because I wanted them to see what it was like."

Doug averred that he was "obsessed" with Houston. "I guess it's because in my travels I've never found an urban phenomenon quite like this one. It's that old cockeyed American optimism that I find gone in many parts of the country. It's still here."

DANTE'S D.A.

"You've arrived in Dante's Inferno," Terry O'Rourke said to me by way of introduction. "Houston—it's something out of Dickens. In terms of toxic air quality, Harris County is second only to San Bernardino County in Southern California. We're killing ourselves and we're killing the earth!"

This had gotten started around noontime. I had set up the appointment with the county prosecutor and was walking around in the pouring rain, looking for the correct address amid the gray high rises. Every other sane person was underground in the city's catacomb of walkways, shops, and restaurants. Except one—a handsome, fortyish man in an old trench coat and well-worn cowboy hat, who just happened to be entering the same building I was looking for. We rode the elevator together and got off at the same floor. O'Rourke put two and two together and with friendly exuberance herded me into his cluttered office. It was like he'd been waiting all year to talk to some weird ecology writer from the West Coast.

I was barely settled into my chair opposite his desk before O'Rourke was well into his impassioned rap, going on and on about the city's endless influx of cars and its gagging, smoke-belching, petrochemical plants. "Where there's smoke, there's jobs," he said. "If you're going to take the tour through hell in the Inferno, the looters and polluters will be there. In terms of the Savings and Loans scandals, Houston has to be among the lead looters. But in polluting we're number one in the nation. I'm the senior system county attorney and my job is pollution prosecution. I'm familiar with all the jingoism and the bullshit and the Houston-proud movement, all of that. Usually the more proud people are is a reflection of their ignorance of realities. I urge you to look at the petrochemical complex found along the Houston Ship Channel in Pasadena. 'Stinkadena,' it's called. There are refineries and all types of petrochemical plants: butylene, polyvinylchloride, the stuff that makes your clothes, your credit cards, and all that. It's just a complex that runs all the way to Texas City. In the sense of being Houston-proud as being ignorant, this complex is what people are ignorant of.

"Clearly, the biggest environmental problem is the channel industries, the production of petrochemicals with inadequate control. That's in terms of air pollution, water pollution, and soil pollution—air, water, and earth. It's a threat to the ecology which is distinct from any other large city in the United States. This county has 2.8 million people in it, about seventeen hundred square miles. So, it's big. It's like L.A. in population and pattern and density. You get a lot of cars.

"Most of those petrochemicals are related to the car because a lot of them are from refineries. You'll find the price of gasoline here the cheapest place anywhere in the United States. When you're near small refineries you'll have competitive, smaller, unbranded gasoline on the market, which will keep the majors from having their prices too high.

"Also, this is the most air-conditioned city in the world. Everybody has AC in their home, car, and office. Freon is *rolling* out this place. So you take the freon plus the cars plus the really killer chemicals from hell that're coming out of that complex and we've got to be the leading city in killing the earth. You're here. And you're talking to the guy who is the chief environmental prosecutor who's trying to protect the earth.

"Right now I'm trying to do the first corporate death penalty in the Houston Ship Channel industry on a company called Allwaste. They are the second most profitable small company in America; they were in *Forbes* magazine. They're an 'environmental services' company, a truck-washing operation. The only problem is that they're getting rid of the shit into the atmosphere and the Galveston Bay. It's called bare-air flocculation. I am trying to kill these guys. I'm asking for a death penalty against this company—close them down, shut them down for good. I lost in the district court; I hope to win in the Court of Appeals. I knew from the start I had to go to the Supreme Court anyway. Nobody's ever got one shut down here. This is a death penalty case. I'd like to take everything they have. I said in court, 'Judge, it's time for the earth. I'm speaking here for the earth.'

"Do you know that I appear in the same courts, I prosecute in the same courts, that defended slavery? It's the same consciousness that made slavery possible. I think they're insensitive to human experience, generally. In Houston, environmental quality is like chrome on a Cadillac. You can go down to the Houston Club and still have oil men talk about how proud they are to pollute. It's still like exploiting minorities, or sex with prostitutes. It's still a common problem. It's a mentality of taking, of rape. Somehow it's connected to capitalism. I believe it's in our physics. Newtonian physics is an objectification of the world. When I had physics in college we used to do these experiments—there was no sense of awe or majesty, it was all mechanical. It was just something to fuck with, something for us to handle, play with, manipulate, and control as opposed to understanding that we had some crucial role in the whole system.

"As a society in Texas, we've always been able to say, Well, there's always Alabama and Mississippi; there's always Arkansas. We're forty-fifth in literacy, we're forty-sixth in inoculation of people for epidemics like measles, but, see, there's always Alabama or Mississippi. There's always south Louisiana. It's an environmental disaster over there compared to here. We've always been able to look down, the holier-than-thou thing. As a culture, we're insensitive. The dominant culture is Calvinist, cavalier, Southern, and redneck—it's not about human sensitivity. Human values, human dignity, human rights just aren't part of the culture.

"You see, I'm a Catholic. I mean I was trained a Catholic. But it's the same right-wing theology. I say Calvinist because of the force of laissez-faire capitalism. The veneer here is just thinner than other places. People are schizophrenic. They want business and profits, and they want to drive that car right into their living room. They want to have their VCR and they want to have food in the supermarket that's been trucked in. But really, they would also like to eat food that doesn't have chemical shit all over it and would like to be able to breathe and that their kid will have two eyes when it's born. I believe people know that they're going to have to eventually have some reduction in what they used to call the standard of living—but not the *quality of living*.

"I've driven cars that get fifty or thirty-five miles to the gallon. You can have zippy little cars without having hog-mobiles. There are all kinds of things. Your quality can actually go up as your consumption goes down—in terms of gasoline, benzene crap, freon—the bullshit in your life. You can have assets. You don't have to have a three-thousand-square-foot house. The mentality of conspicuous consumption doesn't fit society anymore. You can have lots of fine things without, for example, having Styrofoam cups to drink out of. I was in India and they had clay cups they baked in the sun. You drink your tea and you throw the cup away. The energy loss is real low."

I asked Terry if he thought people were becoming more aware of environmental hazards and as a result were more willing to change their habits. Yes, yes, he exclaimed, that's exactly what he thought. (I was worried he was going to leap over his desk.) He handled the county's civil prosecutions, and from his vantage point in the courtrooms he had a clear view of people's mind-set. "I see it in the juries, in the collective wisdom: the people are way ahead of the politicians and the cultural leaders. I've talked to the people that work in the chemical factories who know they'll have a shorter life span as a result of being there. The fact that they're aware of it and making decisions is great. The juries here are giving fairly significant awards, multimillion-dollar awards, on pollution-related litigation. The juries are just tired of the bullshit. When they get down and look at the facts, they don't want to be exposed to chemicals. I see it in the hearings. They are becoming more aware, especially in terms of their own health consciousness. The environmental stuff goes through their health consciousness. Chemical abuse and drugs are the same thing. Whether I'm snorting X or breathing air-conditioned air or car exhaust, it's the same thing. If you look at them as part of the same spectrum, they're polluting the earth and your body. People don't smoke as many cigarettes, they don't drink as much whiskey, they don't do as many drugs, they don't eat as much fat. They are, even right here in Houston, healthier. So yes, it's a larger awareness. Since I've been doing these prosecutions I've seen a change in the mentality."

The prosecutor felt that what got us into all this trouble in the first place was a fundamental flaw in America's basic myth structure. "It's that deep," he said. "Consumer democratic capitalism, the system that we're in, has a huge, huge hole in it. Capitalism is wonderful in its historical sense, but the greed connected with it has to be corrected somehow. As the rest of the world, including the Soviets, try to imitate us, it's somehow our duty to look closely at our system. It's also true in Japan and Western Europe. I watch the Japanese destroying the environment of East Asia on a capitalist system. I have traveled seventy-five countries or so. I've seen the Asiatic cities, South American cities, São Paulo, Santos, some of the areas in Brazil. You look at America from outer space, you can see from the satellite photos what it looks like, and America really looks like the Garden of Eden compared to the rest of the world. But that doesn't mean that we don't have enormous environmental problems and that our system itself doesn't need to be fixed.

"The basic mythic flaw is that wealth still runs the system. The ninety-day quarterly statements of the corporation being more important than the long-term good of society. The budget cycle of government being more important than looking to the future. It comes from Judeo-Christian culture, from some notion that 'you're no good,' as the Linda Ronstadt song says. Mustang used to have an ad that said, 'Mustang makes it happen.' It was not very subtle: You'll get fucked if you buy a Mustang. If you get a Mustang you'll get more pussy than if you don't have one. You won't get any at all. Virtually all advertising in our country is somehow related to Mrs. Olsen with Folger's coffee. You're not getting along so well with your husband? Drink some Folger's coffee and you will. Advertising is saying 'you're no good' without these products.

"In Calvinism you became good by being rich—the Doctrine of the Elect. If you had money that was the selection process to prove that you were in the sight of God, that you were productive as opposed to the lazy people. But what's happened to community values and morals? The same is true in Roman Catholicism. It's rampant. I see it reflected in politics. The politics is controlled by money now. Politics is now down to the thirty-second spot. It is: How much money can I get to do the polls? The polls will tell me what the people want, and then I hire the ad firm to frame for me what the people want. You don't like black people? I'm not going to say I hate niggers. You can't get away with that. What you say is: 'It's time we start thinking more about production quotas instead of racial quotas in this country.' That's the message; all the people know what the real message is.

"I believe that the view of the earth as something to be taken and used by humans is excessively anthropomorphic. This is the Judeo-Christian culture, and it has to be reimaged or altered. I believe the automobile is literally and metaphorically the vehicle for the destruction of the earth. It is rare that metaphor and object are so much the same. The vehicle is the vehicle. It is the automobile society that everybody in the world worships. They all want one, and they want the gasoline and the highways that go with it.

"I used to be with the Carter administration and travel all over the world giving Jimmy Carter's energy pitch, which the Reagan administration just threw out the window. But the idea of having conservation and renewable energy was a wonderful effort. And people would talk to me and say, 'Why don't you do more things to limit automobiles?' I said that the relationship between a man and his automobile was very intimate. Getting between him and his car and the gas pump was more serious than getting between him and his girlfriend or wife. What the car and gasoline meant for the American was freedom. It was the freedom to go wherever the fuck you wanted, whenever you wanted to. As long as you had your valid driver's license, your safety inspection sticker, and your insurance certificate in the glove box, you can go anywhere in the nation the size of a continent. It's amazing! That's freedom like nobody on earth has ever experienced anywhere. As long as you have the object of worship of the entire society, the dollar, in your pocket, you can think anything, you can be anything, do anything, go anywhere. That's it. That's the object of worship in society. It means freedom. And that's wonderful.

"What's wrong with it? It lacks value. When I was in the hydroelectric business in California, I was so happy. This was the first time I lived in a rural area. It was in Redding. I took essentially sunlight and gravity to make electricity. The company, Consolidated Hydroelectric, bought the equipment in Red China and had it installed. It's in receivership now, but is still producing electricity into the San Francisco Bay Area, to PG&E, the largest private power company in the world. The only pollution we produced was heat because the machines themselves produced heat. That was the only thing you lost. I used to be so happy to think that I could participate in a small way in the solution to the problems of earth. I saw electrons, these almost massless objects, as the replacement commodity to a lot of things. And it created value. It was value different than land or wealth or cars. The raw material was electrons, which in turn produced light, heat, data, art. I'd think with the light that I was producing in the power plant, the one thing I was taking away from civilization was the sight of stars in the sky. When you travel, especially at night, you realize that for almost the entire history of humans, until the last hundred years and the advent of electricity, half of their life was spent with the awareness of things that were way beyond them. They had no problem with the mystery or the majesty of the universe.

"Now it's so tightly focused on the TV screen and on the odometer and speedometer of a car. It's a stimulation just like drugs. The TV is on a thirty-minute cycle with three to four interruptions; the programs are actually made to fit the commercial messages. Ultimately, they're one and the same. The message is: Buy me, buy me, buy me—buy me because you'll become better, you'll be good, you'll become happier with this *thing*.

"Ultimately, that's a bunch of shit. We have so much overcapacity in the United States. Waste is so much a part of our life as a society. We call ourselves consumers—that's what we do. It's a function. We're loyal because we consume. Saving is a threat. I can remember an old episode of 'Dragnet' where they had one of those old L.A. trolleys in it. They're not that far out of our horizon, but in my lifetime they were gone. Public transportation was something for poor people. They even smelled like poor people. Nobody wanted that. I grew up in the suburbs, and having a used car or a used house was something to be ashamed of. Getting a used car was like marrying a girl who was not a virgin. It was the fifties mentality."

Terry admitted he didn't know if we would ever break our addiction to the car. He said that there were other, more favorable sides to cars. Driving was a time when people could truly be alone; the car was a place where many people had their most memorable sexual experiences; and as a beast of burden, it allowed us to carry home the fruits of our hard labor from the local Target or K mart. Nevertheless, our car-dependent transportation system *must* change if we are going to save ol' Mother Earth. "The answer has to be something along the idea that there's got to be more variety. I've often wondered why they don't have almost all electric cars in the cities. Even with today's battery. There's no reason why they couldn't find some photovoltaic system to recharge the batteries off the sun. Clearly, if we spent the kind of money that we spent in the Persian Gulf in the production of photovoltaic electricity, things would be different.

"I believe the revolution is going to happen. It already is in the sense that you can get jury verdicts for chemical pollution. In that sense, people are a lot higher evolved. And the outrage—people don't want to be polluted. They treat it like assault, like rape. It's something they don't want. That's not so hard to get into their mentality, that you've been penetrated or violated by this company or group of people. This is not Alabama in the fifties when they let people who lynched blacks off. Still, the political system is perverted by capitalism, which is a destruction of the earth mentality. Something has to be reimaged in capitalism itself. I don't have that solution. Perhaps grass roots movements have to be reflected in religion, in politics. In the lounges, the bars, wherever people meet. Consciousness builds very slowly. The question is, is it fast enough?

"I think it's happening here in Texas. I believe it is because maybe I'm a true Buddhist and maybe I'm a Hindu. I believe that the most beautiful lotus flower really does blossom in the filthiest swamp, and that we may be here to watch it. The elements of revolution, the same kind of things that got people to stand up and kill the Mexicans after the Alamo, are still strong here. If you can see the Civil War in a way other than the protection of slavery, as people just wanting to be left alone to lead their lives their own way—that will to fight is still very strong here in terms of individualism. They do not want to be destroyed by toxins and pollution. Texans may have the courage that they don't have in other places to stand up and fight."

I took Terry up on his recommendation and went sightseeing along the Ship Channel in Pasadena. (Navigated by barges all day long, the channel runs a sinuous trail from the Galveston Bay practically to downtown Houston.) It was indeed a tour of the Inferno. A labyrinth of chemical factories, steel plants, and oil refineries surrounded the channel and adjacent highway for miles, spewing gray and angry smoke from a towering array of cylindrical chimneys and vats. A sour sulfuric odor permeated the area. Welcome to Pasadena signs appeared along the highway, as if they were someone's idea of black humor. I'm not sure who stayed at the Rodeway Inn or ate at the Denny's that looked out on the petrochemical complex. Who called this home? One of the mooring berths I drove by seemed to say it all: thousands of new Fords filled the dock, waiting to hit the streets.

"Both the good and bad aspects of America are exaggerated in Texas," Doug Milburn had said. "And the relationship with the car is an example of that exaggeration. The car mystique is still alive and well here, despite the pollution." That captured my thoughts precisely. Pasadena is a palpable experience of industrial pollution, and an extraordinary symbol of the pernicious fallout of cars and driving. That this symbol exists in Texas drives home the ecological paradox of cars like nowhere else in America. Texas is second only to California in registered cars, with a total of nearly 13 million. Yet despite serious traffic in the Metroplex and Houston areas, the romance of cars and driving seems not to have dimmed a shade. As in all the western states I visited, the car is so deeply entrenched in the way of life that alternative modes of travel are not even imagined. It is still the Wild West, where the wide-open spaces speak of freedom, where individualism is madly revered. As I headed out of the Houston megalopolis, I couldn't shake the deep sense of irreconcilable differences. The kingdom of cars and driving is here to stay. So too are places like Pasadena. So too is the smoke.

Five

Lay
of
the
Land

*When you begin to realize the depth of the land, you begin
by understanding the depth of your particular land, wherever it is
that you live. When you enter that land, you begin to feel connected.*
—William Least Heat-Moon

Within two miles of crossing the border into Louisiana, I counted three human-machine entities with Texas license plates being preyed upon by Louisiana state troopers. Either the Louisianans didn't like the high-speed high rollers zooming out of the cowboy state or they'd long decided what was the Wild West on one side of the border was revenue meat on the other. Pat Shannon, an oil refinery engineer, told me he once got pulled over and the highway patrolman said, "Guy, you'd get off cheaper for murder in Louisiana than for speeding." I slowed down.

In the South, I planned to look deeper into the automobile's impact on the lay of the land, the ways in which auto dependence was remapping central urban regions and affecting the indigenous environment. Los Angelesization—the fanning out of freeways, housing, and commercial developments from the urban core—was playing itself out with a new fury below the Mason-Dixon Line. Traditionally, through history and literature, the South has inspired a strong sense of place, so how were drivers and transportation experts here responding to the car's increasing rule over themselves and their land?

I knew this issue would be the hottest in southern Florida and Atlanta—

two regions forever bursting at the seams—yet I wasn't about to abandon my individual drivers en route. Besides, in amassing my biological inventory of America's auto environs, I would be sorely remiss if I bypassed New Orleans, which is reputed to have a look, culture, and attitude all its own. A mix of abject poverty and storybook mansions, of the Old South and Caribbean and French influence, it's the bottom of the nation, where pirates and misfits and the rich river could go no farther.

It was evening and raining as I pulled into the outskirts. Despite being good and lost, my expectations of being steeped in the Big Easy ran high. But where I pulled in for directions, a busy intersection with your generic convenience store on one corner, a fast-food joint and gas station next to a motel on the other, could have, literally, been anywhere in America. Once again, I was in Anywhere, U.S.A. My only encouragement came when I got back out on the road—an old Volkswagen went flying around me. It was hand-painted, badly rusting, and nearly entirely wallpapered with various stickers, most of them half peeled off. Only one sticker stood out, centered neatly in the middle of the rear bumper. It read: "How's my driving? 1-800-EAT-SHIT."

MINDING THE SWAMP

The next morning I sat on a rusted chair opposite Macon Fry, thirty-five, on the back porch of his patchwork shack overlooking the Mississippi River. Through a tangle of black willows I could see the wide brown waters rolling past the factory chimneys and modern skyline of New Orleans. Macon's meager residence sat between the levee and the water's edge on a thin strip of land called the batture. His house was constructed of bargeboard and other odd assortments of whatever was handy. "Whatever you need," Macon said, "sooner or later floats down. You just have to ask yourself, how bad do you want it and will it float? Then you wait."

Macon taught autistic high school students in the city and had just spent the summer crisscrossing western Louisiana—Cajun country— putting together a travel book. "Talking to people and eating, you know. Listening to music." His computer sat on an old cable spool behind us in one of the shack's two burlap-walled rooms. Out on the levee sat the battered green fifty-seven Ford F-100 van Macon used as his safari swamp wagon.

New Orleans, he said, was an exotic area to drive around in. After he'd been upcountry, he always loved coming back to the city. But the actual driving experience soon wore thin. This was partly due to the fact that Macon didn't have any insurance, there was a big hole in his windshield, and his inspection sticker was long dead. The sticker regulated not the car's emissions ("Down here they're not too sticky about the exhaust thing") but its mechanical shipshapeness.

"Then there's the roads," he said. "That's a whole different matter. If you talk to somebody that just moved here, the first thing they're gonna say is, 'Like, man, the roads, I can't believe it!'

"Like, for the last year the budget wasn't looking too good. Louisiana's got a lot of financial loads, particularly in New Orleans. And so to help resolve the budget issues here, Mayor Sidney decided that the best thing to do was eliminate the pothole-repair program. Now, the streets here are virtually one continuous pothole. To eliminate the pothole-repair program is ridiculous. Driving here, it's something you get accultured to. Whoop, another pothole! and you're off the road. There's potholes that my girl-friend's Hyundai can easily fall into. I mean, her Hyundai's great for going and traveling around the state, but here in the city, you'd best have a truck or something big like an Oldsmobile where, at worst, maybe only the front end's gonna fall in."

Macon didn't think New Orleans was much of a car town—for eco-nomic reasons and because the actual terrain was largely wetlands. "There's so many people here that are very poor," he explained. "I don't know what percentage own cars, but a very large percentage of the people here ride public transportation, or they walk to work. And the city has a heritage. It's a boat town. It's a river town. Roads here are a fairly new development. There's so much water. Louisiana has more wetlands than any state in the country. Something like half the nation drains through south Louisiana. There's no place to build a road unless you're gonna build it up in the air. Which is what they did. You came in on I-10, which runs through the Atchafalaya Basin and down to New Orleans. It's all up on columns and the inside lanes are settling into the muck. The only firm land is beside the water. If you look at a map of Louisiana, the towns are all snaking along various waterways, and a lot of them snake right down until the waterway ends. You'll find a lot of dead-end roads between Lafayette and New Orleans—the Mississippi Alluvial Plain, they call it. They're like crow's-feet. Down toward the Gulf the roads follow each side of the bayou. Make a right or left turn and you'll end up in the swamp."

Macon stressed that to him the most important environmental issue was the increasing loss of wetlands. He told me of his love for the fantastically beautiful swamps ("The Atchafalaya Basin is Louisiana's Grand Canyon") and of the outlandish forms of exploitation. "Most people who go out on swamp tours, all they want is to see alligators. These tour guys, a lot of them, they go out in the boat to an area where they know there's alligators, and it may be beautiful or, more likely, it'll be next to a damn oil rig. They'll go out there and they got names for the alligators. You know, Here Missy, Here Elvira, *bang, bang, bang,* hit the side of the boat, right? They come like a dog or a cat. The alligators come out and these guys throw 'em doughnuts, glazed doughnuts. And, of course, that has an impact in itself, because the next time people fish out there, or some kids go out on the bayous on their little surfboards and, you know, make noise against the boat—alligators aren't that smart. Differentiating between, say, a seven-year-old and a doughnut, that may be beyond the recognition powers of an alligator.

"I love the swamps and that's related to the car. It's more important than emissions. You can see the oil companies and industries that're cutting canals, which are subsequently eroding, causing wetlands loss. And they're also dumping shit into those canals. They call the Mississippi River the American Sewer. The Old River Road here—it's a plantation then a factory, a plantation and then another factory, and on up the river. And it's not just what the plants are dumping in. They'll drill a well and they'll use different chemicals to pump the oil out with radioactive chemicals, salt, and all kind of by-products. Texas and Louisiana are the only states that don't have a law saying that oil by-products can't be dumped right back into the swamp. Now, anybody with half a brain knows that's not a good idea. So much of this state is wetlands, and so much of it is still potentially a wild area that I think we need to preserve those areas.

"There's miles and miles of pipes out there in the wetlands and nobody knows who put them there. You go on a swamp tour and there's oil pipes. They run out into the Gulf, across the bayous; they run all over the place. The land is eroded around the pipes and they're hanging in the air—and they're not being used. But no oil company has said, 'Well, we're not using this pipe so we're gonna take it out of here,' because a lot of oil companies went out of business after the oil glut in the seventies. Shit, they have no idea whose pipes those are. It's like south Louisiana is a big boneyard of leftover industrial pipes.

"There's not a whole lot of environmental concern in the state of Louisiana. But I definitely feel like there is beginning to be a curb to what's happening. In the past it hasn't been in vogue to support environmental issues because the oil companies have been putting so much money into the economy. But in the last five years it has fortunately become more fashionable for politicians to support environmental causes because no longer is the oil company the sugar daddy. They had to fire people, they had to close down, they left their stuff in the swamps. Now more people are visiting the swamps and beginning to see entire stands of dead cypress trees. Some people say, 'Oh, that's because of saltwater incursion,' but half the time they know it's because the oil companies have been dumping shit out there. This area has the potential to become a real hellhole. But it has the potential to reverse the process, too."

DEATH WISH

It was late at night. A woman in a sequined white leather dress and white boots stood near the window with her band singing something they called Western Zydeco. I sat to the rear of the funky storefront bar somewhere (I think) near the French Quarter at a table with several new acquaintances, including a rather exuberant and precocious twenty-year-old named Nicole Vance. Nicole did not lack conviction on any subject, driving and cars being no exception. "She's convinced she should teach everyone how to drive," her friend Dina said. Nicole agreed. She told me she was studying to be a mortician and was enrolled in a funeral service "practiceship." Eventually she wanted to have enough money to open a bar along some levee somewhere. Accessible only by foot or bicycle. No cars.

Nicole drove a 1976 Toyota Corona that her mother bought her. "I got a car because my mother didn't like the way I drove hers," she said. "My friends would burn the seats with their cigarettes. I had a guy jump on the hood and leave a big dent. Then I ran it into my friend's house one night. I was drivin' home and I was doing something I shouldn't have been doing. We were drunk and driving, something I don't ever do, and will never do again, and I, ah, dropped a lit cigarette in my crotch and sort of ran into a brick building. I knocked the bumper out about two feet. We went, 'Ah, God.' We got back in the car and drove into a utility pole about fourteen times to push the bumper back, though it was still bashed in. So my mother was tired of all that and got the Corona.

"I would rather have had an Oldsmobile, though. There's something about the name of it that I like. And it has lots of chrome. It's something that doesn't look like every other car you see driving down the street. I don't think I'd ever buy a new car because they're so ugly. My friend who just moved in with me, she has this nice new Volkswagen Jetta, and every time we pass an old beaten-up car she's like, 'Ohhhh, if only I had one like that.' She just hates her new car; she hates the fact that it's fiberglass, she hates the fact that it's just new and she has to keep it in good condition 'cause her father bought it and he'll go crazy if . . . She just wants an old car she can junk around in. Having a car that you don't have to worry about how it looks—it's just another dimension I don't have to worry about. There's just too many things to fit into your mind."

Although her friends didn't always agree, Nicole felt she was a good driver. It was other drivers who were inconsiderate. As if to underline her point, she told me a harrowing tale that began on her way to the bank during a recent lunch hour. "I was driving down this street called Jefferson and coming to the infamous St. Charles. I turn left at the light and I see this car behind me, he just shoots around the cars stopped for the red light, he doesn't want to wait in line, and he comes up on me real fast. I'm driving in the middle of the road and I won't let him pass me. It's one lane but it's real wide. So he just starts blaring his horn at me. And it's like, God, give me a break. This guy's going back and forth trying to get around me, and there's not enough room 'cause I'm driving right in the middle of the lane. He was in a new Honda, a business-suit type of guy. And blowing his horn. You could see he was getting all red in the face and going crazy. From St. Charles to Broadway, *honk, honk, honk*, and he's swerving back and forth. I turn and he turns. I turn down a back street that leads to my bank and he turns too. And then he really goes crazy—he tries to come alongside me. He's after me. And I look in the rearview mirror and I see him waving a gun. And I'm going, Ohhh my! OK, I can't let him get alongside me now. I'm slipping down in my seat going, Oh, God, please don't shoot me. There was no way I was gonna stop. And I look back again and I see him fooling with—he's putting a silencer on the gun. I kept driving, and then there's a red light. And I couldn't get around the traffic, so I had to stop. He stops and I see him gettin' outta the car and he's running. He comes right up to my door, and I roll up my windows frantically. And I say, 'What's your problem?' And he says, 'You're my problem.' He has the gun in his hand at my window. And I'm just breathless. Then he puts the gun away in his holster, and he starts hitting on my window, hitting on my car with his hands. I still have the dent in my car where he hit it. Then he ran back to his car and backed up so quickly I couldn't see his license number."

Nicole felt she was OK and proceeded to the bank. But standing opposite the teller she became discombobulated: she couldn't remember why she was there, she could barely remember her name. "I apologized to the woman. I said, 'Just give me a break and I'll remember everything, I just had a gun pulled on me.' The bank called the cops, who took a careful description of the culprit and his gun.

"Now, I try not to piss people off too much," Nicole said. "I have a bike now. Whenever possible I ride my bike now. I know I'll be in a much better mood when I get to where I'm going."

SOCIAL RESPONSIBILITY

The next day, driving down St. Charles Avenue (with me occasionally glancing back over my shoulder), Tracy Santa was providing a running commentary on the adjacent mansions. This one housed the president of Tulane University, this one some erstwhile Civil War statesman; mainly, however, these picturesque homes belonged to regular families. Here, incredibly, was a huge two-story beauty that recently sold for $60,000. Down the center of the avenue ran the St. Charles streetcar, on a wide grassy median shaded by palm trees. Tracy was showing me his daily route to Loyola University, where he taught English. As we got closer to down-town, a statue of Robert E. Lee appeared briefly between several buildings. Tracy grunted to himself. "Talk about irony. The local grammar school, which is over ninety percent black kids, is called Robert E. Lee School." On the way back to Tracy's house we stopped at a "convenience" store that sold nothing but daiquiris. Behind the counter were twenty different fruit-flavored daiquiri mixtures swirling in Slurpee-like machines. People of all ages pulled up for a quick pit stop, then jumped back in their cars and took off sucking on their straws. I stood in the parking lot and sucked on my own. I found it unskimping on the rum.

Tracy, thirty-seven, lived with his wife, Dina, and one-year-old daughter, Bebe, in a "shotgun"-style house in the Riverbend area. He had been in New Orleans for three years. When not teaching, he played guitar and sang in rock bands around town. He grew up in Connecticut, lived in San Francisco for ten years, then Cambridge for a few more. Dina was an AIDS health educator at New Orleans Charity Hospital. She'd never had a driver's license and always rode mass transportation to work. Tracy, who "exclusively owned junkers," drove everywhere. Asking why he didn't take the streetcar to Loyola, which was less than a mile away, opened the door on a lively, personal discussion about social responsibility.

"You say it's great to live right on the streetcar line, that I can take the bus to work and all that. The fact is, I have never taken the streetcar there because I'm so used to working with a car. If I have to prepare for a class and my time's down to minutes, I want to be able to get in the car, turn the key, have it start, and be there in four minutes. It's a seven-minute ride down there on the streetcar, and you have to wait a bit. When I was younger in San Francisco, I was more patient about waiting for public transportation."

He might be hooked on driving, but he couldn't say the same about cars themselves. "When someone asks me what kind of car I have, I say a blue car. I look for cheapness in a car. I don't put much value on what I drive. Whatever keeps working. It's just a utility. I don't anthropomorphize the car. I don't go build a little temple in the backyard to it. I just try to keep the thing functioning. I treat it well not because I feel close to it but so it will get me where I want to go with the least amount of hassle. I don't resent my dependency on it, because it's not that costly. I've never had car payments. When people pay a lot of money for a car they feel more connected to it. A car is a recreational vehicle, whether it's called that or not. It's a way to get out.

"Driving is also a rite of passage. Try to think of someone who was sixteen or seventeen who didn't want to get their driver's license. I was happy to get mine. I didn't have to hitchhike, or wait for friends to come over and weasel me for gas money. It's just simpler to do it yourself. I like driving. It relaxes me. I don't see it as a negative thing, although on the relaxation scale, it's not like taking a shower.

"Driving across town can be draining at times, but driving in the suburbs is worse. That does raise my blood pressure. That's because it is completely a car culture. There is nothing going on. I see the suburbs as a less well integrated way to live. You have your paneled sleeping module off here, and you have to take a car to get food, or to pick up the paper, or to go to school. I use the car around here because it's a little faster, but in the suburbs you *have* to use the car. I also like living around people who don't have such a high value, or high need, for automobiles. I like living where there's less need for them."

Tracy bemoaned the inefficiencies of public transportation and admitted that while the poor service was directly proportional to flagging usage, that was still no incentive for him to alter his life-style. As for helping the environment, he would do so if *everybody* was called on to make a sacrifice. "I wouldn't have a problem with driving less if it was an across-the-board sort of thing," he said. "But I'm not willing to singularly make an example of myself in terms of the environmental impact that the car has. If I stop driving, unfortunately it's going to have very little effect. Whereas if the major motor companies decided to make cars that would run on non- or less-polluting fuel, and I know the technology is viable, that would actually cause an impact. It's naive to think that my behavior could actually make a difference. If people were really concerned, they would lobby against the major motor companies and get something done about the kind of cars that are built, the kind of fuel they use. I do to an extent, but then I consistently vote for people who lose elections."

"Do you think people are concerned with acting toward a 'common good'?" I asked.

"The assumption there is that you can determine what the common good is, but I'm not sure there are that many things where there is a consensus opinion in a large society. We choose to do what we do professionally for a number of different reasons. I wouldn't be happy being strictly a businessperson. That's just a morally bankrupt way to live your life. What I do is based on that personal belief. But I wouldn't want to stand around and try to talk other people into becoming college professors or nurses. If there was a hypothetical situation where there was a viable solar-powered car on the market, and it worked reasonably well, and it was reasonably priced in relation to gas cars, I could see myself buying that kind of car for 'environmental reasons.' But that's not an option. Until it's an option, I'm not sure what sort of impact individuals can have.

"People here just don't see a physical connection between cars and pollution. Part of it is because pollution is a way of life here. It really is. People have always just trashed this area. Has the political consciousness back in the San Francisco Bay Area helped congestion or air pollution due to cars? No, it's gotten substantially worse. In the Bay Area you're looking at a place that's relatively liberal, politically active on social issues, and things are getting progressively and physically worse. What does that say for the rest of the country?"

The situation had to get to the point where it was flat-out unbearable. "What's the incentive to do something here?" he asked. "In Los Angeles they're trying to do something, not out of some altruistic reasons, but because they're saying, 'I'm fucking dying because of the air. It's crazy. People are shooting at each other. I can't breathe. I spend three hours in the car every day!'" Tracy was convinced we live in a *re*-active society. "I'm reading a gun-control article in my class tomorrow. A lot of the support for this person's point of view, eight paragraphs, is from Sarah Brady, Jim Brady's wife. I didn't see Sarah Brady out campaigning for gun control in 1978 or 1980. She had to get her husband's head shot off first. That's the way America works."

"But you personally would act," I said, "if, say, the mayor asked you and all New Orleans citizens to give up your cars and ride a bicycle for two days a week to cut down on air pollution. You would do it?"

"First, I have to know that all the CEOs downtown are doing the same thing. That the mayor and his staff are doing the same thing. Look, if you want something to have an impact, you have to get at least thirty percent of the people doing it. And the way that you do it is by having high-profile civic leaders set an example that this is what a responsible person should do. That influences other people to consider doing it. I want to know that the people who are at the root of the economic system that's created this problem are willing to make the sacrifice. My criteria for my action is that if I'm going to make a sacrifice, I want it to have an impact. That's important. I do not want to rush the machine gunners by myself just because I think that's a good thing to do.

"You say there's a problem and something needs to be done. But I don't think that not driving my car is going to do it. You're not going to get enough people in the United States who feel strongly enough to act frequently. You haven't sold your car yet. You've got a van out there that you're driving around the country asking these questions. I just think there is a more efficient way of going at the problem. We need to have different kinds of engines. And we need better pollution controls. Make gasoline so expensive that people don't want to drive. I think some smart entrepreneur is going to take the pulse of the nation and realize there is going to be a market for an electric car, and they're going to find that it's going to be profitable for them. But electric cars, or any one solution, is not the way to go. Offering them as an alternative, and creating cars that burn gas more efficiently, and public transportation, should all be done up better. I don't think the gas-driven car will disappear quite as quickly as the LP in the face of the compact disc. But then the Styrofoam boxes that the electric cars come in will become an issue.

"I think I'm relatively optimistic that some changes are going to be made. It's gruesome to think that something positive has come out of sending four hundred thousand troops and billions of dollars to Saudi Arabia, but I think the more that war dragged on, the more it played into the hands of people who want to make a real serious issue of overconsumption in the United States. I see it as an initiating force for some sort of reform.

"Another good thing about the way things in the United States seem to be shaping up for the next century is that there's going to be more of a tangible world community. There will be some pressure brought to bear on the United States from other countries to get their shit together. We burn so much more gasoline, we drive so much more than other countries, that people are going to find some way to turn the screws on this country.

"I can foresee a situation where activists might educate the population by using Los Angeles as some sort of example: This is what could happen. These are figures that show this could very well happen in other cities unless we do something. That way you might be able to persuade a significant number of people to change. But it's an enormous amount of work to change people's minds and convince them that's the case."

I heard from Tracy some months later. He had just bought a new car, a Geo Metro. What? Driving the car with the best fuel-efficiency rating on the market would surely ruin his reputation for driving vintage gas-guzzlers. "Oh, no," he said, anticipating my next response. "Don't even consider thinking I went from the Cutlass to the Metro so the world will be a better place." He bought the Geo because his seventy-eight Olds Cutlass was stolen, apparently an inevitability, as three times as many Oldsmobiles were stolen in New Orleans than any other car. Besides, Tracy explained, the Geo was relatively cheap, and he had been worrying about the Cutlass breaking down while traveling with his daughter. "OK," I said. I just grinned.

STOCKS AND CBS

Beneath a warm gray sky, my drive along the Gulf coast was pleasantly uneventful. I conducted interviews in Biloxi and Mobile, where transportation wasn't a worry. Just stay out of Houston and everything would be all right, I was told. And watch out for "country bumpkins driving at a snail's pace on city streets," said a structural engineer for Brown and Root U.S.A. Inc., the nation's largest builder of chemical plants. Neither of my interviewees felt the rapid growth in their cities in the last decade negatively affected their quality of life. Both believed the economic benefits to the community from the expansion of companies like Litton Industries and Brown and Root far outweighed any environmental detriments caused by more cars. As if in chorus, both chided me about my L.A. upbringing: "How could anybody live in that smog?"

In Ocala, a no-man's-land of northern Florida, I zipped off the interstate to pay a visit to the "Big Daddy" Don Garlits Drag Racing Museum. Here was a fossil record no car biologist dare pass up. Inside I walked along the path tracing the history of the race car, from plump four-cylinder Ford coupes to aerodynamically sleek turbo-charged dragsters. What a brilliant tour of American culture! I particularly liked the room that featured nothing but engines, like the 1937 Ford V-8—or "Arkansas Offenhauser"—on pedestals under domed glass. I had to laugh. Forget sculptors like Alexander Calder. Here were works of art forged in the heart of the country, the perfect expressions of American energy and ingenuity.

Like rock and roll, drag racing has provided a universal culture among teenagers. From California to Kansas to New York, wherever you could find a straight road out in the sticks and a person to wave "Go," you could have a party with screeching tires and overrevved engines. Here in the South, moonshine runners racing cops over the state line was not only one of the

earliest forms of drag racing but also gave birth to the car culture phenomenon that inspired generations of starry-eyed gearheads—stock car racing.
As Tom Wolfe wrote in "The Last American Hero," his 1964 *Esquire*
profile of stock car champion Junior Johnson, "Here was a sport not using
any abstract devices, any *bat* and *ball*, but the same automobile that was
changing a man's own life, his own symbol of liberation, and it didn't
require size, strength and all that, all it required was a taste for speed, and
the guts."

Scott Schuette, thirty-five, met all the requirements. As a stock car
racer, he had collected a few "upside down" trophies. That is, to end a
racing season "in a blaze of glory" he would come speeding around the
corner in front of the grandstand and purposely flip the car over to see how
far he could slide on the hood, sparks flying, down the straightaway. Then
there was the time he jumped a school bus over six cars, the floorboard
literally caving in as he hit the ground.

Scott lives in a trailer park in Lake Worth, just north of West Palm
Beach. After navigating a confusing series of back streets, I pulled into his
berth and parked near his Ford Bronco, red 1988 Thunderbird, and two
Harley-Davidson Sportsters. Scott gave up racing and now worked for John
Deere, hauling machinery in an eighteen-wheel truck to distributors and
retailers in south Florida. He loved the drag racing museum. That I had
been there immediately established a common bond between us. Inside his
dimly lit trailer a score of colorful caps were strewn about his kitchen table
and counter, each one featuring the insignia of a stock car track where Scott
had raced. His phone was shaped like a Corvette. However, the first thing I
noticed, sitting beneath the TV on a metal rack of shelves, was an eight-
track tape player. Surrounded by eight-track tapes! "You wouldn't believe
where I had to go to find that damn recorder so I could transfer my eight-
tracks onto cassettes," he said.

During his racing years, Scott lived in Chicago, where he worked as a
commodities broker in the Chicago Mercantile Exchange. "Being a broker
is what financed my racing. I didn't have a drug problem like all the other
brokers, I had a racing problem. Instead of going out buying cocaine like
the other commodities brokers, I went out and bought racing fuel and tires
and a lot of body parts."

It was night and Scott appeared tired. He awoke every day at five o'clock
and this was past his bedtime. Recalling his driving life, though, he gained

a second wind, and I could see the daredevil's mad glimmer push the fatigue from his face. Driving a truck was stressful, but it was nothing like the job he had left behind.

"I made very good money as a broker," Scott said. "But it gave me two bleeding ulcers and it was killing me. The last year was not a good year, and since my health and finances were going, I just sold the homestead and moved down here. I figured I'd sleep at night, and I *can* sleep at night. Driving a truck is just not as intense. It's not the kind of stress that I know is going to kill me, like one mistake up north could wipe me out financially.

"I was a floor trader. I was on the floor screaming and gesturing wildly with my hand trying to get to whoever has what I want. There was an old fart who had a heart attack right in the middle. Trading went on, we stepped right over him. They had to have the paramedics come. Trading never even slowed down. Finance is everybody's life up there. It's a real-life game of screw your buddy. It's an unfortunate thing."

Scott never went to school to learn the stock market trade. He started as a $60-a-week runner for his broker father and learned the ropes from experience. "I saw a lot of Daddy's boys, people who were pampered all their lives and not very intelligent, making a lot of money. I said, 'Well, if this guy can do it and he's got the IQ of a pet rock, I can clean up.' I got into it that way."

Scott got involved in stock car racing when, not wanting to drive his fancy Corvette in the winter slush, he bought a $50 car for the season. "When the thaw came, I said, 'What the hell, I got this thing sitting here, what am I going to do with it? I can't get my fifty bucks back.' So I entered in a spectator race in a dirt track, and I'll be damned if I didn't win. It was a race against other junkers. There was no work that had to be done on it except to put some good shocks on it and move the battery around because you're going to hit the guy in front of you to get him out of your way. Not unlike today on the highway.

"I raced that whole season. All my friends got involved with it and they started buying fifty-dollar cars. Next thing you know we're trying to corner the market on old Chryslers because you could do the most damage with them. Are you familiar with Roller Derby, where they have runners and blockers and smashers? They had team demolition derby races just like that. We were called the Crazy Eights. We were all black cars. There's a blocker, a smasher, a runner, and there was always a reserve car. One car was the runner, that was the scorer. All the other cars tried to protect him and take out the other team. The smasher would always go after their runner. So when they dropped the green flag, the runner would go out and make laps, but the other teammates could cut across the track after this guy, or go backwards around the track to try and hit him head-on. Head-on hits and driver's door hits were illegal. You could actually aim for a driver's door, and just try to peel each other's fender off. You would take cushions from discarded furniture and line the car on the inside so you're pretty well protected."

Scott advanced from demolition derbies to figure-eight tracks to sportsmen racing. He earned a sponsorship with Aamco Transmissions and became sanctioned by NASCAR, racing alongside the biggest names in the business. "I got a picture back here of David Pearson and Bobby Allison all going through the same turn and me hitting the wall," he boasted. Scott attributed his success to his love of driving and to an unusual talent. "In some way I think I'm better than the guy in front of me. That's why I got to get past him, to prove to myself that I can get past him. Then I am better because I am in front of him. But I don't know. I don't consider myself a winner in anything other than that. I live in a trailer, I drive a truck for a living. I don't know if that would be called winning."

Like many other race drivers, Scott had felt close to cars since he was a small child. "Probably since I was five, I was trying to figure out how to put a motor on a bicycle, anything to get out of work. I was totally engulfed in growing up around loud cars, hot rods. I stole my father's car when I was eleven years old and drove it around the neighborhood. In fact, I was a pretty darn good driver. I used to pull up in front of my friend's house, beep the horn, and lay up the tires and stuff. I even stole my father's car in downtown Chicago once when he parked it on the street. I was twelve. Regardless to say when I got back, the parking space was gone. I got caught. Big-time. But my dad was pretty good, he just lectured me and told me not to do it again. So the next time I took the car I made sure it was parked inside the garage.

"My first car was a Baja Bug, which was a pretty wild car. You had to have the airplane tires in the back—big bouncy tires. I was probably sixteen. Before that I had motorcycles—a dirt bike and a street bike. I rode the street bike on my brother's license illegally for a year. My first real fast car was a Ford. It was my Mustang, the second car I ever owned. It was a cream puff that I got for five hundred dollars. It was a sixty-six Mustang two-plus-two, stick shift. I didn't even want to buy the car. My mother bought it for me with money I had earned delivering bundles of newspapers. I learned how to use the clutch, took it down the street, and just laid a patch of rubber the length of the block. I said, 'This is it, I'm in heaven.' "

In Florida, Scott started "reverse drag racing." "There was a little side road called Roebuck Road. It was a two-lane road with wide-open shoulders, real grassy shoulders, and was straight as an arrow. We would go out there to drink beers with our girlfriends in high school. I was always good at backwards driving with my mirrors. Everybody else put their arms behind the seat and turned their heads. I would fix my mirror on the white line on the side of the road and just follow it. So I got real good. One of my friends challenged me to it. That was my Mustang versus his Duster. At the end of the road we'd just hit the brakes and do some bootlegger turns and laugh and have another beer. We carried it up north to the spectator races. We tried to get the track to sanction these backward races, but they couldn't get it for insurance purposes. We demonstrated it to the track official. He loved it. He thought the crowd would go nuts. So he let us do it on Sundays when the track was closed. People would be out there working on their cars, we would get out there, and the next thing you know you have thirty guys racing backwards in stock cars around the track. It's the funniest thing you've ever seen in your life. The racers will get out of their cars and they will be laughing so hard they have to sit on the ground and shake. It's the most fun you've ever had in your life in a car."

Driving a truck, however, was not nearly as enjoyable. Just too many idiots out there. "People in their cars—they don't pay attention. They have become too lax with their driving skills and abilities. They just focus straight ahead and they think about what they've got to do, going to the beauty parlor or shopping. They don't read signs along the highway, whether it's a speed limit, exit, or a lane restriction. Before, you didn't have power brakes, power steering, air-conditioning with climate control, or stereos from hell. Today you're just sitting in your Barcalounger with the scenery rushing past you. Gallagher, the comedian, had a good way of dealing with bad drivers. He said everybody should have a dart gun that shot stupid stickers. When a car gets enough stupid stickers on it, the cop pulls him over for being an idiot. I think that would work fantastic.

"I see just some of the most stupid things I've ever seen in my life down here, and I've driven on the County Expressway in Chicago and survived. This is total madness. I have two chains that are as wide as my two fingers together holding down thirty tons of equipment, and some fool will cut across from the fast lane to an exit. Or I'll be coming over the hill and find somebody doing twenty-five in a fast lane. The fact that I have thirty tons right behind my head and I have to put on the brakes suddenly is a scary thought. With most truckers you're going to find that problem because they're legal to carry eighty thousand pounds and it's always right behind them.

"I enjoy driving once I'm on the road. But I don't enjoy having to put up with customers who are wondering why you're late, and having to explain that I've got eighteen tires and a seventy-five percent chance that one of them is going to go out at any given time. That's always the case with a truck—it's always behind schedule, but it's got to be there now! You've got some old guy who is just putting along in the fast lane and you can't get around him by any means, and you're going to get right up on his butt and show him your bumper, then back off a couple of times. If that doesn't do it, you're going to start getting aggravated, and you're really going to think about nailing this guy. I mean, you just want to ram all eighty thousand pounds right up his trunk. But, of course, you don't. What you do is get on the CB and talk to the next trucker over and say, 'Can you believe this stupid . . .' Then everybody will get on there and start saying stuff like 'I don't believe the drivers down here.' They go, 'Jesus, I thought they were bad in New York, but this is ridiculous.' Then I get on and I say, 'That's because everybody from New York *is* down here.' Then they say, 'You got a big ten-four there.'"

Then there was the Department of Transportation personnel who got a perverse thrill out of stopping heavy-equipment haulers and meticulously checking the weight of the load and eyeballing every piece of paperwork. Scott had to keep a careful watch; his CB handle was "The Outlaw" because he often ran with an illegally heavy load. All in all, big rig driving was exhausting.

"There's a lot of fatigue involved in driving. There's a lot of time when you'll be going down the road following a Toyota, next minute you snap out of it again and the Toyota is behind you. You passed him while you were in kind of a daze. Sometimes you nod out a little bit. After a while, after your hundredth mile or so when you're starting to get into the day, and praying for a Snickers bar or something to give you some energy to open your eyes again. The old adage about truckers and road dope is not true anymore. That might have been true in the seventies and into the eighties. But it's not common at all now. You go to a truck stop and you will have prostitute problems, and you will have people trying to sell you drugs, but eighty-five percent or more of the drivers will either report the drug dealer, knock them out, or tell them to get the hell away from them. Most truckers will go for the second. They will physically knock the son of a bitch off his butt. They're tired of being called druggies."

Changing the subject, I asked if Scott considered the car's impact on the environment. "I do think about it, but I try not to let it get to me. I know something has to be done, but it's really going to put a damper on my weekend fun, and in the long run it's probably going to hurt my business. Now they're finding diesels are just as harmful as automobiles because of the particles. That's the black smoke you see. So it's going to hurt me both ways—working and recreation."

Reluctantly, Scott said he would do his part for the environment—he might even consider buying an electric car. "If they can come up with one that's not a pain in the butt. Technology has come a long way, but they haven't come up with a way to make that damn battery small enough or last long enough. If everybody has an electric car, I wouldn't object to it because I could figure out a way to rewire it, put bigger brushes in the motor, and go faster than the guy next to me."

MIAMI VICES

Scott told me that driving in Miami was like the opening scene from the Walt Disney movie *The Boatniks*. But instead of boats there were a thousand cars coming at you in "mass confusion." That's I-95, he said, "morning, noon, and night." I figured it couldn't be that bad. Everywhere I went people had been telling me horror stories about traffic and bad drivers. Yet I hadn't experienced anything that would qualify as more than an ordinary day on the Bay Area roads. "Wait till you get to Boston," I must have heard twenty times. "Not only do people regard red lights as only a suggestion, there's no rhyme or reason to the streets and highways. It's complete chaos." (Well, I did get to Boston, and although I got hopelessly lost one evening trying to find my way to Rosalindale in the southern part of the city—it seems that provincial New Englanders are not big on street signs that may offer the slightest bit of help to someone from out of town—I didn't find the roads particularly chaotic or dangerous.)

Then I got to Miami.

Driving in a strange city leaves you feeling disoriented and a little unsafe. Keeping one eye on the road and the other on unfamiliar freeway exit and street signs makes driving a bit of a chore. Yet I had grown used to that feeling of disorientation, and in fact had become something of an expert in navigating around strange cities. I don't know what it was in Miami, though—maybe my equanimity had been derailed by the late summer humidity—but during my four days there I feared for my life on the roads. Honestly, I didn't go three miles on any road without being forced to steer around someone cutting willy-nilly across three lanes or slowing down in front of me for no apparent reason. I think I set a new world record for being forced to slam on my brakes in the course of a fifteen-minute drive. And the traffic on I-95, State Highway 836, Collins Avenue in Miami Beach, and especially on the Dixie Highway heading south would make Los Angeles proud. However, I don't hesitate to say that I'd rather be stuck in L.A., where at least you don't feel like you're going to be impaled at any minute by a rusted chrome bumper.

Biologists have been known to go a little insane from being in the field too long, and maybe that was happening to me. Then again, maybe the craziness on Miami's roads really was the norm. I phoned the *Miami Herald* in search of insight. "You don't want to talk to me," said the transportation reporter, "you need to speak to the Lane Ranger." The Lane Ranger, it turned out, was the paper's popular columnist. He drove around Dade County and reported firsthand on the "vehicular mayhem" on south Florida's roads. Self-proclaimed "voice of the outraged motorist," his weekly columns provided a vicarious release of drivers' pent-up frustrations and anger. "The Lane Ranger has had it with Dade's tailgating, lead-footed red light runners," he wrote in his maiden column in late 1986. "I'm fed up with cocaine-snorting, brake-jamming lane jockeys."

The Lane Ranger tackled Miami's indigenous driving problems with mad glee. He took on highway design ("If highways were human relationships, the junction of Interstate 95 and State Road 836 would be a barroom brawl"); people who ate in their cars ("Hogging out while in gear should be taboo for the common herd"); street peddlers who solicit drivers ("It's getting so you can't cross town anymore without involuntarily shopping for exotic fruits or . . . feeling like a heel for telling some doe-eyed little kid with a tin can to stuff it"); and the Department of Transportation ("Bureaucrats are out of their minds to think they can actually improve Dade's roads without nuking them").

The Lane Ranger became an instant celebrity. There were bumper stickers and contests, like guessing the date the roadwork on the Dixie Highway would be finished. (Most readers responded with April Fool's Day.) He received nearly two hundred letters a week. "Only in Vietnam were the driving conditions worse," wrote a local retired Marine sergeant. "Nowhere, not even Saigon or Da Nang, have I wanted to open up with my M-16 on full automatic as much as I have in Dade County!" "The Ignorant Moron Driver," wrote a police sergeant, "is the driver who insists on driving in the left-hand lane on the expressway, usually next to another Ignorant Moron, door-to-door at 47 mph." One Miami motorist, after reading the Lane Ranger for months, felt inclined to summarize: "Somewhere I read that a person's personality is reflected in the way they drive. I certainly wouldn't want to meet the people who have expressed their views in your column!"

There was nothing dangerous about meeting the Lane Ranger himself. Sitting in a glitzy Holiday Inn bar near his home in Coral Gables, he was a friendly Irish bear of a man. His real name was Patrick May, and he was actually the *Herald's* star crime reporter. He had just returned from Gainesville, where he was investigating a series of murders at the University of Florida. He had plenty of experience amid Miami's seamy characters and drug dungeons and plenty of attitude to go along with it. Originally from Oakland, California, Patrick loved his job, but was none too fond of his adopted city. In fact, after listening to him rail against Miami for a while, I knew his gonzo persona as the Lane Ranger was no act.

"I've gotten into the psychology of why drivers are so particularly bad here," Patrick began. "And one is we've got a lot of elderly, so we have little old ladies and little old men that can't even see over the steering wheel. You see them in Miami Beach in these big Cadillacs, and you see this little, teeny head. It's so cute. They're just little, teeny heads sticking up and they're driving along, usually huge cars, and they're driving real slowly on the roads and creating all sorts of problems.

"And we have drugs, maybe not as much now, but in the mid-eighties it was pretty crazy. It was like 'Miami Vice,' it really was. I've covered stories that you wouldn't believe, where people stop on the interstate, push a couple guys out the door, blow them away, and take off. You know, that kind of stuff.

"I see people tooting up cocaine while they're at red lights. You look over to the right and you see people smoking joints. You got the Rastafarians, you got the Jamaicans, and they're all stoned. And you got these macho young Cubans and Colombians that are all coked up. There's this hot-blooded Latin veneer to the whole place. It's really a tough, macho city. And the guys that are driving live that out. Crackheads are all over the place, too. I got hit by one of them.

"Then you've got a lot of immigrants, and they're coming from a country where they have either no rules for driving, or different rules. They're from Guatemala City, El Salvador, Colombia, Venezuela, and then there's the Islanders: Bahamians, Jamaicans, and Haitians. I did a Lane Ranger story on this driving school where most of the people didn't even speak English. And they can't read English. And I said to the instructor, 'How do you teach people things like "No Right Turn" if they can't read English?' And she said she would teach them to look for something like the letter R. It was something that simple. I mean, these people just blew into town and you can't expect them to learn English overnight, but they get their licenses anyway. I understand it's tough being an immigrant. But, God.

"Just last week we had a shootout on the freeway. While two cars were going down I-95, one of them opened fire on another one. We have a neighbor section of the paper which is real local, regional news. And it had this running column called 'Car Wars.' Twice a week it would be an update on incidents reported to the police where somebody was either shot or assaulted or had a gun pulled on him in a traffic incident. It happens that often that we had this ongoing column for it. It was amazing.

"Your threshold of losing it here is lower because everybody's irritable anyway because of the weather. Just ask any Miamian—you've got to be very careful who you honk at because there are people that have been literally shot to death for honking. So you learn to survive.

"I never flip anybody off, I'll only yell. I had an incident where I was driving down this street right here, Le Jeune. I pulled onto Le Jeune one Friday night to visit a friend and this little Porsche was coming down the street at about eighty miles an hour, you know—way out of line. And he's not only coming real fast, but he's endangering all these people's lives by going down the wrong side of Le Jeune to get around these cars. He's out of control. So I chase him. I've got a Honda Civic. I get up next to him at a red light and I'm going, Oh, shit. But I was so pissed off. And I pulled right up next to him on the passenger side, and he's got a passenger in there. It's two Latin guys with gold chains, just drug dealers and bodybuilding guys. The last guys you ever want to mess with. And his window's down. And I was pissed. I just unleashed this line of profanity at him. And they both looked at me and smiled. Then the driver says, 'OK, you want to die, mother-fucker?' And he starts to reach down under his seat. And I just hit my gas and I took off.

"I chased another driver, the only time I've been hit in Miami. I'm coming home from a party over by the *Herald* and we're near a place called Overtown. It's a black area, and a heavy crack area. And I'm driving down the street and this car comes out of nowhere, one of those out-of-nowhere cars, like monster cars. They come out of the darkness and all of a sudden they're on top of you. And he's coming down on the right, and the lanes merge into one. And it turns out to be a she. And she scrapes me all the way down, passes me at about fifty and just like scrapes me all the way down. And I just lost it. I was losing my clutch, too, but even with a lost clutch, I chased her. She was in this old, beat-up, brown Chevy.

"And I chase her down a couple streets as fast as I can. I'm just swearing, I'm out of control. And she knows she's being chased, so she's really hauling now. She runs a red light, and she cleans another guy. He spins around. It was just this little Nicaraguan kid in from Managua, you know, speaks like no English. And I go, 'Come on, come on, let's get her!' And he's going, 'OK, *amigo*.' He jumps in his car—which is now half totaled—and we're both chasing her now into Overtown in the projects. And it's like Saturday night at midnight, the worst possible part to be in. There are crack dealers everywhere, they're like cockroaches. I'm honking my horn, I'm trying to get her to stop, we're chasing her. Finally she pulls up a dark alley and comes to a screeching halt. And I stop and I realize, you know, my better reason sets in. I thought, We're going to go in there and she's going to pull a gun on us and blow us away. And I stopped this Nicaraguan kid. I said, 'Go find the police.'

"So we go back to Biscayne Boulevard where we'd been hit, and we're at a red light waiting to go over to the *Herald* to call the cops, and this car pulls up next to me on my right. And I look over and it's the woman! She sees me and takes off again over to Miami Beach. And I chase her across the causeway. All these guys are fishing out on Saturday night, there's hundreds of fishermen and their families. And I'm going up the wrong side of this causeway! I was as bad as she was. She goes through the pay booth and we chased her all the way to Miami Beach, but we lost her."

Blaming his anger on his Irish temperament, Patrick didn't quite know what he'd do if he actually caught any of these people. "All you think of is, I just want to get her. It's insane."

As Patrick saw it, most of Miami's problems had to do with outsiders. Not only immigrants, but seasonal vacationers and, worst of all, greedy developers. "Oh, God. All they do is build, they keep building out toward the Everglades and to the east, more and more homes. And the developers in this town are so corrupt and crooked. I mean, every politician around is on the take. And so the developers run the town and get whatever they want. They go out there and build these huge—I write about these things—these ugly tract homes. And then the city and the county has to come along later and try to build roads. Down by Metro Zoo, there are thousands and thousands of people out living in these new homes that have sprung up over the last couple of years. There's one road down there called Quail Road that goes out past the zoo. It's a two-lane road and it's supposed to handle thousands and thousands of commuters every day, and it just can't. Rescue vehicles have to take this long, narrow roadway to get out to these homes for an emergency. It's ridiculous.

"Thank God we have the Everglades. They say the Everglades are dying, but at least they marked off this big hunk of land in the center of the state for them. But if it weren't for that, developers would have just built clear across to Naples—which is on the other side of the state—with nothing but homes. The beaches, as you know, are wall-to-wall condos. Miami Beach has these condo canyons. Oh, it's just disgusting. I mean, they've ruined the beaches. That's one of the reasons it's not too much fun living here. It's totally raped. This place has just been raped again and again and again. It's always been exploited. It has a history of scam artists and dreamers with their crazy dreams.

"That's another thing that explains a lot of this town's problems—the transients. People come in and they just don't care. There's not a strong sense of community, which explains why people on the roads don't care about each other. Everybody just sort of cares about themselves. Because they're going to be gone a week from now or next season. A lot of people just come down here for the season. A lot of people live in New York and they come down here for the winter. And they don't have anything invested here. I mean, they live in their condos. They don't give a shit about south Florida. You know? They just sort of come down here and kick back and relax and use the place and then take off. There's a real lack of community here, and without it, no change will ever be possible."

Patrick's portrait of Miami explained the chaotic roads all right. He certainly stoked the fear in me—I drove around on my best behavior. The regional issues he kicked up—increasing surliness among drivers, unbridled development, lack of community—were also national ones, affecting lane rangers across the country. Not since I had left Los Angeles, though, had I encountered these issues so high on the list of an area's daily concerns. On my way to Miami I had stopped in Orlando and visited the Disney World Epcot Center. I rode the little tram through the General Motors–sponsored exhibit of the automobile's history, "World in Motion." Throughout the Norman Rockwell–inspired re-creation of Americans and their cars, voices chirped the singsongy tune "It's Fun to Be Free." To hear Patrick and the letter writers who cheered on the Lane Ranger, though, was to understand just how silly that chime of freedom now sounded.

Mercy Dominguez, though, changed the tune. Wearing an elegant red dress and makeup, she was dressed in concert with the hotel in which we sat near Little Havana. A computer systems designer for Southern Bell, Mercy, forty, was personable and forthright, and no doubt made a good manager. Yes, she agreed, Miami was totally car-dependent (most of her friends, because it didn't service their neighborhoods, called the new high-tech Metro Rail system "Metro Fail"), and yes, the legacy of the 100,000 Cubans that arrived in 1980 during the Mariel boatlift was rampant overpopulation, and yes, there has been no coordinated effort by city planners to alleviate the resultant gridlock, but, in the end, so what? Her 1990 Mercedes and 1980 MGB certainly meant more to her than a few lost hours in traffic.

"There was a book written by a lady here who says that Cubans typically drive Mercedeses and BMWs because we are always very concerned with our image," Mercy said. "So maybe that's why I've always bought a

Mercedes. When I first came here from Cuba I had nothing to eat. I was eleven years old, I came by myself, my parents were left behind, and I was taken over by a government agency that put me in a foster home. So now it's my tradition: on the first day I buy my new Mercedes I always drive it through those real old terrible places in Little Havana where I used to live. And I think, Hey, look at me now. That makes me feel good."

Mercy said that Miami (52 percent of which is Hispanic) was a "very special place" to her. "You can live here and think you are in Cuba and never have to speak a word of English. Of course that's not a problem for me, but I relate to people a lot better in Spanish. My feelings are in Spanish. I dream in Spanish." Her sense of community, though, did not include the environment, for which she was not about to change her driving habits. "If gas goes up to six dollars, I'll pay six dollars, but don't take my car away. See, you're talking to somebody who never thinks about the environment. And the people I deal with don't ever talk to me about it. Well, OK, I don't put trash in the street. But no, I'm not thinking about forty years from now. Let people forty years from now worry about forty years from now. I'm concerned with today. I learned a lesson. My parents were in Cuba, and they were so concerned with the future ten years from now, twenty years from now, and Fidel got in there and took everything away and they landed with zero. So why concern yourself? Live today. Tomorrow will take care of itself. Live it up!"

ROAD TO NOWHERE

Well, whether south Floridians bear the driving hassles with Mercy's composure or the Lane Ranger's fury, there is no denying their ecosystem is getting worse. Fifteen hundred people pour into the state every day, while only six hundred leave. With so many new residents, not to mention the year-round influx of tourists in search of golden beaches, it's no wonder that the roads have become clogged like bad plumbing. But traffic is merely the effect and not the cause of the problem. Developers have been living it up in Dade County since the thirties, accommodating the stream of new residents, tourists, and transients with ever more housing tracts, condominiums, and hotels. From 1950 to 1990, the population has quadrupled from 500,000 to nearly 2 million. Clearly the root of the problem is rampant development, the environmental wreckage of roads and cars its mutant offspring. At least that's how it was explained to me by the boisterous and passionate Joe Podgor, a lifetime resident of Miami and executive director of the environmental group Friends of the Everglades.

"Transportation in Dade County has been manipulated in order to meet every need there is except moving people from place to place," announced Joe. He was plopped behind a desk in his cramped office above a post office in the Miami Springs neighborhood. "The highways are more an arm for sprawling development than they are for actually moving people." Roads not only sprang up in the wake of new development plats like the "white flight" suburb of Kendall, forty miles southwest of central Miami, but in fact spawned more development themselves. Joe liked to explain this phenomenon with a little tale he called "The Road to Nowhere."

"A road to nowhere is a publicly funded dog path that runs out to a private developer's previously unaccessible land," he said in his best sardonic voice. As an example he referred to the southerly extension of Interstate 75 from Broward County to Miami. "Our previous governor, Bob Graham, was one of the beneficiaries of that. His family is behind the Graham Companies, which is the major developer in Dade County. And Interstate I-75 just *happens* through their property in Miami Lakes. But there was already a preexisting four-laned parallel road that could have been the route. It would only have cost them about eight hundred dollars to put blue I-75 signs on that road and it would have covered the same distance and achieved the same effect.

"Now, the fella who was the secretary of the Department of Transportation at the time the road was sited is now the president of an engineering corporation. His company had contracts to engineer a study by the Department of Transportation—aside from his previous role as the Department of Transportation secretary—to see the feasibility of putting this road through the wetlands, to see whether it would hurt the water resources. Interestingly, they came to the conclusion it didn't. That company also had engineering contracts with developers whose developments would occur on yet-to-be-built intersections along the route of the road.

"None of which," he added, laying on the sarcasm, "has any link; nor does it in any way implicate anyone in anything that's anything but aboveboard and ethical."

Since 1969, Friends of the Everglades has joined with civic groups and national organizations like the Audubon Society to support lawsuits against the asphalting of southern Florida. The publicity surrounding the cases has allowed the environmental group to spread its message that the mayhem of development will soon completely destroy the area's fragile wetlands eco-system.

The ground under all those buildings and beltways in south Florida is basically thin mounds of porous limestone encrusted to a rock plateau. (This plateau, which makes up the tip of Florida, forms a coastal shelf on the continent.) Like marbles in a bowl of water, where the mounds rise out of the water there is land, and where they dip under there are the wetlands, or Everglades. As the ocean began receding about 100,000 years ago, the heavy rains—spawned by water vapors rising off the shallow warm ocean—filled up the Everglades. Like a huge river, fresh water flowed through the Everglades toward the sea, forming deep aquifers in the limestone on its way. Thus ran southern Florida's natural water cycle until Henry Flagler's railroad came to town. With a corps of bulldozers not far behind.

It doesn't take a geologist to know that houses and hotels couldn't be built on mushy land, so beginning in the forties the city fathers dug canals to reroute the water and dry up wide parcels of land. The water was channeled into storage tanks and managed by a branch of local govern-ment. (Today south Floridians still get their water from the storage tanks and wells tapped into the natural aquifers, which yield up to 7,000 gallons a minute from wells no bigger than one foot in diameter.) Siphoning off the natural flow of fresh water, however, drastically altered the local ecology. Salt water seeped into the aquifers and ponds, wreaking havoc on freshwater fish and wildlife, while the newly dry areas killed off estuaries and shellfish and led to destructive brush fires.

Furthermore, Joe pointed out, runaway development resulted in pollu-tion funneling into the entire water ecosystem. To build on limestone, developers must scrape away the soft peat topsoil and replace it with sand and gravel. However, unlike peat, which acts as a natural filter, sand and gravel allow toxins and contaminants to seep directly into the ground, where they eventually wash into the wetlands and into the water table—which is a mere two feet beneath the ground wherever you go in Miami. "The water table is taking a hell of a beating," said Joe.

Another main culprit is the daily trek of hundreds of thousands of cars, leaving a crust of oil and gasoline on south Florida's roads, a crust that the rains eventually flush into the aquifers. In fact, explained Joe, the highways themselves are "pollution-creating devices." To build up intersections or cloverleafs, workers dig holes nearby for the dirt. Those holes then become ponds of petroleum-tainted water that slowly spreads across the land like a toxic blot.

"Then you've got the *real* problem," added the never-flagging environmentalist. "We've got roads going through and around drinking water well fields. Those wells are located on the west side of town because we've frankly polluted the aquifer to the east where the people and most of the houses are located. So we put these new wells out west in open land where it's still uncontaminated. The groundwater flows from the west to the east in Dade County, so if you put the wells out there, where there's still wetlands, there's a certain amount of natural treatment that goes on if there are any pollutants. Then you can draw clean water.

"To the west of those fields they're talking about four-laning a new bypass, Krome Avenue, on which will travel all the agricultural pesticide trucks and oil trucks and gasoline trucks. That, of course, would put the source of pollutants directly upstream and over the new wells, which would be a very serious business. So we leapfrog. We pollute the ground, we move the well; we pollute the ground, we move the well. Now we're at a point on the aquifer where the wells are so far to the western edge that we've painted ourselves into a corner—there's no place else to move the wells. So now we're at a last stand. Custer had his and we have ours."

CATCH-UP GAME

South Florida's driving ecosystem sure looked like a lost cause: fossil fuels had returned to wreak a nasty vengeance on the land and drivers seemed locked in a perpetual battle. Maybe the cavalry should just let the place go up in flames. No, David Fierro said, that wasn't quite the plan. The state had mounted a strategy to save it.

David was the public information officer (read: PR, spin-control man) of the Florida Department of Transportation, located twenty miles outside of Miami. Like all PR types who are hired to put a spin on the truth, David found a way to paint a happy face on the department; but he was also forthcoming. A former newspaperman with his own personal opinions and feelings, he could juggle contradictions with great dexterity, but couldn't mask the fact that south Florida's transportation is a mess. "If I had to face that commute into downtown Miami every afternoon, I probably would not have taken this job." He laughed nervously. "Here I am, I work for the Department of Transportation yet I have moved away from the urban area because I don't want to deal with the traffic."

David admitted, "We're not going to be able to concrete our way out of this crisis. To be successful in Miami, there's no way we're ever gonna build enough roads or widen enough lanes." A systematic approach was needed, one that included mass transportation and attacked traffic at its root: over-development. In fact, Florida had begun translating such a view into legislation. In 1987 it passed a growth-management plan, called the Local Government Comprehensive Planning Act, which made developers responsible to each county for the infrastructure—notably roads and intersections—of their housing tracts and industrial parks. No longer could they slap down the buildings and depend on the city to build the streets and freeway exits leading to them.

"For a long time the whole notion of Florida was: encourage development. Give them anything they want if they'll come and bring their plant here. During those years development was rampant. It was unchecked. Now we're having to live with the consequences of that. In many ways that was good, we've grown as an economic state. But in many ways our quality of life has suffered.

"The state government is now playing a catch-up game. You can't go back and change growth patterns that have already occurred over the last fifteen years. And because there's no state income tax, Florida is still known as a tax haven state. So of course people keep coming here. But for the first time, the county government here is heavily involved with growth management. And the whole philosophy behind growth management is that growth must pay for itself. If I'm gonna put in that development, I've gotta also widen roads, I've gotta put in water and sewage. Before, because of the property tax revenue, you had local government saying, 'Well, I don't care where you put it as long as you build it, because that's gonna mean so much coming in property taxes.' But Florida's finally realizing you've gotta control it or it's gonna control you. South Florida is being looked at by the rest of Florida and the rest of the states as the mistake. 'OK, they messed up down there, now let's avoid what south Florida did.'

"So now before a development approval is given, a builder has to go to

Dade County and say, 'I want to develop this,' and the county has to approve the plat. Then the state is coming in on top of that and saying, 'OK, before that's approved, you gotta do this and this.' There are more hoops the development community has to jump through.

"Still, we're gonna have growth. You're not gonna erect a wall at the Florida-Georgia line and say, 'OK, no one else is coming in.' They're gonna keep coming. The point is: we need to, as governments, say, 'Where's the growth gonna occur, what kind of growth is gonna occur?' We need to manage."

To illustrate the county's newborn involvement, David pointed to the Krome Avenue widening project that upset Joe Podgor of Friends of the Everglades. "We said we need to four-lane that road. But Dade County said, 'No, we don't want to encourage any more development out there. We don't want you to four-lane.' So they removed the widening of Krome Avenue out of the work program. It's not in our five-year plan."

Another example was the developers' attempt to subdivide farmland in the southwest section of the county. Again, county officials said no— there was plenty of available land with highway access within the northern urban area. "So you see, with these new planning laws, for the first time we have government entities working in concert. It's definitely a sign of progress."

As for Dade County residents themselves, David said they were growing increasingly "sensitive" to environmental issues. "And I think the Department of Transportation mirrors that," he continued. "In 1969 the federal government created the National Environmental Protection Act. And since then we have been required to do environmental studies for our plans. And that's a good thing. Because that means before we widen a road, before we build a bridge over a wetlands area or a lake or river, we've gotta show how we can do that without any negative environmental impact. I think the age-old stereotype is that we pretty much have our bulldozer and we're gonna build our road and we really don't care. And that might have been true back at a certain time.

"Obviously when we build a project it's gonna have some impact environmentally. Our point is, how are we gonna keep that to a minimum? I think it's impossible to say we're gonna build a project and not have any kind of environmental impact. If you have a situation where there's a piece of land that does not have a road on it today, and you come and build a road on it, you're gonna have an impact on that environment, whether it's air quality or noise quality, whether it's endangered species or plants. Whatever it might be, something there is gonna be affected. And it's not gonna be positive.

"Of course this is a very, very delicate ecosystem. And a prime example is that we are proposing to widen Highway 1, roughly from the end of Dade County to Key Largo, to four lanes. But our major concern is safety. Two-lane roads that carry any amount of traffic are dangerous because you have people trying to pass slower vehicles and honking and jamming up traffic. The other thing is hurricane evacuation. The Keys are very vulnerable to a hurricane. And evacuation is a big issue to people who live in the Keys. But there's a whole menu full of environmental issues involving this project. We believe we've been responsible in how we've addressed those concerns; we say, 'We'll take the minimal amount of wetlands, we'll do as much bridging as possible to increase the water circulation a little bit.' However, there's some no-growth groups, some environmental groups, that say, 'Look, I don't care what you say you're gonna do, it's not good enough, leave it alone.'

"And I can respect where they're coming from. At some point something's gonna give, you know. As much as I can appreciate the wetlands issues, as much as I can appreciate endangered species, I also have to appreciate human life and how many people are dying on a highway. So how do you weigh this? What values do you place on that? Do you say, 'OK, we're not gonna do anything, we know we're gonna lose so many people every year'?"

I asked David why we continually have to pit one issue against another. "I know what you mean," he responded. "Can the two exist in better harmony somehow in the future; that is, can the transportation system meet the needs of the urban area *and* help the environment? But I don't know of any place in the world where man has encroached upon a pristine or natural area and something else didn't have to suffer."

Still, David believed Dade County residents had a way to go before they would change their commuting habits. "If people were really concerned about the environment—and this is true of south Florida and any area— they would get out of their car and get on mass transportation. Or carpool. I grew up in Los Angeles, and Los Angeles and California are known for their love affair with the car, but I think the whole country's that way. People just love the personal freedom. I do. But if there was a viable transportation system for me, a Metro Rail, that came all the way to where I live, I would use it. I feel responsible when I do. I work in transportation and I realize that driving my own car on the highway at my own convenience is pretty selfish. I think like anybody else over the last few years I've been bombarded with environmental issues. You know, *Time* magazine cover stories telling me what we're doing to our environment. Bette Midler is Mother Earth on a TV special. All those things can make you think, Gee, we really are trashing our world. Is there something I can do? And one of the prime causes is the emission that we're all producing. And if we could cut that down, if we could all get out of our cars, I for one would do it. It's the responsible thing to do for the earth. I know that sounds kind of corny, but it's really how I feel. I have a four-year-old daughter and it frightens me what we're gonna leave children of her generation or the generation after that. What are they gonna inherit? Toxic dumps. It's sobering to think about what we're doing with our environment. It's an emotional issue for me because I feel real responsible.

"Unfortunately, because of the system we operate in, departments of transportation around the country are measured by performance. We're measured by how much we produce, how many projects we contract, how many contracts were completed, how many miles of new road or resurfaced road. In the final summation we're gonna be judged by, 'OK, we gave you X amount of dollars, how many miles of road did you rebuild or build?' So that has to be our number one objective. Not too many legislatures or governors are gonna say, 'Well, how sensitive were you to the environment?' Our whole culture is, 'Look, if I don't get it in eighteen months, it's not worth doing.' It's that immediate gratification philosophy that's put us in the situation we're in today."

THE PEACH STATE

I tracked out of Florida in one long run toward the border, through pelting rain so fierce most sensible people pulled over. But I put my nose to the windshield until I crossed into the bright sunshine of peaceful, pastoral Georgia. It was flat and pretty country, lightly wooded, with a relaxed feel about it. I settled into the long stretch of highway and enjoyed the ride— and remembered a story that a young man named Kurt Zinser told me in

Denver. As often happened at the end of an interview, we got to swapping
driving stories.

"I have a friend that probably had the best one," Kurt said. "He had a
Porsche 911 and he and a buddy were driving down the coast—he went to
school out east—and he had cruise control. They were going to Florida for
the weekend, and somewhere in Georgia he let his buddy drive so he could
sleep. And his friend set the cruise control at about one-ten and promptly
fell asleep himself. And off the road they went, across a Georgia cotton field
at about a hundred and ten miles an hour with the cruise control on. He
said pretty soon the cotton on the bottom of the car started to catch fire and
it was leaving this fire trail through the cotton field. Finally the car stopped.
The brake jiggled, or whatever, and they woke up. It was dark and they were
just too tired, so they fell asleep in the field.

"Well, the next day they pulled out of there, drove back through the
field the way they came because they didn't want to hurt the car any more.
There was just that one black burnt trail in the middle of nowhere. And
somebody called it in to the police because they thought a meteor went in
there. They read about it in one of the local papers the next day. There was a
picture and everything. And they said, 'That looks real familiar. Oh, my
gosh!' It was a short piece of how this meteor had crashed to earth through
this cotton field and burned a long strip. At the end of the story it said there
was no actual rock found. Maybe they thought it melted down or something."

BACK TO THE FUTURE

All ecosystems go through stages of development, or "succession." The
more complex and diverse an ecosystem—the more species and environmental conditions—the more mature and stable it becomes. The final
result is called a climax community—something you'd be hard-pressed to
label south Florida or, in fact, most of America's urban areas. Unless,
perhaps, you lived in Atlanta.

I came flowing in on the fast, fluid currents of I-75. It was rush hour,
but never mind: without a hitch, or a lost beat, I rolled into the greater
Atlanta area. I was going seventy in the far right lane, and drivers were still
pressing on my rear to Move It Along.

In an unassuming way, Atlanta was very pretty. The city floated on a gently rolling sea of trees and hillocks, at reasonable distances denoted by modern clusters of gray and glistening buildings: Downtown, the classy Midtown, the chic Lenox-Buckhead mall complex, as well as several urban villages that rose above the trees like ship masts along the sixty-three-mile I-285 perimeter freeway that encircled the area. Beneath the trees, north of Ponce de Leon Avenue (the demarcation between the affluent north side and poorer south side) stood some of the most beautiful inner-city homes you'll find in America. It's a sophisticated, cosmopolitan, historical city (the home of Martin Luther King), and despite having one of the highest crime rates and the second worst poverty in the country, the area's prosperous and growing. People were thoroughly delighted with themselves and their town. The second day I was there they were literally dancing in the streets, thanks to Atlanta's winning the bid to host the 1996 Summer Olympics. (The following autumn they would be dancing and doing "the chop" as fortune continued to smile and their erstwhile dud Braves played in one of the most exciting World Series of all time.) Everything was upbeat!

Good heavens, they even had efficient public transit, the relatively new MARTA bus and rail system. I had traveled over 3,000 miles and I *finally* could talk to people who, at least now and then, ride the bus. But make no mistake, this was a car-oriented region. The area's seven counties of 2.3 million people relied heavily on the four-wheeled beast. As in L.A. and Houston, commuters thought nothing of traveling seventy miles to work every day alone. Traffic's just not that bad, people kept telling me. Atlanta was experiencing its Golden Age of Transportation. DOT (Department of Transportation) had just completed its "free the freeways" program and significantly widened all the trouble spots. And despite a little ozone, mostly emitted by all those trees, I was told, the sky was clear. All was peachy!

But . . .

There was something vaguely Faustian about all this auto-minded good cheer and enthusiasm. As if, perhaps, one day there would be some sort of recompense. For thus far, no American city has maintained its autopian age as a climax community. After all, only about thirty years ago south Florida was boasting of its Golden Age of Transportation.

DOT, DOT, DOT

Like most proverbial newspapermen, Doug Monroe of the *Atlanta Journal* was a bit of a sourpuss. Recently divorced, he no longer made the marathon commute to town, having opted for an inner-city bachelor apartment. The Atlanta area lacked a cohesive transportation program, he said, thanks to the "concrete-oriented" DOT. "I'm concerned that we're blithely going into the next century in our cars. We're not really looking at alternatives. In ten years the traffic's gonna be much worse and people are still gonna be scratchin' their heads, saying, 'Well, I wish we had done something in 1990.' There's going to be gridlock."

Doug had no faith in DOT. "The state of Georgia doesn't allow one penny of gas money to be used for anything but roads and bridges. DOT's orientation is, 'Don't do anything about alternative transportation.' Because if they take cars off the road their revenue is lower. The less gas you use, the less money they get. DOT wants to lay pavement from now till the end of time."

But a few blocks away, in a small white structure across from the Capitol, came the loud, opposing, pro-cement view. "I in-vite people tah cum tah Georgia an' travel ar highways," said Hal Reize, head cheese of Georgia's DOT. I sat opposite Hal's sprawling desk in a beautifully paneled showcase office. A large man with a wide ruddy face and cocky air, the DOT chief was a picture of perfect composure and bureaucratic royalty. Unlike the slick-talking David Fierro of Florida's DOT, Hal seemed a throwback to the good ol' days of Huey Long–type politicking. With a thick, sticky Southern accent, he wasted no time selling me on Atlanta's roads.

"Far as I'm concerned we have the best maintained highway system in the United States," Hal told me. "Drive out in our rural areas. If you find a pothole, call me. It's axiomatic to our maintenance force: you don't go to bed at night with a pothole on your section of highway. You do and your job is in serious jeopardy. As respect to our freeway system, it's *excellent*. The best freeway of any city of comparable size in the United States. Course, growth is goin' to detract from that."

Hal admitted, however, that their ability to expand the freeway system was limited—they were simply running out of room. "We can't widen anymore. Our northern perimeter freeway's carryin' the traffic but if any little incident or accident happens, it's so critical, the whole thing just falls apart. We're gonna build an outer circle—an outer perimeter freeway. Our engineers are seriously on it. But what I think we gotta learn in the Atlanta area is to use public transportation more. I'm on the MARTA board. The more people that can get on the rails, the happier I am. It's an excellent system that's expandin'—the outlying areas are trying to adapt it."

But not too successfully, as it turns out. The northern counties have consistently voted against MARTA. Seems they don't want to allow access to their area by the "criminal element" who allegedly reside on Atlanta's south side.

"But far as traffic goes," said Hal, "we need to balance out our growth. All the growth in the north needs to shift. I been preachin' this for several years now. We need different zonin' laws. Clamp down on the north. If this area was a ship heading east to west we would'a already capsized to the north.

"There's no coordination. We have regional planning, the Atlanta Regional Commission, but they have no zoning power or authority. No authority over land use. And developers, they's cagey people, see. The developers play these counties off each other. They go to DeKalb County and say, 'I want at least thirty-thousand-square-feet-per-acre zoning.' No, we can't do that, we'll give you twenty thousand because we think that's all we can accommodate. The developers say, 'OK, we'll go to Fulton County.' No, no, come back, we don't want yah to go to Fulton County. I mean, seriously. It's a matter of zoning. And they play cities off one another. Well, a developer told me, 'Hell, if I don't get it I'll go to Dallas.' I said: 'Go pack your bags.' I'm serious about it. These are the problems that give bureaucrats gray hairs. Because although we have metro area planning, we don't have metro area zoning authority."

Although Hal wanted more zoning clout, he was not eager to tell people what to do. DOT had built carpool lanes on some of the freeways but, fearful of infringing on personal freedoms, never actually enforced them as such. I asked him why, but he waved me off. "It's just like the lawsuit we had on doin' some upgradings here a while back. Some planner was saying, 'Well, we gonna put so many people on a bus, so many on rail, gonna put so many people in cars.' He's sittin' up there on the witness stand. So the judge looked down on him and said, very sarcastic: 'I drive out that way. Which one you plannin' on puttin' me on?' You can't control people. Not like that. But you can provide the services."

When I asked Hal about the environment, he quickly replied that highways have a *very positive* impact on the environment. *The human environment.* He said the worst thing you could do was to have growth, attract industry and jobs, and not provide supporting facilities. "You need water, you need power, you need sewers, you need schools, and you need transportation. In terms of the quality of the human environment, the worst thing you can do is pack a bunch of people into a confined space without providing facilities to serve them reasonably. With all the controversy around the Georgia 400 extension [a connector freeway being built in the lush northern counties to service the Lenox-Buckhead mall complex], planners say it will decrease traffic on I-285 by fifteen percent. Decrease traffic and you decrease pollution. Though we don't really have any. We have no carbon monoxide problem. The federal standards for ozone are one-point-two parts per billion, and last year we exceeded that nine-point-three days. That's all. But when I talk about the environment, I look at the quality of the human environment. I look at it in that context."

So did Kay Baynart, of the North Buckhead Civic Association, a community action group that had been fighting the Georgia 400 freeway extension for twenty years. In a fancy restaurant amid the high rises, hotels, and department stores, I talked with Kay about the freeway. But not before driving around the construction site myself. Ultimately the six-mile extension will be a six-lane toll road featuring a space down the middle for a MARTA rail line. One person's description of the current site as a "war zone" seemed appropriate. Through a dense cover of trees and homes and wetlands was cut a wide, muddy, skag-strewn swath. Smoke hung above the trees in small pockets, and chain saws buzzed like incredibly amplified cicadas.

"It's hideous," Kay said. She was a polite and sincere middle-aged woman, well dressed and well educated. She drove a white Ford Taurus.

"Nobody wants a highway in their backyard. I feel so very sad for the people that live near this thing." Kay and her husband's own home was 1,000 feet away. "But it's the congestion and the pollution that we're also worried about. Obviously from an environmental point of view you don't want tens of thousands of belching cars replacing hundreds of acres of trees. When you fly over Atlanta all you see is trees. And under them are all these homes and churches and communities. Being ruined.

"This's an automobile city. You have to educate people out of their bad habits. They say you can't take people out of their cars, but my feeling is that you can if you make it painful enough. If it takes forever to get somewhere, if you're constantly stopping, if gas prices go high enough. But not if you keep building freeways. DOT has no real interest in MARTA. Hal Reize is a very . . . interesting person. But the attitude is: close the barn door after the horses are gone.

"I'm horribly worried about environmental problems. We already have serious air quality problems. But our legislation—it's a dark ages mentality with a lot of internecine warfare and fiefdoms. It's very sad because we have terrible schools statewide, terrible poverty statewide, we have infrastructure problems—except for highways. We have a lot of highways that don't go anywhere or do anything, but they're beautiful.

"This new highway corridor is nothing but a marketing tool for the developers who want to move the central business district northward. We don't need it. The extension will dump cars into this area in a confusion of traffic. In the city, we already have a glut of office and hotel space. The people who make those decisions to build more buildings and hotels, for which there is clearly no market right now, are the same ones pushing for this road. I mean, that's the mentality. What we see is: there's no long-term thinking. Like my husband says, the worst invention was the quarterly report. You need visionaries that think twenty years down the road.

"Yes, I think we've finally lost. What's the opposite of fair and square? Down and dirty. We lost down and dirty. The road's being built. After two hundred thousand dollars in legal fees, we just lost a major appeal. It's so political—things won't change until something changes in the way decisions are made. And remember, advocacy groups here are not as powerful as they are on the West Coast." Kay sighed. "Maybe next time."

Freeways like the Georgia 400 were once considered the crowning achievements of modern city transportation. The defeat of Kay Baynart and her ad hoc group would once have been considered a victory for city planners. But there is no triumph when autopia is succeeded by gridlock and sprawl. The car is no longer a harmonious part of its ecology, like, say, the gray wolf is part of the relatively stable and ancient northern temperate forest, interwoven with and dependent upon factors such as the weather, availability of prey animals, and the vagaries of disease. This creature, the car, literally dominates and creates its environment. "The car is now the defining technology of our built environment," wrote urban planner and architect Peter Calthorpe. "It sets the form of our cities and towns. It dictates the scale of streets, the relationship between buildings, the need for vast parking spaces, and the speed at which we experience our environment. . . . The car wants lots of pavement and the low-density development that preserves plenty of space for it." In other words, the car has taken over, bending the urban ecosystem to its will. It's like the forest has become filled with souped-up wolves—better eyesight, sharper teeth, inoculated against all diseases. It's a lopsided and dangerous development—something soon is going to crash.

But before it does, it sure is a pleasure to drive. I intentionally got on the I-285 perimeter freeway at five P.M. and drove the whole sixty-three miles' worth. My conclusion? Los Angeles circa 1960. No need for brakes. Cruising with remarkable ease along Atlanta's concrete encasement, you really had to look hard for problems. But, hey, I found one. A disease that, according to the National Institute of Mental Health, affects about 4 percent of all hucars prowling the highways.

CAR PHOBIA

Knowing she had to negotiate the Tom Moreland Freeway Interchange with its twelve ramps, fourteen bridges, and thirty-six retaining walls, Leigh, twenty-eight, confessed, "I started getting weak before I had to leave the driveway. I usually went into a panic attack. I'd get a feeling of doom. I felt like I was going to pass out. I had sweaty palms, a pounding heart, and feelings of unreality." Another of the afflicted, Kay, forty-seven, contemplated the I-85/I-285 junction and said, "Oh, my gosh, I'll never go over that." And for several years she didn't, wearing out one Atlanta map after the next traversing surface streets.

These women all paid regular visits to Dr. Charles Melville in his nice red-brick town house office in Buckhead. I, too, went to see the good psychologist, who, as part of the Atlanta Area Phobic Program, treated anxiety disorders and ran an ongoing therapy group called Mastering Spaghetti Junction: A Course for Fearful Drivers. This, basically, was how he made his living.

Originally from Cleveland, Dr. Melville earned his Ph. D. from Purdue

University; his dissertation was on snake phobia. He drove a five-year-old Honda Accord, which fit, he said, his ideal self-concept. "I'm sort of a mainstream kinda guy." His manner was relaxed and, befitting a therapist, poker-faced. "Some of these people have just a simple fear of driving," he said. "Where for other people the fear of driving is one subpart of a larger condition now called 'panic disorder with agoraphobia.' That fancy term means that these people are having panic attacks, sudden rushes of overwhelming anxiety that you or I might have if we came this close to being hit by a semi going down the highway. They have these sudden rushes of panic in any host of situations where they're a distance from home and do not feel like they're with someone who can take over in a case of incapacitation. They often upset themselves with frightening self-statements like 'I'm going to lose control of the car and kill someone.' These are people who can't be adults in the normal sense. The most common situations they fear are bridges and congested interstates where there's no escape. They feel trapped, in their mind." No exit.

"Some never go beyond a certain 'safety zone' from home," he continued. "Some drive only in the right lane, while some people never get on the interstates. It prevents them from doing things, like mother-things." Two-thirds of Dr. Melville's clients were women, but he estimated that the incidence of male phobics was just as high, though men were more effective at hiding their fears—or covering them up with alcohol.

Dr. Melville's method of cure included behavioral modification, cognitive therapy, body relaxation, and group pressure. The first half of the Spaghetti Junction course takes place indoors, while the second half actually entails getting out there on the road, practicing a prearranged hierarchical list of driving situations—from sitting in your car in the driveway with the motor off to braving the interstate and the horrific Tom Moreland Interchange—first with good ol' Dr. Melville, and then . . . Oh God! . . . alone.

"How many wrecks have you gotten into with these people?" I asked.

"None," he claimed. "In fact, I feel safer driving with phobics than with inattentive drivers, those who get distracted easily."

Dr. Melville's success rate was pretty impressive—about 80 percent, excluding those who would, for one reason or the next, drop out of the group, and those who were just "too invested" in their malady: they had too many "primary and secondary gains" (getting out of doing things and accumulating a lot of nice sympathy). He told of a gentleman who, for eighteen years, never made a left-hand turn nor set one wheel on the freeway. Now he was a happy fella. The doctor's systematic method worked well. "But some people," he said, "never have a gradual approach to anything. I had this woman who even after many sessions could not get out of her safety zone. Then one day I got a postcard from her from the Smoky Mountain National Park. I had gotten her angry that last session. She left my office and drove to Tennessee. She said she'd had enough of this pussyfooting around and she just went out and did it."

Dr. Melville said that driving in Atlanta had become substantially more challenging in the last twenty years. Whether this produced more car phobics, he couldn't say. But he knew it was more congested out there, that drivers were more reckless and aggressive.

MARTA

So why didn't these people take the bus or train? Probably because these vehicles inspire another phobia: fear of minorities, the infirm, the poor, and the just plain crazy. In the minds of many people buses represent "second-class" transportation. So goes the myth, anyway.

I rode the MARTA system, beginning with the immaculately clean rail line. Then I switched to one of MARTA's immaculately clean buses, getting on the 19 Claremont. The driver, Mike Hawkins, was a nineteen-year veteran. I asked if his riders were confined to low-income folks. "I don't think so," he said. "If I had to say, I'd guess the majority would be middle to low income. But if you go through the routes up in north Atlanta, those people are wealthy and they ride the bus. I think it's just according to what route you're on." No gangs? He shook his head. "We have some trouble with school kids, but nothing serious." And your buses seem so . . . immaculate. City ordinance, he said. No food or drink. No radios, with or without headphones. Security was maintained by MARTA's own police force, the eighth largest police force in Georgia. "We haven't had that many accidents either," Mike said. "We've won the Safest Transit System in the World award numerous times." Uh-oh, I thought, this was beginning to sound like their damn flawless freeway system.

At the end of his shift, Mike and I sat in one of the generic MARTA depot offices. I asked for the lowdown truth on driving in Atlanta.

"I was born and raised in Atlanta," he said. "It's a totally different town than I grew up in. Just so many people have moved into the South, especially the Atlanta area. They're coming from different towns and I think they're bringing some of their habits with them. They got a saying in Atlanta that the red light is just a suggestion to stop. You got to count three cars before you go because there's three cars that are going to come through that traffic light after it turns red. It's getting worse and worse. Everybody is in a hurry.

"I don't know what happened all of a sudden. It's just been coming on for years, but no one cares about running traffic lights or stop signs. They're bold, especially these small cars. And it's very aggressive. I attribute it to the influx of Northerners. I hate to say Northerners, but just people coming from all over. Of course, Atlantans are just as bad. I know people who have lived here all their lives and drive like maniacs. There's just too many people and not enough roadway.

"It really amazes me that people will do the things they do. I had this woman the other day, we were going side by side. All of a sudden she cut in front of me. She just had it timed perfect. She cut right in front of me and went right into this driveway to this shopping center. She was in a small Honda with Florida tags. If I would have hit her, I would've drove all over the top of her.

"A couple of days later, I was stopped at a traffic light. The right-turn-only lane was next to me. There was nobody in it, and I always check. The light turned green and I started to go across the intersection and pull over to the bus stop. Well, I was just about to start pulling over, and here comes this Camaro from the right. By the time I got slowed down, he didn't hardly have room to get between me and the curb, but he made it. There was a woman at the curb waiting for the bus. If she had stepped onto the street, he would have killed her. I got his tag number. If I'd caught him at a red light, I probably would have got out and choked him, but he was long gone."

The best thing about being a bus driver, Mike said, was being his own boss. No one was looking over his shoulder. He enjoyed people, though he admitted that dealing with the public had to be one of the most difficult jobs there was. The customers, the traffic—it could get to you. "Evidently my attitude must be right because I don't get too shook up about it. There are times I probably boil over, but there's no one looking over my shoulder, and that's a nice feeling. We have some drivers that have been here twenty-five to thirty years that I don't see how they go from day to day. They're just nervous wrecks."

Yet ugly situations were enough to send anyone into stress overdrive. "Just a few months ago I had a guy threaten to kill me," Mike offered. "He got on the bus at the end of the line. He wanted to go to the VA hospital, he said, then went and sat down. I got to the VA hospital and I let everybody off. He didn't get off, he just sat there. A couple miles later, he rang the bell and came up. When he got off, he stood in the doorway and said, 'If I'm late for work I'm going to kill you.' I said, 'What are you talking about?' He said, 'I'm going to kill you. I'm going to shoot you in a place where you'll be slow to die.' I just said, 'OK,' and shut the door and drove off. There wasn't any use for me to pursue it.

"The most problems we have are with drunks. I don't even like to pick them up. But if they're standing there with a bunch of people it's hard to pick out a drunk. Most of the time I tell them, 'Buddy, I'll let you ride, but if you start raising hell, I'm going to throw you off.' They'll promise you everything to get on, and five minutes later they're crawling over every woman, hollering and cussing.

"You do get to learn the people. I've met people on some of my routes. I've been to Christmas parties with some of the passengers. I've gotten to know a lot of people in this town. I've dated a few of the passengers. And we have a lot of drivers that have married their passengers. I do enjoy some of the people. It's not like it used to be. Before the rail, it was almost like family. Everybody rode at a certain time, and you saw everybody every morning going to work, and in the afternoon coming home. Now, with the rail, it's spread out. A lot of people just drive their car to the rail system and catch the train."

Unfortunately, Mike himself was forced to commute twenty-five miles to work because MARTA did not service the area where he lived. Since driving was his job he tried not to complain, but personally the traffic was wearing him out. "There's just too many people and not enough asphalt," he said. DOT and company might have been doing a good job trying to keep up with the growth, but the minute they added a new lane it filled up with cars. "I would love to catch the bus to work. Sometimes I'm just so tired when I get off work because I have a lot of twelve- to fourteen-hour days. I'm putting my daughter through college. I'm so tired, I don't even feel like driving home. It would be *so nice* just to sit on the rail or bus and go home."

A Voice in the Wilderness

"I'm not sure that people drive themselves only by cars," said Leon Eplan. "They drive themselves in a lot of ways." We were sitting on the screened-in porch of his exquisite home along a deeply shaded lane in the midtown area. Inside, his wife was preparing for Rosh Hashanah that evening. "We're a driven culture. And I'm not sure that cars don't represent something of that."

Perhaps we've driven ourselves into some sort of ecological pothole, I thought. But I didn't say that. "I drove in from Athens this morning," is what I said. "People were starting in for town well before it got light. It took me an hour just to get to the freeway, and once on the freeway, though moving right along, it was packed. And I thought, This's what it's like right now in every urban area in the country. And people do this every day."

"I have to say that the great pleasure of living where we live is I've never been more than ten minutes from any job I've ever had."

The jobs Leon Eplan has had are impressive. A city planner by trade, he was head of the largest urban planning firm in the Southwest, and helped plan MARTA in the seventies. Under Mayor Maynard, he was the Commissioner of Budget and Planning for the city of Atlanta, giving him a rare opportunity to combine two functions that had not been combined in any other city, allowing him to be in charge of budget policy as well as development. He served as national president of the American Institute of Planners and head of the graduate city planning program at Georgia Tech. Presently he was a private consultant and worked out of his home.

Eplan was a prime exponent of "regionalism," which fosters a holistic view of urban areas. For all practical purposes, regionalism was spawned in 1931 by Benton MacKaye in his book *The New Exploration: A Philosophy of Regional Planning*. Along with Aldo Leopold and other conservationists, MacKaye was a founder of the Wilderness Society, a nonprofit Washington group that pioneered the preservation of federally owned lands. MacKaye started planners thinking about people's place in, and psychological connection with, their urban environments. He blamed urbanites' increasing sense of alienation on "hideous" structures and haphazard development. Looking around cities he saw "not the slum of poverty but the slum of commerce. . . . These souls live all in a single environment: not city, not country, but wilderness—the wilderness not of an integrated, ordered nature but of a standardized, unordered civilization."

Eplan had been trying to reconcile unordered nature through integrated planning throughout his career. Yet he constantly found himself smack up against one barrier or another. A born teacher and frictionless talker, he only had to be prodded gently to get him going. And straight into the Big Picture he went, holding Atlanta as a mirror of the transportation, land-use, and very real psychological problems that cities around the country face.

"The main problem with transportation," Eplan explained, "is that we tend to pull it apart from the other urban functions, such as land development. So that decisions that largely influence the nature of transportation aren't under the aegis of transportation people, and vice versa. Decisions are made strictly on immediate single-issue needs and not on the larger issues of how you manage growth and the kinds of things that would make life endurable and tolerable in the city.

"So you've got engineers trying to solve the problem the best they can. But it's like the generals running the war: we don't achieve the notion of peace. We've always resisted putting the generals in charge of our foreign policy; we have people we regard as larger than the generals. The generals who run wars are out there in the field; they have a very narrow mission, and they're out to attain that mission. A traffic engineer is out to move cars."

To illustrate the lack of harmony among departments, Eplan offered the example of a school system, which is made up of a diverse array of bureaucrats, teachers, accountants, and architects. It is an entire technical culture drenched in mystique because no one person feels adequate to comment on the whole. The same is true of transportation. Urban planners are inadequate to comment on transportation because they aren't traffic engineers.

"I'm not at all diminishing the importance of expertise," he said. "What I am diminishing is separating that expertise from the larger issues that we need to be dealing with. We don't achieve higher aims. And the best example in transportation is that the transportation person has no control over land-use decisions. It's the land-use issues that are ultimately stymieing their best efforts to solve transportation. I mean, we build an interchange on the interstate with state and federal funds, and then we allow the local community jurisdiction and authority to determine what goes around that interchange. And what ultimately happens is they build with such intensity around it that we draw heavy traffic to that interchange and defeat its purpose. Traffic doesn't flow off the interstate right onto the arterial; it stops, it gathers. Ultimately, it reduces the capacity of that interchange.

"This is all to illustrate the isolation that we've allowed transportation to achieve and operate in. And it works to the detriment of building a decent city. Instead, you sit on the expressway and waste your time. There is all this stress and environmental pollution—you're being poisoned because that person has been allowed to move a car from this point to that point without proper planning.

"Atlanta is one of the very best single examples. I mean, people talk about Los Angeles and Houston. But Atlanta is different. Just the scale itself—it's small enough where you can see what's happened. And we've built a tremendous amount of roads in Atlanta. You can see the difference between this inner city where I live, which is not as expressway-dependent as the new city, the doughnut city which came after World War II. And you compare that outer city with the inner city, compare the quality of life. And what you see is, until we began to burst forth with development out in the suburbs in the fifties and sixties, all of our transportation solutions were aimed at the problem of getting people from the rim to the center through specific corridors. The expressways, they were radial routes. And they came from the outside to the interior, where the jobs or the services were, the bands, all of the government functions, the entertainment, everything.

"What happened over a period of the last few decades is a totally changed urban pattern. And you see it in every city. We began to extend, through federal policy primarily, our system outward. Our rail, our highway systems, our utility systems, our school systems. We began to put public investments out on the edge. Remember, all of this was in the fifties and sixties where the federal government underwrote all of these things. There were two choices. We could have rebuilt things in the inner cities and kept people close by. Or we could extend things. And we chose to extend our systems outward.

"My point is that we put these public investments in the extension rather than the renewal, which also drew people to the suburbs. Then in the seventies, the next function that went out was the retail trade. It left the city and went out and built huge shopping centers to serve that population. The new condition that occurred in the eighties was that we began to have a substantial number of jobs going outward. The economy flipped over from a manufacturing economy to a service economy, so that people worked in office buildings and in shopping centers and things of that sort. So we began for the first time to have a significant amount of service jobs in office buildings, office parks, business parks out in the suburbs. Now we've got people living fifty, sixty, seventy miles from Atlanta in Athens, Gainesville, wherever. People now commute to jobs, but they don't come down to Atlanta. They come to the edge of the growth because that's where the jobs are.

"So the form of development in the eighties and nineties is people living very far out and commuting to the edge of the regions for jobs, and going back in the evening. And their commuting is now more than half an hour or forty minutes. But they can live in a small town. Until those jobs moved out, though, people were still coming into the central city. And then the transportation problem was in corridors. And therefore large systems— systems with enormous capacities like expressways and a rail system— could be justified. They could be justified because there was a large capacity moving through those corridors.

"But what began in the eighties, and is going to be the problem with the nineties in transportation, is that once we put jobs out on the edges—and those jobs were scattered around this huge area—the chief transportation movement is not going to be radial but lateral. And unfortunately, because of this scattered development, there are no corridors. There are no major roads that can be built to go from this point to that point. Therefore people wander along these nonradial lines through neighborhoods and through these small towns, along small, old roads. The problem today is not the traditional one of coming into the city and going back out. The major problem of the nineties is this cross-lateral movement. And that can't be solved by the automobile.

"The value of the automobile in transportation has always been its flexibility. All you need is a road. And you wind around where you want because we have roads everywhere. So you've got maximum freedom to find your own way. The problem is, that works only to a certain level of capacity. But when that capacity is used up, meaning you can't tolerate any more cars, there's no alternative. That's because we can't build expressways, because we no longer have what's called in transportation 'many-to-one.' Let me explain.

"When there's a lot of people at one point, and they're all going to one point, you can build a tremendous capacity. And in fact that's where transit really works best. The one-to-one. From Atlanta airport to downtown Atlanta, you've got millions of people going to one location area. And so transit is just absolutely fantastic. Disney World works wonderfully under those arrangements. Everybody's in sync at the parking lot ready to go inside.

"More characteristic of our life-style, over the last fifty years, has been what is called many-to-one. And that is many people scattered around trying to get to one place, like downtown, some large military base, or whatever. So what happens is everyone comes to these corridors so that they funnel in. Expressways are designed to deal with many-to-one. You've got all these lateral connector roads, neighborhood roads, arterials coming into the interstate and they shift you into that one spot.

"Now, we're many-to-many. And no transportation system can tolerate that. The automobile is ideal up to a certain level of capacity. But we cannot build enough roads to continue to allow many people who want this maximum freedom to leave the house when they want to leave, to move wherever they want to go, to make certain stops along the way, to have this enormous freedom that the automobile offers. There comes a point, a tipping point, beyond which the capacities of all of our capillaries in our system cannot function.

"The reason we got to this is because the people trying to solve the transportation problem had no say in the land-use questions, or vice versa. And the land-use questions have been so fragmented. There's no overall planning. Planning implies control. An evil word, *control*. The C word that you don't even mention. What planning does, it removes individual choice and says there's a public interest that needs to have some control or have some say in your life-style.

"We've gotten used to a level of that in this country because of zoning. You cannot do what you want to do with your own property. But we've agreed on that because we see that giving up some degree of freedom allows us to be free in other ways in an urban society. As long as you're way out in the rural society and the jungle, you could keep all the freedom you want. But once people come together, they have to give up a certain degree of freedom. And that's what zoning does.

"That's what utility systems do. You can no longer have a well, you can no longer dump your waste in your backyard. You are required to plug into the central sewer system because what you're doing in your house pollutes the next house. That's why cities were formed—to deal with problems the state had never been involved with, problems created by people living close together. When people get in close together, they have an effect on each other's lives. And so they have to create a cooperative, it's called a public corporation, which is called a city.

"They come together and say, 'Look here, I'm willing to give up my powers if you're willing to give up your powers in order for me to do what I want to do, and you can do what you do.' What happens is that we've come to the point where we have to give up a certain amount of freedom that the automobile offers. We've already given up some by pollution controls and speed limits and a lot of other things. But as for the use of the automobile, what is the solution that we all can live with? What will I agree to live with when I have to give up some of my freedom? How should that public control be effectuated?

"The problem is there's so many interests involved. And I might say, there's so much money involved. So we're not willing to give up our individual control. We've given up some control. Zoning is an example. But we've not been able or willing to give up the control necessary to solve this movement problem.

"And it is the land-use controls that say whether or not we're going to solve our transportation problem. It is not a transportation issue per se. It is a land-use question. Because land is in the private sector, we haven't been able to marshal enough public concern to control the problem. Because you have the private interest, you've got every city that wants its own control over its own zoning. Even in the public sector, in each little city, you've got a fragmentation of the power, and therefore the unwillingness of a lot of people to give up the necessary control.

"We have fifty municipalities and counties in the Atlanta area. The question is, How do you come up with a single concept? If you look at the plans of the Atlanta Regional Commission, when it comes to transportation planning, they've supposedly got the problem solved. But then you look at their land-use planning in a regional situation, and you have to go to the lowest common denominator to get agreement, and that agreement is so minimal that it has no effect. So what happens is you take whatever's given to you. You're not a leading edge. You're not controlling or directing it. But you're following it. In all the cities, it's no different.

"There is no major problem facing Atlanta right now—transportation, crime, air pollution, poverty, drugs—there's not a single problem that can be solved in Atlanta by Atlanta operating alone. The new thing that's come out of the Bush war era is that people no longer live in cities, they live in urban regions. Before World War II, people lived in cities and there were a few regions, a handful of regions in which I'd have to guess twenty-five percent of the people lived: New York, Boston, Detroit, San Francisco, Los Angeles. Today, over eighty percent of the people live in urban regions. Those urban regions are fragmented. The problems that people face are not city problems, problems of a single government, but problems that are regional in scale: transportation, crime, pollution. And so what happens is that you no longer have anybody in charge.

"If the problems are on a regional scale and you don't have a public entity dealing with that, you kick it up to the next level of government, which is, theoretically, the regional government. Well, we don't believe in regional government in America. So what happens is you kick it up to the next level, which is the state. And the states' functions have never been urban. The states' functions have been traditionally and very specifically in health and welfare and civic functions. But the created cities, the public entities, the public corporations, solved the urban problems. The state didn't want to deal with those. They turned those over to the city. The problem is the cities are no longer in charge because of the scale of the problem. Then you have to kick it up to the next level, which is the federal government. But at the very moment that these problems became regional in scale we elected this antigovernment guy. Your favorite Californian."

"You mean the Cowboy," I said.

"And so what's happened now, since we don't believe in regional government and the states refuse to get involved and the federal government has gone away—what we have done to solve some of these problems is that we've created a new kind of government, a special-purpose government to solve a specific need. And usually they can tax to carry out their function. In transportation we created MARTA, which is a government agency, it's a seat of authority set up to solve a single problem. Because MARTA, for instance, doesn't care about land-use problems. They don't care what kind of zoning goes around their stations.

"So how are you going to solve the problem? I'm just telling you how we have been *trying* to recognize the problem. That the nature of our problems has been regionalized; they have been fragmented, and no one is in charge. The reason we were able to deal with transportation in the past is that in 1963 we passed the Federal Highway Act, which required that regions come together and agree on a transportation policy. It's known as the three-C process. You don't get any federal money unless you come up with a 'comprehensive, continuing, and coordinated' transportation plan. Do you see something like that happening now? Can you see George Bush saying, 'Hey, we're going to have a regional school system.' 'Hey, we're going to have a regional land-use policy'?"

"Why can't regional planning, which makes so much sense, be implemented today?" I asked. "What prevents some governor, or soon-to-be governor, from listening to someone like you? Is it philosophy? Is there no money behind regional planners?"

"I think that's part of it. I mean, who do I represent? I only represent logic. For people to give up power, for people to give up freedom, they've got to want to do this. It all goes back to the unwillingness of people to give up their land-use decisions. The larger control."

"So that's why the Reagans and the like are so popular, because they're touting individual rights and not recognizing the collective?"

"That's right, their larger interest. Exactly right. When someone like Reagan says we're going to get the federal government off our shoulders, what he's saying is there is no national interest to be expressed except war. I mean, there are no national interests. Therefore all the poor people living in the city of Atlanta means the city of Atlanta has to solve that poverty problem. Hell, the number of people who were born and raised in poverty in Atlanta is minimal. A lot of the poor people came from Iowa, and wherever, because they heard Atlanta was the Golden Fleece.

"We're not going to deal with the issues, whether those issues are transportation or school or environmental issues, until the federal government has the will to say, 'We're not going to tell you how to solve your problems, but we're going to tell you that either you solve your problems or have a plan for solving your problems, or we're going to cut you off at the knees.' It's not just the ability to plan, it's the power, the control, to *implement* the plan that's missing. That power is conferred on the states. The federal government can also mandate. But that regional power is sadly missing.

"Let me tell you. The way we began to address our housing needs in cities in the fifties with Eisenhower . . . I mean, you talk about a lack of government. Eisenhower is the predecessor to Reagan. In the Eisenhower administration, in 1954, we passed a law saying that if you want urban-renewal funds, you must tell us how you're going to solve your slum problems in the future. And we were filled with slums. I know that slums have become sort of passé, although now we're getting back to them. But then we had slums everywhere. In the '54 Housing Act there was 'The Workable Program.' That required that to get urban-renewal funds you had to do six or seven things. You had to have a building code, you had to have a comprehensive plan. No cities had a comprehensive plan. That act began urban planning in America."

Eplan didn't see much hope for increasing the paucity of planning and cooperation. Yet he insisted he was one of the least cynical people I'd meet. "I'm a person of incredible optimism," he said. "I could not have survived for thirty-two years as a planner. When I lectured the students at Georgia Tech, they asked me, 'What does it take to be a good planner?' I said you have to have a sense of humor and you have to be an optimist. Because you're not going to win many of them.

"I do win a few, I have won a few. But for every one you win, you're battered. I'm a planner, and planning implies some degree of control. But since we've moved away from control at a time when we need more control to turn this big sucker around, it's going to take a Kennedy, it's going to take someone, to inspire us. The only time in American history where people have helped out was in times of national leadership. When Roosevelt was in, he said, 'We've got to come together and overcome fear and rebuild this country.' And they came, and they believed him, and they went and backed him up."

"Couldn't it come from grass roots movements?"

"That's a good question. But I don't think so. I don't think it's going to happen at the scale you're talking about until we're inspired to do it by leadership. Inspired to want to make it work."

"Do you think environmental issues are going to inspire some sort of action?"

"I think that's probably the best chance we've got. I think people are truly frightened by what's happened to the environment. I don't know for sure, but I think all the polls indicate that if there is anything the people want more action in, it's the environment. I suspect that's the most fertile ground for building a national consensus and a national will."

Six

Engine
Voices
of
the
Heartland

—a car wash flyer from Louisville

Heading north, I made a little side jag into the Great Smoky Mountains National Park, the most frequented park in the national park system, with nearly 10 million visitors a year. It was *really* being visited now. In fact, it was being invaded by the largest motorcycle gang I'd ever seen. As I inched my way through Cherokee they were everywhere, packed into every motel and drive-in, lining every road that wound into the Smokies; there must have been at least 5,000 of them. But this "convention" bore no resemblance to the bedraggled outlaw Harley gangs you saw terrorizing teenagers in TV cop shows. This was the Middle America version of the motorcycle gang—the final realization of Japanese advertising campaigns to legitimize street bikes—mostly moms and pops riding tandem on their beautifully polished monster Honda Gold Wings 1500-cc motorcycles.

These Chrysler LeBarons of the motorcycle world, which dress out to about $11,000 new, came from all over the country, some with saddlebags, many others pulling small trailers. Many couples wore matching helmets equipped with two-way radios so they could talk to one another above the muffled rumble of the four-cylinder engines they were sitting on. At the park outlook near Newfound Gap, I stopped and talked to the owners of a shiny, candy blue Gold Wing from Phoenix. "The only way to see the country is out in the open," the man said. "My wife has been videotaping the whole trip from the backseat." His wife smiled, then stuck me in the viewfinder of her camcorder; she panned from me to my van, with its "The Great American Driving Survey" blazoned across the side. "We've gone twenty-five hundred miles on this outing so far," the husband said, claiming the bike was much more comfortable than sitting in car seats. They proudly showed me their tricked-out bike: glistening chrome, CB radio, stereo, heater, windshield—the gearbox even included reverse. The husband said there were currently 90,000 Gold Wing members across the country.

I stood with the couple and looked out over the mountaintops, rounded with age, dissolving into a grayish haze in the distance. This smoky haze gave the mountains, home of the last virgin forest in eastern America and the oldest range in North America, their name. It was supposed to be a *blue* haze, but it had a decidedly brown tinge. Yeah, Ranger Tom Robbins later told me, the haze, a natural combination of humidity, temperature, and plant transpiration, was getting browner, "like a ring around a tub," thanks to air pollution (from factories and our friends, automobiles) that came floating in on upper-air currents from as far away as Chicago. Yeah, way out here in the middle of the mountains, there was definitely a problem with air quality. Sulfur and nitrogen oxides and unburned hydrocarbons from industry and car emissions were the major components of acid rain, which, evidently, was playing havoc with the Smokies' unique forest of red spruce and Fraser fir. Fifty percent of the spruce had lost previous levels of growth and vigor, and 95 percent of the mature Fraser firs, weakened by acid rain, had been killed outright by an insect infestation.

THE BAD HRUDUDIL

Obviously, the car is not as ecologically friendly to its fellow creatures, green flora and furry fauna, as it could be. It eats up habitat, pollutes, and often just plain squashes living things into nonexistence. In Richard Adams's novel *Watership Down,* the protagonists, all rabbits, come upon a strange phenomenon running through the middle of the forest.

> For a moment, [Hazel] thought that he was looking at another river—black, smooth and straight between its banks. Then he saw the gravel embedded in the tar and watched a spider running over the surface.
>
> "But that's not natural," he said, sniffing the strange, strong smells of tar and oil. "What is it? How did it come there?"
>
> "It's a man thing," said Bigwig. "They put that stuff there and then the hrududil run on it—faster than we can; and what else can run faster than we?"
>
> "It's dangerous, then? They can catch us?"
>
> "No, that's what's so odd. They don't take any notice of us at all . . . I must admit I can't altogether make it out."
>
> Although the hrududil meant no intentional harm to Hazel and his warren, it was nonetheless ruled "elil," enemy.

No one knows for sure how many wild animals are killed each year on this nation's roads, but the best estimates put the figure at around 100 million. Road kills are second only to the meat industry in numbers of animal deaths. Certainly, cars kill many more deer than hunters do.

"I pick up about three hundred deer a year that're killed on the road," Leon Taylor told me back in Marin County, north of San Francisco, where he has a contract with the county to retrieve dead wildlife. One afternoon I rode shotgun with him in his Toyota truck to get the flavor (and the stench) of the wildlife-pickup business.

Leon, sixty-four, drove about 70,000 miles a year scooping up flattened critters, earning $36 if it was under fifty pounds, $46 if it was over. He loved his job—"What could be better than driving around, at your own easy pace, such beautiful areas all day long?"—and had been doing it for nine years. Possum, raccoon, and skunks were the dumbest animals in Leon's experienced estimate: they just didn't pay attention to traffic. He rarely picked up a fox or a bobcat—and a coyote, never. Deer were frequent targets, especially during the mating season, starting in mid-October, when the bucks, preoccupied and dumb with love, fell right and left. It was nothing for Leon to pick up six bucks a day during the fall rut. Out-of-the-ordinary specimens like brown pelicans or blue herons he would take to the Willingham Education Center, which would have them prepared by a taxidermist and used as exhibits for schools. The rest of the sad creatures, dead and bloated in the bed of Leon's Toyota, were hauled to a rendering factory (the Royal Tallow and Soap Company) and dumped in a large steel pit that narrowed into a turning corkscrew blade that ground them into mash. The animals ended up as industrial grease, chicken feed, and lipstick.

By late afternoon we had hoisted three deer into the truck, plus a possum and a pancaked skunk with little left save its bushy tail. We were out in the western, rural section of the county looking for another customer, a deer the Sheriff's Department had alerted us about. We drove to the spot, back and forth, but we didn't find a thing. "It's a GOA," Leon said, not surprised. Gone On Arrival. Where could it've gone? I wanted to know. Leon shrugged and said someone might have kicked it into the ditch; that, or they took it home. What for? "For food." He said he'd once come upon a site just in time to see a car go tearing off down the highway, leaving behind a smear of blood and maggots on the macadam. "They boil it, then they boil it some more. Once I came upon another car with its trunk open and two guys about to load in a road-killed deer. 'No, boys,' I said, 'that's been dead for a while.' "

Leon had a high respect for the animals he retrieved. "They were here long before we were," he said. He disliked people who summoned him to remove a dead animal only to complain that "the things are everywhere" and are "nothing but a bother." He didn't understand people like that. He told me of a tiny fawn that was killed in front of a grammar school. He said that when he arrived the children had festooned the dead animal with wildflowers.

The naturalist Barry Lopez, in an essay in *Harper's*, wrote: "We treat the attrition of lives on the road like the attrition of lives in war: horrifying, unavoidable, justified." He told of a recent journey he made from his home in Oregon to visit friends in Indiana. Along the entire way he stopped by nearly every road kill and wondered, "Who are these animals, their lights gone out? What journeys have fallen apart here?" He carried each animal off the roadway into a cover of grass or brush as an apology, "a semblance of burial . . . as an act of respect, a technique of awareness." It was a sentimental essay, but it grabbed you in a strange way. Lopez seemed to capture a feeling we've always had, seeing these poor dead animals beside the road, but could never quite get a grip on.

IT'S ALL HAPPENING AT THE ZOO

In Louisville, Kentucky, I was visiting *live* animals at the Louisville Zoological Gardens. I walked quickly by the fenced and moated containment on my way to see the zoo's curator of education, Marcelle Gianelloni, my next driver contact.

I found her at the Metazoo, which was filled with scurrying schoolchildren, in a cramped office behind glassed-in exhibits of sundry snakes and small mammals. Fortysomething, a handsome woman with dark-complexioned skin, she was very busy—"I'm acting director of the zoo today," she explained—but as head of the zoo's Educational Center and the president of the local Audubon Society, she was eager to talk about all creatures of ecology—especially a beast confined in no cage or exhibit. Commenting on a recent column written about the new Infiniti automobile, she said, "It's interesting they picked a name for a car that talks about going on forever and ever. We *can't* go on forever driving cars, and the environment doesn't go on forever and ever. If we don't put serious money into a transportation system that's not related to cars, we're in serious trouble.

"I live three miles from here but I cannot take a bus here. People commute between here and as far away as Frankfort and Lexington, but there's no train. There was a train when I first came here fourteen years ago. Now, some cities have turned their beautiful old train stations into shopping malls. Like in Indianapolis; it's so sad to me. The trains have become hotel rooms, and in Indianapolis they even have little statues next to the train, like the porters. There's people who have never spent a night on a train. A moving one, anyway. It's so sad.

"All people are thinking about is, I've got to get there. Look at the car phone. As our life-styles have gotten busier, we absolutely have to have a car, because we just can't wait. What if you're a housewife or a father that has to take the kids to day care and then get to work? Our life-style has changed so much in the past fifteen years with both parents working; we've got kids going to different schools, going to ballet, tutoring. If you had to take public transportation, forget it, folks! The car alienates us from the environment, accelerates our life-style; we don't know how to sit back. And if you're not willing to sit back and look at what's around you, well . . ." We were interrupted by an assistant who came into the office area with a huge owl on a portable perch. She wanted to know if it was OK to take the bird out to the school where she was giving a talk. No, Marcelle told her, it was too hot and humid outside. Maybe she could take a hedgehog instead.

In seven years at the zoo, Marcelle was beginning to see a shift in people's attitudes toward ecology. "When I first gave teacher workshops, I'd ask them who Rachel Carson was, about recycling, about the Greenhouse Effect. 'Do you know what ecology is?' I mean, half the people couldn't even define the word. These are teachers from all levels, from elementary through college. But, in the past two years, when I get out there and talk they're going, 'Oh, yeah!' They really are so much more aware. And I feel that, if the teachers don't know, forget it. Because they're supposed to be out there educating the future of the world.

"And also I want to give you an idea of zoos. We're so involved with our own land and what's going on in our exhibits and, you know, breeding endangered species. But now zoos are beginning to adopt projects in the wild. This zoo is adopting acres in Costa Rica to help a park. I went to Colombia last summer and worked with some people who're trying to save part of their tropical forest there. And zoos are networking and handing out information. I think this's what keeps me going. I'm seeing change. Last year one hundred and thirty million people visited zoos. More people visit zoos than go to professional baseball and football games. What a perfect place to educate people about our environment and being responsible for it. We're centers of conservation and education.

"I feel that education is the way to get the word out to your average Joe. Made aware by the endeavors of zoos and conservation groups like the Audubon Society and the Sierra Club and Kentuckians for the Common-wealth. But I think change must come from up above. You know, us little folks say what we want—educate, or publish, or lobby for whatever we want—but I wonder if we'll ever have an enlightened car manufacturer. I wonder if GM would ever come out and say, 'Here's an ecologically sound car.' I feel strongly that our government needs to push. We need more politicians to get up there and say, 'This's what I'm committed to.' The big car companies are not going to take the lead; they're going to keep building those big cars if they think they can sell them. So more and more of us are asking our congressmen or aldermen, 'Where do you stand?' Most are rather nebulous, but the more we push and ask, the better off we're gonna be."

IN A HURRY

Louisville, bordering the Ohio River, usually tops magazine surveys that name the most favorable cities in which to live. I could understand why. Amid its downtown high rises, it seemed remarkably clean and comfortable. There was also a small-town feel in its tree-lined neighborhoods. From its residents, though, I heard the same refrain heard in urban areas many times its size: drivers were in a bigger hurry, more intense, more uptight, more discourteous. People complained that the freeways were filling up (especially the I-264 loop around the city) and that sprawl was ever-expanding—"Every time I look around I see a new mall going up," Marcelle moaned—out into the beautiful bluegrass countryside. And beyond. Like in many urban areas, many people lived on the far outer edge known as exurbia.

Joy Barber and her husband, Rob, and their small son lived in their own little house out in Shelbyville, thirty-two miles from Louisville, where Joy worked as a market coordinator for a national ambulance company. She was easygoing and good-natured, her statements often punctuated with laughter. She drove an eighty-eight Beretta, but it was just a step toward a sports car such as a Maserati or a Ferrari. She was big on visualization technique. "I had a sales manager once. He said, 'I want you to think of the car you want in five years. And you write it down. And then the next step is go out and get a Polaroid. Drag your husband along to the dealer, sit in that dealer's car, put your hands on the steering wheel, and have him take your picture. And you put that picture on the bathroom mirror where you look at it every single day. And then you figure out a way to get it.' Let's face it, a car is a part of your personal property. You have to like your car or you're in bad shape. You take things a step at a time. My next step will be a Celica convertible."

I told Joy that she returned my questionnaire with one of the highest scores for being an unbounded lover of cars and driving. And an environmental score best rated as . . . dismal.

"Although it seems I'm not concerned about the environment, that isn't actually correct," she bristled. "My 'commute time' is my *free time*—a think tank, so to speak. And as a working mother I value my time alone. If an efficient rail or subway system were available—not the bus—and it worked with my schedule, I would consider it.

"And, yes, I feel transportation is a problem in this world, and in this area. And, yes, in this valley, what they call the Ohio Valley, because of the river holding it in, there's smog. But I'm a hyper-type person, generally speaking. I need time by myself to sit and unwind. And I think that's something you get when you're behind the wheel: you're in your own little world. Your car is your world and you're in control of it. And I think it puts you in a different mode, especially from your work situation or home situation, where you have to rush to get certain things done. In your car, you're just there. You're your own master. There's no pressure. If I wanna listen to sixties music and turn it up and blast my ears out I can do that. Or if I want quiet, I can do that, too. You're separate from the world—there could be an earthquake and I wouldn't know it.

"Now some days it's not so pleasant, when there's accidents and backups where you sit in traffic. But for the most part it's a pleasant commute to work. I see the same people in their cars every morning. I can pinpoint cars. And if it's slowed down or stopped, on one radio station they have the joke of the day. And you can always tell the people who're listening to the same radio station 'cause they'll be laughing. You feel a bonding with those people."

Joy said that if large companies and manufacturers were not doing their part to clean up the environment, she certainly wasn't going to feel guilty driving. "We had this tire company just move into our area just so they wouldn't have to worry about pollution controls, because we don't have any. These companies just see dollar signs in front of them, they don't care about the environment. Let's come down on those guys, let's clear those people up, and then you can go to the driver and say, 'Well, we got rid of those terrible polluters. And the car manufacturers are now making economical and efficient cars for you. So now we'd like you to cut back on your driving.' *Then* I might have a more positive attitude about it.

"You talk about my working commute. But like today we'll go into Louisville. Practically every day we go into town; we shop in Louisville, we eat out. So not only do you have your commute but your pleasure driving, and that's going to be hard to deal with, too. You have so many things to feel guilty for. My goodness, on a daily basis, every time you turn on the news or every time you do anything there are these guilt trips thrown on you. I smoke, so I'm killing myself, I'm killing my family, I'm killing the world. You have a drink, I'm gonna have liver cirrhosis. You're gonna die from this, you're gonna die from that. Every day you have all these internal pressures, they're there, you have to deal with them. So when you're driving—no, I'm not gonna deal with that. Yes, it's there. Yes, I know about it. But when I get in my car I don't think about it. I don't *want* to think about it."

Joy admitted that people may buy more fuel-efficient cars as they become more aware of the environmental hazards of driving, but she was quick to add: "People are not going to give up their cars. 'That is my car, that is my vehicle—I care what it's doing, but I don't care, because this is my privilege. I worked hard to buy the car, to insure the car, to put gas and oil in the car. So . . . life's tough, but this's mine. I'm very protective of my car. I'm not going to have it taken away.' I'm protective of my car, too. I have no intention of giving it up." I assured Joy I had no intention of taking away her car. She laughed. "Good."

People's attachment to cars was indicative of the self-interest that governed society, Joy said. She pointed out that while the city of Shelbyville may profit from the creation of jobs at a new Toyota factory on the edge of town, everyone else in the community suffered from the inevitable increase in traffic. Where was the long-range planning, she lamented, to deal with the growth? But then, who had time to look out for the larger welfare of the community? "We're not living in Beaver Cleaver days," she said, "where everybody knew everybody, where June meets Ward at the door with her pearls and dress on, OK? That's not life in America today. And I think part of the problem is economical, problems that force us, both adult members in the family, to work. So you don't have the time to involve yourself in a lot of community functions. And I'm sure there're a lot of things that go on that you would want to be involved with if you had the time. But time is such a crisis. You have no time. And so to keep up, you're not as involved as you should be.

"When you're driving, you notice people not paying attention to traffic laws. Running stop signs, not using their turn signals, going faster. Why? People are in a hurry. Why? Look at your life, my life, Rob's life. You get up, you have X amount of time. From time to time I get up, and get Robert ready for school, and get ready to go to work, take him to school, leave the school—if I hit any traffic at all, my schedule is off. So, you're gonna go faster to get there, to be on time. You're gonna do what it takes to get where you're going and be there when you're supposed to be there."

TIME ON MY HANDS?

It's been called "The Great American Time Squeeze." According to a recent study by the Economic Policy Institute in Washington, Americans have added 158 hours (a full month) to their annual work and commute loads in the last two decades. So-called leisure time, time to spend relaxing, with our children or avocations, with community-oriented organizations or issues, is seriously missing. Although the automobile may be the fastest way to connect all the points of our helter-skelter lives, the car itself has helped create this fast-paced more-more-more world in the first place. We spend 20 percent of our incomes on the things. We average nearly two hours a day sitting in them. And the fact that everything in our urban regions is so far apart has a great deal to do with cars. You have to wonder: Who's driving whom?

Cities are always formed around the up-to-date transportation mode. St. Louis, the city and its satellite suburbs, sprang up at the confluence of the mighty Missouri and Mississippi rivers. Once the center of the nation and the gateway to the West, St. Louis was now formed around the confluence of I-70, I-44, I-64, and I-55. I stood outside my hotel near Old Man River and the permanently docked paddle wheelers (now home to McDonald's and Burger King) and watched with envy people filing by on their way to Busch Stadium to see the final game of the year between the Cardinals and the Pirates (the Pirates would clinch the division with a win). I had no time for leisure and was soon in the van, on I-70, on my way across town to visit my next hucar family: Jim (eighty-six Chevy pickup) and Mary (eighty-three Buick Regal) Hicks.

Jim, sixty-three, was a recently retired sign erector. Along with his questionnaire, he had sent me a wonderful pen-and-ink drawing titled

Man-Nature-Technology/Leaves of three or harmony. In the foreground stood a tree wrapped in vines; behind it, in the pine grove, as though it grew there, sat an old Model A, rusting, its tires gone, partly wrapped in barbed wire from a weathered fence pole. The drawing was difficult to figure. The car seemed a scar on the landscape, yet it blended perfectly into the landscape nonetheless.

We sat and drank beer over ice cubes in Jim's homebuilt studio behind their modest home. As Jim, the obvious family head, talked, Mary echoed practically everything he said, repeating, commenting, adding—a conversational merging so rehearsed over so many years it was barely noticeable. Jim said early in their marriage they'd lived in L.A. for two years, but one afternoon Mary came home from work and Jim said he'd had enough. They packed up that evening and returned to St. Louis. Since then they have lived on this street—"Our Little Village"—for thirty-four years and watched two generations' worth of neighbors and friends grow up. They have no plans to ever live anywhere else.

"Driving has always been very relaxing to me," Jim said. "Other people, they fight it. A lot of people get up too late for work, and they rush. I've told a lot of people: 'I think you get too tense, and I think the time element is what causes that.' Got to get from point A to point B *as fast as you can.* I'd get up at five, leave at seven. People are driving fast, honking their horn. I'm just driving along, with my coffee, listening to the radio, just having a ball."

"In the drawing you sent me," I said, "you seem very appreciative of technology, yet ambiguous about its effects."

"It's like TV when it first came out. There was no problem with it. There wasn't no cable with all the pornography. We had Milton Berle and all that, it was a fun thing. But over the years TV has ruined a lot of children. And ruined a lot of adults. I never watch TV. But automobiles are the same. When they first came out, you know, they were just great. I say that the forties and the fifties were the heyday, the most beautiful two decades of the automobile. In the forties the roads weren't all crowded, there weren't that many people with cars. Talk about a romance with automobiles. Like every Sunday everybody would be out in the park washing their cars, polishing them. Most people in the forties didn't use their cars for work, they used public transportation. They only used their cars on the weekend, to take a drive or something. When the fifties came, why, ah, it went into the speed thing. They wanted higher-powered cars. For the young people it was a big romance. It was a beautiful era. But after that, automobiles started to become problematic. There was too many of them, and they had to start building all these highways, and it became pandemonium. It's gradually getting worse and worse.

"There's no prestige in automobiles anymore. There's so many cars now—and they all look alike to me. Used to be you'd see a Cadillac, you knew that was a Cadillac. Or a Thunderbird. You would say to me, 'Hey, Jim, what kind of car is that over there?' And I'd tell you. But not now. Now they've become more of a necessity and a problem than an attachment."

"How would you reconcile nature and technology today?" I asked.

"You need to educate people. To change their attitude about driving. People are always in their cars. Theresa across the street—seems like every time I look she's gettin' into her Suburban. She loads the kids and goes someplace, and then comes back, and then she's going out again. Also, people are lazy. Like parking spots. You go to the store and instead of parking where there's a space, they'll sit and wait, close to the store, for a place to open up.

"One way to eliminate problems is economically. That's how they got busing through—said, 'Well, if you don't bus you're not going to get this money.' Well, I thought, why don't they have some sort of tax incentive where if you live so many miles from your job—for instance, if your house is less than fifteen miles—you get a tax break on your income tax. Or, to put it the other way, if you don't live close enough, it's going to cost you so much tax per year.

"The other thing is pollution. When I was down there in Los Angeles, that was in '56, I went downtown and my eyes were burnin'. But, boy, I bet they'd fall outta your head now. Your eyes probably would be gone. Here, under some weather conditions, we have haze. It's not a serious problem, but we have problems with the refineries.

"I would be willing to change to help the environment. I wouldn't drive at all unless it was necessary. I had an uncle, he lived in Arkansas. I always admired him. I admired him as a man. He reminds me of myself. He was my mother's brother. I think he was eighty-four when he died. But he lived in a small town; he was born in this house in Corning, Arkansas. Grew up, got married, and the house he bought to live in was right across the street. He lived there his entire life. And he had four girls. And he walked to work.

I used to go down there and visit them when I was a kid, and I'd be sittin' on the front porch and he'd come walking down. He'd leave in the morning, have a big breakfast, kiss my Aunt Bess good-bye and he'd walk off to work; he worked in a cotton gin. At noon, he'd come walking down the road to eat lunch. Then at night the same thing, he'd come walking down the road. He never drove an automobile in his entire life. And he hated to ride in an automobile. Hated to come to St. Louis. And they brought him up here, the daughter did, to visit one time. And guess what? They had an accident. And he was injured, broke a rib or something. He was happy in Corning. He didn't wanna go anywhere. Couldn't wait to get back there.

"So that's the way I think about the car. As far as I'm concerned, I wouldn't drive anywhere."

North by Northwest

Heading north by northwest, speeding across America's prairie breadbasket, I picked up little interest in any automobile conflict—though in Lawrence, Kansas, a Volvo-driving librarian did tell me that "the automobile, especially in today's mass quantities, is a cause of environmental destruction, many diseases, social alienation, crime, social and economic decay." I wasn't quite sure what she meant by "diseases" and "crime," but she didn't elaborate because she refused further interviewing. And a Lincoln-driving rancher in Cimarron told me he felt closer to a triphammer than to an automobile. There was concern about the price of oil (you can't farm or ranch without running your equipment) affecting an already shaky market, but as for traffic, the most you had to look out for was some teenager maneuvering his dad's eight-row combine down the lane.

Finally, I spent an evening talking with one Martin Sieverding, a friendly bachelor high school music director and teacher in the small farm town of Menno, isolated in the rolling wheat fields of the southeast corner of South Dakota. The tiny town was supposed to have been called Midway (Menno, derived from the large Mennonite settlement in the area, was to be down the road a piece), but the railroad company got the signs mixed up when the towns were formed. Martin lived in a small house on Teacher Street, so-called because many of the town's teachers lived there. There was an Alfalfa Street, because they started growing alfalfa next to it. And then there was Main Street—just a post office, a few stores, and the wink of an eye. "Driving here is unique," Martin said, "because you sort of have to know personally who's in front of you, because this person or that is probably going to turn this way and they're not going to tell you. I've been here twelve years and there are some people I know to watch out for. Course, it's not what you'd call a traffic jam kinda place."

Seventy percent of the kids at the school were from farms; sixth and seventh graders drove on the farm, though only eighth graders were allowed to drive to school. He believed not much had really changed: high school kids still liked to drive fast; many of the parents were still naive. "Like one father who wonders why his kid goes through a set of tires every three months. 'Gosh, they must not be very good tires we gave him.'" Menno had only one drunk driving arrest last year, and the school was still blessed by the fact that it had never lost a student on the highway. Martin, though, did notice one difference about high school drivers now—they preferred loud, really loud, car stereos. "It's like, a half mile away, 'Here comes Toby.'" Martin himself walked to school, "so the birds don't drop on my car and I have to wash it again." He just bought a brand-new Chevy Lumina. "I like it. The kids like it, too. That's important. I had a Celebrity before, four years old, silver and gray two-tone with maroon interior, and the kids thought that was OK. Then I got the Lumina, which is a lot more sportier—blue with a red pinstripe and spoiler on the back. The kids really think that's sharp. I just have a stock stereo in my car, but I can rattle my rearview mirror with it. Push the bass all up, put on the right music and *ba-dam, ba-dam*. I kinda like it. Every once in a while I have to drive with my windows down and turn my stereo up so the kids can hear me. So they know I'm still young at heart."

THE COLD OMAHA THEORY

From Menno I crossed the state of Minnesota and entered what had been labeled by a few wiseacres as "the city designed by Walt Disney"—the Twin Cities, Minneapolis–St. Paul.

It wasn't Disney World, not exactly. I didn't have to pay an admission, but it did have that symmetrical, squeaky-clean look to it: nice neat flower beds, little parks with lakes, tall buildings with skywalks, as though . . . well, it had been designed. Certainly the cars on the freeways (as usual, I liked to get on them at rush hour) seemed perfectly spaced apart, like a ride.

"I never sit in traffic," a somber 3M Company chemist who lived ten miles away in White Bear Lake told me. "Cars . . . ummph," he shrugged without expression. No big deal. Sure, Minneapolis was an easy city to live in, Tom Kaiser, a teacher, told me; though, like Japan, it was a little too homogenous for his taste. But then he'd just gotten back from West Africa, where he'd spent the last two and a half years in the Peace Corps. The traffic here now? It was flowing faster, as far as he could tell.

Minnesota boasted (rightfully so) of its Metropolitan Council, a regional planning body that has helped keep the Twin Cities area single-minded and efficient. The council, a model organization that is near unique in the country, has facilitated land-use issues with a regionwide revenue-sharing plan; it has initiated a unified sewer system that has cleaned up the Mississippi River; has consolidated a regional health-planning process; and, among other things, helped integrate highway planning.

Scott Anderson, a young (and somewhat sarcastic) graphic artist I sat with one morning in one of Minneapolis's pristine office buildings, explained that most of the credit for making the Twin Cities a model modern city went to ol' Hubert Humphrey, former Minneapolis mayor and U.S. senator. Humphrey was behind the Cold Omaha Theory, whereby if the Twin Cities didn't want to be left, literally and figuratively, out in the cold, like Omaha, Nebraska, then great effort needed to go into constructing a showcase city. They brought in major sports and gave each team a fancy stadium; they constructed, and continue to construct, an effective highway system ("There's basically two seasons in Minneapolis–St. Paul," Scott said. "Winter and road construction"); and they spruced up their downtowns. "Right now, there's a postmodern orgy going on, with lots of mauve and forest green buildings. And pyramids. *They* got a pyramid building, *we* want one, too, sort of thing."

Scott complimented the freeway system—"maybe crowded sometimes but never stop-and-go"—but complained that the off and on ramps were too damn short. He'd just totaled his "rice-burner" Dodge Colt on such a ramp and now commuted with his wife in their Honda CRX. He liked the money they saved being a one-car family and carpooling; it also helped with the costs to the environment, he said. He was especially sensitive to acid rain and the damage it was doing to the Boundary Waters Canoe Area and the Northwoods, for which he had a great affinity. Locally, there was smog, he said, but it wasn't yet a huge problem. Besides, he quipped, it made for pretty sunsets.

Scott enjoyed living in the city proper; he liked the neighborhoods, the racial mix. "I just got married about a month ago, and the attitude was, Well, now that you're married you'll probably have a kid and move away to the suburbs. Oh, really? I like older neighborhoods, I like having the neighborhood grocery store on the corner. And I definitely have an aversion to the type of subdivision mentality of 'Let's take over another farmer's field. Let's buy up another farmer's field so we can carve out a couple of little fake streams and put a little bridge over it when you drive in and we'll call it Stone Bridge Pass.'"

Public transportation was not what it could be, Scott said. "In the early sixties, they ripped up the light-rail system we had. In fact, they're using our trolleys in Mexico City, somebody tracked them down. They thought they took up too much road, I guess. The cynical thing is that now the city, which is so fashion conscious, wants to put the system back for aesthetic reasons. 'Oh, wouldn't it be quaint? Hark back to the old time.' It's a big political football. But if we had a more comprehensive public transit system I think people would use it—especially in winter. Winter is a joke. Everything shuts down. Cars try to plow through it. They're scattered to the side like the *Road Warrior* movies, abandoned. They have a snow plow crew—it's an army."

I asked if he planned to buy a new car. "Well, every once in a while I get this little subconscious tweak that comes like, *You deserve and need a hot sexy car!* But since I've been married, the voices are fewer and far between. I think I'll keep with the carpooling. We're planning to move our office downtown soon, and then I'll take the bus. I like the idea of just being able to sit there."

MESSENGERS OF DOOM

Back on the road, down through the fine state of Wisconsin, the trees glowed in their autumnal oranges, yellows, and reds, a glorious sight to a mono-seasonal Californian. I cruised along I-94 through spacious green dairy farms and cattle ranches. Outside the town of Osseo one rancher entertained motorists with a sign that announced: "New Cuds on the Block."

It was late in the afternoon when I picked up the Edens Expressway in the northern suburbs of Chicago. While those of us bound for the city moved along fairly briskly, I could see the traffic headed north grow more congested with each passing mile. By the time I got on the John Kennedy Expressway within the city limits I was smack-dab in the middle of an endless bumper-to-bumper crawl. Only the Metro train, sailing along the median, seemed to be making any progress.

The next morning I experienced Chicago's traffic as everyone should experience it—ninety-four stories above it. I was on the lookout floor of the John Hancock Building in the heart of downtown, viewing the expressways through a telescope. From the north, west, and south, Chicago was being invaded by a huge, slothful army of cars. To the east was a breathtaking view of Lake Michigan. I was accompanied by Rick Sirovatka, the operations manager of the Shadow Traffic Network, a broadcasting group that provided traffic reports to fifty-two of the area's radio and television stations. Shadow Traffic employed reporters in helicopters, planes, and cars to keep motorists informed of the road conditions, and initiated a unique method of doing so. On-air reporters didn't announce typical banalities like "There's a stall near the Washington Street off ramp," but instead gave listeners constantly updated "travel times," such as: "Twenty minutes from downtown to O'Hare Airport." The greater Chicago area was referred to in numerous grids, allowing commuters to judge how long it would take to get from their current locations to their destinations by the travel times. Shadow Traffic couldn't do anything about the congestion, of course, but they could make commuters feel a little better by advising them to relax, they weren't going anywhere soon.

Transforming traffic information into instantaneous and intelligible broadcasts requires a massive coordinated effort. Inside the Shadow Traffic control room, I watched the employees shape order out of chaos. Eight editors wearing headphones sat at a bank of computer terminals, listening to reports and madly typing various codes. Eight broadcasting booths surrounded the bank of terminals. Inside the dark booths stood the Shadow Traffic air personalities, translating—in their heads—the rapidly changing computer codes into pithy traffic reports, often trading banter with the wisecracking disc jockeys in the process. Editor and reporter Ric Federighi was particularly dazzling. He consistently dashed from computer bank to broadcast booth, all within a split second of his designated air time on a specific station. The whole thing was making me dizzy.

At eleven in the morning, after the frenzy in the control room came to a simmer, Rick, the operations manager, took a break to discuss Chicago's world of traffic with me. What would he tell me if I was someone considering moving to Chicago?

"I'd tell you either to live downtown and take public transportation or, if you're coming in from the 'burbs, try to use Metro, because to drive from the suburbs you've got to have a lot of patience. It's so unpredictable how long it's going to take. I only live about twenty-five to thirty miles away from here. There are some days where it only takes me thirty-five to forty minutes and there are other days where it takes me up to two hours to get in to work. It's almost like the weather. A lot of people say, 'Those traffic guys are just like those weather guys; they don't know what they're talking about.' But the thing is, you can't predict traffic anytime. Traffic is a perishable commodity—it's always changing. The weather is a little bit more predictable because you can see the front coming in, whereas with traffic it's happening now, right at that second."

But of course the weather itself has a major impact on traffic. "We've had some unbelievable days," Rick said. "Last Valentine's Day we had a major snowstorm and there were people who needed to go just a few miles and it took them maybe four hours to get there because the weather hit right in the middle of rush hour and the snow plows were stuck in the middle of traffic and they couldn't get the snow off the roads. So instead of just giving backup reports and travel times on the expressways, we told people to get off the expressway and find a hotel and stay the night because they weren't going anywhere. If you wanted to drive, plan to sit in your car anywhere from five to seven hours. But most people just abandoned their cars. The next day it looked like Vietnam because you had to drive around all these cars on the roads."

Editor and air personality Dorothy Humphrey, known to most Chicagoans as "Bunny" (because of her squeaky voice) of the "Bernie and Bunny" show on the popular radio station AM 1000, entered the conference room. She mentioned another factor that made the traffic unpredictable—a factor that drivers everywhere complained about with exasperation: construction. "During construction it's all up for grabs because you don't know what's going to happen," she said. "I live in the city, but I do drive to work. But when they start working on Lake Shore Drive next year, I'm going to take the train. I work during hours when there's not supposed to be traffic, but there is anyway. And me being a traffic reporter, I freak out. But we're smart enough to listen to our own reporters. A lot of people with telephones call us and ask how things are. I can tell them it's clear, but by the time they drive for fifteen minutes something could happen and then it's not good anymore. Then their whole life is up for grabs at that point because I told them it was good. Then they call me back and get upset."

"We talk to a lot of people on their cellular phones," Rick added. "We get a lot of attitude. We tell them what's going on and they'll cuss at us and be pissed. You know, kill the messenger. There's a lot of frustrated people out there."

"What we started doing for the past couple weeks is stuff for people who are stuck in a backup to help them," said Dorothy. "They're just sitting there and they're bored. One week we had them stick their arms out of the car and pretend they were flying. We were amazed at how many people were actually doing it."

I said I always had this impression of Chicago as a great urban city where everyone used mass transit and driving wasn't that big a problem.

"That's completely false," Dorothy said. "When I first started here seven years ago, midday traffic wasn't a big deal. Now it's a very big deal because all of a sudden you're driving from one business meeting to another, and you think there's nothing happening, and they do a lot of construction in the middle of the day. So it doesn't matter if it's nine in the morning or four in the morning, there could be backups. Weekends are terrible too. Oh, my God, are they terrible."

"What's also happening is our rush hours are no longer hours," Rick said. "They're rush periods. When I started, the main rush hours were seven-thirty to eight-thirty and everything before and after that really wasn't too bad. Now, things are solid by six-thirty in the morning and they don't clear up until ten. Rush hours are now three, sometimes four, hours long. The amount of traffic in the nine-year period that I've been here has really escalated tremendously."

Rick confirmed what Leon Eplan had explained to me in Atlanta: the spread of traffic resulted from businesses moving out of the central city and an increase in suburb-to-suburb commuters. Rick also noted a new pattern of people commuting from the city to the suburbs. Just imagine, he said, what would happen if everybody wanted to move in the same direction at the same time. In fact, during Bears football games or a Fourth of July parade downtown, that's exactly what happens. "So you'll have sixty-mile backups," Rick uttered. "*Sixty miles.* And people are going maybe ten miles an hour. Figure it out: six hours!"

I commented that Chicago had quite a little transportation crisis on its hands. "It's definitely a crisis," Rick asserted. "What's going on is the same thing in New York, where rush hour starts at four in the morning and goes to about eleven at night. Eventually that will happen to Chicago. I think it will take quite a bit of time because unlike New York we have the room to go out to the suburbs, and we just keep moving outward more and more. But the traffic will someday be as bad. Instead of having trains run every twenty minutes on the commuter rails just during the peak periods, they're going to have them twenty-four hours a day to get all these people in and out of the city."

Looking fatigued, Cherie Lanz, one of Shadow Traffic's senior drivers who radio in dispatches from the front lines, joined the discussion. I asked her if Chicago drivers had reached a boiling point of frustration.

"Oh, you should see it," she said. "People slamming on their steering wheel, their heads hung down, swearing out the windows and honking their horns. I can see the frustration. And it's definitely getting worse—the congestion and people's tempers." How did she deal with it personally? "Oh," she said philosophically, "since I've been driving I know all the shortcuts. Besides, I'm used to it. Sitting in traffic is my job. It's my life."

Was it true that there were different types of drivers on the city's two main expressways, the Dan Ryan and Kennedy? "That's definitely true," Rick said. "A lot of blue-collar people live down to the south and down into Indiana, whereas people on the Kennedy and Edens expressways are more white-collar, high-paid executives coming down with their Porsches and Mercedeses and car phones. So you've got a totally different group of people coming in from different directions. It's like night and day. But I don't think that any one social group is any more patient than the other. They're all upset about being stuck in traffic."

"I'd be more nervous to be broken down on the Ryan than on the Kennedy," Cherie said. "I'll tell you that right now."

"To tell you the truth," Rick added, "I think that maybe the people on the Ryan, even though they don't have the luxury to be sitting in an expensive sports car with a car phone, they might be a little more patient about it because they expect it. Whereas the people that are on the Kennedy have the attitude anyway because they're a little snooty: 'Why should I be stuck in this and how come I can't be doing eighty-five in my Porsche and I'm late for my meeting?' "

Given the ever-increasing gridlock, did Shadow Traffic see itself as a kind of missionary in keeping Chicago functioning?

"Well, yeah," Rick said. "Something we have to realize as traffic reporters is, technically, you're on duty twenty-four hours a day, every day of the year. If there's something going on, it's up to you to let people know about it. I don't mean this to be geeky, but we as traffic reporters really owe it to our clients and listeners to let them know what's happening. It's a community service. When you're out in your car you just want to know what's happening. Whether it's good or bad, people just like to know what's up ahead. It's like getting hit in the side of the head with a pie. It'd be better if you saw it coming."

THE CHICAGO THREE

Resignation to the auto treadmill has become the normal way of life in urban America. We have grown up with cars, designed our cities around them, and are now stuck with them, for better or worse. Like watching television, driving has become an act of mass conformity. But in every system there're mavericks, nonconformists. In Chicago I discovered such a contingent, represented by three people who passionately resented America's—and their own—dependence on automobiles. Curiously, their ire stemmed in part from their own upbringings. Educated and outspoken, they repudiated their parents' auto-addicted life-styles as they distanced themselves from the car's destructive legacy.

Joanne Trestrail, thirty-nine, lived in a small comfortable house in the Lincoln Square neighborhood, a few minutes' walk from an "el" station, the city's elevated mass-transit rail system. She was the managing editor of *Chicago* magazine and could easily hop on the "el" to take her to and from her downtown office. But she feared violence while waiting alone at the train stations and so begrudgingly battled the inner-city traffic every day in her Honda Civic. "My car is protection," she said.

Still, she "hated the feeling" of driving. "Like at the end of a weekend, to think I spent my whole weekend in my car. That's a terrible feeling. My fingers clenched, just in the habit of being in a car all the time." To Joanne, a car was strictly a utilitarian device; status be damned. "I drive a new Honda Civic because the old Honda Civic was finally so rusty and so gross I could barely sell it. I liked it because it totally left me alone, I never had to think about it at all, and the less I have to think about it the happier I am. If it hadn't really given out at the end I probably would have driven it forever, because, especially in the city, it's important to have a car that nobody wants to steal, and a car that was banged up on all four corners. I remember how happy I was when the fourth fender was finally smashed. I thought, Bingo, nobody can hurt me now." Joanne was hit by a bus twice, and once by a van.

Her solution for America's transportation woes was simple: "I think that cars shouldn't exist, period. I think that would be the solution, to just not have them. I mean, it's just incredible to me that people are allowed to have them. Just completely dangerous. It's giving everybody a loaded gun, everybody. I'm amazed there's as few accidents as there are. I'm just surprised the roads aren't strewn with wreckage and bodies. And they're terrible for the air. It's so stupid that we're using up oil in order to run them. Ridiculous running around digging up oil."

I reminded her that we were all attached to our cars, in one way or another. "Yeah, people will never give them up, but they never should have been allowed to have them in the first place." Did she remember her first car? "Ohhh"—and her mood seemed to brighten—"it was a yellow Karmann Ghia. Just a physically beautiful car, just beautiful to look at. It was the perfect combination of reliability and beauty. I couldn't drive it, but that's what I wanted. It was completely irrational that I wanted that car. I have a picture somewhere if you'd like to see it?" I said I would, and she disappeared out of the room, quickly returning with a faded snapshot of the yellow sports car. She confessed she had been unfaithful to her Karmann Ghia: when it began breaking down, she sold it. She then bought a renegade Rabbit, and found out what a "real lemon" was like. It cost her a fortune in repairs, and she sold it for the practical Civic. "Hmmm," she mused. "I guess I'm not getting pleasure out of my cars anymore."

Bill Wyman, thirty, most assuredly didn't get pleasure out of cars: he refused to own one. Well, actually, he did own a car once. He grew up in Phoenix, and when he turned seventeen he bought a used "huge yellow Impala." He kept the Impala when he moved to Berkeley to attend college but often forgot where he parked it, and one day lost it entirely. He has ridden mass transit ever since. We talked in his house, located just a few blocks from Wrigley Field. Bill was a free-lance journalist and music critic for various national publications; books, magazines, and records were strewn across his living room. He talked a mile a minute, leaving a wealth of personal experiences and political convictions in his path.

"My two small contributions to the world are: I don't drive, and I don't write about Madonna. As for driving, I'm not precious or anything about it. I ride in other people's cars. I'm happy to get a ride from someone. But otherwise I get there by public transit."

Bill confessed that his antipathy toward cars was part of his "systematic rejection" of his suburban upbringing in Phoenix, where people would drive five blocks to get a quart of milk. By not driving, he said, "It's not another fucking car on the street! I mean, the idea of just one person driving is just really crazy. When you go to a place like Honduras or to China or somewhere like that, you see people never drive without a full car. They just don't. People here have way too many cars anyway. There really is this indolence. It's like wherever you go down the highway, you look over and every car has a single person. I just think that's really awful.

"And isn't one person having one car sort of decadent? It's bad enough in a place like Chicago or Berkeley, but in Phoenix, you know, where there's more than one car per capita. I think that's correct: a million cars in Phoenix. Amazing. In my neighborhood, when the girl turns sixteen she gets a little Datsun truck and the guys all have Camaros. And the parents all have a car. They have a nice car like a Mercedes and then they have, like, their running-around car, the mom's car, which is, like, a Datsun. And then they have, like, some sort of a Bronco wagon or RV or boat. And they have fucking motorcycles. And then you got the daughter's boyfriend's car. The driveways are always filled with cars."

As a form of rebellion, Bill rode the buses in Phoenix, despite the long waits at bus stops, and in spite of his father's constant complaints that buses tied up traffic. "I just don't think cars should be allowed," he declared. "Period. It's a very, very complex thing, but it really causes a lot of the decline in the quality of life in our cities. All these things are a part of zoning. All politics is zoning. What they've done is they've enforced land use in a way that works against public transit and almost requires you to have cars. All these suburban settlements where there's not good-enough public transportation so people just drive—that clogs the highways and the streets and the parking, and causes more pollution. That makes the cities crummier.

"So what happens? The large corporations say, 'Well, we don't need to be in the central city, it's ugly and dirty and expensive, so let's relocate to a suburb where they'll give us ridiculous tax breaks.' And of course the companies relocate to a suburb where they probably already have the highest spending for, say, schools in the state. So the taxes from the company then go to the already rich school district, even as it is being taken away from the tax base of the city, which needs it more.

"Then what you wind up with is two or three or ten thousand people who don't have access to public transportation who are now making a suburb-to-suburb commute, which further skews the region's transportation problems—freeways were designed to get from the cities to the suburbs, not suburb to suburb. This is what's causing a lot of the current problems in what were once the bedroom communities of the San Francisco Bay Area and Long Island in New York, and all these suburbs here in Chicago. All of these pressures come together to cost society money, further deteriorate the schools, make life miserable for people who have to commute to work, and so forth.

"What really kills me about public transit is how biased the public and the press are against it. Reading about public transit in the papers is like reading a debate about unions in the thirties. I've been a reporter for about twelve years, and have kept files on public transit for most of that time, and I don't think I could produce for you, even from the alternative press, an article that carefully laid out the problem of public transit. This is how public transit works: government subsidizes it fifty percent or seventy-five percent or eighty percent. Like every time I get on the 'el,' I pay a dollar. It's costing Chicago a dollar, a dollar-fifty. Very few systems get more than fifty percent of their operating costs through fares. No transit system in history has ever supported itself. Bus companies are like the opera. They don't make enough money to support themselves. I mean, they just don't. It's just the way things are. So, is that good, or is it bad? Sewer systems cost money, so do cops. And they're a good use of it, because they're improving the overall quality of life in a city. So does transit.

"I just love some guy on the freeway complaining about money for mass transit. He's not subsidizing me; I'm subsidizing him! I'm paying for his roads, his insurance, and for the pollution of his car, and I'm also paying for the goddamn army we need to have to protect the source of the oil he's running his car on. And I can take it further; I'm also paying for the general cost to the economy that accrues from being so dependent on nonrenewable energy resources."

"Are you telling me you ride mass transportation because it's good for the community?" I asked.

"Well, I was in London recently, and there's signs up all around town: 'The bus system is the lifeblood of the city.' It's true there, of course, and in Paris, where the Métro is just so huge and impressive. Besides, say, New York and Hong Kong, I don't know if there's any other place with that size of a mass transit system that is so intertwined in the life of the city. Chicago's is still pretty impressive, but how long that will last is a little in doubt right now, the way things are going. What you get in other places, particularly in California, is a system that starts becoming the mode of transportation for poor people, or nonwhite people. And, of course, the way things are in America, that's just a better reason not to fund it properly. Transit systems can't really survive without middle-class support. That's a shame.

"But then you have to understand: I love mass transit. I'm a total bus freak. I could ride the 'el' all day long. Seriously. It's the greatest thing in the world. It's not like I'm one of these train buffs. I just love the idea of mass transit. I love getting on the subway and holding on the strap. I even like being huddled on an overheated, crowded bus in the middle of winter, or a sticky and hot one in summer. Riding the 'el,' you feel like you're part of the city, part of the flow of it all. Again, maybe it's because I grew up in a place where it was almost nonexistent, where a lot of the whole idea of people working together to live together well is just deteriorating. It's still a miracle that a place like New York or Chicago just doesn't collapse under its own improbability. But I think mass transit is a really key part of it because it's really a part of the standard of living. You get on it, you're in downtown Chicago in twelve minutes. It's the most amazing thing in the world."

Kelly Bulkley, a doctoral student who taught courses on modern Western culture at the University of Chicago, was the internal, or psychological, counterpart to Bill. Whereas Bill wanted to liberate society from cars, Kelly wanted to liberate individuals from them. Kelly is a strikingly sensitive man. He had thought a lot about the psychic implications of cars and driving, and unabashedly revealed how they had shaped his own inner life. He lived with his wife in Hyde Park near the university.

"After high school the car diminished in importance to me," he began. "Then when I went away to grad school to Boston I didn't have a car. Suddenly I didn't care as much and I started to see the environmental effects of cars and I sort of had a guilty memory of how blatant my wastefulness as a driver had been. Suddenly I became very anticar. I got real down on cars. And I thought, Wow, I can live without one. Suddenly I didn't have to worry about repairs, insurance, accidents. I'd always taken those things for granted as something that was just part of life. But then I didn't have to deal with it—it was like, whoa, freedom, liberation. I don't need this.

"But then we moved back here and my wife went to law school. And she had a car. So then I started driving again on a regular basis and was very ambivalent about it. Because, you know, here I had decided that cars were the root of much of the evil in the world. It was sort of a reversed independence in relation to cars, where suddenly I didn't like the idea that I could ever be dependent on a car again. I liked being independent of cars.

"I'm caught up with guilt about driving—from two sources. One, the environment stuff. Here I am driving again. I know I'm spewing out X amount of pollution. What it makes me feel is alienated from nature. More than at any other time, when I'm driving, I'm very aware of how distant I am, alienated I am from the environment. It makes me realize how I am not in a natural setting. In other places, when I'm in my apartment or walking around or whatever, that's not as powerful a sensation. But driving really brings that out, and I guess that's one of the reasons I don't enjoy driving.

"About an hour south of Chicago is the Indiana Dunes National Lakeshore, which is a stretch of lakeshore that's been preserved in its natural condition. This summer I went there about three times just because I had to get out of the city. Well, this's the nicest place you can get to but you still gotta drive. I mean, it's exactly fifty-five minutes of driving on I-94 with just these huge trucks spewing exhaust in your face. And it's the worst possible driving setting. Just like I said, there's huge trucks, ugly as sin, you're going through Gary, Indiana—oh, man, really, really foul, ugly scenery. I mean the dunes are nice, but even when you're there you can still see the smokestacks of Gary just down the end of the park. God, I mean, here I am, this's the reason I'm going to this place, because I want to feel closer to nature, but the very process of getting there and back is so destructive to me. How much gas am I burning up, how much rubber am I burning up to get here and back just for me to have my little nature experience? You know, I mean, I'm not sure if it really balances out.

"The other thing is that, for me, driving is very caught up in a sort of psychology of this mass human aggressiveness. Being able to drive, being the driver, is an important part of masculine identity. At least as I've grown up, Dad was the driver, right? And I wanted to be like Dad in lots of ways and that was one of them.

"Since then I've realized, well, I want to be like my dad in some ways and not in other ways. The whole issue of what is masculine identity in this culture and in connection with aggressiveness and the need to dominate, those sorts of things, suddenly made me look on my driving tendencies in a different way. Every time I now get behind the wheel I find that conflict within me. Where otherwise I can be relaxed, calm, happy about things, as soon as I get behind the wheel, that bastard in front of me had better hurry up! And, you know, I honk at him, and I cut people off, I shift gears and get frustrated, and I flip people off, and . . . I mean, Chicago is an aggressive area. Anyplace where there's lots of cabs, it's like high-competition driving. I hate that in myself.

"I can't stop myself from being that way. It's one of the few areas in my life where that conflict within me still flares up so strongly. And not coincidentally, my wife—driving to Mexico once, she got in a near-fatal accident—she's very scared of driving, so she gets upset at me when I drive aggressively. It scares her. And we get in the same identical bickering relationship that my parents did with my dad driving and my mother scared of his driving.

"What I'm trying to say is that driving is a setting that channels those energies. Suddenly I'm driving in my little metal box and there are clear-cut aggressors and I lose myself to that situation. People become someone else when they drive. One thing I've noticed driving in Chicago is that some of the most aggressive and reckless drivers appear to be poorer men, poorer men in cars that tend to be beat-up. And in this society where inequalities of wealth are increasing, where we've got a serious underclass, how can these people have power in any meaningful way? One way is to get behind the wheel of a car. That is a sanctioned, time-honored means of having an expression of power in our society.

"I think cars are a very tangible and accessible means of gaining power.

But it's not real power. I mean, it almost serves the purpose of the very wealthy to let the lower classes drive around because that gives them the illusion that they've got real power. That's a very cynical and probably paranoid way of looking at it. But I see these people cruising around very recklessly, with fairly little regard for safety. I mean, there's this overwhelming urge to express that power.

"Now, to me, I think all that comes around to greed, individual greed. In my experience cars often appear in dreams as symbols of one's power and control, or a lack of those. For me and for other people, cars are symbols of the way we get around in this society, how we relate to others, in a way. The distinctive thing about cars, these self symbols, is that cars are too radically individual. I think that says something about modern individuality, to the extent that we identify so strongly with cars. And one of the dangers of driving around with so much power and individual aggressiveness, cruising around so recklessly—one of the constant dangers is crashing.

"I've found in my dreams I'll blast through traffic signals, or I'll crash into somebody and drive away. One of the underlying meanings there is that I'm struggling against some sort of social stricture or constraint; I'm wanting to, you know—fuck everyone else. I'm not gonna stop. I'm gonna keep going. I got someplace to get to. Another thing that's interesting in our society is how a major element in our car consciousness is being intoxicated while driving. I mean, it's clearly a profound social problem. And again, that's something, a behavior, that says to hell with everyone else. In my dreams I've also been drunk and driving—and feeling intensely guilty about it.

"I just feel that we all need a little more social conformity of thought and behavior in our individual lives. Not to take our individuality too far. So far that it becomes greedy and recklessly aggressive."

EDGE CITY

The Chicagoans' anti-car/anti-'burb attitude may well be prevalent among deep-city urbanites, but it most definitely represents the minority. Elitism aside, Americans' aversion to dense city living is a clear trait of our national character. Only 8 percent of the nation's population actually live within the inner confines of major cities; furthermore, as Joel Garreau points out in his book *Edge City*, "we have not built a single old-style downtown from raw dirt in seventy-five years." Literally, our country's suburbs have been designed to suit that part of our character that doesn't like to be cramped. Besides, for a number of complex reasons, one of which is our affinity for open spaces, most of our inner cities have been abandoned and left to die like worthless appliances. They have become dire and unlivable. So who's to blame for wanting to live in the suburbs?

"I was raised in Chicago, and you do get used to living there," said David Jones, of Batavia, a bedroom community fifty miles west of the city. "It's kind of nice if you like to be close to the theater, variety shows, shopping, museums, zoos, the conservatory, the lakefront, and things like that." I was seated with David, a tool repairman for a plastic flowerpot factory, at his dining room table in his pleasant split-level home. "What drives people away from the city," he continued, "is the high population density and the traffic. Chicago has a very good rapid transit system, but you get tired of being jammed in with people all the time, especially if you're not from the area. My wife never liked it. She always felt uncomfortable anywhere she went, and said she didn't want to live there and didn't want to raise our son there. The schools don't have the best reputation." David moved to Batavia in 1973, yet like many exurbanites, he now feared that some of the worst aspects of the city had followed him to "the promised land."

"The people who lived here before us had a deer come through the downstairs and run around the rec room," he said. "Now it's all houses. It is a very rapidly growing area and they're not building roads to match the amount of people coming in. The roads that we used to ride our bikes across are now very heavily traveled and are very dangerous to ride a bike on. There's just a lot more cars and a lot more people. You move away from an area where there's more people to one where there's less people. But it's kind of self-defeating. More and more people move out and the whole point of moving out here is lost because now there's so many people that you have traffic problems again. People that are moving out make more money than the people that live here in a lot of cases. Housing prices go up. Shopping prices go up.

"People are saying it's really nice and pretty out here, it's one of the prettiest areas of northern Illinois, but let's not make the same mistake that Du Page County made where you've got umpteen million people, not enough roads, constant congestion. That's not my idea of paradise, the way people live further east in areas like Naperville or Schaumberg. Everybody has two cars so there's got to be parking for everybody. You have constant movement of cars. People don't walk anymore. You have this constant turmoil twenty-four hours a day, and it's starting to get that way out here.

"Kane County is trying to limit the amount of growth. They're trying to increase the lot sizes. There's a push to say that if developers are going to buy property, he's going to have to put houses on one-acre, or acre-and-a-quarter, lots, so you don't get these large houses on small lots. I don't know how successful they're going to be because property values are so high. If somebody buys a piece of property it gives them a lot of clout. The feeling is we can generate X amount of tax revenue dollars if we build X number of houses. I imagine there's a lot of pressure to build more rather than less houses.

"And they're not building any more roads. Of course, they're expanding some roads, but they can't expand them at the rate of the population growth. There's only so much money in the economy of a state budget. How many construction crews can you hire even if you had the money? In a lot of places, they can really use mass transportation, but nobody wants it because there's no money, there's no place to put it. The stuff that was here is long gone, you can't bring it back. Everything is cars.

"At the time I was growing up, a car was something you used to go places on Sunday and visit relatives that lived a long ways away. If you want to go downtown you take a bus. If you went to school you didn't drive. But you get used to having a car right away when you buy one. You immediately give up mass transportation. 'Why take a bus? I got a car.' Out here you have to have a car if you want to go anywhere at all, if you want to go further than a mile. I never thought in a million years that I'd ever have three cars, but here I am. But recently I did something that I thought was very unique. I got on my bike to go to the store. Holy cow, it takes less time than a car."

I asked David if he worried about cars' impact on air quality, and if he believed we'd ever see an alternative to the internal combustion engine. "I'm aware that they do have quite an impact on air quality. All you have to do is look toward Chicago on a clear day and you can see the haze over the city. That can't all be generated by oil and stuff like that. It's got to be cars. But I don't think there's any viable alternatives to the internal combustion engine at this time. The internal combustion engine has been around for a hundred and twenty years. The reciprocating part is old technology, but all the stuff they do to the rest of it to make it efficient is very modern. I don't think they can replace the reciprocating engine with anything that wouldn't require this incredibly long lead time, and an incredible amount of money. I'm sure there's other alternatives. If somebody comes up with a reasonable battery-powered car, that would be great except it brings up the question of where are you going to get the power to recharge the cars at night? Nobody is addressing the issue of adequate power supplies to major metropolitan areas. The technology exists to generate all kinds of power with safe nuclear energy and safe disposal, but nobody wants to make a commitment to doing that.

"It's like cutting your own throat, because they could build very safe nuclear reactors and they can dispose of fuel very safely if people have the political will to do it. Nuclear power is almost like gun control in some places. It's such a heated issue. It's not as bad as it seems, but what politician is going to touch nuclear power? A politician is like anybody else. He's got a job, he's got power, and he's going to make money. Why throw that all away for something which people don't want to deal with? It's unfortunate, but it's true. People don't want small cars that get good gas economy that take half an hour to get to sixty miles an hour. I don't want that. But depending on the Middle East for our oil supply is stupid. It's also nothing new. It's all old hat. For seventeen years this country has been very obviously dependent on foreign oil. Nobody wants to do anything about it. We're still in the same place we were seventeen years ago. We're the most technically sophisticated country in the world, and by far the richest, and we depend on an area that's unstable politically for all our oil. It's stupid. It's like having a very nasty next-door neighbor and hoping he's always going to be willing, in exchange for money, to give you food."

David had little faith in politicians to reduce America's consumption of oil because they "make a hash out of so much they do." He believed raising gas prices to $3.50 a gallon would certainly cause people to drive less and force the automobile manufacturers to build more fuel-efficient cars, but David knew that "politically, they'll never get away with it." When you really think about the problem, he admitted, "there's not any swift cure, just like there's no swift cure for drug problems or anything else in this country. People are hooked on cars. People grow up and say, 'I'm going to get a car.' They don't say, 'I'm going to get laid.' They say, 'I'm going to get a car, *then* I'm going to get laid.' Nobody really thinks about the problems.

"I never thought of it in those terms until tonight, but the car *is* like a drug addiction. Where you live is set up for cars. Look at the size of my driveway. Look at the size of the streets. You just can't give it up."

SUPER SUBURBIA

I joined the Monday morning commuters out of Batavia, and began a long day's journey east across the Indiana-Michigan border. It was my first extended experience on the highway phenomenon unknown to a Californian: toll roads. Cruising along the slick pale roads with their median service areas of gas stations, McDonald's, and postcard stores, I was beginning to feel that I was back in Disney World. Furthermore, I must have spent a small fortune on tolls by the time I reached Ohio. But reach it I did. The Buckeye State. Flatland, middle earth, and home of super suburbia and whatever open space was left over. Here also was the birthplace of both my mother and father, home of baseball's first major league team, and the former stomping ground of one of my favorite rock bands, the Pretenders:

> I went back to Ohio
> But my pretty countryside
> Had been paved down the middle
> By a government that had no pride
> The farms of Ohio
> Had been replaced by shopping malls
> And Muzak filled the air
> From Seneca to Cuyahoga Falls
> Hey, ho, way to go, Ohio

This was also dangerous territory for hucars. I had been warned to be *very wary* of the police on all Ohio roads and highways. Watch your step! (I didn't.) And enjoy your stay.

WILLOUGHBY TO BEAVERCREEK

By the time I pulled in for a late lunch in Cleveland, the Cuyahoga River wasn't on fire. Oh, well. I ate at one of the face-lift restaurants on the riverfront wharf, known as the Flats, and looked up instead at the trestle drawbridges and the sooty backsides of old brick office buildings that hung on the edge of the spectacularly drab and melancholy downtown. If ever there was a place where you wanted a souvenir mug, this was it. To my back, Lake Erie stretched out into a gray horizon foreboding another cold, dismal winter. Upriver, in the distance, smoke erupted from an endless string of factories and refineries. Ancient neighborhoods fanned out with tight-fitted little houses, bunker-style schools, and people with long faces. It was, to my mind, the perfect picture: the last true functioning bastion of the Industrial Revolution.

I traveled along the lake on I-90 to the eastern suburb of Willoughby, and once again found myself weaving through Middle (it-could-be-anywhere-in-the-country) America, ending up in a condominium complex and the home of Laurel Smith, where a slew of small children spilled out the back door.

Divorced and engaged, Laurel spent her day doing child care. A couple of the mothers scooped up their broods and loaded them in cars parked next to Laurel's Volvo station wagon. I was invited in, stepping over toys and a little redheaded toddler whose mother was yet to arrive. Settling down to a cup of tea, keeping one eye on little Aaron, Laurel said her own kids were still at school. As for small children in general, she said, "I look at them as little people. They're little adults. You can talk to them, you can treat them just like you would a friend or an adult. You know, some people think they have to be trained. But they all have their opinions. They may be little opinions, but they have their opinions." Laurel herself had big and rather strong opinions; presently, she was rip-roaring mad over the fact that we didn't have electric cars for sale in this country.

"I *do not* understand why we don't have electric cars," she told me. "They've been developed for decades and the car companies are dragging their feet—it really gets your goat! They say, 'Well, we can only get them to go a hundred miles.' What? I don't use a car more than a hundred miles per day. That would be great. That would be excellent. I could bring it home and plug it in and— Hey, I mean, I don't know what's holding them up. Give us a choice. So you limit them to a hundred miles. We can't drive them on vacations. So, two-car families have one gas and one electric."

I told her that if every two-car family in the United States replaced one car with an electric car, that would eliminate the need for Middle Eastern oil. "Let's go, guys!" she exclaimed. "What we have to do is we have to bring Detroit to its knees again. They came to their knees before over wanting us to replace our cars every two years. And when Japan starts making electric cars and exporting them, those things will go like hotcakes. Even if they started at fifteen thousand dollars, I bet you'd sell them fast. And Detroit will be on its knees again. The government's stalling; the oil lobbies are sitting up there with their feet standing on it. We have the technologies. We sent people to the moon and we can't get an electric car? Give me a break! I'll write them a letter today. There's no reason why we should be bowing down to Iraq or anyone. It's crazy. You know what I'm saying? I just wish they'd give us a choice on the cars. It's like abortion. Give us the option. I don't like somebody else to make my decisions for me. I want the option."

Laurel was equally adamant that the environment should be protected at all costs. "I don't think anybody has thought that we have been given this planet to take care of, and that if we cover it with concrete, plants will die and people will get sicker. We just have to wake up! I'm concerned about fresh air. I think we have air problems everywhere, unless you're up in the mountains somewhere. But even then we're all dumping acid rain on places like Canada. I suppose there's a lot we can do, we just haven't. I think the consciousness is shifting, though. It's not so way out there any-more. Still, people'll have to be forced to change. But it's there now. The solutions are there. The government and industry could change it right now and nobody would grumble.

"But I think the only thing that's going forward with the industrial part of it is making money. I mean, you could still make money with the environment, but they're going for the megabucks. You don't need mega-bucks. You need a nice comfortable living that pays your bills, and just the things you need to do in life to be creative or whatever. You don't need megabucks. These people are going for big, big, you know, estates and billions of dollars. Who needs billions of dollars? What are you ever gonna do with it?

"America was brought up—myself included—with 'Keep up with the Joneses and what can you attain material-wise.' And the manufacturers perpetuate this with all their ad campaigns: You need this because you need that because you need . . . You have to be intelligent enough to sit down and think, Hey, I don't need that. I could live without that in my life and my life will be just as rich. You have to be able to think about it and not go with the flow of the masses. The environment has gotta be more important than thinking about money.

"But I think there's a lot of good happening here also. I think spirituality has raised consciousness. People are really thinking about, you know, Well, what are we doing to this planet? Most people I know are at least thinking about it. And I think it's all positive energy coming together. Each little bit keeps adding on. And it's just a matter of when is it gonna snowball and really take off."

Despite her optimism, Laurel feared the countervailing snowball effect of sprawl and congestion. "A lot of people live this far out from Cleveland and just commute in. Even a lot farther than here. Traffic in Willoughby's not a problem, not yet, but the next community north, Mentor, is very, very bad. You don't want to live in Mentor, because you've got nothing but little communities, little developments and not a whole lot of industry. Mentor's real bad. Their schools are gigantic. And they've got fabulous facilities for kids, which is what's bringing people out there. They've got skating rinks, swimming pools, all kinds of stuff for the kids they really poured into the community. But they're getting so many people out there that you can't move. You don't dare get out on the streets at rush time anymore.

"Willoughby itself just happens to be a hot community right now because it's the next one that's underdeveloped coming out of Cleveland. It'll be next. So it's hot for selling and I'm getting out. This condo is for sale now. I'm heading down south to the country suburb of Chagrin Falls. It's a small community, self-contained, with groceries and theater, so I won't have to travel much. I don't like traffic. I don't."

But I do. That was what a car biologist's job entailed. I turned the Caravan south and began my descent into the state. Down I went, through the suburbs of Akron, deeper, around Columbus and the I-270 loop with suburbs radiating out in every direction, down through the suburbs of Springfield, dropping finally into the suburban maze of Dayton and the Miami Valley, where I meandered through the suburban development of Beavercreek until I located Spicer Heights and the suburban home of my next questionnaire respondent.

The face and hands of Basil Maxwell, age seventy-two, bore the lines of a life of hard work. After twenty years in the military and twenty more in the post office, he was still working, "more now than I did then," doing general home maintenance, plus catering weddings and the like. He spoke softly though forthrightly and was extremely knowledgeable of and active in local Beavercreek civic matters. He was a sort of local historian of sprawl.

"When I first came to this area in 1950, it was all farms," he said. "Our local church was all farmers, and there were about fifty people in the church. They were all related. A lot of people in the local area would like to have seen Beavercreek stay like it was back then. It's impossible. No place in the United States can stay isolated. If you have a nice area, people are going to congregate to it. And if you have job opportunities and all the associated businesses, you're going to have expansion. And when you have expansion, you're going to have even more business. We've got local people that just put down their feet and just say no. They fight everything.

"The developers are putting in a mall south in Centerville which will be the same size as the Dayton Mall. It's a large mall, and it's built up with business all around it. A lot of people complain because of traffic. Business generates traffic and generates more development. It's just like a snowball effect. This's what's going to happen up here close to Wright State University, and they'll fight that. A developer bought up the land and he's going to put up another mall. In Centerville they tried every way they could to stop the building of that mall. They've done everything. Harassment. Everything. Just a small group, but very vocal. As you see in other parts of the state, a small group can make more noise than a majority because a majority stays quiet. They don't speak up. But every time it comes to voting or it comes to court, like this one did, they lose. But they can sure make a lot of noise.

"They're putting in a private golf course just to the east of the river over here. Jack Nicklaus will develop the golf course and a big builder named Arnold is developing homes around the course; it's going to be millionaire homes all around this fancy golf course which is right beside the river. That's going to open up the land between Beavercreek and Zenia, which is all farm now. The area's expanding. Beavercreek, now, we're the largest city in Green County [Dayton is in Montgomery County, just down the road a mile]. In the last ten years, we've grown to about forty thousand population."

Basil believed Beavercreek was still free of big-city problems but wasn't sure how long the town would retain its community feel. "We've got a very good planning commission. They're trying to keep it under control but they're limited. You can only do so much with your laws. A developer will do what he can get away with; he'll even take them to court to gain his point. If the developer's got a block of land and the planning commission says, 'You can only have so many buildings per acre, only so many stories high,' and all this, and those restrictions are going to lower his profit on that land, he'll go to court. It's selfish, yes. In a surrounding community a developer wanted to build this mall. Well, people closest to it immediately started finding fault. Too much pollution, too much water runoff, too much traffic congestion. They moved into the area in the last three to four years and bought next to this vacant land and they expected that the vacant land was owned by a farmer, they expected him to leave it vacant for the next hundred years. They like to look out there and see the trees. Things don't work that way."

Basil said he would like to see less development in the area, or at least development that wasn't so dependent on cars, but added, "It won't happen in my day. I won't have to worry about it because I won't be around when it happens. Especially in the outlying areas like we've got here, because our society is geared to the automobile and our industry is geared to the automobile. General Motors, Ford, Chrysler—look at our economy and how much is tied in with gasoline, oil, and automobile-related—all your parts stores, your highway construction. All your fast-food stores built right next to where there's traffic. Drive in, get it quick, and get out. If it was possible to take gasoline and automobiles out of the system completely, the economy would collapse. There's no way. The businesses would fail. All your chain stores. Look at the trucking industry. We've done away with trains, you might as well say we don't have trains anymore. Everything went to diesel trucks. If you don't have automobiles and trucks, there's a lot of towns that would starve because you just have no way of transporting stuff.

"It's the main reason we're over in Iraq. And it isn't just the United States. It's all the industrial nations. Every mechanized country. Your Third World countries which aren't dependent on oil as much, they can get by because it's just like somebody that's never had the taste of ice cream, he doesn't know what it is so he doesn't eat it. But somebody who likes ice cream has got to have it. We like our oil, we got to have it.

"All of Ohio has a good road system. But the areas have changed so much our big problem is the roads can't support the traffic. The more people you got, the more traffic you got, and it just gets to be a bottleneck. It gets pretty congested around here. Everybody drives an automobile. There's two or three cars in every driveway and you don't go anywhere without an automobile because you're always ten miles away from everything. It's so spread out and isolated from one business to another business, and there's very little bus service or alternate means of transportation around.

"Overall, most people are pretty courteous drivers, but it builds up frustration. They get in a roadblock and they're sitting there bumper-to-bumper and they can't get no place, they get frustrated. Then you have people do crazy things, or take chances they shouldn't take. You start getting people that want to honk their horn. There's just getting to be more people. They run tests with rats and mice the same way. Anything that gets confined, where you get a restricted thing and it's very densely populated. Then you have explosions.

"The only answer I can see is carpooling, unless it gets to the point where a gas crunch gets so high that people start riding motorcycles and bicycles. Take your foreign countries. I've been to most of them through the military service, and that's their transportation: bicycle or walk! So you start a little earlier in the morning and you walk to work, or you start a little earlier and you ride a bicycle. But the Americans, they don't like to walk and they don't like to ride a bicycle very much, not so long as they got an automobile. As long as they can afford it, they're going to continue."

Basil added that the Persian Gulf crisis had made people more aware of their dependence on oil and automobiles, "but so did the last crunch, which was about 1979. Everybody got aware of it then, too. But as soon as the price dropped back down, everybody relaxes. It's like you was cold and then the sun came out and you started warming up, and it feels fine."

If we were going to break our dependence on oil, Basil believed, "the automotive industry is just going to have to be pushed. Back in the thirties the Germans in World War Two developed an engine that would run on any kind of fuel. They took potatoes and made alcohol out of it. Ran their airplanes on them. They made alcohol out of coal. They used any alternative fuel because we had cut off their oil supply. Well, we haven't had a war to cut off our oil supply, we've just run out of a supply. We're going to have to go to an alternative source if we're going to continue to run these gas-guzzlers.

"Our atmosphere is fast becoming contaminated. The CFCs, it goes into the air and you don't see it so you don't think about it. It's up there. There's a lot of things that you can't see, taste, or feel that can kill you. Most people can realize that they're going to have to change. It may not be in their immediate lifetime, but if they have children or grandchildren, they better start thinking about it. Are we going to have a world to pass on to somebody else? Because if you start cutting down the rain forests, for instance, at the scale we're cutting them down, you're not only destroying the land, you're cutting down trees that absorb carbon dioxide and create oxygen. It's a natural rejuvenation. So you're destroying the whole system and it's the basic system of the earth. The automobiles and pollution is the same. It's all tied in together—it's interrelated. When you start controlling one, then you're going to control another and another. So when you start reversing it, hopefully, you're reversing all the way down the line.

"I hope somebody can come up with an answer. But that's what frustrates a lot of people. They would like to do something, but they're a little guy and they say, 'What can I do? What I say doesn't have an effect.' You've got to take somebody like Ralph Nader, or somebody like that to get the people together. People that spoke up. That French fellow, Cousteau, he's been preaching for years about the oceans. But they're like people crying in the wilderness. There's one voice here, one voice there, and nobody's paying any attention to them. But they're going to have to start listening pretty soon because we're getting to the point where ruin is getting closer all the time."

HIT AND SKIP

Basil was a revelation to me. His belief that a solution to environmental problems must arise from a vision of interrelatedness and his faith in the power of grass roots leaders to initiate change were heartening. Here was a World War II veteran, no stranger to manual labor, firmly planted in suburban America, whose convictions would give college-educated progressives half his age a run for their money. But there was something more to Basil that gripped me, something that had to do with his cantankerous view of women drivers. He reminded me of my father. It was a feeling deepened by the fact that I was near my dad's hometown, the legendary Minersville. Legendary because I had heard about Minersville my whole life, about the farm where he took care of cows and chickens, where he made his own toys out of thread spools, where he rode his horse to school in the snow, where on weekends he rode in the neighbor's car to the county seat of Pomeroy to buy candy. Since I was so close I had to see this idyllic land for myself. Furthermore, as a car biologist, I would be exploring the evolution of one of my subjects, who insisted I take pictures.

But then photographs weren't really necessary, as Pomeroy didn't appear to have changed since right before the Depression when my dad lived there. I arrived after a 120-mile drive on two-lane roads through endless acres of cornfields and one-horse towns like Greenfield, whose welcoming sign proclaimed: "Ain't no gridlock in Greenfield." Pomeroy curved around a sharp bend of the Ohio River, and was nestled under shrub-and-tree-lined hills. Across the river, reachable by a steel trellis bridge, sat poverty-struck West Virginia. But Pomeroy was no better off. Along the river road stood a rickety wooden boardwalk that harbored a generic drugstore, a shoe store, a small market, and a bait-and-tackle store. Muffled country music was coming out of a dank bar filled with men slouched over a counter and drinking beer in the middle of the afternoon. As I walked along the boardwalk with my camera around my neck, people in dusty work clothes eyed me suspiciously. I turned around and saw the paranoid faces of store clerks pressed against their windows, watching me as I walked by. On my way here I hadn't seen one mobile home or camper on the road. I was convinced that Pomeroy residents had never seen a tourist, and never wanted to. This was definitely a town that time forgot.

At the west end of town, however, there was a little burst of modernity. Today marked the grand opening of a McDonald's, and a small crowd had gathered. A policeman stood in the middle of the road and directed cars into and out of the parking lot. Kids strolled out of the restaurant clutching balloons, their moms handling the bags of food. There were a number of men in white shirts and ties milling about and eating on the benches overlooking the muddy river. I figured they were regional McDonald's representatives or employees from the teachers' college in the northerly city of Athens, down for the big event. It was a weirdly anachronistic scene.

The late founder of McDonald's, Ray Kroc, created his multibillion-dollar restaurant chain with places exactly like Pomeroy in mind. In the early sixties, he flew his company plane over the country looking for small towns that would benefit from friendly service and familiar food. These were areas that didn't have such services but were ripe for them for one major reason: expanding roads and interstates made them easily accessible by car. Here in the backwaters of Ohio, as people from surrounding small towns pulled into the new McDonald's, I felt I was witnessing the birth of America's fast-food life-style. Chain restaurants, of which McDonald's is king, turned the daily necessity of eating into an event no longer associated with home and hearth but with cars and driving. Only I was witnessing this development thirty years later!

I left McDonald's—I got a Coke—and drove east on the river road to Minersville, which was a couple of miles away. Since there was only one road out of Pomeroy, there was a minor traffic jam created by the cars leaving the restaurant. Approaching the town's one stoplight, the string of cars was moving at less than five miles an hour. As I was coming to a stop I saw a beautiful old house that I was sure my dad would recognize. I reached for my camera and bumped into the car in front of me. Oops. I pulled over into the dirt lane, and so did the other car, a Ford Granada. A young woman got out, I greeted her, and we both looked at our bumpers. There was nary a nick on either one. We exchanged license numbers, I made a joke about being a long way from home, and we said good-bye.

Minersville was even more depressed than Pomeroy. Near the town entrance stood an abandoned coal mine, its rusted smokestack crushed like a tin can. The mine must have been booming with men when my dad was a boy. I took a picture. Across the river I could see the ominous fat cement stacks of a nuclear power plant. I drove into the hills along a canyon road. Barely standing beneath groves of trees were houses held together by frayed boards and corrugated roofs, with beat-up cars and trucks junked out front. The canyon road merged into a wide green valley, and I drove past a few sparse farms. Here was where my dad was raised—the fabled Minersville. Suddenly all his stories about growing up dirt-poor materialized in front of me. They were real. And so was the fact that he had gotten out of this place. I didn't understand that part of his story until now.

Along the road back to Pomeroy a county sheriff deputy pulled me over. I couldn't imagine why. Maybe he wanted to know what "The Great American Driving Survey" meant on the side of my van. "Your license plate number just showed up on my on-board computer," he said. "I have to take you in for 'hit and skip.' " What? Did he mean "hit and run"? I assured him I didn't run or skip out on anyone. I courteously exchanged license numbers with the woman in the Granada, whose name was Mary Wolfe. The deputy appeared to believe me, but nevertheless said he would have to escort me back to the Pomeroy Police Department. I got in the van and drove slowly to Pomeroy, the deputy right behind me. I felt like a criminal in one of those Burt Reynolds movies about cars and moonshiners in the South.

Inside the police station, which was actually an old stucco courthouse that resembled a high school, I approached a counter where some Hell's Angels type was talking to a corpulent secretary and a razor-thin cop whose face was frozen in rancor. He looked like Barney Fife in a terminally bad mood. Finally the cop turned to me. He was wearing—I swear to God— wide aviator glasses with yellow lenses. I politely explained to him that I had merely tapped Ms. Wolfe's bumper with my own bumper at less than five miles an hour. "That's impossible," he countered with unremitting nastiness. He had just returned from the Pomeroy Ford dealer, where he and the local mechanic had examined the car. There was a deep dent on the bumper and structural damage to the chassis. He then grabbed a clipboard and walked outside to my van. He walked around it, and even curled underneath the front end, jotting down notes.

Back inside the courthouse, he told me I was a liar, and was writing me a ticket for reckless driving and improper lookout. "You weren't even there," I pointed out. "I saw the evidence," he sniped back. "Is this how you treat everyone from out of town—with such courtesy?" I remarked. "Forty dollars," he said, handing me the ticket. "Pay it now in cash or wait to appear before a judge next Tuesday. And you can wait in jail." I gave the money to the dour secretary and headed for the door. Barney assured me I'd be paying for big damages to the Wolfes' car.

I immediately left Ohio, anxious to return to civilization. I decided to detour through West Virginia to Pittsburgh, my next destination. I figured my license number was still on the Ohio state police computer and I didn't want to go through this charade again. Once across the border, I called my insurance company, instructing them not to pay. But, alas, back home in San Francisco a few months later, I got a call from a very nice Farmer's Insurance agent from Athens, Ohio. She told me my little adventure was not terribly uncommon, that the Pomeroy cop was no doubt in cahoots with the Wolfes and the Ford dealership (each probably getting a small piece of change), but it would cost Farmer's more money in legal fees to fight the case than settle. They settled.

Hey, ho, way to go, Ohio.

ROAD ROMANCE

Pittsburgh at night is a glory of lights and a maze of bridges and tunnels and narrow streets up and down hills, across and along river bluffs. I liked it, though while driving through it, I never knew exactly where I was. I passed over another river, and glowing through the girders of the bridge, like a phantasm, was a fully illuminated Three Rivers Stadium. Below, in the dark, flowed either the Ohio, the Allegheny, or the Monogahela. I took my time and eventually found the restaurant as instructed, a glaring neon affair against a rocky palisade, and the bright fire-engine red eighty-nine F-150 Ford pickup and its exuberant driver. "It's my boyfriend's truck," she said. "He bought it red because I like the color red. I love this truck. I love being up in the cab. I would drive a tractor trailer if I could."

Sherry Murray, thirty-two, actually drove a courier van for U.S. Cargo. She had two basic routes: Pittsburgh to Cleveland and Pittsburgh to Parkersburg, West Virginia. Including her twenty-minute commute to work, she drove over 450 miles a day. On weekends, to visit her boyfriend in Akron, she drove another 130 miles. The way she told it, she had one of the best jobs in the country. Pittsburgh was a great city to drive in: drivers were "kind, considerate, and had a good attitude." In fact, all aspects of her life were tangled up with the highway, and she veritably glowed as she told me about it.

"I met my boyfriend on the road," she said. "I would go through the same place every night around the same time and I always had the CB on channel nineteen, the truckers' channel. This was between Pittsburgh and Cleveland. I always met quite a few people that went the same way I did on different nights. Like UPS drivers who drive eighteen-wheelers, or drivers for different soda pops and Hostess Twinkies—just different companies. So we would talk all the way up and down the turnpike. It's hard for me to look up into them so I really don't know who I'm talking to. But they can see down real well. So I pull up into the tollbooth one night and I hear one of them saying, 'There's one of them little U.S. Cargo vans giving pennies to the toll collector.' I laughed. He says, 'Will you pay my way?' I said sure. So he asked me where I was going and I told him down into Pittsburgh. He said he was heading the same way. We start to pull out of the tollbooth and get back on the interstate. I hadn't seen him at this point and I don't think he saw me either, he just knew I was a girl because of my voice. He says, 'Turn

on that porch light,' which is your interior light in truck driver talk. They
like to see who they're looking at. So I turn the light on and he didn't say
anything. He just stayed beside me and didn't say a word. So I shut the
light off.

"When they say, 'Turn your porch light on,' I always say, 'You're not
missing nothing.' They'll say, 'Oh, but that's up to me to decide.' Well, he
didn't say anything for, like, three miles, and we were side by side. So I
said, 'Are you all right?' And he says, 'Oh, my God, you're pretty.' Like he
was so stunned. And I was like, 'Well, thanks for the flowers, dear, but I bet
you've seen better.' So he asked me just where I go and what I do and
everything. Well, here he had picked a route that's right in time with mine
for the next four years. And then one night I took a break and we stopped for
coffee and we finally met. That was on January eighth, and February
fourteenth he told me he loved me. He got my phone number and came
over. It was pretty neat. So we've been going on for five and a half years now,
and we'll be married next year.

"He's an over-the-road, but a home-every-night type of truck driver. He's
not your typical gone-for-a-long-time, big-belly-talkin'-like-thizz-'ear,
hasn't-taken-a-bath-in-three-weeks-swears-incessantly kind of truck driver.
He doesn't fit the image. He drives eighteen-wheelers for Commercial
Carriers, and they drive for Coca-Cola. So it's a pretty big outfit.

"We talked all the time on the road. He made sure that he would pick a
route where he'd be going the same time I was. We had it down to a T. I'll
see you at such-and-such an exit at such-and-such a time, and if you're not
there I'll know that I'll see you here. Not see each other physically, but talk
to each other on the CB. But usually we're right behind each other."

Sherry never gave a second thought to how much time she spent behind
the wheel. "I don't mind it a bit," she said. "Nobody's breathing over my
shoulder every minute of the day. I can smoke as much as I want. I can sing
as off-key as I want. It's like I'm my own boss. And you get to meet different
people from all over. Though some's not so good. It definitely is different
sometimes. Getting flashed, that happens a lot. From my van, I can look
down into these cars and there's these guys that drive next to you for miles
doing, you know, their thing. That's happened many a time. Because they
know I'm alone. Truck drivers do that, too. There's a lot of perverted people
out there and many are on the road.

"But nobody's ever really physically attacked me. But this one guy, he'd get on the radio and I'd hear, 'Nightflight, you're a fox.' Nightflight, that's my handle. And I'd be like, 'Who is that?' He'd just laugh. It was like out of the twilight zone. This would go on for weeks. It really spooked me. I met the guy finally, his name is Rich, and he said he just saw me in the Circus Plaza one day and thought he'd just play with my mind a little bit. But he had me scared. I was always looking out for him, thinking he could be anywhere. But I like meeting people. I meet people at rest stops. Other people that I met once were mail haulers, driving for the post office. We still get together once a year.

I commented that her whole social network seemed to revolve around driving and wondered if she had any friends who, you know, walked. "Oh, yeah." She laughed. "I have friends that don't know how to drive, who do drive but shouldn't be on the road. One lives right up the street here. She can't read a road sign. She couldn't talk to me and drive at the same time. She couldn't chew gum and steer at the same time."

"But you feel comfortable out there?"

"Always. I have a fear of icy weather. In the winter, it's ice and snow big-time. Right through the snow belt is where I drive. Big-time. Blizzard conditions where you have to shut your headlights off at night. You can't even see the lines. You drive by your parking lights. You don't even know if you're on the road or off the road. Then, like, I've sat, just sat, in traffic in the middle of the night because of a jackknifed truck for six hours because the plows couldn't get through to get them out. Things like that. You get to meet people there, too. You run out of cigarettes; it's fun. It's like a tailgate party."

"Do you ever worry that your car or van has a negative impact on the environment—you know, air pollution, adding to congestion, acid rain, that sort of thing?"

"No. Cars and trucks and vans and bikes have been there long before I got here and they're going to be there long after I go. It's just something that's a fact of life. I never really thought about it."

"Has Pittsburgh changed over the years in terms of congestion?"

"It's just gotten worse. I can't say exactly when it started, but it's gotten worse."

"You don't consider it personally, but if your local government or someone asked you to help out in some way to protect the environment, would you do it? Like voting for certain legislation, maybe driving less miles one week, riding your Metro system one day a week to work?"

"If it was feasible. Sure, I'd consider some of those things. If it really is that much of a problem and it's going to help. If pollution and things were going to have some long-term effects here, some damage, sure, I'd do it."

THE ENGINEER

Following a bracingly clear morning drive along the Pennsylvania Turnpike through the Appalachians, I encountered quite a contrast to Sherry's wide-eyed enthusiasm in the studied ruminations of a veteran IBM computer scientist and former teacher. Across the Susquehanna River from the state capital of Harrisburg in the Cumberland Valley, Mechanicsburg still felt like small-town America. "Yeah, Small Town, U.S.A.," Barrett Bower chided. "Where Superman came from. Clark Kent. The Kents live right down the street. I know the boy's a little weird, but he's OK. He's very polite and says 'sir' and 'ma'am.'"

Small Town, U.S.A., however, was now part of the fastest growing area in Pennsylvania. The regional population had doubled in the last ten years, while heavy traffic had become a burden in just the last three. All brought on, claimed Barrett, by "parochial" townships and boroughs. "It was not planned in terms of the whole environment," he said. "The problem is that as far as community development, where housing is going to be, where light industrial is going to be, where commercial is going to be, where shopping centers are going to be, there was not good planning. I think that has been true of our culture across the board. It's no different than the planning that goes on in New York or San Francisco or Los Angeles. Except there you see it right away because the city fills up with smog."

Sitting in his small, windowless office, Barrett, forty-nine, said he loved to drive. Yet today's sleek and sporty cars were not for him; he drove an Olds Cutlass 88 nicknamed "the Tank." "But what I'd really like to have for everyday driving is a thirty-nine Packard. It's big, roomy, has a heater in it that would blow you out, and if you hit anything you just apologize to the guy and tell him that the wrecker will be there soon, and you drive away."

It was obvious, though, that Barrett was itching to talk about matters beyond the joy of old cars. He said he had thought a lot about my questionnaire; he had, in fact, made copies of it and went through it several times. So I asked him what he thought it was in our culture that had caused the runaway problems of automobilism, thereby kicking him into high (high!) teaching mode.

"I think that culture is very lax in wanting to know about the environment. And I don't mean just trees and leaves. I don't mean just ecological systems. But interpersonal systems, technological systems, political systems. I mean, a lot of people can use a computer but they don't understand how the government works. Things like how a bill gets through Congress. And all that's because I think you go through three stages with technology. The first stage is the gee-whiz stage: Ain't that neat? Isn't it wonderful? The next stage is: Let's commercialize it. And the last phase is: Well, what can it do for me?

"This country runs on electricity. Now there's a whole technological system that has broader implications than the automobile. And yet I think the attitudes we have toward the automobile are the same thing people carry toward the light switch. All they know is: If it doesn't work, I'm pissed off."

"Why do you think people don't know or care about how things interrelate?" I asked.

"Because we've gotten a lazy education. And I don't mean at a public level, I mean at a very private level. It's not only the desire to know, but the desire to have my children want to know. I have eight children and they range from age twenty to two. I get a full point spread of family living these days. All the way from college-level down.

"What I see in a predominance of families is a laxity, an almost disinterest, an almost passiveness, in promoting learning, wanting to learn and be interested. But don't you want to know how this works? I don't mean the intricate workings, but just have the basic idea of how an automobile works, what an internal combustion engine does as opposed to an external combustion engine?

"We still have external combustion engines around here. We have a great Amish sector here who will not use internal combustion engines. It's against their religion. Internal combustion is the work of the devil. The logic behind it is probably because of some very fundamentalist interpretation of a passage in the Bible. They won't use electricity, for example. They will not have television or radios or electric lights. They use candles and lanterns; they use steam engines to farm. Because that's all natural. Fire and steam are natural. Water boils and makes steam and that's OK.

"But most people just don't want to know how something works. I think it's a very selfish attitude: What can it do for me? And the kids are being reared that way. Their attitudes are: Does it look good and is it the same as everybody else's? Because if it's not, I don't look good." Barrett was constantly trying to steer his own kids away from conformity. If they wanted to buy, say, Reebok sneakers, they had to convince him that they were high-quality sneakers, not just what everybody else was wearing. "Everybody has to be identified by some image," he stated. "Why? Whatever happened to individualism?"

"OK," I said. "But how do you get people back to being curious, to being aware and involved?"

"I hate to tell you this, but I think it's a losing battle. Why don't people want to think about it? Because it's too much of a damn bother. It's much easier to go watch the latest TV program, or rent a VCR tape, go to the movies, or be more involved with myself, getting myself in physical shape. I see nothing in our society that is significantly helping to steer us to more aware attitudes toward other people and the environment around us. And I'm talking about the whole environment, the technological as well as the culture and the people. I think our values toward people, including our own children, is such that it takes too much time away from myself. What I notice about parents is that it takes too much time to do personal educating, caretaking, guidance, to sit down and have a nice philosophical talk. It takes away from my watching television, or my whatever it is."

"In the questionnaire you answered that technology is part of nature. Why?"

"Technology to me—I'll be very candid—it's a toy. And I don't mean that in the sense of just a plaything. Working and playing to me are not separate things. Everything is play if you have the right attitude toward it. Let me put it this way. I'm a Christian, OK? I don't believe that God allows anything to be created, even by our own hands, that is inherently evil. It's how it is used and how it is interpreted. It's like, you explain to me that all of this [he taps his computer complex] did not come from natural material. Now everybody will say, 'No, it's got synthetic stuff in it.' Well, if it's synthetic, then you made it from nothing. Bullshit! You made it from something which was natural material to begin with."

"The point is that this computer was designed by man. But man is as much a part of nature as oak trees and amoebas. Therefore, why isn't this part of nature? I mean, there's no difference between the atomic bomb and a sharp stick. It's how I use it. The same is true of an automobile. It's how I use it. To me it's essentially a toy. It serves a purpose that makes some things handier for me. I can get more things done in a day instead of having to live in the middle of Mechanicsburg. I don't have to walk half an hour. I can live two miles away, twenty miles away, forty miles away, depending on what ecological price I want to pay for that. What difference is a shovel? I can dig a hole with my hands, OK? Or I can use a shovel and a pick and do the same thing. Or I can go next door and say, 'Hey, Charlie, bring your backhoe over here,' and I can dig the hole in thirty seconds.

"What price do I want to pay for it? What trade-offs do I make? Our technology is really our tools, and toys because they are fun. But an automobile is not a benign toy. Its usage has consequences."

"The list is pretty long: air pollution, highway deaths, urban sprawl. Are you concerned about these things?"

"Yeah, I am. Am I going to do something about it? Probably not. Because until it gets really bad for some particular problem, we don't solve it. And so because of the attitude of the whole culture today, I think there is very little you can do from an activist standpoint to motivate people on a large scale to introduce mass transportation, electric automobiles, those kinds of things. Though I'm all for them. But as long as people are rushing about—I don't have time for my kids, I don't have time for my wife because I've gotta be doing something else. That's the way society is today. And they live it out in their automobiles.

"I came from a very small town, a farming community. Saturday you went to town. You got all the food, you visited your friends, people talked on the street, you did your shopping, picked up the hardware, went to the doctor, maybe went to a movie. Here, today, if I need it, I need it now, so I go get it now. I don't wait and say, 'OK, on Saturday, I'll go to the hardware store and I'll pick it up.' Everybody does it now. Mass transportation? People will say, 'Well, that's fine as long as it doesn't ruin the back of my house because that's where it's gonna go through.' Or, 'It's not convenient for me because I want to go home at two-thirty instead of two-thirty-five.' Gee, too bad.

"So I have very mixed feelings about the effects of ecological awareness. Let me explain. My mixed feelings extend to the point of whether the awareness needed for change is a capable goal. Like, simply, when Adlai

Stevenson was running for election way back. When he was campaigning at Harvard, he was in an open car and a young woman yelled, 'The intelligent people are with you, Mr. Stevenson.' And he said, 'I don't need the intelligent people, I need the vote.' OK?

"I have a negative attitude, but I'm not pessimistic. I don't think we're heading for doom and gloom, but I think it's going to have to get real bad before the average middle-class Joe Blow in the street is gonna say it's time to do something."

"But I assume you're concerned about your children's future and the world they're going to inherit."

"Yes, I am concerned about that. But I'm not going to convert this environment because I'm concerned about them. OK? What I'm going to do is teach them how to survive in what I think the environment will be. If I'm a Jew in the middle of Europe prior to the 1930s and I know that some fascist government is going to come along, I will do one of two things, either move out of there—a smart move—or teach my children to survive in that environment somehow. Well, I'm not moving out; I don't want to go to Australia.

"I want to teach them to have the proper attitude to all things. I want them to understand their environment. I want you to have a chicken in every pot but you don't need two cars in the garage. What you need is some way to get somewhere. Whatever that is."

Leaving Mechanicsburg (the name of the town somehow seemed apt), I wondered about Mr. Barrett Bower and his rather lofty approach to matters. He had told me his fellow workers and friends constantly avoided his homilizing. I was curious if his eight kids were similarly embarrassed by him ("Look out, here comes Dad; he's gonna explain how something works again"). But then I thought, No, they probably saw him as a little weird and old-fashioned but loved him. While he seemed to me too disparaging of the country's citizenry, he was a heartfelt man filled with genuine passion.

I drove south through some of the most beautiful and picturesque farmland (now known in land-planning parlance as "working landscapes") in the country—in any country—and eventually entered the urban labyrinth of Baltimore and our nation's capital.

I was early for my next rendezvous in Washington's Brightwood neighborhood. I unfolded one of my lounge chairs and sat on the sidewalk, whiling away the time by watching the stop sign at the corner. By my count, three out of every ten cars *almost* stopped. Later I was told this was representative of D.C. drivers. They were either in a big hurry, government workers in a steady state of psychomotor anxiety (around town you saw bumper stickers that warned: "I stop for red lights"), or diplomats from afar who had no inkling how to navigate the streets and expressways of a modern American city.

THE GATHERING

That evening I sat among three couples, all in their thirties, to discuss the vicissitudes of driving. There was Ed, who worked for the National Education Association; his wife, Pat, who taught high school; Helen and Doug, both nurses; Mary, a lobbyist, and her husband, Marty, an accountant. Everyone offered their opinions on the social consequences of driving but seemed to reserve their passion for personal tales of growing up behind the wheel. It was a scene out of *The Big Chill* by way of *Road & Track* magazine.

Ed worked downtown. "I put three miles a week on my car. I pay six hundred dollars insurance a year and I drive it three miles a week. I ride my bike to work. It's a six- to seven-mile ride through the park and some heavy traffic. It takes thirty-five minutes one way. Not many people do what I'm doing. This town's difficult and dangerous to ride a bike in. I used to live in Virginia, and the bike commute was much easier. And it was kind of a relaxing time. I could let my mind wander, riding through the cemetery or something. But now I have to be totally awake, aware of what's going on around me. My biggest problem is pedestrians who walk between two cars in the middle of the street, and stunts like that. Cars are fairly considerate, though they come pretty close to you.

"I ride my bike to work for the cost saving and the physical fitness. I think about the environment. I breathe in all the fumes and realize this's terrible and complain to my employer that they don't do anything to encourage bike riding. But to tell the truth, that whole environmental issue is secondary to me in commuting to work. I wish more people would bike, I wish the city would do things to make it more safe, to encourage bikers, but I do it because it's the quickest way to work."

Pat commuted to a high school ten minutes away. "A real easy drive," she said. The car for her was mainly for escaping town and visiting friends.

All trips, because of heavy traffic and increasing population in surrounding areas like Silver Spring and Tysons Corner, had to be carefully planned.

"I only have six minutes to work," Doug said. "Not enough time to get frustrated. However, there are many other ample opportunities to get frustrated. Like any large urban area, it's more trouble than it's worth. You just do it. And now and then you get 'auto anger.' All the frustrations you've been holding in with the dizzy drive come out."

Helen rode her bike to the Metro, Washington's much-touted rail system, then took the train to Virginia to the hospital where she worked. To drive in the D.C. area was "a pain!" "It's too populated. It's like an anthill. When I moved out here from Boston, it was really uncongested and I really liked it then. But it's the 'burbs, they're the problem."

Mary also rode the Metro, yet her daily destination was the city's palatial and spectacularly revamped Union Station. "I don't drive much, and that's great," she said. "I enjoy driving, but I enjoy walking more. Walking from Metro allows me to be alone before I get home, and I can switch gears. It's better than in a car because I don't have to pay attention to traffic or think about driving. I just walk. One of the big key benefits of living here is that I don't have to drive. Driving is so bad downtown and parking is terrible, and very, very expensive. Also Metro riding, it's a great equalizer of the classes and I love that. Everybody that gets on—I was thinking about this today—is so different. And everyone's considerate. Everybody wears headphones when listening to their stereo. Everyone really does abide by the rules, even though there's nobody there to enforce them. There's never a guard around. And that includes kids and teenagers. It's real different from New York.

"The biggest problem in Washington is poor planning. And, yes, I consider the car the biggest problem in the environment. I think that people are making choices and not really acknowledging the fact that they're the ones controlling those choices. We chose to live in an area that's Metro-accessible. I made that choice. I chose not to live in a place where we had to buy a second car. Now, we're lucky because we can control that, but I think a lot of people could control it and don't understand that choice is in their life. They don't really know. I know and I choose to ride Metro—unlike Mr. Environmentalist here." She indicated her husband.

Marty looked around, feigning surprise. "I *can't* take the train or bus," he said sheepishly. He commuted to Rockville, which was twenty-five miles away. "There's no convenient direct line. My work's a mile and a half from the Metro, in the middle of suburban nowhere. Out there it's a real car culture, there's not even any sidewalks. I kinda have to walk in the street. So you're going along and you look like you just ran out of gas. People'll pick you up because they feel sorry for you. Walking's just not part of the culture there. You know, there's a degree as to how far out of your way you're going to go to help the environment. Maybe the best way to help the environment is to quit and not go to work."

"When you start talking about curtailing driving, you're talking about major life-style changes," said Pat. "The ability to run to the store when you want, things like that. I think it has to hurt before people are willing to make some real radical changes. People say they're concerned about the environment. I say I'm concerned, but I rarely think twice about going where I need to go. I feel a lot better living close to my work, but that's just sort of happenstance."

"I agree," Mary said. "My personal sense is that unless people personally feel something, dollar-wise or a personal loss of something, they don't relate to the environment. Something has to happen to each individual before they'll take responsibility. When you can see and taste the air, you know it's bad. All of a sudden you realize things are more finite than they used to be.

"I think people will start demanding more action. The thing that's frustrating is that I know we have the technology to do other things. The government needs to make them more feasible. But I get a sense that people are getting really sick of the politics that's going on now. And when a politician is threatened with his job he'll start doing things a little bit out of the norm.

"I went to a lecture recently, it was really interesting. It was that field poll person, Lou Harris, giving a talk up on the Hill. The subject was the environment. He'd just completed a global survey of where people stood on the environment, and what they were willing to do about it. And it was fascinating because for the first time—he had done this survey over the last decade—it was impacting their lives, families dying of cancer and pollution, all these different global problems. People were beginning to say, 'Yes, I'm willing to make the changes, I'm willing to pay more taxes, I'm willing to do these things personally.' So Harris thought that it was a real new time happening in the United States and globally. People are starting to get real worried."

As everyone agreed that environmentalism was rising in the culture (this was clearly a gathering of people who, according to Barrett Bower, would have voted for Adlai Stevenson), the conversation came to an ebb. And switched to a more lively mood. Although car ownership held no magical glow for this group, there was, as was the case with everyone I talked with, no lack of car tales.

Mary and Marty owned a Ford LTD "bumper car"—Mary's aunt had it after her husband suddenly died, and when the aunt died shortly thereafter, Mary inherited the car. It was a 1984 model but had only six hundred miles on it. They named the car Bob (after the uncle, who no one actually liked). There was a mystery about Bob, for when Bob was driven down the street he didn't look quite right. His body paint resembled cottage cheese, and upon close inspection it appeared as though someone had rewelded his frame. "If my aunt and uncle came back from the dead, and I could ask them one question," Mary said, "I'd ask: What happened to Bob?" Mary's theory was the car had fallen off the truck when it was delivered to the dealer. At any rate, Mary had been in two fender benders since she'd been driving Bob.

"Maybe the car's haunted," I said. "Mysterious accidents and two people have died."

"Not in the car," Mary said.

"But close enough," Marty said. "Tell them what the mechanic said after he worked on it. Although it was mechanically sound, he said, 'That car is butt-ugly.' I wonder, is that an extension of our personality? It's so dull. It's like driving a government car. In the movies all the undercover guys are driving Bobs, so people get nervous when we're around." Marty said he missed his Mazda RX7.

"My family weren't real car people," Helen announced. She had grown up in Minnesota and Maine. "They were so boring, like they kept buying the same cars over and over again. They had a navy blue Malibu and this big gold Impala station wagon. And then we moved to Japan, and then when we came back, they bought a navy blue Malibu and a gold Impala station wagon. That's pretty weird—don't you think that's weird?

"I snuck out in the gold station wagon when I was only fourteen. I drove around the woods, cut the curves a little tight, hit a couple of trees. The car was just so big and I had to get it back into the garage. What was I supposed to do? Oh, hell, I'll just, *rrrrrr*, I stuck it in gear—and there was this horrible sound of wood ripping. I hated waiting for my mom to come home and tell her. Oh, God, it was terrible. I had to tell her, the wood was falling off the garage. My father was in Europe so I had to write him and say: 'Dad, I borrowed the car and I don't have my license yet and there was a bit of damage.' "

And so began Helen's storied driving career. She continued. "Once, I was driving away from the library. I did have my license by then. But as I was pulling away I heard this *urrrrttt*, and I said, 'Oh, someone's having an accident.' We called 'em 'accies.' And all of a sudden this guy's at my window at me. I just didn't look and had hit his car. I went to my girlfriend's house and called my mom and told her I had a little accie. I had to write another letter to my dad.

"It was a weird family. Christmas Eve—we all had to go to Christmas Eve services and none of us wanted to. And it was in the sixties and it was a bad time in America. It was a bad time at our house. My brother had taken acid, my sister had taken acid. And my little brother was drunk, and my mother was drunk, and my father was in Europe. And my mother says, 'OK, we're all going to church.' And we all get in the gold station wagon, and I was the only one who was able to drive. We drove about two miles and I kinda yawned and went, 'Ahhh, that was such a nice service.' And Mom said, 'Yeah, what a nice service it was.' I said, 'I think we should all go home now and go to bed.' She said, 'Uh-huh.' So I just turned the car around and drove back home. I don't think anybody in the car knew whether we'd gone or not.

"I remember I once completely drove off the road once in a snowstorm because I turned the lights off. I thought, Oh, it'd be so nice to watch the snowflakes coming down without the lights on. I had my little dog with me and I was sixteen. I can't recall how I got out of that one. Must'a had a tow truck. Then there was my aunt's old truck, a forty-six Chevy pickup. I loved driving that truck. I turned it over in Maine, though. Only I wasn't driving that time, thank God! My girlfriend Sal was driving. We were coming home from work. I think we had a couple of beers. We had some hitch-hikers in the back, too. And Sal took a corner too fast, and it was just an old truck, so the tires were probably pretty gone, and we went just sliding toward the cliff and the sea, then we went toward this hill, and finally we crashed into the wall near the cliff. And I fell on top of Sal. And I'm sitting on top of her saying, 'Are you OK?' 'Yeah, are you OK?' And we're OK and we're climbing out and I go, 'Ohhh, the hitchhikers!' I'd forgotten about the hitchhikers. But they were really drunk, two drunk kids. And they just rolled out. And they were just lying on the road. They were OK. So I had to tell my aunt we'd rolled the truck.

"When I was driving to my wedding, I almost . . . this was really bad. It was a Hyundai and it's a really light car and I was driving down through Kentucky with my sister and I was really tired. I'd been driving all day and I went off the shoulder and I was going about sixty-five. I went right into this grass median. The car was so light—maybe it was the wind? So anyway, we went down this median, then out onto the other side of the freeway with cars going the other way. And then we were sorta going toward the guard-rail, and I'm doing fifty, and I thought, Well, I have to do something here, so I just sort of hit the brakes and turned the wheel at the same time. We spun around and around, but we didn't hit anything.

"Yeah, I used to go off the road all the time. The thing is, I'm a good driver. I really am."

End
of
the
Road

Today we are well underway to a solution of the traffic problem.
—Robert Moses, 1948

D riving up the New Jersey Turnpike, my feelings seemed to shift with the landscape, from the freedom of the rolling hills, to the comfort of small towns like Woodbridge, to the claustrophobia of gray, industrial Newark. Then a touch of dread and menace became lodged in my chest. Every weekday up to a million cars poured into the unthinkably crowded island of Manhattan, and this cold afternoon I was about to be one of them.

I fell in line at the tollbooth, handed over my three dollars, and followed a stream of cars down into the Holland Tunnel, a long cement dungeon of carbon monoxide. As I emerged into lower Manhattan, cars fanned out and I was greeted by the cacophony that is New York City. Cars, taxis, and trucks of all sizes jockeyed for position beneath the towering buildings. Horns, squealing brakes, revving engines, screeching tires, and sirens blended into a loud and never-dissipating blare. I joined the antagonistic herd and headed up the Avenue of the Americas to Greenwich Village, where I was staying in a friend's apartment. They say the average speed in Manhattan is 7.3 miles per hour, and as I jostled from stoplight to stoplight, I knew they were right.

In measuring the car's impact on an urban area, I could go no further than New York. I was at the end of the road. Even the far coast was no fair comparison. "I do not accept the conclusion that Los Angeles has amazingly bad traffic," UCLA professor of urban planning Martin Wachs had told me. "I grew up in New York, and I still marvel at the fact that you can be stuck in traffic in New York for hours, and New Yorkers will still say, 'How can you live in Los Angeles with that terrible traffic?' The traffic is clearly worse in New York; it is completely unacceptable."

Here, in New York, was a habitat whose carrying capacity, its ability to sustain a particular species, had crashed. Hucars had taken over the urban island, hastening the destruction of both the habitat and themselves. It was a vision of the final future of driving in America, a metropolis where automobility had evolved into complete and total gridlock.

My goal at the end of the road was to understand how the inhabitants coped with the madness. If there was a place to document how cars and driving at century's end were stripping away sanity in the human psyche, it was Manhattan. The island's 22.2 square miles are filled with over 200,000 registered passenger cars and commercial vehicles, thousands of trucks, and 890,000 daily commuters. But the ones to take a close look at are those drivers who fight their way through this congested madness ten hours a day, every day, year after year. Of course I'm talking about everybody's favorite New Yorkers, the cabdrivers, all 12,000 of them. Here was a breed of driver whose mentality has got to represent the decline of Western civilization— proof that humans will adapt to anything! Then I met Willie Bly. He tried to set me straight on what to think of New York cabbies.

A taxi driver for twelve years, Willie was now president of the ITOC (Independent Taxi Owners Council, Inc.), an organization that represented "medallion" taxi drivers in their dealings with city regulatory agencies. Purchased from the city for $127,000, a medallion grants drivers an independent business license to operate a cab. Willie was also the manager of a credit union that loaned drivers money. He was forced into his bureaucratic roles after being disabled in an accident in 1986. He was getting into his cab outside a coffee shop when a limousine, whose accelerator stuck, smashed into him and broke his legs. Willie regretted the accident mostly because it took him off the streets as a cabbie.

I met Willie at ITOC's old and cramped office building on Ninth Avenue at Forty-second Street, two blocks from Times Square. Born and raised in Queens, Willie talked a mile a minute and loudly issued orders in stride. At sixty-seven, he was short and balding and bared an uncanny resemblance to former New York City mayor Ed Koch. We climbed a narrow metal staircase toward a vacant office, but the keys wouldn't open the door. "Where's da damn keys for da door?" he yelled to no one in particular. "Get me da right keys!" "Calm down, Willie," said a man in a white shirt with rolled-up sleeves in an adjacent office. "I'll find them." "Stay dare!" Willie growled; "I'll geddem!"

Once inside the office, Willie gave me a good looking over. I was doing my best to hold back a huge grin, partly because of Willie's brusqueness and classic New York accent, and partly because I was thinking of my jolting, Mr. Toad's taxi ride through traffic to get here. "The first thing I've got to ask," I said, finally giving in to laughter, "is how do taxi drivers do it?"

"Don't laugh. Don't even say, 'My first question.' Just say, 'How do you do it?' 'Cause now you're normal. And you're sensible. You're on the right track. Let me tell you something, it's a rough way to make a dollar. I started to drive in 1974. I bought my own medallion. On Monday I went in to my wife and I says, 'Babe, I'm going to drive a taxi.' She says, 'Really?' Because I never spoke about it. I says, 'I need about twelve to fifteen thousand dollars for a down payment, do we have it? 'Cause ya know, I can't take orders from anyone. Once I buy my own medallion, I'm the boss.' She says, 'I hope you know what you're doing.' So why did I do it? I love people. Anything that I've got to do with people, I'll do, because I was always in the people business. I had coffee shops, what we call in New York candy stores, luncheonettes, egg cream stores.

"She says, 'Willie, you don't know all the streets.' I have to say something. I'm married to a very sensible woman. How dumb could she be if she married me? I was fifty years old, and that's kind of old to buy your own medallion. But I keep on looking in front of me. I love people and I wanted to make a living that way. I'm not a dope pusher where I can also deal with the people selling crack. 'Cause I happen to be a very honest person. It's a corny statement to make, but I am.

"There's an old saying: Only ten percent of the people like what they're doing. I was in that ten percent so I was lucky. I never had a partition in my cab because I enjoyed talking to my people. So when you come to the traffic, the traffic didn't bother me because while I was standing in traffic, my meter was clicking away. I used to grin at the traffic, like a moron. I was making money. It's not my fault that I was stuck in traffic. I felt like Jesse James making money just standing still, but that's the laws of the game of the taxi business. I'm an oddity because I was able to tolerate the traffic, tolerate the stress.

"Today when I get to a corner where the traffic is so bad, so backed up, and I see drivers hitting the dashboard or blowing the horn or they want to press a button and fly over the traffic. None of those things they can do. Or they take out a cigarette and forget they already have a cigarette in their mouth—it's stupid. It's stupid because at the end of the day, you wanna know something? You go home with your same money, but you go home aggravated.

"I'm a very bad guy to talk to because I love my work. If it wasn't for my wife, I think I never would come home. My kids are married, they're out of the house. I have five grandchildren. So my wife would make dinner. I used to keep my cab in my backyard. I used to sit and eat and look at the cab. I'd say to myself, What am I doing eating here when I've got a tool out there I can make money with? A lot of times, I used to eat fast and say, 'I'm going out for a couple of hours.' My wife used to say, 'Willie, go get some hot bagels, and I need two quarts of milk.' I'd go out at eight o'clock and come back at one-thirty. Because I snuck away to work. I didn't have to open a factory and borrow the key. I just went to work. She used to say to me, 'Willie, why did you do that? You're tired. Why do you have to kill yourself?' 'Honey, we're gonna eat out tonight and we're going to a movie. I want to make my expenses.'

"But to say the traffic isn't stressful is a lie. Because exactly two years ago this month, I had open-heart surgery. I don't think I can attribute it to driving a taxi. I am a very stressful person. Right now I enjoy talking to you, I really do, but I worry about what's going on downstairs in my office. When I worked at the taxi school, I used to have twenty-four students. If I had one or two Americans, that was a lot. It was rough, but I loved teaching so much because it was related to the taxi business. I used to teach from nine to twelve and one to five. From twelve to one was my lunch hour, right? I used to say, 'I'm not hungry, anyone who wants to stay and talk through the lunch hour, I'm OK.' One guy would run out and get me a small Coke and a doughnut. And we would work.

"What I taught was driver-customer relationships, which is very important. I practice what I preach. When I used to go to work I used to shower the night before. I would always wash up good. My hair was groomed. I did not wear a suit and tie, I'm not going to lie. I wore a nice sport shirt or a nice shirt with a collar. I was always clean-shaven. I wore a nice pair of dungarees. I never wore white sneakers because they get dirty fast. In other words, self-appearance is very important. And don't forget when I get in a cab on a July seventeenth early in the morning, when it's still maybe seventy-two degrees out, and a person only sat three feet from me, I make sure I don't have body odor. These are important. I used Right Guard. I used to brush my teeth, which I always did. I wanted my car to be clean. I never had any of this crap in my car, these refresheners and all that stuff. I didn't need them because my car always smelled clean. Every two and a half years I would buy a new cab. That's unheard of, but I had to have the biggest and the best of everything because I was the smartest and the best-looking of everybody.

"Then I used to do something that the taxi drivers used to do years ago. They don't do it anymore. If a gentleman or older lady would get into my cab, I would run out—and I got pleasure out of it—I would open the door for the lady and help them in. I used to do forty jobs a day, so I was jumping in and out thirty to forty times a day. Or if I picked up a youngster like you, and my baby is much older than you, and if they had packages, I would help them with their packages. For two reasons. I didn't want them to trip or drop anything. But the most important thing was I visualized a bigger gratuity. And I got it. I made a lot of money. That was part of the money. If you give them terrible service, they're going to give you a nickel. That never happened to me. I heard stories where they gave a nickel or dime. They were trying to give you a message.

"The only thing that hurt me a lot, that I didn't like, was the dangerous aspect of the job. Getting stuck up and cut up, the fear they were going to put a bullet in my left ear. You're playing Russian roulette with your life. When I pick you up, and you ask me to take you somewhere, how do I know three blocks down the road you're not going to put a gun to my head? I once said that to my wife. So you know what she told me? Don't pick up any strangers."

"Have you ever been held up?"

"I used to leave my house at four-thirty and at a quarter to five I was driving someplace and I got a flat. I had to fix my own flat. That was in the summertime. It was still dark out. That was in Long Island City, and two black guys—black, white, they all do it; I'm not picking black 'cause it's black, or, I should say, I'm picking black 'cause they were black—they both came at me with bread knives. I says, 'Take it easy.' I always started out with some money. They get very angry if you have no money. I gave them eighty-five dollars, but it wasn't enough and they started to slash me. Somebody scared them off and they ran and I chased them. But the blood was just gushing out till I collapsed. Then they took me to the hospital and stitched me up. So I says to the nurse, I says, 'Could I go back to work?' She says, 'Well, I'd go home and rest up, you lost a lot of blood.' I says, 'Yeah, maybe you're right.' On the way home, somebody hailed a cab and I just kept on working. They stitched me up and I worked. Some of my colleagues weren't that lucky. They're six feet under today. It's something that can't be controlled.

"But I'm a fighter. It's stupid. Another time a guy had a gun in my nostril and I took the gun away from him. He bent over—remember I told you I didn't have a partition—and with my elbow I busted his nose. I was able to get the gun, but he had a partner who also came with a gun. All he wanted was the gun, because he wanted to help his friend who was bleeding profusely."

"Tell me about some of your favorite fares."

"You take Senator Bradley. It was one of those days before a holiday. The airports were what we called 'stripped and working.' You know what I mean when I say 'stripped and working'? 'Stripped' means the flights are coming in very fast and there's not enough cabs. 'Working' means working, going after fares. So I got on the cab line. I think it was Pan Am. I am very very sports-minded. I'm into sports. I was always a New York Knickerbockers fan and everybody knows that Bill Bradley played for the Knicks, and at that time he was a senator. He's that big, his wife is this big, and I'm about the fourth car out. He comes out and I said, Oh, God, why wasn't I number one and he would get into my cab? All of a sudden, I look up and he's walking toward me. I couldn't imagine what's going on. He's arguing with the dispatcher, saying 'I want to go in his cab,' pointing to me, not because I'm good-looking, but the first three drivers had partitions. He would have to sit like a monkey in a cage, all shriveled up. He says, 'I'm going to New Jersey.' He lived in Tenafly, I think. He says to the dispatcher, 'Don't tell me how to spend my money.' So he got into my cab and I put his luggage in and we drove away. His wife sat in the back doing her needlepoint work and he sat in the front and we talked sports and New York all the way.

"I picked up Senator Javits once. He was waving good-bye to Governor Rockefeller. He says, 'No, Nelson, I'm going to jump in the cab and go home.' He jumped into my cab. I had stopped. There was traffic backed up at the light, so I heard the conversation. He got into my cab and was very friendly right off the bat, so I had no problem talking to him. And you know, we all have our names right in the cab, so right away he was my friend. 'Willie, can you explain to me how insurance works with the New York taxicabs?' Because he was having an insurance meeting the following day, so he wanted to know what he was talking about. Here I'm giving advice to a New York senator. We became very friendly. When we got to his house, which was maybe only fifteen blocks away on Fifty-seventh Street, he wouldn't get out, he enjoyed our conversation so much. I turned around, I says, 'Senator, I got work to do.'

"I picked up Stiller of Stiller and Meara. You know the team? He was dressed like a bum with a cap and a muffler. It was sometime in August. It was about a hundred and fourteen degrees out. I turned around and I says, 'Stiller, why are you dressed like that there? You look like a bum.' He says, 'When we get to the theater I'll show you why.' I knew right away what he meant. He didn't want to be bothered with autographs. I started to kid around with him and I told him all true stories that happened to me. I couldn't get him out of my cab. I says, 'We're here.' He says, 'I got time, continue, I'm enjoying you.' And he's a comedian, and he was enjoying *me*.

"I picked up what's-his-name, Strawberry, and Gooden, at Bloomingdale's. I was taking them to Shea Stadium. I think the fare came out to about seven-sixty and he gave me eight dollars. Now, that's a lousy tip. I said, 'Wait a minute, wait a minute, we did very good coming here. You're gonna really leave me with sixty cents?' So Doc Gooden says, 'Come on, man, take care of the fella!' Not the boy, the fella. Take care of him. He took out ten bucks and give it to me. I only said it in a joking way. I was just kidding around. But you have to have balls to talk like that. You got to know how to talk and who to talk to."

"Do you feel like a psychologist sometimes?"

"You got another good point there. I was a rabbi, I was a priest, I was a bartender, I was a psychologist, I was a medical doctor. I was everything. I was riding up Fifth Avenue up in the upper Eighties. There were three women and a little older woman with them. I picked them up and they got in the cab. 'Please take us to Penn Station.' This was about four-fifteen; traffic was pretty heavy that time. It's quite a ride from about Eighty-eighth Street to Penn Station. I knew they were Jewish. And I'm Jewish. I started to talk about Jewish life, but again, all truthful things that would happen. Like I would insult my wife, or my three jerky son-in-laws. But I got good son-in-laws. I'm kidding around. When I got to Penn Station the fare was about six dollars and change. She gave me a ten-dollar bill and said keep the change. But I said, 'Wait a minute, wait a minute, you have two tens here.' She said, 'No, it's all for you.' I says, 'Why are you giving me so much money?' This is how I was. The average cabdriver don't do that. She says, 'Do you know where we came from when you picked us up, driver? We came from my mother's psychiatrist. My mother's been depressed for four years. That's the first time we saw her smile for a long time. You made her laugh. We just gave that doctor one hundred and seventy-five dollars, we got a *pill* out of it.' She said, 'Keep the change.' I pulled up at the corner and started to cry. I started to cry. It's things like that that make you want to love the business. Because again, I love people."

"What happens if people don't want to talk?"

"That only happens with men. Women want to talk. *Women* want to talk. Sometimes I get a little angry because I want to talk, too, and they don't let *me* talk. But the men are a little harder to crack. I pick up a gentleman on Madison Avenue and he's going to La Guardia Field. Twenty minutes to five, the height of the rush hour. When he got in he said, 'To La Guardia.' But they never tell you what terminal. There's fourteen terminals there. 'La Guardia, driver.' I drive him half a block. I says, 'Could I pick out my own terminal?'

"Just the way you're laughing, that's how they would laugh. Whether the guy had a big red nose and he was the chairman of a big board where his wife or his secretary or his first wife would be afraid to talk to him, I can say what I want. Before you know it we're talking sports, politics, the way of life. There's only one thing that I would never talk on."

"Religion."

"What am I doing here with you? You know the answers. Religion. I gave advice, too. A lot of times a man and a woman would get in my cab and they were arguing. You know what a yenta is? A nosy guy. So if I had a radio on I would shut it because I wanted to try to hear everything. Little by little, I would stop at a light, I would never turn around while I'm driving, I would look around and say, 'Can I say something? But if you want me to I'll mind my own business.' 'No, no, let me hear your opinion.' They always invited me into the conversation. And I'm not going to brag, but more times than not I was right.

"I tell you something, driving a cab in New York is an honest day's work, it's an honest living, and you should be proud to be a taxi driver. You know why? Because when you sit behind the wheel of the taxi and you pick up a man that came from England for the first time in his life at Kennedy Airport, you're not just a taxi driver, you're a goodwill ambassador. In 1962 we used to have a gentleman who was a multimillionaire, but his salary was one dollar a year. He was what we called the goodwill ambassador. His job was to greet all the VIPs that came from foreign lands. That's what Willie Bly was to these people, but not only to the VIPs."

And Willie would still be driving today if it weren't for his accident. "You're damn right I would be driving," he yelped. "You're damn right. I'm just sixty-seven, but I'm a bald-headed teenager. I wouldn't mind the stickups, I wouldn't mind the traffic. I wouldn't mind anything because if you weighed it, the driving made me happy. It was like going to a show, to a party. I enjoyed it. You want to know the truth? New York City is the only place that has taxi drivers. If you could make it in New York as a taxi driver you could make it anywhere. I've been to Chicago, Philadelphia, they're pretty rough in Boston. In California, you're a bunch of farmers—it's like office work in a cab. There's nothing like driving a cab in New York City."

A THREE-HOUR TOUR

"Of course Willie says he likes to drive," protested Nabil Lakah. "He's not driving anymore!"

Nabil and I were stationed in his cab at a red light at Water and Wall streets in the Financial District. Cars and delivery trucks jammed the streets in every direction. Bicycle messengers darted in and out of the fray. Pedestrians packed the sidewalks. Through the buildings to the east stood the grand Brooklyn Bridge. Nabil was giving me a "tour" of Manhattan. He was an Egyptian in his "early fifties," and had lived and driven a taxi in New York City for ten years. When he came to America he wanted to start his own business, perhaps open an electronics store, but he believed his broken English would make him ripe for exploitation. "It would be very tough for me to go through deals," he said, "because people know that I'm a foreigner so they are going to try by all means to take advantage of everything I do." He continued to take college courses in English and computer electronics, holding on to the hope that he could someday get out from behind the wheel of a cab.

We inched our way through Chinatown, where trucks whined and screeched as they stopped in front of stores and small markets. Construction workers on the Bowery near Delancey Street froze us at an intersection. A tractor with a huge iron claw crept across the street in front of us. A chain saw ripping through the asphalt added a loud grinding noise to the agglomerate of impatiently idling cars. Then a semitrailer driver behind us pounded on his horn. Nabil remained calm. "Because of bad manners he has to blow his horn every two seconds. We are living under a big amount of pressure in this city." Nabil rolled up the window. A homeless man on the median walked by us and Nabil rolled it back down. "Here!" Nabil yelled to the man, holding out two quarters he had ejected from the money changer on his belt. "You give up?" "Oh, no," said the homeless man. "You was talking to your passenger, and I didn't want to bother you. Thank you very much."

"We've been sitting here for what," said Nabil, "about ten minutes? Tell me, how can I make money if I'm stuck in traffic like this?" He explained that when his speed dropped below ten miles per hour, his expense meter slowed down and in effect only charged passengers about nine dollars an hour. "Does that make sense to you? My benefit is to keep my passenger ten minutes, fifteen minutes at the most. So when I'm not on the move, I'm losing money."

As we headed up Third Avenue amid the apartment buildings, Nabil's spirits picked up with the speed—about thirty-five miles per hour. He waved to a coffee shop owner in Gramercy Park. How did he deal with the traffic and potential danger from passengers? "I have no other choice," he said. "My philosophy is the same as a doctor that has to treat patients with AIDS. They have to treat patients with AIDS. It's not everybody that has to go there just for a cough or sneezing. You have the good passenger, you have the bad passenger. And the only thing that gives me help to deal with everything is I like people. I couldn't make it if I didn't like to talk to people, to understand people, to give them solutions to their problem. They talk to me like a confidant. I have about forty passengers a day, and every one has a different problem than the other one. I know how to deal with most every problem."

As he maneuvered through lighter traffic, Nabil often took his hands off the wheel to highlight something he was saying. I admitted he was making me a trifle nervous.

"You just let that guy cut in front of you," I said.

"In my way of driving, I'm not aggressive. I tell you that because driving over the years, I got the lesson to be very patient. When I have bad traffic, or people like that, I don't curse. I turn my head and look to the left side, and look to the other side, but I never look ahead of me. Because if I have to look ahead of me I will drive myself crazy." A driver behind us, duly unimpressed with our speed, darted around us, horn blaring. "You see?" said Nabil. "So I forget about him. Finished. He's out of my mind."

We crept through sheer gridlock in Midtown, a moving dot in a daunting canyon of high rises. We drove along the Upper East Side, across the Third Street Bridge and into the Bronx to get a look at Yankee Stadium. We headed down a vacant street lined with warehouses. A fat woman in tight shorts was walking backward down the middle of the road while another man near an underpass appeared to be walking in figure-eights. "We choose the wrong street here," said Nabil. "Better go back into the civilized area." We crossed the 145th Street Bridge into Harlem. Along Lenox Avenue we pulled over for a fire engine blaring its pulsating siren and wailing on its horn, which started a chain reaction of horn honkers for a good block. "Manhattan is a very noisy place to live," offered Nabil. "I don't want to live in Manhattan, even if it's for free. You have all day long the fires, the ambulance, and the police. It's noisy as hell." A monumental understatement.

Heading south on Park Avenue we melded into a sea of yellow taxis. We had been in the car over two hours, and whatever benign and rational face Nabil had put on for me earlier had vanished. He was sweating and looked fatigued and restless. Glaring at the traffic, he admitted, "For me, driving in Manhattan is like those people going in the mines underground. I think that we cannot do that job more than a certain period of time. We are destroying ourself. Sometime I have pain in my chest. I don't know if this pain in my chest is coming because of the pressure or because of the pollution. I don't know. Maybe could be the pressure. Because I'm under pressure. You imagine you have to make a certain amount of money during the day. If you don't make two hundred and twenty-five dollars you are not going to be able to pay your bills. And you see in three hours you are not going to make it. One day you can let it go. But after a while you say, 'Oh, oh, how am I going to pay my bills now? I have to make it faster, I have to blow my horn, I have to cut off other people. I have to make money.' "

It took us nearly an hour to get across Manhattan on Forty-seventh Street, which was literally at a dead stop. Nabil leaned on his elbow and occasionally stuck his head out the window to look up ahead. People on foot streamed past us on the sidewalk. Along with the cars, our conversation had come to a standstill. Finally, Nabil said, "You know what? I'm going to amaze you. I don't like driving. When I'm not working my wife drives. Even when I take her in the morning to her office, she drives my cab. It's against regulations, but I let her drive. The least I drive, the better it is for my health."

Back in the Village apartment, I felt positively exhausted. My skin felt permanently soiled. I had done nothing but sit in the front seat of a car all afternoon, but my mind was drained. I could think only of the absurdity of driving in Manhattan and wonder how America's great urban area could have become so enslaved to the steel-fisted rule of the car.

HOLY MOSES

Geographically, the answer was easy: too little space, too many cars, with Manhattan as the focal point of New York City's five boroughs. In fact, New York City has meant gridlock since the first car-buying boom in the late twenties. In 1932 nearly 800,000 vehicles made their way along the same narrow roads that horse carriages crossed in 1918. During rush hour in the thirties it took drivers forty-three minutes to cross the 1,182 feet of the Queensboro Bridge. At the height of the second car boom of the postwar era, drivers could look forward to a good two-hour crawl across Manhattan, a snarl frequently exacerbated by frustrated drivers making abrupt U-turns in the middle of the street. Yet the people have kept coming and the cars have kept multiplying. As for commuting into Manhattan today, Joseph Bierman, regional director of operations for Metro Traffic Control, had this to say: "It's still very, very silly." And getting sillier still, as experts predict a

13 percent increase in commuting into New York City by 2005, bringing the total of cars in the metropolitan area to 15.4 million.

Here was the ultimate example of the cycle I had encountered elsewhere in the country: a boom in population generated more development, which generated more roads, which generated more development, which generated a boom in population. And on and on, leaving residents shackled to their cars. However, there is one significant difference to this cycle of growth in New York—it was fostered by one very powerful man. No other driving ecosystem in the country has been shaped so extensively by a singular force, a force that belonged to New York City Park Commissioner and City Construction Coordinator Robert Moses.

From 1924 to 1968, Moses was responsible for the development of 627 miles of roads in and around New York City, including the Triboro Bridge, linking Queens and the Bronx to Manhattan; the Brooklyn Battery Tunnel, joining south Manhattan to Brooklyn; the Cross-Bronx Expressway; the Cross-Westchester Expressway; most of the major causeways crisscrossing once rural and now suburban Long Island; and, last but not least, Manhattan's West Side Highway. The West Side Highway was symbolic of Moses's land-use practices. He designed the highway to run along the edge of Riverside Park, granting drivers a nice glimpse of the Hudson River. That left pedestrians and picnickers seeking a tranquil moment in the park with a view not of the waterfront but of a river of noisy cars. Today, however, the West Side Highway is falling apart—engineers recently cited fifty hazardous road conditions on a fifteen-block stretch—and Moses's roads are jammed with cars morning, noon, and night. They demonstrate how the dominance of a single ecological force can wreak havoc on an environment and its inhabitants.

Historically minded commuters today may feel inclined to stick their heads out their windows in traffic on the Triboro Bridge and curse the memory of the great city coordinator. But they would be cursing not the man so much as the times in which he was able to exercise his power. Moses's dedication to roads as the solution to New York City's horrendous traffic sprang from the aspirations of the New Deal era to enlarge the American frontier both physically and psychically. (Moses derived billions of dollars in funds from Franklin D. Roosevelt's public works agencies.) And of course the symbol of this burgeoning commitment to social equality and freedom was the automobile. In fact, the city coordinator was so committed to the car and the good life it represented that he blocked the construction of mass transportation at every level. Subways, buses, and trains catered to inner-city residents and were anathema to his vision of happy families with two cars in every suburban garage. Never mind that in 1945 two out of every three New York City residents didn't own a car. Never mind, too, that Moses never drove, but was chauffeured everywhere in a plush limousine.

In *The Power Broker: Robert Moses and the Fall of New York*, Robert A. Caro details Moses's legacy: "By building his highways, Moses flooded the city with cars. By systematically starving the subways and the suburban commuter railroads, he swelled that flood to city-destroying dimensions. By making sure that the vast suburbs, rural and empty when he came to power, were filled on a sprawling, low-density development pattern relying primarily on roads instead of mass transportation, he insured that that flood would continue for generations if not centuries, that the New York metropolitan area would be—perhaps forever—an area in which transportation—getting from one place to another—would be an irritating life-consuming concern for its . . . residents."

But as Caro proves, Moses's legacy has been far more than aggravating traffic. By literally remaking New York City over in the image of the car, he "tore out the hearts of a score of neighborhoods, communities the size of small cities themselves, communities that had been lively, friendly places to live, the vital parts of the city that made New York a home to its people." Moses uprooted 250,000 people, sending the poorest ones into already overcrowded slums. Neighborhoods gutted for roads, intersections, and bridges lost their humane character and urban blight spread like cancer. As New York political science professor Marshall Berman points out in his book *All That Is Solid Melts into Air*, a cultural history of the "experience of modernity," no place was more devastated than the Bronx. Referring to Moses's Cross-Bronx Expressway, Berman writes: "Ten minutes on this road is especially dreadful for people who remember the Bronx as it used to be; who remember these neighborhoods as they once lived and thrived, until this road itself cut through their heart and made the Bronx, above all, a place to get out of. For children of the Bronx like myself, this road bears a load of special irony: as we race through our childhood world, rushing to get out, relieved to see the end in sight, we are not merely spectators but active participants in the process of destruction that tears out our hearts. We fight back the tears, and step on the gas."

For other children of the Bronx, though, those who couldn't afford to step on the gas, the fate of the Bronx doesn't bear special irony as much as plain sorrow. Yet Larry Fleischer wasn't shedding any tears. At sixty-three, he was hardened toward the Bronx's decline, though he still clearly relished his feelings for his hometown. I talked with Larry; his companion, Cindy, thirty-seven, who taught nursery school; and Cindy's daughter, Jessica, fourteen, in their brownstone apartment on Manhattan's Upper West Side. Larry's parents were Communist Hungarians who came to New York at the turn of the century, settling on Seventy-ninth Street in the Yorkville neighborhood of Manhattan. Larry's father was a toymaker. In the fifties and sixties, Larry worked as an editor for men's adventure magazines and paperback books—"You know, spy stories, cowboy nonsense." Today, he conducts surveys for an electronics market research firm, though he insisted it was just a dumb job that allowed him to read the paper all day. He kept telling me he wasn't a good subject because, as a native New Yorker, he didn't drive, never had, and never wanted to. Still, while growing up, didn't he experience peer pressure to own a car?

"No, no, no! You didn't think of it. Nobody had a car. I grew up with the subway and buses. It was the perfectly normal way to get around. I would take the train to school and walk home. When I was a kid we used to go trooping around the museums to see art shows. We would get on a Fifth Avenue bus, one that ran down Riverside Drive, a double-decker, and we'd sit up on top. I would take the train and the subway to some place I had not been before, and just go out walking, exploring the city. There were streets of leather tanners, and streets of ship chandlers. My uncle had a sewing machine repair shop on Twenty-fifth Street, which was a street full of sewing machine repair shops. And these guys would throw their toolboxes on their shoulders and they'd walk to where they had to repair machines. If they had to take a machine back to the shop, they'd throw it on their arm and walk back with it. I did the same thing.

"I would do all these things because they were cheap enough. So for me to walk or take the subway was simply normal. Just as it's normal for you to have a car or to think of having a car. Even now it's normal for me to get around the city on what used to be a much better transportation system."

"Did you ever feel that you were missing out on some crucial part of the American experience by not driving?" I asked.

"Definitely. But New York is not the typical American experience. It's an experience of its own. It's a city. And you've got to understand what it is to be a smart-ass kid growing up in New York. You don't really think anything on the other side of the Hudson is worth knowing about. It's an attitude. They're all rubes out there. Course, it isn't true. You know it isn't true. It's this New York attitude. Now New York has got no New Yorkers left in it. All the New Yorkers have moved to the suburbs or Los Angeles or Florida. The place is full of yuppies from Indiana.

"At one time it was a living city. It had its working population in the outer boroughs. There was industry in Manhattan. There was industry along the river. It was a major seaport. And the subways and buses cost a nickel. It was necessary to subsidize these things in order to get the working population into the garment trade, the dockworkers to the docks. But then the garment trade left New York for cheaper labor, and the port business dried up, and the reason for this enormous city has disappeared along with them. It's now a tourist center and everybody wants to be in the hamburger business and forget about the city. There's entertainment, there's publishing, there's the financial business. But that can all be done by button pushing. You don't have to be in the city anymore. You can fax things around the world faster than you can get to the airport. The city is an anachronism. It's become so in my lifetime.

"There is almost nothing being produced in New York now. Nothing can come into Manhattan anymore except through a few tunnels and a couple of bridges. The ships aren't piling up anymore and unloading their goods. We got through World War Two moving all these goods and troops by train. But right after the war everybody wanted the American Dream. Everybody was living in some slum tenement and wanted a piece of grass around his house. And wanted to drive to it. There had been suburbs along the train lines, but those were already built up, and they built new suburbs that needed motor roads. Everybody wanted a car anyway. Everybody wanted the American Dream, but it was unrealizable to move out of the city, and then it became realizable. You could get these ticky-tacky houses cheap, and move out there.

"The Bronx became just as urbanized as Manhattan, and there was a flight from the Bronx. Originally there was a flight *to* the Bronx. That's how come I grew up there. People left the Lower East Side or, in the case of my family, Yorkville, and moved up to the Bronx where it was more open, the houses were newer, the streets were wider. Yorkville was getting awfully crowded, like those old Dead End Kids movies, so we wanted to move up to the Bronx. And when we originally moved up there, there were cows in sight. Now the Bronx is where the undesirables get exiled to. It's a place of last resort. Nobody cares for those slobs in the Bronx, which is why it is devastated. Much of the population there is considered surplus and is so treated. That's one of the reasons we got all these kids with military submachine guns selling crack to other kids and blowing away the neighbor's babies. There's nothing for them to look forward to. It's that or flip hamburgers at McDonald's. If they live.

"I guess this doesn't have anything to do with cars. But having a car here has always been a big burden. When my father got prosperous and got a car, he couldn't leave it parked on the street. He had to get a garage for it and that was several blocks away. He spent almost as much rent for the car as for his apartment. Then he got a heart attack—and he lived in a hilly part of the Bronx—and he had to have the car delivered and picked up again to save his heart. He was paying more for the car than he was when he moved to California.

"A car is just a bother. I mean, maybe one day a week I go to work and I see this little grazed glass on the street and it'll mean somebody's car has been broken into. We rented a car one night, we left it parked here and it was broken into. It was one of these minimum cars. There was nothing to it, nothing to steal. The guy, in fact, left a ballpoint pen. Maybe he wanted to sleep in it."

Cindy, who had been nodding her head in agreement with Larry, piped up that cars were indeed a hassle. "I've driven across country in a van," she said, "all the way to California and Mexico. I remember what a great relief it was to give up the car. One of the things I like about living in New York is that I don't have that ball and chain. For years I was very happy not to own a car until the public transportation went down the tubes. And the price of a bus ticket to take you out of New York City went sky-high. You wouldn't believe how much the bus cost. Just to go up to Hudson for the three of us costs almost two hundred dollars. It's really outrageous. You can rent a car cheaper. And that's what we do.

"But I long for the day when I leave New York City and can have a car again. I know how to drive. I've been driving since I was fifteen. I know about this American Dream. One of the things I wanted to hand down to my daughter was to teach her to drive. When we talk about moving out of New York, one of the advantages was to have her grow up as a driver. If you wait till you're twenty-five, it's awfully hard to learn how to drive. But I can't teach her how to drive in New York.

"She takes the subway every day to school and back, about five different trains, but I have an aversion to the subway. I went down to a parent/teacher conference today on the subway. It took forty-five minutes, which wasn't bad. But in the course of forty-five minutes a man with only one leg went by looking for money, a man selling a newspaper went by looking for money, great big stereo-looking people went by. I'm glad I don't have to ride it every day. I work right here in the neighborhood and I rarely go into the subway. I avoid it. And I've been living here for fifteen years now."

"They dug these subways a long time ago," Larry asserted. "They designed them on the cheap. They got dirtier and there was no way of cleaning them. Then they fell apart and they're not well maintained. The infrastructure in society is collapsing. Things are getting worse. The homeless people inhabit the subways. They sleep in the subways. They live in the tunnels. This is all fairly recent. The deterioration has accelerated. So only now is it becoming noticeably unpleasant.

"But then it's ridiculous to think of having a life under optimum conditions. It never existed before. Life has always been dangerous and filthy. Why are we in that damn war for cheap oil in the Persian Gulf? It's because we're so dependent on oil. The last scare before this one, some steps were taken to explore such things as solar power or alternative fuels. But Reagan changed it all. Reagan announced a new individualism. Morning comes to America. The idea was to drain the public treasury. To make social services impossible. To encourage rampant individualism on the part of the small people so that these large groups, these S and Ls, could sell junk bonds unregulated. It was a scam which this gullible public bought into. Because it seemed to promise them . . . God knows what. It didn't promise me anything. It allowed them to turn their backs on the chaos that the Vietnam War had brought. But you can't blame the Republicans for that one.

"I just think modern technological society has gone farther than we want to go. But we cannot stop the momentum of it. What will stop it is breakdown. It's hard for me to imagine what a decent life will be for Jessica. Maybe not Jessica. Maybe her kids. My parents were assured my life would be better than theirs. Boy, were they ever wrong."

ASPHALT COUNTRY

The western side of the Hudson Valley provided one of the most striking topographical contrasts in my travels. Just an hour north of the country's most dense and daunting metropolis stretched miles of pastoral farmland, small lakes, and forests. The natural beauty of New York's Orange County may be no surprise to the locals, but to me it delivered a much-needed dose of calm. I was on my way to meet a land-use and transportation planner in the village of Goshen. Committed to a leisurely pace, I avoided the New York State Thruway and cruised along Route 17, a mountain pass that wound along the western edge of Harriman State Park. I passed through a number of small towns where I occasionally caught a glimpse of cars and trucks speeding along the six-lane Thruway.

As I cruised down Main Street in central Goshen, there wasn't a crass shopping mall in sight. This was my idea of a classic village. Churches with steeples. Wooden storefronts. Brick houses. A stone courthouse. It was as if I had fallen asleep on the road and awakened in a Nathaniel Hawthorne novel. A town of 5,000, Goshen had as its main tourist attraction the Trotter Hall of Fame, a shrine to old horses and jockeys born to race at a leisurely pace. You could even take a stroll along the oval "Historic Track."

In Goshen's standard-issue county building, I rode a rickety elevator up to the second floor. There I met Fred Budde, the transportation planner, sitting in front of a computer, manipulating colorful grids and lines. Fred, thirty-three, a laid-back gent, suggested we grab a sandwich and talk at his house, a couple of miles away. Actually, his house, which we reached after driving a few hundred yards on a dirt road, was more like a cabin on a hill. Fred had grown up on Long Island, lived in Germany for a couple of years after college, and was now glad to call Goshen his home.

"This area right now is great for me," he said. "There's a variety of development patterns: a small village, rural lands, dairy farms. It's very pleasing. In the morning I jog past horse farms and dairy farms. Meanwhile, if I want to see a movie or go shopping, it's fifteen miles away in Walkill."

At work, Fred forecast the amount and whereabouts of new roads needed to service the industrial parks and shopping malls being planned and developed for Orange County. He also gauged new development's impact on existing roads, which usually meant suggesting more and wider lanes. Fred was a busy man. Blue Shield/Blue Cross had recently moved its regional headquarters to the area, and developers had just broken ground for ten million square feet of office and warehouse space in northerly Newburgh. "That project is going to produce thousands and thousands more cars on the road network," he said. "In fact, in my model, I'm supposed to subtract those people using mass transit. But I won't even bother because that number's so small."

Fred's models served only as advisories for developers and city commissions, leaving him with little actual power. He may predict gridlock and wetlands damage, but that wouldn't prevent developers and city-planning boards from running roughshod over his predictions, if not his principles. "I like to see areas keep their rural character," he said. "Growth should be predominantly kept within the village areas. The rural areas should be left green so we can keep our New England small-town atmosphere and not have this endless sea of shops and homes that you experience in the suburbs of Manhattan."

By law, Fred said, the only thing that could harness developers was a federally mandated EIS (environmental impact study). "If you can show that what they plan to do will have a detrimental effect on the environment, then you can get them to scale down their project." However, too often Fred had seen that process corrupted. Recently he reviewed an EIS for an 800,000-square-foot mall under construction in nearby Walkill. Yet the study wasn't conducted by an independent group but in essence by the developers themselves.

"That's a very common practice," he said. "The developers hire consultants that only write positive statements—not only positive, but they gloss over a lot of the negative aspects. In this case it was wetlands damage and flood control. They were going to fill in a wetland area. But because Walkill is pro-growth—you're talking about millions of dollars in taxes each year—the town is basically concerned with the impact to the roads of traffic. They're not concerned with wetlands and flood protection. The bottom line is, How many cars is it going to put on the roads, and is this amount of traffic going to stop development in other areas? That's all they're concerned with. And this is a big corporation. If they don't get their approvals from the city, they'll wait a certain time and fund the opposite political party that'll come into power and change the zoning for them. They've done it in the past.

"We're talking about a hundred-million-dollar mall. The developers are willing to give ten million in road infrastructure to the town. They'll build cloverleafs, widen roads, and even build a bridge over I-84 for access. We've been telling them that their zoning is just too intense, that the roads can't accommodate all this traffic in the future. But they want the ratables, they want that tax base. So they just keep going, stay the course, and haven't really listened to our recommendations.

"County government in New York doesn't have very much power. The town has the ultimate power. Nobody else can reprimand them. We have what we call 'Local Home Rule.' Each individual village, city, and town has the right to develop themselves. And each has their own separate political government. They don't get along for whatever reasons, it could be clashing personalities. So trying to get anything done is extremely difficult. It's very frustrating.

"Sometimes I think there is no effective land-use planning in this country. You go to Europe and the cities there have been around for hundreds of years. You travel from one city to another and you travel through rural areas. Why is that? Because people aren't permitted to develop their single-family homes and industry. It's just zoned for farming. But here, it's not only zoned for farming, it's developed for single-family developments. So you get sprawl, and I think the way things are now, sprawl is inevitable out here. It's just a matter of time. Even though we try through the environmental review process to slow it down. I guess my views aren't very optimistic."

Fred gave me a map and marked directions to the burgeoning areas he had been talking about, just in case I wanted to see them for myself. I thanked him for the map but ignored his directions. I'd seen industrial parks and malls before. Instead I headed back down Highway 17 to Bear Mountain State Park, crossed the Hudson River over a small bridge, and headed north to my next interview. It was rather depressing to think that this gorgeous land would soon be rampant with freeways, cars, and trucks. It wasn't hard to imagine how Long Islanders must have felt when Moses's expressways first began appearing in their rural front yards. But the times were different. For all his power and corruption, Moses really believed the automobile would usher in a better life. Pillager that he was, at least he functioned under a somewhat positive ideal. But what ideal did developers function under today? Must the pastoral Orange County and mountainous Putnam County that I now drove through really be stripped for another mall? Just how many Kinney's shoe stores did America need anyway? Moses wanted to open up the country to individuals. Today's exurban developers and city politicians were closing it off. Through their dubious properties and deals, their greed was transparent.

That evening I landed in the tiny town of Fishkill—or, more precisely, at the Fishkill Maximum Security Prison. I drove through the gates and crept up a windy unlighted road, where I found Superintendent Patrick McGann's brick red house amid a row of such houses on the prison grounds. Patrick greeted me wearing sweats and immediately put me at ease with his cordiality. So much for expecting a grim and stern prison warden type. "It's amazing you're here," he said. "I remember filling out your questionnaire and mailing it in. But I never thought anything would actually come of it."

Patrick was actually the deputy superintendent of administration. "The bean counter," he said. "A realist." He grew up in Illinois and had lived in various locations in upstate New York since he was fifteen. As a teenager he was a car fanatic. "I had a forty-nine Ford five-window coupe with a fifty-six Merc engine." He laughed. "I built the head, put on four-barrel carburetors, raced in the streets, cruised—the whole nine yards. I was Jimmy Dean." But those days were long gone. "The world's gotten more crowded, and the sense of freedom that we had has vanished, too. Now we tend to feel more confined. I had my love affair with cars, and even though I probably never traveled as far as I do now, I always had a sense that I could. Now, driving's only a hassle. There's nowhere you can go where it's fun, where it doesn't seem like the rest of the world wants to go at the same time."

Patrick graduated college with a degree in history and remained attuned to political currents. I asked him if he believed our country's ever-worsening traffic was linked to our land-use policies.

"I think there's no question about it. The way the land is developed in this country is dictated by our relationship with cars. I remember riding trolleys and trains when I was a kid in Illinois, in Chicago, Detroit, but they just don't exist anymore. And I think that's something this country has to address. When John Anderson ran for president, I thought he had one of the most sensible ideas, which was to subsidize mass transit and make it attractive for people.

"My parents live near Redlands [east of Los Angeles], which is in the middle of nowhere. The goddamn freeway is eight lanes wide and wall-to-wall traffic twenty-four hours a day. Out here, you can go as far north as Hudson, which is a hundred and twenty miles from New York City, and they're commuting to New York. When is it going to stop? Well, unless there's some dramatic change in our policy, nothing is going to stop. We're going to become an asphalt country."

I asked who should take the initiative in setting these types of policies in motion. "Just today at work we were talking about whether *anyone's* capable of taking initiatives of any kind in this country anymore," he said. "Not just on transportation issues but . . . We waffle on this war, we waffle on taxes and the economy. Everybody says, 'Not me, somebody else.' The old folks say, 'Don't hit Medicaid, don't hit Social Security.' The military-industrial complex says, 'We've got to have strong defense.' For what? Who knows anymore? Who the hell are we going to fight? But no one makes decisions anymore. Congress doesn't want to make decisions, all they want to do is pass blame. Make the Republicans the scapegoats or the Democrats the scapegoats. Who gets the blame? That's much more important to them than solving problems. That's the whole world.

"I just wish the government would recognize what's in this nation's interest. And one thing that's certainly not in our interest is relying on the Middle East for what amounts to our whole way of life. But the only people who are in a position to take initiative and show courage, and probably at the expense of their careers, are our politicians. They're the ones who can adopt and follow a policy that leads people into what's best for them. I can't see people being driven to change by themselves. I know I'm part of it. I make excuses about why I don't walk to work. The guy next door is my boss, I could ride with him. I'm probably as bad as the next guy about it. People have become so selfish that everything is OK as long as the other guy does it. So the only hope is the politicians, but I don't see them doing anything because they are so poll-oriented. If the wind blows in this direction, they do, too. But they're the only chance other than crisis. Somehow they must miraculously develop leadership.

Someone says, 'Listen, we've been screwing around too long, and over this horizon here there's going to be chaos if we don't do something. And that means we've got to raise your gasoline tax. We've got to siphon that money into encouraging you to ride a bus or a train instead of doing it the way you have been. We've got to make the trains attractive enough to you that it's worth your while.'

"I think there's a growing recognition that these things have to be done, and I think people would accept them. I really do."

In the meantime, drivers have to cope the best they can with today's traffic conditions. And demand change. Or so believes Brian Murphy, a sales and marketing "guru" based in southwestern Connecticut. I stayed the night in upstate New York, and leisurely made my way down the verdant corner of the Constitution State to Westport, where I met Brian in a cozy Italian restaurant. Born and raised in lower Connecticut, Brian, forty-one, was an incredibly direct man who boomed out matter-of-fact assessments of the state of driving in New York and the role of the government in transportation. As a teenager, Brian had cracked up his fair share of cars "playing chicken with telephone poles" and "thruway racing" with friends into New York. Today he still got a kick out of racing around—when the roads weren't jammed—in his eighty-eight Toyota Celica. He commuted regularly into and around New York City, putting over 30,000 miles a year on his car. Yes, the congestion was "horrendous," but he didn't let the stress get to him.

"Driving doesn't have a negative impact for me because I enjoy it," he declared. "My car is outfitted to be in traffic. I have the car phone, I have a great stereo system with separate speakers in the back. It's a convertible and it's got enough balls to make it worthwhile when you're on an interesting road. So when I'm in my car, I'm in a fairly relaxed environment. I'm not in a stressed-out environment because I'm in a Chevy Nova with an AM radio and all the other shit that goes along with it. If I'm in my car it could be just like being in bed. All I gotta do is pay attention to what's going on around me.

"Having the car phone is the biggest difference in the world. 'Cause you're instantly accessible. The biggest thing is when you get in a traffic jam or that kind of bullshit. Without a car phone you have that sense of frustration and isolation that there's no solution to what's happening to you right then and there. You're helpless. OK? You have a car phone and you're not helpless. You can call ahead and say you're going to be late so you relieve the stress of trying to get there on time. You can occupy your time by making other calls that you would normally have to wait until you got somewhere to make. So you relieve the stress of saying, 'Oh, God, even after I get outta this mess, I still got to do this and this.' So traffic's not time lost for me. Even if I get tired of doing business, I usually have a well-stocked supply of music."

In New York, Brian said, "you are defined by your car. Not to the extent as in L.A., where your personality is an *extension* of your car. It was interesting, the timing in my life, when I got the Celica. I was separated. I had nothing that was mine. I was living in a furnished bedroom apartment, I had a car that was leased, the lease was due up. I could do anything I wanted for the first time. I've always wanted a convertible and I've never gotten one. I've always been able to afford one since I've been an adult. There's certainly nothing that stopped me except probity and sanity. I finally realized that there's just no reason for me not to have one.

"All those boxy cars we've been driving for the last twenty years are part of the lie we tell ourselves. Which is that we're protecting the environment and economizing our resources. And we're telling ourselves that as we build the same cars now that use up just as much fuel as before, if not in the engine then in their accessories. It's society that's changed. It's become much more of a scared place to be. You know? Society is now designed around protecting people. That's much more of a focus than allowing people the opportunity to just do whatever they want to do. If you translate that down into automobiles, it's the idea that you don't need to go beyond fifty-five miles an hour because you might get hurt. Which, you know, that may or may not be true, but it has nothing to do with the actual flow of traffic and moving people efficiently from point A to point B. OK? It has to do with building square, boxy-looking cars, which we did for the past twenty to twenty-five years, and it's only recently that they're starting to look like cars again. It's doing things like talking about air bags as being something that is a necessity. I don't think it makes that much difference. It's all that kind of shit that doesn't really impact on things, but sounds good."

Government had nothing to do with helping people live better or more civil lives, Brian maintained. "You want to go to work and do whatever you do with a minimal amount of interference in your life. Government is a maximum amount of interference from the moment you wake up until the moment you go to bed. And really the only thing they should be doing is providing you with police protection and making sure that your ability to move from point A to point B is protected as long as you're not impacting on other people. That's about all the government should do. But they don't.

"There's no question that we have a transportation crisis. We have bridges collapsing, people driving into the water. In Greenwich, Connecticut, of all places. Probably the richest town in the United States. The Mianus River Bridge collapsed. People didn't know it because it was nighttime, and eighteen cars went *vrrp*, right off the edge. That's why you have no more tolls on the Connecticut highway. Because that was the government's way of saying, 'Oh, I'm sorry. Here, we'll get rid of the tolls.' New York City? That whole infrastructure is just crumbling, period. I'm not talking about services just breaking down. I'm talking about physically crumbling. It's ridiculous trying to move around in New York. And I don't care whether you use public or private transportation, it's equally as ridiculous. It's horrible in New York. Just horrible. The whole thing. I mean, the city does not work, period. It just does not work. End of story.

"OK, driving in Manhattan can be a challenge. If I'm in an aggressive mood and want to kick the shit out of somebody, that's as good a way to do it as any. But mostly it's not worth it. It's just not. The emotional price you pay is too severe. The subways? You could die, and that's not from accidents. Taking the subways is a crapshoot. I have the same feeling taking the subway as I used to have when I used to go hang out in low-rent bars looking for fights. You know, scuzzball bars. If you go in there looking for a fight, you usually find one. Well, on the subway I have that same attitude.

"Here's my thoughts on where we're at, OK? I think that over the next decade U.S. society as a whole will have gone beyond the crisis point to where the American population has no choice but to react and do something. I don't know exactly how that'll be defined, but it will be. There'll be a convulsive change of sorts. Because things are at that point where they're just not working, and I think transportation is just another symptom of that. Whether we're talking about airline transportation, whether we're talking about local transportation, whether we're talking about the infrastructure of the highway system. None of it is working.

"When we go through that convulsive change and make our government responsive to ourselves again, the problem will probably be addressed, because it has to be a government-solved solution. But it's gonna take something like what Eisenhower did in the fifties. It's gonna take a federal mandate. It's gonna take selling it to the American public on why it's important."

Brian was unresolved about what he could do personally to alleviate the problems of driving. Sure, he could drive less, but the impact would be negligible. He was willing to buy a fuel-efficient car—no problem there. In fact, he said, put whatever you need on the car to make it environmentally sound. "I'll pay the price. I think I'm benign towards the environment. As I become aware of things I shouldn't do, I don't do them. But would I give up the car? No, I wouldn't do that. That's ridiculous. The trade-off of freedom is just too big. And that's the name of that tune."

With evening I got on the New England Thruway and headed back to Manhattan. As I drove south through Westchester County, I watched the mass exodus headed north. An avalanche of cars and trucks poured out of New York City on every road in sight. It was as if a nuclear power plant had erupted downtown and now everyone was getting out of there as fast as they could. Only, of course, they weren't moving fast at all, while I was motoring along fairly briskly. That is, until I got to the Cross-Bronx Expressway, which was a frozen mass of steel and rubber in both directions. Finally I emerged in Manhattan, where I crept along the West Side Highway and back into the Village. My friend, Sean, reading the fatigue on my face, offered me a drink. "So how was your trip out of the city?" he asked. All I could think of was, "Another day in America."

FINAL EXIT

Everyone I met in Manhattan, either professionally or socially, told me that the only reason for owning a car in Manhattan was to get out. Daily affairs on the island were easily managed on the subways or by walking. "As I go about my normal routine the car is the furthest thing from my mind," said native New Yorker Gregg Geller, forty-three, who lived on Manhattan's Upper West Side. "I don't know anybody who lives here in town and drives to work. It's crazy, and it's impractical. The only reason I submit myself to the pains of having a car is to escape." But the real pain wasn't only the traffic. To own a car in Manhattan was to suffer the unceasing nightmare known as parking. There are four times as many cars as there are parking spaces, creating a constant scramble to bring your car to a legal rest. Like

Gregg, most residents pay on the average of $500 a month to keep their beasts in a private garage. However, the scarcity of parking is gold to the city, whose coffers are stuffed with $25 million a month from parking tickets. In 1991, drivers in New York City received 13.2 million of the nasty slips.

Furthermore, no Manhattan drivers are busier than those behind the wheels of tow trucks. On the average they haul in four hundred illegally parked cars a day, resulting in another $17 million in annual city revenues. Nor do the city's legion of parking cops and tow operators discriminate. Tourists in rented Ford Tempos, cab and limousine drivers, pizza delivery drivers, telephone company repairmen—anyone and everyone—are fair game on Manhattan's streets. To make matters worse, parking on many residential streets is ruled off-limits at certain times of day due to street cleaning or alternate rights-of-way for traffic. I was warned to study the rules posted on street signs. You don't want to end up in the tow yard, I was told.

The next morning marked the end of my personal interviews. I had been on the road a long time, exploring America's driving ecosystems, excited and practically overwhelmed by all the people I had met. I was looking forward to returning to my own niche in the San Francisco Bay Area and assembling my findings. My drive home would be relatively peaceful, a private appreciation of the nation's interstates and environs. I walked out to Hudson Street to retrieve the Caravan to begin packing it up.

But it was gone. A dirty white Honda Accord sat in its place. The night before I had done my duty and read the closest street sign, which was a block away. It was like deciphering a tax form, but I was sure I'd figured it out and was legally parked. But what's this near where I was parked? A bare pole. I looked down and read the sign lying on the ground. Indeed, this block would be cleaned this morning. I had been towed.

I called the Violation Tow Pound and read the guy my license number. "Yeah, we got it. A hundred and fifty bucks. Forty bucks more for the ticket." Great. I grabbed my checkbook and hailed a cab to West Thirty-eighth Street and Twelfth Avenue. Behind a chain-link fence topped with barbed wire stood a huge warehouse attached to a white bungalow trailer. I walked along a cement path, gave my license number to a sentry—who flipped through a thick stack of pages—and followed his pointing finger to the trailer. There were three roped-off lines of people waiting to approach a row of clerks sitting behind bulletproof windows. And the lines were long, real long. The next thing I noticed was a big sign on the chintzy paneled wall: CASH ONLY. I made a quick about-face. Another cab. An automatic teller machine. Back to the pound. The sentry waved me through. "Happens all the time," he said.

Now the lines seemed longer, the trailer utterly cramped with humanity. I got in the information line. Having your car towed knew no socio-economic divisions. A man in a three-piece suit waited next to a woman in a postal uniform. A truck mechanic in a greasy jumpsuit restlessly paced behind a young woman in designer jeans. It was a melting pot of races. But there was one thing everybody had in common: a foul mood. Everybody in Manhattan is in a bad mood already, but this was a veritable crucible of dismal feelings. Twisted faces told the story. No one wanted to be here. They were missing work, losing money, falling behind on projects. A buzz of angry phrases boiled out of people's mouths: "This sucks"; "God, I just want to get out of here"; "Two hundred dollars!"; "Shit, why didn't you tell me I had to be in that line"; "There's nowhere to park in this goddamn city." Every new person who walked in sighed the same mantra: "Oh, man, this is ridiculous." The grim buzz was momentarily broken when a young woman bubbled to one of the clerks, "Oh, I'm so glad. I thought my car was stolen. But it was only towed." Derisive laughter filled the stale air of the room. "Tourists," somebody muttered.

At the information window I showed the clerk my driver's license and received a form verifying the van was mine. Then I joined the tail end of the other snaking line to pay my $190. There were four windows for collecting money, but only one had a clerk. The other three windows taunted us with their vacancy, driving aggravation deeper into our chests. "They do it to punish us," a guy behind me said. I was sweating. A Middle Eastern man rushed into the room, slipping out of a policeman's grip. He was yelling. "Let me go! Why did you tow my car? You got no right! You took it from my wife. She was in the store. She was just in the store. You can't do this!" The policeman was losing his patience, trying to explain to the man that he was double-parked. The man wouldn't believe him and continued to stomp around and scream. "I got no money! Where am I gonna get two hundred dollars? I'm going to get a gun and shoot somebody. I'm going to. I'll shoot them and rob them. That's the only way!" Finally the cop dragged the man outside. Meanwhile, a woman and her boyfriend were arguing with the clerk in the complaint line. The complaint clerks were stationed in booths protected not only by bulletproof glass but by steel bars. The couple insisted their car was illegally towed, and therefore they couldn't be forced to pay their outstanding parking tickets to claim it. Five hundred dollars was robbery. Unable to win their battle, they shoved aside the people behind them and stormed out, smacking the walls. "This is fucked!" yelled the woman. "You're all fucked! I'm getting a lawyer!"

I was beginning to lose my breath. I fully expected anything to happen. I was ready to hit the ground if someone came back waving a gun. "Ain't New York grand?" cracked a twentyish guy behind me. "You live here?" someone asked him. "Are you kidding?" he answered. "I would never live in this hellhole." I expected some of the locals to give him grief, but no one cared. They just wanted the whole ordeal to be over.

Finally, for me, it was. I paid, followed the painted arrow on the warehouse floor to my van, and rejoined the traffic on West Thirty-eighth Street along the dirty riverfront. Now I truly understood what people meant when they said that having a car in New York City was absurd. By their sheer numbers, cars had killed their primary value as a convenient means of mobility. They had become obsolete.

Manhattan was the final exit for me—and the rest of the country. Every urban transportation system through which I had traveled appeared headed toward a similar state of ecological ruin, leaving drivers to suffer the consequences. The freedom machine that had helped make America the land of the limitless frontier had become a daily curse to America's quality of life. Chaos reigned. It was madness. And besides, the whole situation tended to make people a bit *uptight*.

How were we supposed to regain our wholeness and peace of mind? Who was actively managing America's transportation ecosystem anyway; who was going to guide it back to health and stability? What steps were being taken to assure that we weren't going to further pollute our land and planet, that we weren't all going to end up basket cases from the traffic nightmares, that we'd have a chance to live in areas undaunted by endless asphalt and ugly ticky-tacky, get-rich-quick suburban sprawl? My field investigations had come to an end. These were questions I would now take to the experts in their respective laboratories in the auto industry, government, and universities.

Just as soon as I got off this damn West Side Highway.

PART III

QUESTIONS

OF

BALANCE

Eight

W h o ' s
D r i v i n g
W h o m

If you ain't the lead horse, the scenery never changes.
—Thomas McGuane, *Keep the Change*

U rban planners and environmentalists all have a favorite analogy for the calamity of cars and driving. At least the ones I spoke to did. In fact, it got to the point that whenever they would begin a sentence "Have you heard about . . . ?" I nodded yes, because I knew they were going to tell me about ecologist Garrett Hardin's 1968 essay "The Tragedy of the Commons."

Hardin's study focuses on the fate of the medieval commons, or public pastures. Ancient farmers brought their cows and goats to the commons to graze, and as long as the population remained low, there was no problem. But as more farmers brought more herds to the commons, the pasture became overgrazed, and everybody was eaten out of house and home. Hardin's point was that satisfying short-term goals defeated long-term prosperity. Furthermore, no one person seeking to act for the benefit of all could make a difference. For as soon as one socially minded farmer brought one less cow to the commons, his neighbor would bring one more. And why not? It was downright irrational to let a patch of the pasture sit there ungrazed. "Therein is the tragedy," wrote Hardin. "Each man is locked into a system that compels him to increase his herd without limit—in a world that is limited. Ruin is the destination toward which all men rush, each pursuing his own best interest in a society that believes in the freedom of the commons."

In the driving ecosystem, it's our freedom machines that are bringing ruin to the commons. Martin Wachs, UCLA urban planning professor, explained the tragedy. "The air we have in Los Angeles is a common. It's free and we are destroying it. But as soon as I say, 'I'm going to get on a bicycle and sweat my way to work,' somebody else is going to say, 'There's less congestion, I can drive now!' So it makes no sense for me to do that in the public interest. I certainly am not going to get in a bus today and spend two hours making a commute downtown for the sake of the environment when I know that if a thousand or even fifty thousand people did that, the result would be the street would be less congested and other people would say, 'Oh, the street's less congested, let's go use it!' " And of course people do, which substantiates countless studies that new highways fill up with cars almost as quickly as the cement is laid.

Hardin believed that averting tragedy would result from realizing that "freedom is the recognition of necessity"—that is, realizing we must curb certain freedoms to sustain a healthy ecosystem—and accepting the need for "mutual coercion." As I discovered on my journey, American drivers have evolved in accord with Hardin on both counts. They recognize the necessity for change and that some form of mutual coercion is needed to keep our cities and spirits from further ruin. Their changing attitude toward cars, from vehicles of pleasure and convenience to vehicles of anxiety and pollution, constitutes a historical cultural force. It's no small revelation to hear former L.A. street-racer Neal Meisenheimer admit, "There's no pleasure in driving anymore because the streets are so crowded. There is not enough room for the cars." But it's not just in Los Angeles where drivers realize the public lands and skies are under siege from the auto herds. It's in Dallas, where cowboy cop Lloyd Richey, worrying about the oxygen, declared that he was "for anything that can be done, within reason, to solve gasoline-burning cars"; it's in Cherokee, North Carolina, where park ranger Tom Robbins fretted that the air over the Smoky Mountains, tainted with auto emissions, was turning brown "like a ring around a tub"; it's in Atlanta, where bus driver Mike Hawkins said, "There's just too many people and not enough roadway"; and it's in New York, where taxi driver Nabil Lakah felt that the traffic and air pollution were literally killing him. If things have to "go to a crisis before this democracy reacts," as J. D. Power said, then the time to react is now.

Drivers are ready to react but are frustrated because they view the auto industry and the government as permanently stalled. Perhaps Patrick McGann, of upstate New York, best summarized drivers' desperation with traffic and pollution when he rhetorically asked, "When is it going to stop? Well, unless there's some dramatic change in our policy, nothing is going to stop. We're going to become an asphalt country. Is anyone capable of taking initiatives of any kind in this country anymore?" Nearly everyone I interviewed decried the ineffectiveness of our elected leaders, yet they hadn't entirely lost faith in a democratic solution. In the land of the automobile, they believed *something* could be done to preserve our common resources, they just wanted to know what. Who *was* in charge, anyway? The carmakers? Scientists? Politicians?

My next journey began in search of answers. I now planned to examine just how we as a nation are attempting to manage the driving ecosystem back to health and stability. Of course, industry, technology, and government are interdependent forces, and more often than not, at war with one another. So I packed my bags and flew into the most embattled zone of them all: Detroit.

UNDER SIEGE

There's no escaping that this city is the dominion of the automotive industry. The first thing that grabbed my attention driving from the airport in a shiny white rented Ford Tempo was a gargantuan Uniroyal tire that dwarfed a grove of wintry trees. The next thing I noticed was a massive electronic Goodyear billboard displaying gold digits ticking off how many cars were produced in Detroit so far that year. It was at 10,112,566. Downtown's sparsely populated avenues of hotels and retail stores seemed confined under the shadow of the boxy brown General Motors Building. I half expected to meet car executives dressed in wool suits and bow ties talking about Eisenhower and the beauties of six-inch Cadillac fins. But I knew better.

When I was in New York, Maryann Keller, Wall Street auto industry analyst and author of *Rude Awakening*, a critical book on General Motors, told me I would be surprised by the executives and engineers I would meet in Detroit. "The misconception that a lot of people have of the auto industry is thirty years old," she said. "It's not an industry run by the backward thinking that ran it then. It's run today by people who are just slightly older than baby boomers, people who have had social experiences that are similar to our own. They are very realistic about the social problems caused by the car."

Keller was right. I never got the impression from the engineers and managers I met that the domestic industry—led by General Motors—operated in a social vacuum. They weren't building huge cars with blind arrogance toward consumers and the environment anymore; on the contrary, they felt Congress, consumer groups, and environmentalists were now the arrogant ones. In fact, the automakers felt so besieged by regulatory demands that they seemed to have adopted an inferiority complex. They believed Detroit was being singled out as the nation's source of pollution because it was an easy target. "When you attack the automobile industry you don't attack really many voters," offered Marv Jackson, GM automotive emissions control engineer, one afternoon in the environmental activities building of the carmaker's Technical Center. Because Detroit is situated in the middle of the country, lawmakers in California and Washington can slap regulations on the auto industry without fear of voter reprisal. "So when they do something, they're not doing it to themselves, they're doing it to Michigan," added Tom Darlington, GM's senior projects engineer. Gerald Stofflet, GM's assistant director of automotive emissions control, gave me a drawing that best captured Detroit's view of the outside world. It featured a car with "U.S. Auto Industry" painted on its side crushed under an avalanche of rocks that read "New Clean Air Act," "New Fuel Economy Standards," "Air Bags," and "California Emission Standards."

So, yes, the domestic auto industry is very realistic in confronting what is being asked of them; they just don't accept the feasibility of the regulations. But they're a well-buttressed opponent, ready for any and all challenges. They're well aware that the Sierra Club took out a full-page ad in the *New York Times* calling them "irresponsible" and blaming them for America's profligate use of oil; they know California senator Barbara Boxer has said that increasing automobile fuel efficiency "would provide a host of environmental benefits, including . . . a significant reduction in carbon dioxide emissions, the leading contributor to global warming"; but, above

all, they are positively bristling to defend themselves against Nevada senator Richard Bryan's pending legislation—supported by all major environmental groups—to improve the CAFE (corporate average fuel economy)
standard of each manufacturer's full line of cars from today's 27.5 miles per
gallon to 40 by 2001. Bryan insists his bill will "save more than four times
the amount of oil we were importing from Iraq and Kuwait before the
invasion," save consumers money on gasoline, and keep the U.S. auto
industry competitive with the fuel-efficient vehicles rolling out of Japan.

Mentioning Senator Bryan's name in Detroit is like watching Jose
Canseco step into the batter's box at Tiger Stadium: instant derision fills the
air. Engineers especially love to point out that the Democratic senator
drives an Oldsmobile 88, which gets less than twenty miles per gallon. In
other words, they say, it's fine for him to drive a behemoth gas-guzzler just as
long as everybody else risks death on the highway in a fuel-efficient "tin
box" like a Geo Metro. Beyond making all of their cars smaller and lighter,
the engineers insist that the technology simply doesn't exist to meet the
standards in Bryan's bill. "If there was something out there like the two-
hundred-mile carburetor—which everybody thinks we've got locked up in
a barn someplace—if that were really true, we'd put it on," said Stofflet,
who has often testified before Congress on behalf of GM. "But there isn't
one piece of technology that's going to get us anywhere near the numbers
they've got in the legislation."

"There's two ways to get better overall fuel economy," said Darlington,
who worked for the U.S. Environmental Protection Agency for nine years
on fuel economy and auto emission problems before joining the private
sector. "One, start making a lot more Geo Metros and trying to get people
to buy them. The other way is to make improvements on the cars that
people want to buy, either by reducing weight or by downsizing the engine
and performance. But people don't like to buy cars with poor performance,
and the main thing is, we've got to worry about being able to sell cars."

Twenty-five miles away, in Dearborn, they're worried about the same
thing. In fact, Dave Kulp, Ford's manager of fuel economy planning,
declared that Bryan's bill would force Ford to stop selling certain cars altogether. "The only way we know of to meet forty miles per gallon is to drop
our Crown Victoria, Grand Marquis, and reduce the sales of some of our
midsize and sports versions," he told me. "So OK, Bryan's people say that
maybe it's not in the picture for people to have big cars. But the question is,

if we don't want people to have that kind of car, why tell us? We're in the business of satisfying the marketplace. Don't give the middleman the message."

Therein lay the gist of the carmakers' opposition to regulation, to both a higher CAFE standard and to the 1990 Clean Air Act mandate to reduce polluting emissions by as much as 60 percent by the year 2000. They believe Washington is causing them to lose billions of dollars by forcing them to create costly new devices that make their popular cars gutless, expensive, and less attractive to customers. Furthermore, they say, with gas prices at little more than a dollar a gallon, there's nothing they can do to coax customers into lighter and more fuel-efficient cars. "Our CAFE is going to stay where it's at because of the market conditions," said Stofflet. "The customer has no incentive to go to a smaller car because he can do all the driving he wants in a bigger car and it doesn't affect him in the pocketbook."

At least it seemed GM employees did all the driving they wanted in big cars. I only mention this because every time I went to a different building inside GM's sprawling Tech Center, which is actually located a little north of Detroit in Warren, I was driven by communications and marketing man Jack Dinan in his boatlike Chevrolet Caprice. A thirty-six-year veteran of GM, the smooth-talking Dinan was as friendly as your favorite uncle and always dressed in dark blue suits, his silver cuff links glittering at the edges of his sleeves. Leaving the environmental activities building, I told Jack I wouldn't mind walking along the small lake to my next interview, that I rather liked the cold brisk air. "Don't be silly," he said. "Get in." And so we took a thirty-second ride to the research engineering lab.

There I met Dr. Robert A. Frosch, vice president in charge of GM's research laboratories. Before he came to GM in 1982, Dr. Frosch was assistant secretary of the navy for research and development and assistant executive director of the United Nations Environment Programme. Seated in a spacious office overlooking the lake, he adopted a philosophic look at the free market. "If the customer asks for, or doesn't ask for, something, then the industry is likely to be responsive," he said. "Now, the government steps in as a surrogate for what customers do or don't ask for. It says customers should have the sense to ask for emission controls but customers don't have the sense to ask for emission controls, so we will represent the social customer, so to speak, and ask for emission controls.

"Why on earth would you do that? Why would any company suddenly say, 'We're going to spend money to put a thing on our car which the customers won't know is there, and wouldn't care about if it was there'? Unless you can create a competitive advantage out of this, why on earth would anybody want to do it?"

"Doesn't GM have a social responsibility?" I asked.

"Yes, GM has a social responsibility. The question is, how can it go about exercising it? And suicide is not one of the better methods. It's easy for people like Ralph Nader—who's one of the more ignorant people in the U.S.—to say, 'Oh, well, you guys get people to do things by advertising.' You can't advertise people into anything. Nobody's ever been terribly successful in getting people to pay attention to things they didn't think were in their own interest. So to what extent can a single business get away with being a social leader? I guess the answer is, it can be a leader when there is a reasonable possibility of followership. The green movement in the U.S. keeps being announced, but it hasn't made it to an informed consumerism yet. It's like, 'Is he coming, Sister Ann?' 'Well, yes, I see the dust. I think I see the dust.' "

Dr. Frosch then seemed to contradict himself. "Look, you could have done customer surveys till you were blue in the face in the fifties, and nobody would have asked for an automatic transmission. Who ever heard of an automatic transmission? You shifted gears. The instant there was an automatic transmission, everybody said, 'Oh, how nice.' And it was a great success. But we spend a lot of time inventing things customers didn't know they wanted. We do that with safety. I think the problem with safety and emissions was, going back to the fifties and sixties, nobody was asking for it. Why would the research and development people be thinking about safety if nobody else was thinking about it? Some of it is leadership, I suppose. Somebody does stand up and says, 'This is important,' and everybody agrees."

"Well," I said, "the car's impact on air quality and its massive oil consumption are pretty important. Yet it seems like the only ones who are standing up and saying anything are groups like the Sierra Club and Natural Resources Defense Council."

"Yes, and I've talked to them. And some of them are perfectly sensible people, but en masse they're as crazy as we are, if not worse. I've talked to people from the NRDC, and they're a little bit mad, they're just a little ideologically mad. But I guess I don't think the air quality problem now and in the coming decades should be as high on the list of big national problems as it's been elevated to. My feeling, quite frankly, is L.A. is going to be unmanageable. I don't know what to do but recognize it. That's my complaint with NRDC. I don't think it has dawned on them, or it hasn't publicly dawned on them, that they are facing a problem that may not be solvable, in the sense they would like to solve it, namely, that every day is a beautiful day in L.A. But then I can find some car buffs in this business who are a little bit ideologically mad about automobiles. It's all right. But neither of them should be allowed to set national policy because they stand up and yell."

"Which is why we have elected leaders who represent various interests," I said. "Yet all you seem to do is yell at one another."

"Well, I think there's a historical reason. And the historical reason was that it started as an adversarial battle. It was never cast as, 'Hey, we have a national problem.' It still isn't cast as, 'Hey, we have a national problem, let's get everybody who knows something in the room and see if we can together figure out what to do.' It was cast as, 'You've done it wrong. We're going to fix you.' And of course what did we say? We said, 'Hey, not us.' And what's happened is that the argument has gotten so polarized that Congress says, 'Well, we don't trust those guys, so we're going to make these regulations more stringent.' And we tend to say, 'Well, there's no sense in telling them what we can do because they'll triple it and then double it for their amusement.' And nobody will believe what it is we can actually do or what's feasible.

"So, you know, it's gotten crazy. This is the whole style of social regulation in the U.S. And, well, it's not overregulation. It's just stupid regulation."

DENIAL AND INVENTION

But wait a minute. Looking back at the recent history of regulations reveals that the regulations are not stupid at all. In fact, they have been tremendously successful in protecting the environment. Examined as catalysts of new technology, they undermine many of the myths that Detroit continues to foster about itself.

Following the 1973–74 Arab oil embargo, Washington figured it better do something about conserving energy. People were also mighty sick of waiting in long gas lines, so the social climate was ripe for political action. In 1975 President Ford signed into law the Energy Policy and Conservation Act, which spawned the CAFE standard. In 1974, American cars on the average sucked down a gallon of gas for every 13 miles; or, to take a more global view, they consumed one out of every seven barrels of oil produced in the world. The Energy Act ruled that automotive fuel efficiency must gradually reach 27.5 miles per gallon by 1985. The industry balked—GM president Elliott Estes declared that "fuel economy standards are not necessary and they are not good for America"—but it didn't dare invoke the social stigma or financial penalty of noncompliance. Already struggling to reduce polluting emissions by 90 percent, as mandated by Senator Edmund Muskie's amendments to the 1970 Clean Air Act, research and development departments kicked into overdrive to meet the new CAFE law.

Initially, the carmakers didn't know how to bend their fleets to the regulations other than by downsizing, so, as J. D. Power said, "they chopped two feet out of the center of the car, put these two big axles closer together," and voilà!—the Gremlin. Yet by the end of the seventies, the regulations had spawned two major technological breakthroughs in reducing emissions and achieving better mileage in cars regardless of size: the PCV valve and the catalytic converter. David Cole, director of the Office for the Study of Automotive Transportation at the University of Michigan, called these breakthroughs the industry's "big hits" of the seventies. He assured me that "most of the improvements we have seen from the standpoint of clean air were really prompted by the laws. So regulation has been a major factor in technology."

Throughout the next decade, executives denied the feasibility of environmental regulations almost as quickly as engineers proved they could meet them. The big hits of the eighties were front-wheel drive, which made cars substantially lighter, and microprocessor-controlled fuel systems and transmissions, which allowed gasoline to be converted to power more efficiently. Together these led to cleaner-burning and better-mileage cars in every weight class and size. However, never ceasing to complain, Ford and GM executives managed to convince the Reagan administration to roll back the CAFE standard from 27.5 to 26 miles per gallon in 1986, though the 27.5 goal was reinstated for 1990.

Anyway, thanks to regulations and fine engineering, new cars rolling off the line in 1990 spewed out nearly 90 percent less polluting emissions than their brethren in 1970. In addition, U.S. petroleum consumption today is over 2 million barrels lower per day than it would have been if fuel economy hadn't improved since 1975. It shouldn't go without mentioning that cars today hug the road more firmly, brake more smoothly, get more horsepower per weight, accelerate better, and are 50 percent safer than their clunker ancestors of two decades ago. It won't win me any status points with teenagers whose idea of cool is a sixty-five Ford Mustang, but this boring Ford Tempo I'm driving around is a better car in every respect. It is more comfortable and pleasant to drive, and in the relative long run it will last a whole lot longer.

So why are we stuck in neutral? Why have we frozen the CAFE standard at 27.5, and why are the carmakers, their political allies, and deep-pocket lobbyists battling the new air quality regulations, especially the strict ones hatched in California, with all their might and millions? Didn't the auto industry just prove over the last two decades that it could meet environmental regulations in cars that customers liked? Well, as I discovered, old habits are hard to break.

BLAME IT ON THE CUSTOMER

First of all, today's automakers are well aware that their credibility is shot to hell because they were able to meet regulations that they initially resisted. Yet, they argue, take a closer look at what technological achievement actually meant. It meant rushing cars into production that, although they satisfied the regulations, weren't exactly built to last. "If you look back in history, from '77 to '84, we met the emissions law, but boy did we pay for it," said Stofflet, GM's auto emissions director. "We hurried up and got the car out, it met the emission standards, it passed the test, but we recalled one bunch of cars. Today we have really improved our emissions, but those first seven years really cost us." And whose fault was that? Why, the customer, who "has no obligation to maintain" his or her car, to keep the engine tuned and therefore running cleaner. So naturally when EPA retested the cars after 30,000 miles, they didn't meet the emission standards and had to be recalled.

As Stofflet saw it, customers also derailed better fuel efficiency. In 1980, in a state of confusion over the energy crisis, GM estimated that gasoline would cost $2.50 a gallon by 1985. Therefore the company retooled its factories to build a mix of cars that would achieve thirty miles per gallon by 1985. (Ford, too, laid plans to achieve the same fuel efficiency by the same year.) When 1985 rolled around, though, GM had lost over $500 million in closed plants and 18,000 people were out of work. Stofflet related that the plants closed because after GM retooled them to build more fuel-efficient cars—which meant junking the Chevy Malibu for a new model called the Cavalier and opening a second plant to produce more bantamweight Chevettes—neither car sold. Why? Well, GM was forced to outfit the family-size Cavalier with an efficient four-cylinder engine, but customers rejected the car because, as Stofflet said, it didn't "get up and go." The Chevette failed because in the wake of the energy crisis, "fuel prices fell, and people just didn't want them anymore."

The poor customer, blamed for everything. What Stofflet neglected to mention, but what Keller documents in her book on GM, was that the Cavalier and the Chevette failed not because regulations robbed them of power and prestige but because they "failed in quality." While GM blamed fluctuating gas prices and government regulations for its poor sales, Honda and Toyota, subject to the exact same economic conditions and regulations, were drawing customers into showrooms by the droves. Their four-cylinder cars had plenty of get-up-and-go. "Contrary to popular belief within GM," writes Keller, "most consumers now expected good performance and high quality to be standard features on their cars. The Japanese had taught them to demand that."

Japanese competition definitely kicked the Big Three into high gear, and most industry experts agree that the carmakers were producing quality cars by 1990 in the Ford Taurus, Chevy Lumina, and Plymouth Acclaim. Not incidentally, these family-size cars all get about thirty miles per gallon, and were designed to do so at a time when gas prices remained stable. The point is that when pushed, Detroit can build a full line of cars that meet the fuel economy and emissions regulations. Yes, that's true, said GM's Stofflet, "but we can't go any further." Added Jack Dinan, "All the great leaps have already been made. Now we're just ticking it away a tenth of a mile and down as new technologies emerge." Well, given Detroit's intransigent history, given the fact that in the mid-eighties it jettisoned its plans of achieving a CAFE of thirty-nine miles per gallon by 2000, it's awfully hard to accept that new technologies will just emerge without pressure from outside the industry. Besides, many respected independent engineers maintain that the carmakers can reach a higher CAFE standard by the end of the century with technology available today.

DEFLATING THE MYTHS

In 1989, engineers from the U.S. Department of Energy and the respected independent firms Energy and Environmental Analysis Inc. and Oak Ridge National Laboratory stated in a joint report that "using technology already included in manufacturers' production plans and based on consumers' willingness to pay for increased fuel economy, domestic mpg could be increased . . . to 31.6 mpg in 1995 without reducing vehicle size or performance from 1987 levels." The engineers also maintained that the "maximum fuel economy achievable without changing market mix [the amount of each different-size car a manufacturer offers for sale] or performance in 2000 is 39.4." The engineers estimate that this high mileage would cost customers $756 more per car than the going price in 1987. It is this study on which the Bryan bill is based. The Detroit engineers were quick to remind me that in 1991 Energy and Environmental Analysis Inc. lowered its estimate for 2001 to 36.8, while Bryan remains focused on 40 miles per gallon. Still, even at 36.8, we'd save over 2 million barrels of gasoline a day in comparison to 1991, and substantially reduce greenhouse gases. And do so while Beverly Hills matrons still cruise to the dry cleaner's in their Cadillac Broughams.

Suffice it to say, Detroit's engineers claim that independent studies may play well with members of Congress courting the environmental vote but have little to do with building cars people actually want. They argue that available technology—such as four-valve cylinders, continuously variable automatic transmissions, plastic side panels that reduce weight, and aerodynamic styling—may all increase fuel efficiency, but their overall impact on big cars is minimal and would not raise the overall CAFE substantially. However, in 1992, the National Academy of Sciences issued a report claiming that with existing technology big cars could indeed reach 33 miles per gallon. So once again you have Detroit speaking through its big-car mentality, seasoned through years of reaping higher profits on luxury cars. Ford, for instance, pulls in a nice $10,000 on a $30,000 Lincoln, whereas it makes a measly grand on a $10,000 Escort.

Yet there is another part to the automakers' CAFE defense, which perhaps forms the most pervasive myth. "The majority of the environmentalists brush away the safety issue," declared Stofflet. "If you wanted to reach thirty-nine miles per gallon you'd have an average fleet of two thousand, two hundred and thirty pounds, which is in the neighborhood of a Geo Metro." And that would mean some serious carnage on the highways. As usual, Jack Dinan's retort was more colorful. "Environmentalists always ask, 'Why can't you develop a safe two-thousand-pound car?' Then you remind them. 'Did you happen to watch the Redskins-Giants game on Sunday? Did you see that two-hundred-and-ninety-pound tackle hit that poor little son of a bitch that weighs one sixty-five and drive him ten yards?' The laws of physics still apply."

However, the Center for Auto Safety, an independent research group in Washington, D.C., proves that the laws of physics do not apply to CAFE, that fuel efficiency does not mean a landscape of Geo Metros turned upside down like turtles. Just as cars' fuel efficiency has increased 100 percent since 1975 and polluting emissions have been reduced by 90 percent, traffic fatalities have decreased by 40 percent. According to the Washington group, the correlation between CAFE and safety has little to do with sheer tonnage. The safety researchers demonstrate that less fatalities and accidents have resulted while cars have become substantially lighter. Better safety is due not to an army of Chrysler New Yorkers on the road but to technological improvements such as front padding, head restraints, steering assemblies, and antilock brakes in all size cars. "The laws of physics do not say small cars cannot be made safe, they just say good engineering must be used to make them safe," the report argues. In the early nineties, good engineering has resulted in new safety features such as improved roof strength and upper lining, air bags, antilock brakes, and padded interiors. The study concludes that with utilization of advanced safety and fuel economy technologies, "CAFE levels of 45 mpg can be attained by 2001 without any shift to smaller cars" and, despite the increase in population and miles driven, "fatalities and injuries will be ten percent lower than current levels."

THE CONSUMER MYTH

Despite mounting evidence to the contrary, the automakers continue to propagate the myth that fuel efficiency can be attained only in small cars.

In the early nineties, as part of its lobby against a higher CAFE standard, Detroit sank $20 million into an advertising campaign to link fuel efficiency to only small cars. The campaign is further proof that the automakers do not want to mess with their lucrative large-car market. And, they argue, why should they? If customers were so concerned about the environment they would buy more Geo Metros, which represent less than 1 percent of GM's sales. I'm certain everyone I met in the auto industry would agree with Maryann Keller's statement that "people are motivated by economics. They may talk about altruistic reasons, but the point of fact is they're motivated by economics. They bought smaller cars because gasoline was expensive, not because they want to save energy." The engaging Keller said she was not blind to the environment but could not turn away from what she saw as the national purview. "The market is not there for cleaner cars. Personally, I wish it were. Personally, I wish the majority of people in this country were literate enough and watched PBS occasionally so that they understood there was a real environmental crisis and behaved in environmentally rational ways. But do I have a great deal of hope about that happening? I'm cynical enough to say probably not."

Throughout my field investigations, though, I found that people resented being constantly reduced to the single-cell species known as "consumer," governed only by financial concerns. I discovered that drivers have an abiding passion for the car's impact on the environment, their communities, and psychic health. They may not know the details, but they know the carmakers are dragging their heels in building cleaner cars. As Laurel Smith, a child-care worker in Willoughby, Ohio, said, "The solutions are there. The government and industry could change it right now and nobody would grumble. . . . We have the technologies. We sent people to the moon and we can't get an electric car? Give me a break! . . . I think the only thing that's going forward with the industrial part of [the U.S.] is making money."

But carmakers don't seem to believe in people like Laurel Smith. They continually uphold sales of big cars as a sign of people's lack of environmental concern, but that doesn't mean they can't build those cars to run cleaner and more efficiently in the first place. Nor does it take into account the fact that Detroit spends great fortunes encouraging the public to buy their large-scale, high-profit meat eaters. As long as carmakers continue in this vein, the industry will never be a social or environmental leader. And if that sounds too lofty a goal, consider General Motors' own publication "General Motors and the Environment," featuring a dreamy blue lake on its cover. Inside, the world's largest industrial corporation promotes itself as a "responsible corporate citizen" and sets forth six Environmental Principles, which include commitments to recycling, environmental education, and reducing factory waste and pollutants. The world's largest carmaker then goes on to trumpet its thirty-year track record of building cars that meet customers concerns for a "clean, healthy environment."

But of course that's merely propaganda. Throughout its history, GM has spent millions of dollars battling environmental legislation at every turn. Similarly, the auto industry continues to spend billions on advertising campaigns to assure us we are getting the best cars for our money. But when we look for a wide selection of cars that uphold customers' concerns for a "clean, healthy environment," we see a practically empty lot. It's great that a new wave of ads respects the consumer's intelligence and celebrates the joy of driving in normal conditions, but in most cases, strip away the propaganda and the automakers do little but reinforce the message best expressed by Terry O'Rourke, the zealous district attorney I met in Houston: "Buy me, buy me, buy me! Buy me because you'll become better, you'll be good, you'll become happier with this *thing.*" As critics have long maintained, this raw consumer message of catering to people's base desires is killing the spirit of our nation. GM's Dr. Frosch is wrong that "you can't advertise people into anything." Look at the various campaigns that promote the notion of the unfettered driver wandering adventurously through the wilds of nature in his or her Ford Explorer (one of the top-selling cars in the country), Jeep Cherokee, or Toyota 4-Runner. These four-wheel-drive hunks of iron get some of the worst gas mileage. Furthermore, as one sarcastic dealer told me, "They never put 'em in four-wheel. How many streams do you gotta cross on your way to work down the Ventura Freeway?"

It's image. And images are created. They're created as you sit in a passive mental state, susceptible to suggestion, in front of your television set, the great leveler of values. In his biography of Aldous Huxley, David King Dunaway notes, "Social critic Neil Postman has compared Orwell's predictions in *1984* with Huxley's: 'Huxley believed it is far more likely that the Western democracies will dance and dream themselves into oblivion than march into it, single file and manacled. Huxley grasped, as Orwell did not, that it is not necessary to conceal anything from a public insensible to contradiction and narcoticized by technological diversions.'

" 'Television is the *soma* of Aldous Huxley's *Brave New World*,' Robert MacNeil observed. 'In the Huxleyan prophecy, Big Brother doesn't watch us, by his choice. We watch him, by ours.' "

The average American TV set is on six hours a day, one-tenth of the commercial time of which is devoted to selling automobiles. Surveying America in 1990, *Harper's* editor Lewis Lapham fears that without industry or government leaders to believe in, "the active presence of the citizen gives way to the passive absence of the consumer, and citizenship devolves into a function of economics."

BACKLASH

From inside Detroit, the future of the driving ecosystem looks pretty grim. All the carmakers have blueprints on the drawing boards for electric cars, less-polluting internal combustion engines such as the two-stroke and lean-burn, new fuel systems to accommodate alternative fuels such as methanol and compressed natural gas, and even urban traffic-reduction systems that would conserve fuel and reduce pollution. But environmental research and development is hindered when automakers spend most of their energy battling regulations. And besides, where is the impetus to implement this new technology to come from? Not from the industry itself. Progress is defeated at the starting line if the participants have no long-term goal. And right now the debt-ridden American auto industry's only goal is the short-term one called selling cars. Yet the industry has its own misguided consumer philosophy to blame for its financial state. By trying to be all things to all people, it produced too many models with only cosmetic differences that sat on the lots uncared for by a public suffering from sensory overload. "Consumers have a propensity to limit their choices to four or five makes," Tom Price, owner of eight car dealerships in the Bay Area, told me. "So what's happened is that there are way too many choices of a given type of car." Price pointed out that consumers today were more educated than ever about automotive quality and fair pricing, and continued to find their needs met more readily by Japanese cars. Still, the Big Three continued to issue huge batches of cars to dealers. "The domestic automakers' continuing losses are largely a symptom of overcapacity," concluded the *New York Times*.

GM waved good-bye to $7 billion in 1991, the largest corporate loss in

American history. In early 1992, proving that it had wised up to its overcapacity, the automaker eliminated 13 of its 20 basic car frames, with plans to close 21 of its 120 North American plants by 1995 and cut production costs by 20 percent. That meant 74,000 people would be out of a job. The company also fired its chairman and president. Chrysler, too, cut $3 billion in costs, paring 3,000 jobs. The domestic industry's decline adds an ironic twist to fifties GM president Charles "Engine Charlie" Wilson's famous remark: "What is good for the country is good for General Motors, and what is good for General Motors is good for the country." Because of bureaucratic inertia, misguided planning, and an inability to meet educated consumers' needs as quickly as the Japanese, GM and company are now bad for the country. Analysts claim that the American auto industry's financial dive is largely responsible for the country's national recession.

With the automakers buried under a mountain of debt, environmental regulations are now more than ever an unwelcome opponent. The Bush administration, though, made the playing field a lot less hazardous. Bush's crusade on behalf of the auto industry began in 1981, when, as vice president, he headed an effort to revoke thirty-four federal safety, fuel, and emissions regulations. As president he vowed to veto Senator Bryan's CAFE bill, which, he claimed, "would destroy the auto industry and cost American jobs." In 1992 he prevented the enactment of up to ten rules in the 1990 Clean Air Act aimed at the auto industry. The rules held hostage include a penalty for high-polluting vehicles, tighter carbon dioxide standards, extended warranties for pollution controls, chlorofluorocarbon recycling for air-conditioners, and improved emissions testing. In the *New York Times*, Congressman Henry A. Waxman, coauthor of the Clean Air Act, claimed that President Bush's warfare on the Clean Air Act was gutting more than the environment: "The President's calculus is entirely political. He thinks few people are paying much attention to complicated regulatory issues. He feels he can please important corporate supporters by undermining the Clean Air Act without tarnishing his claim to be the environmental president. Ultimately . . . our constitutional system is undermined if the President can ignore with impunity the requirements of a law that took a decade of public activism to enact."

The only things the government—especially the executive branch—seems committed to are big business (especially the oil industry) and an entrenched, fallacious rhetoric that, in a free-market economy, regulation and environmental sustainability mean financial ruin and a dearth of jobs. In December 1991, when the driving ecosystem received its best news in decades with the signing into federal law of the Intermodal Surface Transportation Efficiency Act, a six-year, $151 billion provision for national transportation improvements that included a landmark allocation to mass transit and a carrot for local metropolitan planners to clean up their act, Bush did not pass up a chance to espouse the party line. In a photo opportunity under a highway overpass in Euless, Texas, surrounded by a group of road construction workers, Bush signed the bill, claiming, "It is summed up by three words—jobs, jobs, jobs."

During his reelection campaign, Bush consistently pitted the economy against environmental protection, at one point seemingly losing his mind by yelling that if the environmentally inclined Bill Clinton and Al Gore were elected the country would be out of work and "we would all be up to our necks in owls." The reference was to the highly publicized battle in Oregon between the lumber industry and those who wanted to protect the forest as the habitat of the endangered spotted owl. But, of course, those entering the voting booths in November 1992 were not persuaded by Bush's rhetoric. Based on my journey, it was clear that people did not believe the Bush administration was meeting their wider social needs. People as temperamentally dissimilar as Lloyd Richey, the cowboy detective in Dallas, and Marcelle Gianelloni, the zoo director in Louisville, shared the conviction that in addressing environmental problems, notably those due to cars and driving, "the government needs to push." As Marcelle said, "We need more politicians to take the lead." Clinton and Gore may well be those politicians. Gore was a cosponsor of Bryan's Senate bill to raise the CAFE standard to forty miles per gallon by 2001, and in campaign speeches Clinton consistently supported the bill as a means of conserving energy.

Environmentalists, meanwhile, have rallied to play the economy-based game on their own. They no longer draft proposals to mail to backpackers and bird-watchers. They are savvy, rigorous economists, doing battle in courtrooms, state legislatures, and the halls of Congress. Their plans are designed to sustain environmental health *and* serve the marketplace. One of the most sensible plans currently on the table in every state energy office and agency is the Drive+ "feebate." When you buy a new car, you either pay a fee or earn a rebate depending on the car's output of smog and greenhouse emissions. A point in the middle of the fuel economy spectrum would be set at, say, 27.5 miles per gallon. That midpoint would represent the average registration fee of today's new cars. Under Drive+, customers would pay a progressively higher fee for cars that fell below 27.5, while customers who bought cars whose mileage climbed above 27.5 would earn that money back. By balancing fees and rebates, the program would generate the same amount of state registration funds as car sales do now. Most important, Drive+ would reward people for buying efficient cars. Manufacturers who currently offer the cleanest and most efficient cars would experience a boom in sales, and those who don't would be motivated to follow suit. Window stickers would be affixed to cars in the showroom, telling customers just how much they would pay or earn in emissions fees. (Customers could save as much as $700 on a midsize fuel-efficient car.) By allowing customers to make an informed choice about a car's environmental impact, a feebate like Drive+ is an important step in including drivers themselves in a system-wide solution.

Chris Calwell, an energy expert for NRDC, explained to me that the Drive+ program was emblematic of environmentalists' "strong push over the next few years into the following simple concept: Why is it in our country that we tax things that we're trying to encourage, like income and production, and don't tax things we're trying to discourage, like pollution? There are two points of a tax: to raise revenue and send a market signal. We've pitched this one simple idea—without success—to the auto industry: Why not reduce the tax on corporate income, since we're trying to encourage corporate income, which contributes to our GNP, and increase the tax on gasoline, or on carbon, or on some other socially undesirable thing? Make it a revenue-neutral swap. We're not going to raise overall taxes. We're just going to move them around. We call it 'Tax Pollution, Not Jobs.'"

Along with feebates, increasing the gas tax seems the most plausible one-step solution to reducing emissions and conserving energy. Consumer advocate J. D. Power said, flatly, "Put a dollar-a-gallon tax on gasoline. Maybe a dollar-fifty." Auto industry analyst Keller, a free-market apologist who minces fewer words than most car men, said, "What's the public's motivation to accommodate the auto industry's regulatory standard to achieve 27.5 miles per gallon at a time when gasoline in real terms has never been cheaper? It's zero. If the government is going to sit there and say,

'All right you three evil companies, we're going to legislate tougher mileage and you have to do it,' but then says to the public, 'Your birthright is cheap gasoline,' what do you achieve? You achieve exactly what we have now: everybody buying the biggest, least fuel-efficient vehicles they can get, especially lightweight trucks, which are the least efficient form of personal transportation."

Nor, evidently, is the car business itself polarized by the idea of such a tax. Dave Kulp, Ford's fuel economy chief, reminded me that cheap oil remained the economic force with which all parties must contend. "You say we've got to reduce our dependence on foreign oil. OK. But it costs twelve dollars a barrel to get oil out of the ground here, and it costs us two dollars a barrel to get oil out of the ground in the Mideast. So are we going to reduce our energy security? No. If the oil's coming from overseas and it's cheaper, you're not going to be able to say, 'Let's shut off that supply and turn to our own supplies,' and then end up with an economically reasonable alternative. Even if we *double* the fuel efficiency of the fleet, where do you think the oil will come from at twelve dollars and two dollars extraction costs? They'll reduce the amount of expensive oil from the U.S., and the oil that we get from overseas will probably continue to come in. You'll end up totally altering the economy because the price of the gasoline has to go up substantially to support this kind of fuel."

"That sounds like you're supporting a gas tax," I said. "Surely Ford and the other manufacturers would scream about that."

"It's a matter of relative screaming," he replied. "Obviously, having an overall energy tax, the more costly the fuel, the less disposable income, the fewer cars we sell. On the other hand, if you have a CAFE standard that's inordinately high, that's incompatible with today's gas prices, then we have an impasse. What we would like to see, if anybody changes the energy taxes, is a very careful consideration of how fast it goes up. It has to be slowly increased. It can't be so big that it causes the market and the economy to fall apart further than they are now.

"But that's the only way we're going to get there. We're the only people in the world that have fuel prices at such low levels. It's an odd circumstance. So the argument has to be a little bit more carefully crafted. What we're really saying is, 'Yeah, we don't particularly think fuel taxes are exciting, but if we really have concern for all these issues of oil and conservation, let's get everything working together and make the system work compatibly.' If the national agenda is clear, whether we're talking about carbon dioxide emissions or fuel economy, we've all got to be in there trying to do our part. Let's recognize our mutual goals, our mutual concerns, do what we have to do, and come up with some solutions."

I wasn't sure if Kulp was straight shooting, or just shooting the bull, sitting around chatting in his office. At any rate, Chris Calwell was familiar with the automakers' plaints about fuel economy and air pollution restraints and their desire to ease regulations on new cars by introducing legislation such as high gas taxes and feebates and so on. However, he pointed out, "If there is a part of the problem that the auto industry is recommending a solution to, we'll gladly welcome their help. But if the automakers want a gas tax, how come they're never at the hearings where we're trying to get one passed? If they're that excited about it, why don't we get some commitments from them and see if we can get one passed? The auto companies have had a knee-jerk reaction to all forms of air quality and energy legislation for fifty years. Now that these pieces of regulation, like feebates, are taking incentive-based, pro-business angles, the auto industry is *still* opposed." (In 1992 Maryland became the first state to adopt an emissions feebate—albeit a mild one—with fees and rebates totaling no more than 1 percent of a car's price. The auto industry promptly filed suit against the feebate in Maryland state court.)

While political reality forces environmentalists to play the short-term market-driven game with proposals like feebates and gas taxes, they may be the only players in the game with a long-term vision of the planet's health. To create a lasting ecological plan surrounding the automobile, one that would also incorporate today's achievable technologies, the economy would have to undergo a slight shift. As Worldwatch Institute research analyst Michael Renner points out, such a shift is not an irrational demand—it simply requires a new perception:

> For centuries, economy has ruled at the expense of ecology. Global production has depended on the ability to deplete one nonrenewable source after another, to draw down the earth's regenerative capacity, and to treat the world's waterways and atmosphere as mere waste receptacles. Some people assume that the only way to stop this spree of borrowing from the earth is to turn this situation upside down—to sacrifice human well-being on the altar of ecological purity.

But environmental and economic health are interdependent, and one can be pursued without imperiling the other. Contrary to the "jobs versus owls" rhetoric, less damaging ways of producing, consuming, and disposing of goods are completely consistent with the goal of full employment because they tend to be far more labor-intensive. Although there are undoubtedly situations in which new environmental laws throw individual workers out of their jobs, such cases are in fact rare, and often balanced by jobs created in pollution control or in entirely new fields.

As if taking their cue from Worldwatch Institute, Clinton and Gore, in their book *Putting People First: How We Can All Change America*, promised to "shatter the false choice between environmental protection and economic growth by creating a market-based environmental protection strategy that rewards conservation and 'green' business practices while penalizing polluters."

COME TOGETHER

In today's corporate arena, though, an economy based on ecological sustainability is a pie-in-the-sky implausibility. But the skies may not be a picture of total gloom. During my trip to Detroit, while antagonism seemed to echo the loudest in the carmakers' corridors, I heard the creaking sounds of optimism and cooperation. David Cole, director of the Office for the Study of Automotive Transportation at the University of Michigan, said the auto industry and American government were headed for disaster if they "continued to labor on an axis of regulation and confrontation."

I met Cole, son of former GM president Ed Cole, one late afternoon in his Ann Arbor campus office. Friendly and enthusiastic, he echoed Detroit's free-market philosophy during our conversation. While he didn't debate the positive effects of past fuel and air regulations, he maintained that the financial costs of the *current* regulations outweighed the benefits. When viewed as a whole, he said, the economy would suffer from new regulations that demanded retooled factories and technologies. Like a good professor, Cole postulated, "If we believe in a market-oriented economy, then the customers ought to be where the game is." And if clean air could be quantified as a product, Cole wasn't sure that "customers would opt for it."

But then, he pointed out, that option shouldn't be the customer's worry. Individuals didn't write the rules of the game. "Ultimately, what it comes down to is who the individuals let be in charge," he said, "who they assign the authority to govern how we conduct our lives. I think we as a nation make the decision that government should be in charge of protecting the country, and I think the public basically supports issues like emissions control. Individuals themselves are going to pay the extra money to achieve some degree of purity because we don't have the self-discipline to achieve that ourselves. So let's turn that over to the collective body to make that judgment." Unfortunately, Cole believes we are forced to abandon judgment to myopic, "gutless" public leaders who pander to shortsighted and short-term goals to salvage votes, legislators unwilling to address the automobile's environmental problems as a whole—a whole complex system, made up of many different factors, some of which, like the dilemma of old cars, were not being addressed.

"Everybody in the world is for clean air," he said. "But until we get at the bigger source of the problem, and stop attacking the problem at its smallest parts, we'll never get to the place where we can really do something. If we're not attacking the whole problem, we're the greatest problem-mongers. And if you look at the problem in, say, Los Angeles, you've got twenty percent of the in-use vehicles, cars built before 1980, causing eighty percent of the pollution. Somehow we've got to go after that twenty percent. Because we're not going to solve the problem by putting all the investment into new vehicles. Let's say you add five hundred dollars to the cost of a new vehicle, and that higher price defers even a small fraction of buyers from getting rid of their old ones—just that small deferral wipes out any benefit.

"The thing I fear is the problem's going to get worse rather than get better. If it gets worse, what do you do? Do you beat on the new vehicle more? You can make it zero-emission and it doesn't solve the problem. Ultimately, you do change over the fleet and get rid of the bad actors, but until we can get people in Congress to understand that what we've got to do is get the pre–emission control vehicles off the road, and get people to maintain their vehicles properly, we're not going to do something about the problem. I mean, literally, if you have a guy running around with a car where the spark plug wire is falling off on a V-8, he isn't going to know it, and that car might be putting out fifty times the level of hydrocarbon emissions of a car with emission control.

"To me, the problem in our culture is that we are not systems thinkers, in contrast to the Japanese. The Japanese tend to link everything together. Their thought process is very holistic in nature. They have a wonderful ability to think of things at the systems level. The way we think of things here is we take the whole and say, 'I'm going to take this part out, and I'll beat up this part [i.e., the auto industry], and then I'm not going to put it back into the whole.' Now, if I'm worrying about really trying to reduce the problems of emissions and I say, 'Here's an industry that builds, say, ten million cars a year, and if they add an extra five hundred dollars per car for emissions control, that's going to be five billion dollars a year in added costs. And that's going to get rid of so much pollution. But what if I took that five billion and I spent it over here and I could get rid of that much more pollution?' I would do it.

"What Congress says is, 'Oh, wait a minute now. If we do that, we've got this confrontation with the voter, and we're not so sure we want to do that.' A tremendous measure of that is just the reluctance—and I'm not talking about Democrats and Republicans, I'm talking about our system—to initiate a gas tax. There was a five-cent-a-gallon gas tax last year, and the chances of a gas tax increase over the next ten years are probably zero. Congress is so afraid of it because of the perceived negative reaction of the voters.

"So the systems approach, if we can sell it in our culture, is the way to go about this. It really lays a rational basis for decision making when you structure all these linkages. You look at things like competitiveness. You look at the ability to finance change. You look at the critical skills required. You look at a more realistic assessment of the cost of public transit and where that fits. Gas taxation and all of these things then become a reasonable part of the agenda. I'll tell you, if you can create a sense of linking, or getting this country to think more in terms of a systems approach to problem solving, I think you'll find that the arguments between industry and government would become superfluous."

Cole also stressed that in the last five years the American auto manufacturers, taking a lesson from the Japanese, were adapting a systems approach to designing and building cars. "You've heard of 'simultaneous engineering'—getting the manufacturing guys into the design process and getting a better marketing influence in the early stages. That's all systems thinking. In the old approach you would design something, throw a blueprint over the door, and the manufacturing guy would try to figure out how to build the car." Cole also believed that Washington was beginning to understand Detroit's competitive relationship with Japanese and European automakers better.

"I am far more optimistic about the process of applying a systems approach today than I was ten years ago," he said. "In the last couple of years we've seen Detroit and Washington come together *outside* the regulatory connection. So we're beginning to build some of the blocks in the house that will lead to a more systematic approach. It's not that there isn't going to be tough and contentious issues as these things develop. But we're heading in the right direction."

LOCAL HERO

We're in for a very long haul, however. A sweeping change in the driving ecosystem will require an even wider systemic approach than Cole prescribes. And in the meantime, all the bickering—with the government and the car industry and the environmentalists all squared off against one another—will continue. High-tech and alternative fuels will remain under glass in high-tower engineering labs, and solutions such as increased CAFE standards, feebates, gas taxes, and eliminating pre–emissions control clunkers will continue to fly back and forth in the political game room like feathered shuttlecocks.

But there is one place in the country that cannot wait. Cannot wait for a white knight to emerge out of Congress, for a president to realize that preserving the economy and environment are not mutually exclusive goals, for the auto industry to develop a clean and fuel-efficient car that Uncle Roy can tow his trailer with.

Southern California cannot wait.

Hey, it's getting rather funky down there. Downright nasty. It's not labeled the Superbowl of Smog for nothing. People aren't shooting one another on the freeways because of watching too many violent movies. Drivers aren't leaving home at 3:00 A.M. for work and then sleeping in their cars in a parking lot because they're ambitious.

The Los Angeles basin encompasses 11,000 square miles, 12 million people (more than forty-seven individual states), and 8 million vehicles, all vying for a limited amount of highway space—even though two-thirds of

L.A. is already cement and devoted entirely to the automobile. As of 1990, the average driver lives ten miles from where he or she works and travels an average of one hour and twenty minutes to and from that place of employment, an increase of thirty minutes over 1988. And the population continues to burgeon. Currently the cost of congestion—fuel consumption, car maintenance, and lost productivity—comes to about $7 million a day. And that doesn't count the stress. Or the way the city looks. Or the health hazards.

The basin has the filthiest air in the United States, worse than all of the remaining forty-nine states combined. In 1989, the L.A. region violated one or more federal health standards on 215 days. Capture a jar of L.A. air and you'll have enough ozone, carbon monoxide, fine particle matter, nitrogen dioxide, sulfates, carbon dioxide, and other noisome goodies to poison your average entomologist's entire bug collection. Dr. Russell Sherwin, a pathologist with USC, has found extensive damage in 20 to 25 percent of the human lungs he's studied. And those were the lungs of fifteen-to-twenty-five-year-olds. Not counting lung disease, cancer, and death, exposure to ozone in the area causes, each day, 120 million person-days of coughing, 190 million person-days of eye irritation, 100 million person-days of headache, 65 million person-days of chest discomfort, and 18 million person-days of restricted activity. To meet the federal health standards for just ozone and fine particulates alone would result in health benefits totaling more than $9 billion a year. The congestion and air quality: it's *bad*. The L.A. basin ecosystem is in dire need of some remedial wildlife management.

Enter one of the new environmental heroes, a sort of Gary Cooper of the urban rangeland, a tall, quiet-spoken Tennessean (with a chronic eye problem that makes him sensitive to even minor aerial irritants) who has become one of the most powerful people in Southern California. James Lents, hired out of the air wars in Colorado, heads up the South Coast Air Quality Management District (SCAQMD), an agency of over 1,000 employees, empowered by the Lewis Air Quality Management Act of 1976 (uniting pollution-control districts from Los Angeles, Orange, Riverside, and San Bernardino counties) and the fiercely Spartan California Air Resources Board (CARB), which sets emission and fuel standards. Lents took over in 1986 and has fashioned, in his own words, "the nation's most advanced air pollution control program." He makes no bones about it—he aims to clean up L.A.'s air. He wants it as wholesome and pristine as Los Angelenos' grandparents saw it; meaning, he fully intends to meet the state's strict air standards by 2007—*without* the help of the federal government, and despite Detroit.

I paid Dr. Lents (he has a Ph.D. in physics) a visit to see just how he planned to accomplish this herculean feat. SCAQMD's headquarters, located in the heart of the city basin in Rosemead, sat at a most appropriate spot: right next to the region's IRS offices and directly across the street from I-10, the horrendous San Bernardino Freeway. You could almost see the smog, in waves, breaking against the side of the building. (The headquarters has since moved to a brand-new fifteen-acre complex in Diamond Bar, which, coincidentally, is where Lents lives.) Inside, however, it was cool and spacious. A huge mural of blue skies and tumbling white clouds adorned the foyer's wall. A friendly receptionist greeted me and quickly turned me over to the senior public information specialist, Claudia Keith, who took me to her office and prepped me for my audience with the good Dr. Lents. I was then led past executive secretaries into the executive director's chambers, where a tall man with a warm manner shook my hand and invited me to sit on a couch. Keith remained with us, keeping a close eye on me, monitoring my questions, hovering over the regulator as though he was too frail to endure the likes of me. (I might have made the mistake earlier of telling Keith I was sort of a car biologist who loved cars and was worried that, well, you know, they might become extinct. I'm sure it didn't come out right.)

Dr. Lents had a soft and caring manner; the heart and compassion he evinced were more pronounced than his actual words. As I began firing questions at him, he reminded me that he was merely the producer in a very large and complicated operation. "My knowledge is sort of very limited," he said. "Experts are people who know more and more about less and less until they know everything about nothing. What you get in my job is you learn less and less about more and more until you know nothing about everything."

SCAQMD—"a comprehensive program of regulation, research, and communication"—is composed of lawyers, engineers, scientists, inspectors, planners, and public outreach personnel. It takes as its bible the Air Quality Management Plan, a weighty tome that delineates problems from smog in the L.A. airshed to global warming, and outlines a strategy for solution, including hundreds of different measures, from tiny things like eliminating leaf blowers to mandates that truck fleets run a certain percentage of their vehicles on alternative fuels—or don't run them at all. The agency means business: unlike most do-gooder planning commissions, this one has real clout. "It's what they call 'police authority,'" Lents pointed out: the authority to write rules and punish those who do not obey them with fines of up to $25,000. Everything, from the composition of the air, to how people are complying with the latest measures, is monitored twenty-four hours a day.

"One of the points I've attempted to make to people," Lents started off saying, "is in terms of health standards. The public not only wants to deal with health standards . . . I mean, I think that has to be the immediate priority in the short term, but there's secondary standards, quality-of-life issues, how nice the air looks, how it smells. There's a whole aesthetic set of issues that in time I think the citizens of this whole country want dealt with."

"Wherever I went across the country," I said, "L.A. was held up as *the* bad example. All eyes are on you. People're wondering, can you save the Great Southern California Life-style?"

"We think we can, yes. And we think it can be done primarily through technological changes with a sprinkling of sociological changes. I say a sprinkling, but what's in the eye of one person varies. Carpooling will play a major role. And some dependence on mass transit will play a role. But other than that, I think most of what we're going to do is in this area of technological changes. Meaning vehicles that essentially don't pollute. Go back to what a car looked like in 1970. Cars that are sold here in California today will produce eighty percent less air pollution over their life than the car built in 1970. That's pretty good. Now we're going to take cars to where over their life they are eighty percent cleaner than those cars today. In other words, over its lifetime, a car operating after the turn of the century in Los Angeles will produce only four percent the emission that a 1970 vehicle did.

"The state Air Resources Board, which shares responsibility with us, has the authority to specifically set tail pipe standards—which they have already done. The eighty percent requirement I just described has already been adopted by CARB and is state law, or state rules, that must be met if you're going to sell cars in California."

In 1990 the California board, after cooperative exchanges with SCAQMD's technology and planning offices, passed "rules" that translated into a timetable for the auto manufacturers, requiring them to release a proportionally higher percentage of clean cars from 1994 to 2003. The board offers guidelines by breaking new cars into three types: light-emission vehicles (LEVs); ultra-light-emission vehicles (ULEVs); and zero-emission vehicles (ZEVs). The most draconian requirement—to the manufacturers, anyway—is that by 1998 2 percent of all cars sold (about 40,000) in California must be ZEVs; by 2003, 10 percent (an estimated 200,000). While the air board doesn't stipulate exactly how the manufacturers should meet these deadlines, its staff of independent engineers is well versed in automotive technology and knows that ULEVs, for instance, will most likely be cars that run on alternative fuels like methanol, while ZEVs will be electric cars. Bill Sessa, CARB's communications director, assured me that while the air board regularly exchanged information with the auto-makers, the board operated out of its own "very fundamental philosophy, which is: We do not set pollution standards to reflect state-of-the-art tech-nology. We purposely use emissions standards to force the development of new technology."

Interestingly, GM's Tom Darlington had said he preferred GM's rela-tionship with CARB to the one with federal regulators. "Even though CARB does things more stringently, things that are harder for us to do, our relationship is more give-and-take. We can go out there and say there's no way we can make a deadline, and they seem more flexible to work in our concerns than EPA." Still . . . "It's just a nightmare trying to deal with all this stuff!" Darlington had said, letting his emotions get the better of him, though quickly correcting himself. "I mean it's a *technical challenge*." It's a technical challenge that all carmakers cannot afford to pass by. With ten northeastern states perched to adopt the CARB standards, nearly 40 percent of the new-car market will be subject to the strict new standards.

Paralleling CARB's guidelines, SCAQMD's Management Plan has instituted a twenty-year, three-tiered schedule, from measures that require the implementation of currently available technologies, to regulatory ac-tions that force and use "on-the-horizon technologies," to tier III, which "requires commitments to research, development, and widespread com-mercial application of technologies that may not exist yet, but may be reasonably expected given the rapid technological advances experienced over the past 20 years." This last step would include such things as solar cells and superconductors for transportation.

"Can all this *wunderbar* technology really be developed?" I asked Dr. Lents.

"Yes. Unquestionably, in our view. The technology is early, it's right off the shelf, but some of it is already demonstrated—methanol cars are there, cars that burn methanol and gasoline or any combination. Heated catalysts are already operating that do a good job. Natural gas vehicles. And we've seen a lot of activity in research, even the research we're participating in right here at the district."

"You must be the worst thorn in the side of the auto industry. You're forcing them to do something."

"I think if you look at California as a whole that's true. And I'll say it, I think we're doing them a big favor. They don't feel like that at the moment. But, you know, there's some changing attitudes. I see some movement out of General Motors and Ford, different than what I have seen historically coming out of them, and I hope it's just not some environmental rhetoric that they hope will get them through the short term."

MAKING AN IMPACT

It is much more than environmental rhetoric, of course. Although the auto industry has been talking about marketing an electric car (a ZEV, a zero-emission vehicle) since . . . well, since they stopped marketing them back in the 1920s, no one company has been willing to be the first to test the treacherous consumer-market waters. Until now. Spurred on by a clearly delineated market hatched by CARB and Lents's SCAQMD (more cars and light trucks are sold in California than in all but seven *nations* of the world) and an indigenous design by an independent Los Angeles (where else?)–based engineer, General Motors has gotten off its duff.

GM turned to Paul MacCready, an iconoclastic inventor, to develop a marketworthy electric car. MacCready, whose engineering group, AeroVironment, specializes in aerodynamics, has designed streamlined blimps, propellers for energy-generating windmills, and drag-reducing fairings for eighteen-wheelers. In the late seventies MacCready gained mainstream attention for a number of ultralight flying contraptions. First came the radio-controlled replica of a prehistoric pterodactyl with a thirty-six-foot wingspan. Then there was the Gossamer Condor, a bicycle-powered plane made of balsa wood, piano wire, and high-tech plastic, which earned MacCready a prestigious science award for achieving the first human-powered flight over the English Channel. In 1987 GM enlisted Mac-Cready to develop a solar-powered car to compete in a 1,950-mile solar race across Australia. The MacCready-designed vehicle, the GM Sun-raycer, won the event by two days.

After the success of Sunraycer, GM bought 15 percent of AeroViron-ment. MacCready told David H. Freedman of *Discover* magazine: "The point of the investment was to establish a cultural connection." Mac-Cready, though, didn't just want to build prototypical vehicles that earned the carmaker a blue ribbon at auto shows but to build a car with lasting cultural significance. After all, MacCready had founded his com-pany on the environmental principle of energy conservation, and an elec-tric car uses no petroleum and spews out no harmful emissions. In less than a year, MacCready and company threw out all previous designs for electric cars, which essentially revolved around putting a whole bunch of batteries in a standard car chassis and body, and instead produced a superefficient car, named the Impact, from scratch. The car's great advance was in highly efficient engineering and aerodynamics. MacCready reduced the Impact's drag coefficient, which meant the car didn't expend most of its power pushing its own weight. He pointed out that automakers had never de-signed any vehicle as wind-resistant and energy-efficient as the Impact because they had never perceived a reason to. "Who cares if an automobile has lots of drag?" he asked sarcastically. "Gas is cheaper than bottled water." (One retired GM engineer slyly noted that if a standard four-cylinder gasoline engine was installed in the Impact, the car's extraordinary aerody-namics and light weight would demand such little effort from the engine that the car would reach eighty miles per gallon.)

The Impact featured a teardrop fiberglass body, two lightweight AC electric motors connected directly to each of the front wheels (thus obviat-ing the need for a transmission), and thirty-two regular lead batteries and a DC-to-AC power inverter. The car was also equipped with what's called "regenerative" braking: when pressure is taken off the accelerator, the electric system is reconfigured so that the motors then act as generators to replenish the battery, and the rotor, now working against its magnetic field, slows the car down. On a test track in Arizona, the Impact outperformed a

Mazda Miata and a Nissan 300ZX. It accelerated from zero to sixty in eight seconds, reaching a top speed of one hundred miles per hour. The Impact ran 120 miles on an eight-hour battery charge, which translates to a cost of little more than a gallon of gasoline.

Freedman writes: "MacCready cautions that GM will make many compromises to get the design to be as factory-friendly as possible. 'Mass production is a whole different ball game, and it's GM's ball game,' he says. 'We'll probably be advising them along the way, but they'll be deciding what changes to make.' It's not a prospect that fills everyone at AeroViron-ment with joy, but it's necessary, of course, if the car is ever to have the impact that MacCready and his crew originally envisioned."

Potentially, the energy savings from an electric car would be dramatic. For every 2 million vehicles running on electrons, we would save 35 million barrels of oil per year. It's also been estimated that if all families who now own two cars traded one in for an electric car, we could eliminate foreign oil imports entirely. Being forced to recharge the car every 120 miles is less of a burden than most drivers imagine. Less than 4 percent of all commutes are over thirty miles, and Americans drive an average of twenty-two miles a day. Batteries, however, remain the Achilles' heel of electric cars. In a rare instance of cooperation, the Big Three have pooled resources with major utilities companies and the Department of Trans-portation to form the Advanced Battery Consortium in an effort to design the ideal energizer.

An electric car, however, is not the ultimate automotive gift to clean air. Its reduction of air pollutants depends on how its batteries are charged. If you plug your Impact into an electricity system generated by a coal-burning power plant, your effect on smog, ozone, and greenhouse gases will be little more benign than filling up your Cavalier at the corner Chevron. If the electric power stems from one of the country's less prevalent natural gas, solar, or hydro systems, then you have a truly environmental car. Stated Michael Renner of Worldwatch Institute: "Using electricity derived from the current mix of power sources in the United States, an electric car would release about the same amount of CO_2 [a greenhouse gas] as a gasoline-fueled car, more sulfur dioxide, but much lower amounts of other pollutants."

In a little flurry of self-promotion in March 1991, GM announced it would begin building the Impact in the mid-nineties in a Lansing, Michigan, assembly plant, former home of the ill-begotten Buick Reatta. "GM is proud of its history of environmental leadership in the auto industry and today's announcement is a very strong commitment to continuing that role," said president Lloyd E. Reuss.

So much for commitment. By the end of 1992, Reuss was fired and the chary new GM regime pulled the plug on building the Impact until the "late nineties," trotting out the standard excuse that the "market" was not yet ready for an electric car. At the same time, GM announced it was forming another consortium with Ford, Chrysler, and the Electric Power Research Institute, this time to refine some of the components of electric cars themselves. GM electric car program manager Ken Baker declared that it was now "Team U.S.A. against Team Japan."

Well, with the cancellation of the Impact, it appears that Team Japan is once again in the lead. Currently Nissan and Toyota have electric cars in advanced stages of design. Like all Japanese automakers, they have been part of the Japan Electric Vehicle Association since 1976. And MITI, the Japanese government agency, has been orchestrating the development and market viability of electric cars for over a decade. Bringing together the Japanese automakers and battery and utility companies, MITI has set a goal of putting 200,000 electric cars on Japan's roads by the end of the century, up from 1,000 today.

However, the first battery-powered car to hit the commercial market will probably be the LA301, a four-seat hybrid electric car commissioned by the city of Los Angeles and built by a Swedish-British consortium called Clean Air Transport. The car is equipped with a small gasoline engine that kicks in at speeds above 30 miles per hour to extend the 60-mile battery-powered range to over 150 miles. It'll cost about $25,000. Volkswagen has begun a joint venture with Swatch, the Swiss company known for its trendy watches, to build an electric car, assumably a flashy, multicolored one that teenagers will be dying to own. BMW has also produced blueprints for two electric cars that will be powered by motors built by a small American company called Unique Mobility. Located in Englewood, Colorado, Unique Mobility is headed by Ray A. Geddes, former manager of Ford's high-performance sports car division. Made of light iron and copper, the patented Unique motor reportedly will be more electronically efficient than even the Impact's. In an admission that would please many of the environmentally savvy street racers I met during my journey, Geddes told Lesley

Hazelton of the *New York Times Magazine*, "Eventually, electric-drive race cars with a motor in each wheel will run circles around other kinds."

CLEAN GETAWAYS

The other field of study in which engineers are striving to make cars less of an environmental hazard—or, I should say, are striving to make cars meet the California and the federal (Clean Air Act) standards—is nonpetroleum fuels. Right now, the front-runners in the sweepstakes of feasibility are methanol, which can be produced from natural gas or coal; ethanol, which is produced from biomass such as corn or sugar; and compressed natural gas (CNG), a gaseous fuel tapped from the earth's natural resources.

Gasoline-burning beasts emit three basic smog pollutants: hydrocarbons, nitrogen oxides, and carbon monoxide. Hydrocarbons and nitrogen oxides deteriorate the tissue in our lungs, and carbon monoxide arrests our ability to carry oxygen and puts a nasty strain on the heart. Exhaust from a car powered by methanol would carry about 40 percent less smog pollutants; ethanol, about 30 percent. The carmakers prefer methanol because adapting it to their vehicles by 1994 requires the least amount of retooling and therefore expense. They also like it because it has a high octane content that gives cars more muscle (Indy cars are fueled by methanol). All major manufacturers have assembled prototypical cars, based on existing models, capable of running on methanol. Actually, hedging their bets, the cars are "flex-fuel" vehicles, able to run on gasoline at the flip of a switch. Toyota's flex-fuel vehicle is a four-wheel-drive Hilux pickup, Volkswagen's is a Jetta, GM's is a Chevy Lumina, and Ford's is a Taurus. In fact, the Big Three will each have a few thousand flex-fuel cars on California's streets by late 1993. Less effort has gone into converting cars to run on ethanol because the fuel's chemical makeup takes a high corrosive toll on engine parts, and because producing ethanol is so expensive.

Yet neither methanol nor ethanol constitutes an environmental panacea. Although if you burn methanol in your Chevy you'll be emitting far fewer smog-causing particles than if you burned gasoline, it leaves traces of carcinogenic formaldehyde. Furthermore, if methanol is created from coal, production plants will billow out unseemly amounts of greenhouse gases. Ethanol, too, cuts back on some pollutants, but does little for others. CNG burns the cleanest of the three alternative fuels, emitting almost no carbon monoxide, yet the car companies are not exactly rushing it into passenger car production because it requires making room for bulky and expensive pressurized gas tanks. CNG makes more sense for larger trucks, and in fact GM has begun selling a few thousand CNG Sierra pickups in Texas and California.

While lobbying efforts behind each of the respective alternative fuels are bound to intensify over the next decade (chemical companies are mad about methanol; the Corn Belt agribusiness community is hog-wild over ethanol; the utility companies are already sinking untold millions into CNG television commercials), the barriers to implementation are fairly obvious. Where are you going to get a fill-up? In the Bay Area, for instance, where there are four hundred CNG vehicles already in operation, there is a grand total of six places to refuel. There are about seven hundred methanol vehicles in all of California, and no more than nineteen methanol stations. A refueling infrastructure would spread as more alternative-fuel vehicles took to the streets, but although federal and California regulations are providing a healthy push, our consumerist economy is providing a stronger resistance. Analysts figure it would cost the oil industry anywhere from $7 billion to $80 billion to build and retool enough refineries to run the nation's cars on methanol by 2000. The massive changeover would potentially make a gallon of methanol more expensive than gasoline. So it's unlikely that legislators would risk upsetting both consumers and the economy to create subsidies and tax incentives to fund a nation of non-petroleum fuel stations.

A telling side effect of the federal and California regulatory push for alternative fuels is that it has struck fear in the hearts of oil manufacturers and forced them to do what many oil experts figured they could do all along: produce cleaner-burning gasoline. In mid-1991 Arco announced a new gasoline that would burn as cleanly as methanol. (The company complained that methanol would cost it three times as much to make as gasoline.) So why didn't they market this wonder gas before? Not only because it cost more to produce than their standard brands, but because they were now forced to. Although the oil companies fought the laws tooth-and-nail, the 1990 Clean Air Act stipulated that gasoline must burn 25 percent cleaner by 2000, and in 1991 the triumphant CARB insisted that gas emit 30 percent less pollutants by 1996. Now all the oil companies have cauldrons boiling with reformulated gas.

Step off the oil-consumer treadmill into the realm of real dedication to clean energy, though, and you'll find a long-term solution. In the case of alternative fuels, it's hydrogen. Joan Ogden, a physicist at the Center for Energy and Environmental Studies at Princeton, told Sam Flamsteed of *Discover*, "Environmentally, hydrogen is nearly the ideal fuel. Burning it releases zero carbon dioxide, zero sulfur, zero hydrocarbons, zero carbon monoxide. All you generate is water vapor and a small amount of nitrogen oxides." In the seventies, when the energy crises inspired scientists to begin researching hydrogen as an alternative to gasoline, the problem was not resources—which is, after all, water—but separating the H_2 from the O. Initially, passing an electric current through the water performed the splitting procedure, but again, producing electricity from coal-burning plants defeats the goal of clean energy. Today, though, photovoltaic cells, which convert sunlight into electricity, have become sophisticated enough to perform the hydrogen-separating process. And converting internal combustion engines to run on hydrogen is no more arduous than converting the CNG trucks currently in production in Detroit. In fact, Mercedes-Benz, BMW, and Mazda all have hydrogen-fueled prototypes in their showrooms. Although producing energy from photovoltaic cells is more expensive than drumming it out of oil, Ogden points out that the procedure is not nearly as expensive as cleaning up oil spills off coastal areas and treating patients for auto pollution–related diseases. (Congress's Office of Technology Assessment estimates that a gallon of gas would cost about $10 if it reflected the costs of land and water pollution from petroleum, cleanups, and the deployment of military troops in the Mideast to safeguard its overseas delivery.) In fact, producing hydrogen may not be that far off. *Scientific American* reports that "advances in solar technologies during the next two decades should make it feasible to produce electrolytic hydrogen . . . at a cost to consumers that is about twice the present gasoline price in the U.S. on an energy-equivalent basis."

The political feasibility of hydrogen, however, is a different story. President Bush's 1991 National Energy Strategy was essentially a valentine to the oil industry and, as the *Los Angeles Times* reported, "cold comfort to companies that install conservation equipment and firms that generate solar or other alternative forms of energy."

STREET SMARTS

Of course—not to forget the obvious—the biggest cause of pollution and wasted fuel is congestion. A recent study by the California Department of Transportation (known as Caltrans) stated that when rush hour speeds drop from thirty to ten miles per hour, fuel consumption increases 100 percent. Annually, more than 3 billion gallons of gasoline are wasted on the nation's highways, and that means more than 3 billion gallons of burned exhaust emissions are seeping into the atmosphere. At stop-and-start speeds an engine's pollution-control system operates at its worst efficiency.

The new technological methods of moving auto herds along at a brisk pace are filed under the rubric "Intelligent Vehicle Highway Systems" (IVHS). Basically, the term refers to three technologies: sensors implanted in the road to gauge traffic speeds and density; computerized dashboard maps that feed drivers information from a centralized road-traffic controller; and sophisticated road devices that seize the car by sonar and actually steer and control its speed.

Road sensors are currently in operation on a twelve-mile stretch of freeway, called the "Smart Corridor," in Santa Monica, California. Based on information relayed by the sensors, such as the density of cars, managers in Caltrans's downtown headquarters attempt to keep the car herd moving in harmony by synchronizing the traffic lights on freeway on ramps, offering messages about road conditions or alternate routes on electronic billboards, or sending out tow trucks to clear away a stalled car. More detailed information is relayed to twenty-eight Caltrans officials in experimental cars, called Pathfinders, outfitted with on-board computers. These satellite-dependent computers feature a video map of the surrounding area. Central controllers highlight roads to either take or avoid by using various electronic squiggles. The video map also notes the driver's location at every moment. A quick glimpse at the map tells the driver, "You are here." Safety is also enhanced by immediately alerting drivers to hazards. Some computers have voice activators to translate the messages to words so drivers never take their eyes off the road.

In Orlando, Florida, the Pathfinder project has reached a level of commercial sophistication—apropos of the home of Disney World. Called TravTek (travel technology), dashboard computers offer, besides navigation and safety advice, information about restaurants, hotels, tourist attractions, and, presumably, the score of the most recent Magic-Knicks game. The TravTek system maps 1,300 square miles; currently the navigation computers are mounted in one hundred Oldsmobile Trofeos rented to AAA members.

Along with the Federal Highway Administration and both the California and Florida departments of transportation, Pathfinder and TravTek are funded by GM. Clearly these are handy technologies for the manufacturers in their efforts to reduce emissions and meet federal regulations—they don't require redesigning the car. No American auto company, though, has been forthcoming with a sponsorship for the most futuristic IVHS form at California Partners for Advanced Transit and Highways (PATH), located in Richmond. "The auto industry is generally conservative," Steven E. Shladover, PATH's deputy director, told me. "So some of the people in the industry like to pooh-pooh what we're doing. But we need to make a quantum leap in freeway capacity or our cities are going to strangle themselves."

Studies that reveal that maintaining an even flow of traffic saves energy and reduces pollutants form the foundation of PATH's operating goal. PATH plans to squeeze cars closer together, in a technique called platooning, so existing freeways can sustain up to 200 percent more cars. This would be accomplished by a fully automated vehicle-control system installed in cars. The system features an electronic eye that reads special lane markings and sends out an infrared sonar signal that bounces off surrounding cars. Theoretically these signals would keep the cars tightly, evenly, and safely spaced. The system would also preclude the need for building more lanes and roads. Furthermore, as the electronic eye follows the lane markings, the system would take control of the car's steering, speed, and brakes, allowing drivers to sail merrily down the car-filled stream.

During my field investigations in Cambridge, I had met Hans Klein, a thirty-year-old graduate student at the Massachusetts Institute of Technology and a prime researcher of IVHS. Hans was also at work on the effects of technology on public life, so he loved to talk about the nature of IVHS as well as its wider social ramifications. We sat in busy Harvard Square, the kind of casual public meeting ground that Hans lamented was disappearing from U.S. cities. He said he enjoyed studying IVHS as an example of systems theory, in which many interdependent factors had to be managed at once, and which gave individuals more control.

"The idea of IVHS is to make a system that links individuals—through information networks and computer networks—so that all these individuals start to see the system as a whole and operate in a more efficient manner. You have interaction between the road and the car, the road sensing the cars, sensing the traffic, and controlling the traffic flow. Before, the whole system was just passive—nobody really knew what was happening—but now it's very interactive. You might punch into the computer the address of where you're going, and an electric voice would say, 'Take your next left,' or, 'Cambridge, get in the right lane.' "

Hans stressed that the commercial possibilities of IVHS were not lost on savvy entrepreneurs. "Once you have this telecommunications link, any number of private-sector inventors can come up with new services to ride on it. You might have an electronic yellow pages, or you might say, 'Where's the nearest gas station?' or 'Where can I find a restaurant and what's the menu?' " Advertisements for Days Inn and Denny's can't be far behind. "But if you think a car phone's expensive, wait till you see this stuff. Right now the simplest on-board navigation system costs about twelve hundred dollars."

But as he was of many high-tech solutions, Hans was skeptical of IVHS. "The problem is just much bigger than the technology. Remember the following: There's a public sector and there's a private sector. From the business point of view, the question is, will consumers buy this technology? The beauty of that is, I don't have to say I believe in this technology, I just have to say, 'Hey, if General Motors can make it sell, it's not a bad technology. It's trying to do useful things that have some social good. So that's fine. Let them try.'

"But if the public sector, the Department of Transportation, invests fifteen billion dollars in this technology instead of something else, then I'd say the money could be used better somewhere else. For public transit or urban renewal, say. And another danger is that people who build highways are a powerful political lobby, and they say, 'We want jobs, we want money, so we'll think of something that will justify this funding. So why don't we build some more highways, and why don't we put in this electronic material? That'll give you an excuse to fund us.' That's obscene."

Hans worried that IVHS would put more polluting cars on the road and encourage more solitary commuting. He viewed roads as a form of supply, and filling them up as an act of blind consumerism.

"That's the basis of the real environmental problems in the country, isn't it? It's always viewed as supply and demand, and the consumer is always right. You could go so far as to say the meaning of life is to consume as much as you possibly can at all times. As long as you have a total consumer society, then you're always gonna be hunting for ways to get something for nothing. And technology always gives you something for nothing. That's sort of a definition of technology. So we, in our desire to consume and to drive all the time, run into these problems of overcapacity. We want something for nothing. Then we ask, 'Where's the technology, where's the pill that'll make the problem go away?' You want to drive, where's the technology that'll enable you to always drive more and more? IVHS is such a pill. IVHS is such a technology."

REGULATION 15

Meanwhile, back in down-to-earth practicality, back in L.A., James Lents was talking about SCAQMD's "sprinkling of sociological changes" intended to put a realistic dent in the congestion problem.

Over the next decade, these changes would include the area's devotion of about $40 billion in federal, state, and local funds to mass transit, including 412 miles of light-rail trains. In fact, the L.A.–Long Beach "Blue Line" is already humming with devoted train passengers every day. Lents's plan will also make sure each and every freeway in the basin has a high-occupancy-vehicle (HOV) lane added to existing lanes, for his Big Push is toward carpooling. "The state law, and the law we support, wants to have an average ridership in commuting to work here of 1.5 persons per vehicle. The way I usually say it is that we want to deliver fifteen people to work with ten vehicles. Today in Los Angeles we deliver about eleven people to work with ten vehicles. So that's going to mean that we've got to get about half the people in Los Angeles in some sort of ride-sharing arrangement, varying from a car they're sharing to a bus, to a train, something."

"That's a pretty tremendous sprinkling," I said.

"Yes, that's a big change. Sometimes I say 'a sprinkling of social change' because I ride-share myself. I actually consider it the preferable way to go to work. I don't see that as a huge sociological change for the area, although others might." (Actually, since SCAQMD moved, Lents has been riding his bicycle to work.)

Martin Wachs, a UCLA urban planning professor who has done various studies on mass transit ridership, saw carpooling as a huge sociological change. "It's been said so many times it's a cliché, but the single greatest unused resource of transportation is the empty car seats out there on that freeway," he said. "If we could just get a few more people out of their cars into those empty seats, traffic would move more smoothly. And that's being done. Right now, more people are carpooling in the United States than are using public transit. In Los Angeles today about four percent of the people went to work on public transit, and about eighteen percent went to work in car pools."

Wachs added that people enjoyed carpooling. "When you do an attitude survey on carpoolers, eighty percent say they're happy and satisfied. They encourage their friends to do it." He claimed carpoolers didn't miss the time alone. Van pools, for instance, have been very successful. "People sleep in vans. There are some vans that have headphones, you can listen to music. Car pools actually make up their own rules. People will say, 'In the morning nobody talks, in the afternoon we socialize, and on Fridays we bring along a bottle of wine.' Van pools have Christmas parties. People enjoy them."

Whether or not people enjoy car pools, Los Angeles needs them, said Lents. The crown jewel in the district's plan is Regulation 15, or "The Commuter Program." Regulation 15 requires employers of one hundred or more people at a single site to implement a plan to encourage employees to commute to work by any means other than driving alone. Incentives include company vans, free bus tickets, or free parking for carpoolers. Employers who don't comply get their wrists slapped with heavy fines. Throughout my field investigations, I had asked drivers if they would alter their driving habits to help the environment if they were asked to by someone in authority. The answers were always yes, provided it was really needed and others were doing it. Well, it's certainly needed in L.A., and employers were asking nicely.

"We're talking a real antidote," said Lents. "I started right here at the district because we want to be a good example. With my thousand people who work here we're getting more than eighteen people to work with ten cars. And we're doing it without HOV lanes. We're doing it simply by having dollar incentives for people and parking charges." If Regulation 15 works in reducing congestion and toxic emissions (and early tabulations were promising: a 1992 study of 1,635 employers showed an average ridership increase of 5 to 10 percent), Lents planned to apply it to employers of twenty-five or more. Of course, as with any regulation, some saw the imprint of Big Brother. "It's an Orwellian nightmare," squawked L.A. county supervisor Mike Antonovich. "What you have is a group of liberal regulators, under cover of an air quality plan, attempting to engineer human behavior."

Lents and company have confronted the same criticism over a potential strategy of their plan: buying and scrapping 250,000 smog-spewing junkers from L.A. drivers. The buyback would be funded by corporations such as Unocal, which would earn a "pollution credit" for taking the smog machines, most of them made before 1979, off the streets. That credit would allow the oil company to delay or jettison some smog-control devices on its refineries. Although the trade-off re-creates the scenario of bazaar merchants swapping pollution, it would, ideally, reduce the cumulative amount of smog over the L.A. basin. Critics no less than automotive historian James Flink have complained that such laws are biased against low-income people, the most likely owners of old cars. Without adequate public transportation—and, as L.A. resident Char Ghivaan told me, new mass transit lines definitely steer clear of low-income neighborhoods—targeting old cars is impractical at best, social engineering at worst.

Lents said that "those questions have to be answered" before a cash-for-clunkers program could be instigated but added that the program is "something we think is worth doing." But then he stressed that all of the district's measures must be implemented slowly and gradually, precisely to allow the populace to accept them. And so far the measures are succeeding. Sulfur dioxide has been held to acceptable levels, and a 1991 evaluation revealed reactive organic gases and nitrogen oxide close to their 1989 levels. Los Angeles city councilman Marvin Braude predicted: "We are on the verge of a big breakthrough." Did Lents share that sentiment? I asked if he thought ecological awareness was spreading across L.A.

"I think across the board in Los Angeles, from corporate executives to small business people to the average citizen in the street, that people care more about the environment and are more concerned with what's going on. I'm seeing it now more than any time in my career. Probably a similar thing holds for congestion. It's so bad here, everybody recognizes the problem associated with the car. So there is an awareness out there that it's unlikely that it's going to get a lot better without some significant changes to the system. But that awareness, that concern—it's not easy for people to translate into real actions.

"I think you're going to have really horrendous situations before some guy actually says, 'Well, I'd rather be poor, I'd rather get around a lot less, than live in these conditions.' We have not reached that in the United States, or in Los Angeles. The ecological commitment to me says, 'If you can help me find a way to live my life more ecologically acceptably with less congestion, but keep my life close to where I'm at right today, then I'll go along with you.' That's a step forward.

"You know, it's sort of like, well, the barbecue grill's been a great subject of controversy here because we regulated the use of it. [Charcoal lighter fluid dumps tons of hydrocarbons into the air, so Lents banned it.] I think what the average person says is, 'If you're telling me I can't barbecue, I don't think the air pollution problem's that bad, I will really give you trouble. But if you're telling me that I've got to do something a little bit different to start my barbecue, that's reasonable. Help me find a way to do it and you won't have any big fight.' That's the level that people are at today. So our job in government is to help people find those ways of doing it."

"But to really make a difference on congestion and pollution," I offered, "aren't we going to have to change our land-use patterns?"

"Yes, I agree with that. And that is probably where there is the greatest weakness in authority at this stage—to the extent that you want to change overall land-use patterns. Of course, to significantly change those patterns, it's going to take years and years. Our plan is directed at air quality. We can restore air quality here to a great degree with our plan, yes. But it may well be that for purely congestion reasons, as opposed to environmental ones, we're going to have to do more. Our top priority has not been solving the congestion problem. And therefore I'm not saying that we are going to walk away solving it. Even with the carpooling I'm telling you about, even with the mass transit we're talking about putting in, driving's still going to go up in this area. Now, that actually could portend more traffic congestion instead of less."

"And your plan doesn't factor that in?"

"No, it factors it in. It doesn't solve it. Traffic here has been growing faster than the population. It's true almost everywhere. It's true in Colorado. We expect about a thirty-seven percent growth in population in this area. [Three million in the next decade.] If you look at what the system with no constraints on it would look like then, driving here would be almost at a standstill. It would potentially be sixty percent worse than it is now.

"Our plan encompasses a program to only have it at thirty percent worse. So in one sense that's better. In another sense, it's worse than it is today. So we're trying to deal with it in the plan, but we're not solving it. I had hoped we would have a program that would have no growth in driving over the next twenty years. That was actually the original goal that I talked with SCAQMD about. But then they came back and said they cannot come up with a system to do that. That even if we get half the people in ride-sharing and car pools, even if we spend forty billion dollars on mass transit, there will still be growth in driving in this area just because of the fundamental changes in population. And that's where the plan for this area stands today. There will be a net increase in driving.

"Now, the big controversy is, do you add new lanes to accommodate this growth? And the local transportation planners say, 'Yes, we've got to add new multi-occupancy lanes as well as HOV lanes as a way of dealing with this thirty-seven percent growth.' A lot of people feel like in the long term that portends disaster because people will just fill them up. And that gets back to land use. Can you fundamentally deal with this until you fundamentally change land-use decisions? And that gets to this whole question of regional government that we're struggling with."

"So the air looks better, feels better," I said.

"Right."

"But you're still sitting in traffic."

"You're still sitting in traffic. There's a very legitimate question that none of us has answered. I ask the question, what happens after 2010? What happens in 2030? What do you do with the congestion then? I mean, when are we ever going to fundamentally change the way we do business here so that we have a sustainable program for absorbing and maintaining higher and higher levels of population?"

NOPE, NOT ENOUGH

James Lents is among the most laudable managers of the commons in the nation. He and his merry band of regulators may eventually make the air in Los Angeles safe and easy to breathe, but with the inevitable increase in congestion and sprawl, the quality of life in L.A. will—face it—decrease. Unocal can buy my old clunker and I can plant myself in a new electric Impact with an on-board computer and drive it in the carpool lane, but traffic will be worse than it is now (no matter what city I live in) and my job and my home and my friends will be scattered hither and yon in increasingly distant and increasingly bland suburbs. The work of SCAQMD and the California Air Resources Board is exemplary, an inspiration to environmentally committed administrators everywhere, but at best it's only a partial solution; one very large step, but we need more.

But even more drastic measures, such as putting a quota on the amount of cars sold in an area (such as Singapore does), or adding a couple of bucks' tax per gallon of gasoline (as the Europeans do), or even measures now being considered by the L.A. basin's South Coast Association of Governments, such as registration fees based on how many miles you travel— providing, of course, that you could pass such measures without the outlying car-dependent suburbs declaring an out-and-out jihad—would not do it. If we are to achieve genuine composure in the driving ecosystem before all our cities look like Los Angeles in the movie *Blade Runner*, we are going to have to reexamine how we pattern our homes and businesses. When you get right down to it, it's impossible to separate transportation from growth and land-use issues.

"The basic problem on the planet today is the scale of human activities," ecologist Paul Ehrlich told me. He was not in a good mood that day. I had seen him at a public lecture a few nights before, pacing back and forth on the stage, holding the audience breathless with his appraisal of global ecological problems. "One doesn't have to argue pro or con against gasguzzlers so much as to point out that if the U.S. had stopped its population growth in 1945, when we drove gas-guzzlers and were as wasteful of energy as we are today, we wouldn't have to burn one drop of imported oil and we wouldn't have to burn one ounce of coal. The U.S. is growing far beyond any reasonably sustainable level. So goes the population, so goes the automobile. It's a nasty situation. The car itself is not the problem, the problem's the number of cars and the way we've designed our society around the car.

"From 1930 to 1990—sixty years, right?—we've ruined our cities. Between 1990 and 2050 we can re-create them. Maybe even faster, because it doesn't take that long to rebuild things. If you think of the average infrastructure as having a thirty-year half-life, you oughta be able to have huge changes in a few decades. *If* you had some leadership. But we haven't had any leadership from the top in quite a while. I'm not overwhelmingly confident we're going to do something, to say the least. Is that what you wanna hear?"

Vehicle
o f
Integration

If ecological good sense is to prevail, it can do so only through the work
and the will of the people of the local communities.
—Wendell Berry

L ike any diligent biologist, including those observing that part of nature
ruled by twisting black rivers and huge herds of steely, high-speed
beasts, you eventually come to some conclusions about how best to manage
the situation. For there *is* a solution to the ecological calamity of our current
transportation system. But that solution originates so deep in our biology
that its emergence will be something of an evolutionary event. And as with
all evolutionary events, it will be both apparent and incredibly practical.

To preserve the integrity of the species I call the hucar—that human/
car entity that has taken over the American landscape—and to renew the
overall quality of life in our urban regions, certain essential developments
need to unfold. They do not include a laundry list of dos and don'ts, nor
depend, like a child, on the authority of big government, big industry, or
high tech. No smart cars sailing down smart highways. Actual change will
mean waking up to the complex reality in which we live and drive. It will
mean an ongoing *shift* in how we see ourselves ecologically, how we view
and govern the related activities of our urban regions. It will mean envision-
ing a brand-new, never-existed-before, twenty-first-century world. In short,
it will mean something very different from what we have now.

DEEP CHANGE

"The problem is we all suffer from limited cognition," said William Garrison laxly. "We can only express our desires and what we want in terms of what's out there now." Garrison, the doyen of the Department of Transportation Science at the University of California at Berkeley, sat at his banquet-style table cluttered with papers, books, and periodicals that had spilled off surrounding shelves of the same. Composed, almost disinterested, he was like a king too comfortable in his reign.

"Go back through the situations in history and they're very comparable to what we have now," he continued. "Look at England in the 1830s; they had a good system of canals and roads. If you asked anybody what was needed in the world of transportation, they sort of fussed the way people fuss now about congestion. The toll roads are too expensive; there's too much government regulation; they're dragging their heels—all these kinds of things. But that's the system they had, and no one saw beyond it. In America in the 1820s the railroad came along. Nobody could imagine that there's a market for the railroad. What surprised everybody is that people started riding railroads as *passengers*, which they hadn't imagined people would do. Railroads are for crops, cotton bales, textiles, pottery. You had the same thing when the automobile highway system came along—there's no need for it, you already had railroads. You could get anywhere in the country you wanted by railroad.

"That's the kind of situation we have in the United States today. We have enormous resources; it appears as if we have it all. People think that all that needs to be done is tweak things here and there, impose some kind of government monitorship to fix the ills such as air pollution. The lesson from history is that there's always something waiting in the wings to come along and open up new paths for development and managerial problems. It seems to me we're at a point in the automobile highway system where the important thing to do is to think of new ways of doing what we're doing, as opposed to managing our problems by assuming it's always going to be like this, and we've merely got to tighten up here and there: put on more regulations, sacrifice, or ride mass transit.

"Let me put it this way: We have two worlds. One world that's driven by the energy of innovative people. The other half of the world consists of these big systems like transportation where we've got this *big* investment that's surrounded by regulation. Opportunity for innovation is very poor. We start 'path-dependence,' which means that decisions are made and the paths that follow are locked in. The problem of transportation is, how do you move one of these things that's eighty years old and hard to change? The automobile manufacturer can't produce anything different because it's got to fit on the existing roads, got to fit the regulations. The highway people can't produce different kinds of highways because they've got to fit the automobiles. It's a locked-in system. Locked in by standard and convention. Fundamentally it has to do with the life cycle of systems. Something gets started, you work out the technology, you deploy it, and you get all of the technological and social improvement from it that you can very early on. But now ours is an old system. That's what's the matter with it. It just doesn't lend itself to improvement anymore.

"What we need is not so much a new system. We need to evolve and renew. There's no such thing as a new system. The railroad was not a new system. It was built directly out of what was already there. It was a renewal of framework, a regurgitation, a rebuilding, a reemergence. It was a phoenix that burned and regrew.

"The saving grace is that change occurred in the past. That's the view we have, that change occurs. Now that view is held by me and half a dozen other people. But it's not widely held. Most people out there say, 'Well, congestion's getting worse, we can't build any more highways, so what are we gonna do?' And most of the answers are, I think, symbolic of stupid. They're stupid in the sense that people are proposing building mass transit systems, going back to railroads, proposing that we live in the urban village and work next door. If you look back at the history of the city, that's exactly what people have voted with their feet to get away from, for cryin' out loud! We do have this terrible problem of energy, CO_2, things we have to worry about. But the kinds of solutions that are being talked about, like changing to methanol, are not the solution to the problems. They're just a facade. Deeper change is needed."

FRAGMENTATION

J. Krishnamurti, the spiritual leader (who fanatically eschewed followers), used to say that the greatest evil in human consciousness and endeavor is the delusion of fragmentation. He believed it was false to suppose that something existed independently of its surroundings. Every discrete thing (each person, each car, each chipmunk . . .) forms an interdependent part of a complex system, which in turn forms part of another complex system, and any action reverberates through the whole interconnected web. But that holistic view does not inform the normal course of business in our cities and transportation modes. As Leon Eplan enumerated in Atlanta, no one part of a community or government operates in connection with the other. That was true of nearly every place I traveled. Highway construction is separate from the environment and the consequences of growth; driving is separate from alternative means of getting around; transportation is separate from land use; development is separate from traffic buildup; and each little village, township, county, or borough within one urban region operates as if separate from the rest—what upstate New York planner Fred Budde called "Local Home Rule."

One consequence of fragmented urban areas is haphazard growth, indifferent to limits, unplanned in any integrated manner. Look down from an orbiting satellite (and such remote photographs are available) and you'll see suburbs radiating out in all directions. Watch Los Angeles connecting with San Diego; Phoenix spreading out into the desert; San Francisco spilling into the San Joaquin Valley; Miami burgeoning up the coast and into the Everglades; and the huge wave of development in New York, New Jersey, and Connecticut spreading, unchecked, like a brushfire.

"It's terrible," lamented Gregg Geller, who grew up and owns a house in Suffolk County, Long Island. He told me of boyhood farms and forests turned into housing developments, nearby communities that "went from no people to hundreds of thousands. All these little boxes all over the place, and bumper-to-bumper traffic. On the easternmost end of the county, where we have our house, in the summertime it's so crowded you wouldn't want to know from it. It's the most wonderful place in the world, but it's terrible because there're too many people out there. You can't just say, 'It's Saturday night, let's go to a movie.' Even if you could get into the theater, you might not be able to park your car. We've had friends who've gotten a baby-sitter, have gone into town, and haven't been able to park their car. There's no room. It's really a shame."

Gregg's was just one of a hundred similar stories, and in recent years this "post-Interstate boom," as writer Tony Hiss calls it, has intensified. In *The Experience of Place*, Hiss writes, "In this latest development era, 'urban and suburban sprawl' is no longer descriptive, because the sprawl has been transformed into urban and suburban gobbling up and tearing at the ground, and it resembles the work of the great beasts of the last interglacial period, whose browsing destroyed large areas of thick forest."

In place of *urban sprawl* the term *slopalopolis* is making the rounds amid today's urban commentators. It's the product of grabby developers riding the ropes of questionable growth models, corporations fleeing the central cities to sidestep taxes, and the middle class trying to escape urban government and its sweeping expenses. And, of course, it's individual choice. People want space, a house with a lawn, no crime, a nice place to raise the kids. More than half of America now lives in towns far removed from the central city. The inner city conjures up anomic images of dysphoria and bleak sci-fi futures. The AIDS panic in San Francisco, the homeless of New York City, the racial strife of Chicago, the drug crimes of Miami, the bankruptcy of Philadelphia. Out in the suburbs, it's easy to pretend these problems don't exist.

Besides, "the central city has become superfluous," said John Kasarda of the Keenan Institute of Private Enterprise at the University of South Carolina. "You don't need to go there anymore to work or to buy specialty items or even attend a sports event. Look at where the office jobs and industrial jobs are now; they've moved to the suburbs. You really don't have to leave the suburbs anymore." One suburban government official called it the Back-to-Main-Street movement. Millions of renovation dollars are dumped into "cultural centers," mall-like complexes that showcase plays, exhibit art, lend space to sculpture, and attract sophisticated retail shops. Suburbs are doing whatever they can to convince themselves they are self-contained, that each little town and village is protected within its own niche. Yet despite the amenities, lasting culture and character seldom take root in such prefabricated communities.

Author Mike Davis describes L.A. as the perfect model, a "postmodern city of secessionist suburbs." People have burrowed into separate suburban villages, fought urban bureaucracy, waged tax protests, and in efforts to insulate their communities from outside intrusion, set up social and economic barriers, what Davis calls "spatial apartheid." The ideas of public space and social equality have long been forgotten.

There is no integration. In the L.A. basin, the word *planning* is an anathema. Yet L.A. is not alone. Without integration, the quality of urban life declines, inner barrios continue to decay, neighborhoods crumble, and transportation systems bog down. In 1989, UC Berkeley professor Robert Cervero, author of *Suburban Gridlock*, concluded that more suburbanites live farther from their workplaces than they did ten years ago, when most jobs were located in downtowns. As but one example, California's population has increased 50 percent in the last twenty years, yet miles traveled have increased by 125 percent.

Back-to-Main-Street is an illusion. No matter to which distant exurban netherland people flee, suburbs eventually accrue the same problems as the central city: crime, pollution, gridlock; and, what is worse, they extend the delusion that they really are separate, that Chicago or Boston or Dallas isn't just down the interstate a few miles and they're not part of one large, interconnected—tax-wise, population-wise, education-wise, environment-wise, culture-wise, transportation-wise—region.

BACK TO THE WOODS

To understand what we're up against, and to illustrate what must happen to spur deep change, I needed to venture, once again, out into the field. I needed to scrutinize one particular ecosystem until I wrung from it some inkling of a plausible future. Los Angeles, like New York City, was too immense and unwieldy. Besides, in the eyes (stinging, smoggy eyes) of many people, L.A. was already a goner. New York, too, carried the onus of a city gone beyond the pale. I selected a more manageable scale, a region that several government representatives and urban planning experts have pinpointed as a model for potentially sustaining an efficient transportation system. I had to travel no farther than out my front door.

The San Francisco Bay Area, with its multivarious terrain (redwood forests, rolling hills, scenic seascapes), city concentrations (from the Silicon Valley to Santa Rosa to Oakland), and diversified people (soon *all* residents will be members of "minority" groups), is the ideal testing ground. It is certainly populated enough (6.2 million people in an area about the size of Massachusetts or Virginia), and is growing as fast as any urban region in the nation, sprawl fanning out like a metastasizing cancer: south, toward the green forests of Big Sur; east into the rich farmlands; and north into beautiful rolling dairy farms and wine valleys. The traffic congestion is sufficiently horrid; in fact, in terms of delay per mile, it is the worst in the United States. Bay Area drivers spend nearly 100 million hours in traffic jams each year; and the state Department of Transportation (Caltrans) predicts that by 1995 congestion will increase 150 percent. As for air quality, in 1992 the Bay Area Air Quality Management District felt obliged to impose controls even more strict than those of its much-hated sister city down south.

The Bay Area provides a perfect illustration of this country's ecological state of affairs; it's an instructive region in which to take a casual drive up to Mount Tamalpais, overlooking the entire bay, sit back, and watch the next self-organizing click of the evolutionary process. If, indeed, it will be a click for the better.

The Bay Area is as splintered as an urban region can get. Its nine counties branch into ninety-eight separate towns, each with its own mayor and political agenda; 721 special districts, not counting school districts; and twenty-seven operating transit agencies, each with its own schedules, fares, and (often overlapping) routes. The only regional transit system, the heavy-rail BART (Bay Area Rapid Transit), was originally planned to link all nine counties with three hundred miles of electrified routes; but almost twenty years after its onset, only seventy-one miles serve three counties. The other counties voted against BART because they either didn't want to pay for it or because they feared the people and development it would bring.

More and more national urban planners are encouraging metropolitan regions to take responsibility for their transportation systems and to broaden those systems from highways to all forms of transportation, but in reality such efforts are stymied by turf protection, governmental squabbling and infighting, economic self-interest, and slothlike bureaucracies, which make attempting any progressive change a lesson in futility. Angelo Siracusa, president of the Bay Area Council, a regional public affairs organization, blames "political cowardice" for the mess, saying, "I don't think the Bay Area would let us build the Golden Gate Bridge today."

INTO THE FRAY

In the Bay Area, as in most urban regions, transportation policies are forged in the crucible of the public sector (politicians and bureaucrats) and the private sector (developers). Entering the fray with an increasingly stronger presence in the last decade have been the environmentalists. All three parties are united in a game of land use. For it's how and where you lay out the houses, retail stores, and businesses that determines transportation routes and modes of travel. But of course each party comes to the game board with its own set of rules. The developers see dollar signs in open space. They see business parks, housing tracts, and malls with multiple department stores. The environmentalists want to preserve watershed lands, ranches, farms, parks, and open space. They see nourishment in nature that cannot be reduced to a price. Beholden to their local constituencies, politicians simply go with the flow that keeps them in office. When it's their turn to choose the rules, they generally defer to those with the demonstrated power, who are more often than not the monied developers and their allies in the banking industries.

My initial guide through the battlefield of Bay Area transportation was environmentalist Ken Ryan. As the newest members in the game, environmentalists must possess incisive knowledge of their opponents' strategies and put previous land-use skirmishes into perspective. Environmentalists, too, make for trustworthy guides, if only because they have the least to gain financially from promoting their agendas. There is little money in caring for the planet.

For Ryan, there is none. As the California state transportation chair for the Sierra Club, he passionately monitors transportation issues and makes policy recommendations to the state and local governments for no pay whatsoever. I met Ken in his small office in Richmond, the Bay Area's blue-collar town just north of San Francisco. Yes, he said, the car was at ground zero of the area's transportation mess. "The one thing about the automobile is that it allows you to go absolutely anywhere. If you go one square inch in an automobile, then development patterns follow. Sprawl is a pure response to the automobile. But cars are just a symptom. The real problem is the way we build cities and handle growth."

And the Bay Area has handled growth no differently than other areas; it has allowed new development to fan out from the central city, leaving new swaths of highways, cars, and pollution in its path. While from 1980 to 1990 the Bay Area's population grew 16 percent, haphazard land patterns contributed to a 25 percent increase in daily commuters. Because the Bay Area's public transit systems were never designed to serve outlying communities, ridership declined dramatically in the last decade. Carpooling also dwindled as businesses scattered hither and yon, and Bay Area garages filled up with cars. "We're now at the point in suburban living where there's about one and three-quarters car per person," said Ryan. He laughed. "I guess that means you have one car for every adult who can drive, and at least one spare for when one of those is broken down."

To curb growth and halt the spread of cars, environmentalists would like to see the Bay Area adopt "urban limit lines." Geographically drawn around cities, especially the fast-growing cities located forty miles northeast of San Francisco in the rolling hills and green valleys of Contra Costa County, these lines would corral sprawl and ensure open space. Growth would be managed inside the lines, leading to denser patterns of shops, businesses, and housing. Studies show that for every doubling of housing density (people per acre) commuters use the car 30 percent less. Higher densities of homes, shops, and businesses also increase the economic feasibility of mass transit. Greenbelt Alliance, one of the area's more strident and hardworking environmental groups, claims that, properly planned, the existing urban zones of the Bay Area could accommodate projected new growth for the next several decades.

"The key to breaking the suburbia/highway extension cycle lies in revitalizing city centers," said Ryan. "City centers are the economic focus of a community. It's where businesses, entertainment, and government are all located. It used to be the job and retail center as well." Mass transit would also function more readily if businesses and residences were located closer together, and "if you come back to a transit-oriented society, one of the things you come to is some densification of transit stops, a business center of transit stops, and more walkable communities."

Ryan would simply like to see the world slow down and people rediscover a sense of community. "What is this god-awful rush that we try to live in all the time?" he asked. Besides, he said, it was a myth that today's car-oriented transportation system was any faster than the commuter systems of the past. "My wife's grandfather lived in the Adams Point area of Oakland all his life. He was a chemist for the U.S. government. Starting in the 1920s he commuted to work every day for forty-some years. He took the streetcar to the ferry, and the ferry to San Francisco. Shortly after they built the Bay Bridge—and he was one of the first people to cross it in a car—he retired. But by then it took just as long to *drive* from Adams Point to where he worked as when he used to take the ferry."

Ryan continued: "We're not going to get out of the crisis tomorrow. We have allowed the automobile culture to permeate our society and we've encouraged it. But over time, the nature of California cities is going to have to change. We don't have any choice, or at least we don't have any acceptable choice. If we keep on the way we've been going, we'll just have more air pollution and less open space. The choice is simple: Do we continue to grow out, or do we start the process of growing up?"

JOBS NOT HOUSES

If only the choice were that simple. Establishing urban limit lines would have to reverse the forces of sprawl. And in the Bay Area, sprawl and its offspring, traffic, have been powered by a money-hungry drive to boost local coffers. Since the passage of State Proposition 13 in 1978, which significantly lowered property taxes, suburban municipalities have encouraged commercial development over residential. Housing can be a drain on the public till. It requires schools, roads, sidewalks, and sewer systems. On the other hand, commercial properties pay fat taxes. They also attract wealthy developers, major corporations, jobs, and employees spending money on local services. In *Suburban Gridlock*, Robert Cervero reports that one of the nation's most graphic examples of "exclusive zoning run amok" can be found in the Bay Area's Santa Clara County: "There, enough land has been zoned to support 250,000 new jobs but only 70,000 new housing units. Neighboring Alameda and Santa Cruz counties have been saddled with housing many of Santa Clara County's displaced workers. As a consequence, one-way commutes of fifty miles to Santa Clara's Silicon Valley are not uncommon."

But the zoning imbalance doesn't tell the whole story. Relatively few employees can afford to live near their workplaces. In the eastern upper-middle-class suburb of Walnut Creek, writes Cervero, "a community that experienced explosive office growth over the past several years, the median home costs nearly $200,000, requiring roughly a $61,000 annual household income to qualify for, yet the median yearly income of its work force is just under $32,000. Clearly, it will take more than some numerical parity in jobs and housing to reduce suburban commuting." Cervero's book was published in 1986, but seven years later parity has become even more of a pipe dream. The median price for a detached single-family home in the entire Bay Area is now $260,000, the highest in the country. Housing is so expensive around the area's burgeoning office parks (what Joel Garreau calls "monuments to profit") that workers are moving to towns such as Tracy and Dixon in the San Joaquin Valley, once commonly referred to as "the sticks." But the sticks include some of the most productive farmland on earth, as well as crucial wetlands for waterfowl's Pacific Flyway. Now these lands are dotted with tract homes, mini-malls, and car-filled streets.

Another undeniable factor widening the gap between jobs and houses has been the residents themselves. Because its communities have become so disparate, "the Bay Area has no demographic heart anymore," said Ray Brady, of the Association of Bay Area Governments. "It is very balkanized and smug with self-confidence, which motivates people to conserve what they have. So we subtly try to push out people who are different—poor people, for example." One of the most salient examples of residents battling growth has occurred in the suburban cities surrounding the Hacienda and Bishop Ranch business parks in Contra Costa County. Begun in the early eighties, these megaprojects will generate as many as 75,000 jobs by 2005. Initially, both business parks contained plans to provide on-site housing, but the plans were dropped when residents either voted for laws to limit any more development or passed referendums to prohibit zoning changes to residential housing. Affordable homes and apartments were already hard to come by in the towns adjacent to the business parks. Now they were banished to the hinterlands.

THE HIGHWAY GANG AND ICE TEA

But the suburban residents' plans to exclude growth have backfired, as anyone paralyzed in traffic on Walnut Creek's freeways and city streets will assuredly attest. In fact, as more commuters enter the Bay Area from outside its nine counties, traffic continues to spread across the entire region, leaving drivers blind with frustration, screaming for more lanes and roads. It's a scream that echoes loud and clear in the halls of city government, where beleaguered local politicians run to Caltrans (the California Department of Transportation) for help. And Caltrans has been only too willing to oblige. Although in 1973 the department promised to relieve the state's increasing congestion through a coordinated "multimodal" approach that would balance highways and mass transit, the vast majority of its efforts have been in building new roads. According to a study by the Institute for

Transportation Studies at UC Berkeley, Caltrans's love affair with laying cement "reflects both its historical origins and the continuing predominance of highway engineers in its work force."

In an investigation of Caltrans called "The Highway Gang," the *San Francisco Bay Guardian*, the city's weekly newspaper, found that the agency's prohighway bias was so deeply institutionalized that it "has refused to recognize some important dynamics that affect transportation policy: that transportation planning shapes land use; that new highways always fill up and lead to more air pollution; that environmental destruction is a serious problem; that there may be limits on growth; that the way to solve the transportation crisis is to get people out of their cars."

Caltrans, in turn, is overseen by the California Transportation Commission (CTC), which is empowered by the state to determine which projects should be funded. As the *Guardian* revealed, it was clear where the money would be spent, as CTC was composed of members who have "historically benefited from the continued expansion of the state's highway system." In the early nineties its nine members include "five real estate developers and development consultants, two shopping mall moguls, a tire manufacturer and the president of a heavy-machinery supply company."

With a state board of transportation commissioners who privately profit from sprawl, a state transportation agency stacked with road engineers, and local mayors unable to avoid daily complaints about crowded freeways, it's little wonder that the Bay Area has paved over its parcel of Northern Californian paradise. Promises of real change, though, can be heard from Washington. In November 1991, Congress launched into law a bill that would push the Bay Area and other metropolitan areas to break their addiction to highways and cars. Called the Intermodal Surface Transportation Efficiency Act (ISTEA) and affectionately known as "Ice Tea," the new act is the most progressive transportation bill since the one that built the nation's interstate highway system. ISTEA provides historic incentives for metropolitan areas to lay track for mass transit rather than cement for more roads. In New Jersey, for instance, they're wasting no time putting ISTEA to work. In early 1992 state officials announced they were weaning residents from cars by doubling the state's investment in mass transit and creating a statewide system of integrated, low-pollution commuter trains.

On the other hand, though, ISTEA is business as usual. Of its federal allotment of $151 billion for six years, $119 billion is set aside for highways and bridges. So in boardrooms across the country, executives of road-building firms, granite and asphalt companies, steel corporations, and major engineering firms are no doubt smiling like the Cheshire cat, anticipating hefty government contracts. Nevertheless, the $31.5 billion allotted for mass transit represents a 64 percent increase over the allotment in the previous federal transportation bill, and there are other unique aspects as well: nearly $6 billion is earmarked to help urban areas reduce congestion and comply with state air quality standards; and $660 million is set aside for Intelligent Vehicle Highway Systems (IVHS). Clearly, though, the most revolutionary aspect of the bill is its provision for flexible funding. When I was in Atlanta, urban planning expert Leon Eplan complained to me, "We're not going to deal with the issues, whether those issues are transportation or school or environmental issues, until the federal government has the will to say, 'We're not going to tell you how to solve your problems, but we're going to tell you that either you solve your problems or have a plan for solving your problems, or we're going to cut you off at the knees.' "

According to Congressman Norman Mineta, ISTEA's primary architect, and chairman of the House Subcommittee on Surface Transportation, that is precisely what ISTEA was saying. Realizing that it was high time for "the feds" to quit dictating transportation solutions was Mineta's motivating force in drafting the plan. Seated in his district office in San Jose, Mineta explained to me how ISTEA would take hold of the country's transportation crisis by encouraging metropolitan leaders to adopt both mass transit and regional transportation plans. He began with a little history.

"During the sixties and seventies, we spent roughly 2.3 percent of our GNP on transportation infrastructure. In the eighties, that has dropped to four-tenths of one percent. And then people wonder, 'Well, now, why has urban congestion gone up sixty percent in the last ten years? Why are fifty percent of our bridges falling down?' All because we were not making the investment in our transportation systems.

"So now we're increasing the amount by a great deal, and at the same time there's a great deal of flexibility for local jurisdictions to say, through their Metropolitan Planning Organizations, 'I want to forgo this kind of highway improvement and move the highway money over here into the transit side.' Now, remember, transit is not only buses, light rail, heavy rail, but it's also carpooling and van pooling. So this fund transfer makes those kinds of conversions possible. State departments of transportation have always had an automobile bias, but the flexibility in ISTEA allows different means of transportation solutions to be offered in any given community."

In the past, Mineta pointed out, the federal government subsidized 90 percent of the cost of building roads, yet only 50 percent of mass transit. For instance, if the Bay Area suburb of Walnut Creek wanted to make a $1,000 transportation improvement on a stretch of land, the state and city would have to come up with only $100 for a highway (10 percent). If Walnut Creek wanted to build mass transit instead, the state and city would have to pony up $500. "So what happened," continued Mineta, "is everyone went to road building and not to transit." ISTEA, however, provides an 80 percent subsidy for mass transit. "In that way we've taken the tilt out of how local people will be making decisions based on how much they'll be getting back from federal coffers. I've made a level playing field so that local areas can make the best *transportation* decisions, not decisions based on how much money they're going to be getting back into the community."

But Mineta stressed that ISTEA alone was not a solution. "The Clean Air Act without a doubt is going to be the most important driving factor in the transportation future," he said. To attain the ironhanded air standards set by the Clean Air Act in nonattainment metropolitan areas (places where, according to the Environmental Protection Agency, lung-damaging ozone exceeds safe levels), each state would have to instigate tough and efficient transportation measures. "So in places like the San Francisco Bay Area and Los Angeles, where you have two major metropolitan areas with regional transportation authorities, the big problem is clean air. They're going, 'Holy cow, how am I going to be able to comply with these clean air standards?' ISTEA comes along and says, 'Here's a way; we will be a resource for you.' The Clean Air Act without ISTEA would have done nothing. ISTEA now puts the meat on the bone. It says, 'Here's the funds.'"

And of all the places in the country, Los Angeles and the Bay Area need the money most, if only because they have the strictest air quality standards. Mineta added that if any place in the country could make ISTEA work in conjunction with the Clean Air Act, it was the Bay Area. "I always use the Bay Area as a good example of what can be done," he said. "And MTC [the Bay Area's Metropolitan Transportation Commission] is the premier example of what a good regional transportation planning agency can do."

But, I asked, how can MTC or any like agency be effective planners when they just direct federal and state funds to various local transportation projects?

"If we were playing a game and you control land-use planning and I control transportation, I win every time," Mineta said. "Look back to when the wagon trains were being pulled across the country, or railroads, or now take a local community like the Bay Area. It's where, for instance, you set your BART lines that's the signal as to where the development will occur in the future. So a planning agency like MTC becomes very important. Because of their ability to do regional transportation planning, they will be able to deal with congestion management as well as land use. Still, our big problem here is clean air. So to the extent that MTC is able to comply with the Clean Air Act, the faster we'll be able to get the job done."

FREEWAY REVOLT

Congressman Mineta struck me as a savvy legislator, but at the same time ISTEA struck me as the proverbial happy face on the transportation crisis. For there is little evidence that metropolitan planning organizations can wrest power from the politically formidable highway-interest groups—road builders, auto manufacturers, commercial and residential developers—and arrest the forces of sprawl and congestion. It's an unfortunate irony that Mineta holds up the Bay Area's MTC as a model of progressive transportation planning when in fact MTC's recent history illustrates the very ineffectiveness of a metropolitan planning organization.

For years environmentalists and concerned citizens had been searching for a means to curtail sprawl and its resultant pollution in the Bay Area. "The facilities have always filled up faster than Caltrans thought, and the congestion has reappeared much more quickly than anyone believed possible," said Bill Curtiss, an attorney for the Sierra Club Legal Defense Fund, a public-interest, nonprofit law firm not directly connected to the environmental group. He was referring to what has been called the "Treadmill Effect," well-known in places like Miami, Houston, and Los Angeles, whereby the more freeways and highways you build, the faster the area grows and consequently the more crowded the freeways become. "We've been going through that vicious cycle for forty years in the Bay Area," Curtiss said. "It's like drilling holes in the bottom of a leaky boat to let the water out."

In 1989, even before Congressman Mineta actually declared that the Clean Air Act would be the most powerful tool in revamping transportation, the Sierra Club and Curtiss put the Clean Air Act to task. Discovering that four new highway projects planned for the Bay Area would violate federal air standards by inducing growth and adding more polluting cars to the roads, the Sierra Club, along with Citizens for a Better Environment, conscripted Curtiss's legal talents and sued MTC, which had approved the highway funds. The environmentalists claimed that MTC's authorization of the projects reneged on a 1982 regional amendment of the federal Clean Air Act. The regional plan required MTC to adopt a series of transportation-control measures to reduce auto emissions. In May 1990, Judge Thelton E. Henderson of the U.S. District Court in San Francisco ruled that MTC was not making sufficient progress toward meeting the clean air goals, and ordered MTC to provide detailed studies of how it planned to reduce emissions. Despite the ruling, MTC authorized four Caltrans lane-widening projects, prompting Curtiss and company to rush back into court and demand that the work be stopped. In December 1990, Judge Henderson issued a court order halting construction on three of the four projects.

The Sierra Club was not exactly gloating over the temporary injunction. Ken Ryan admitted that it was "absurd" to attack MTC when the real problem was reckless land-use practices of the "local development community." Nevertheless, the suit provided the only course of action for citizens to curb the equally absurd spread of highways. "Ken's sort of a political guru, and I don't claim to be," Curtiss told me one afternoon in his San Francisco office. "I just beat people over the head with this stuff."

Curtiss was enthused by the fact that the case could set a national precedent. "This case is typical of dozens of other major metropolitan areas in that all during the Reagan administration it was said that you don't really have to take the Clean Air Act seriously. Congress laid out a clear message about clean air in 1977, but it was never followed. What this case says is that there is a big penalty if you don't follow the act, and the penalty is that I'll shut down your highway-approval process until you get your house in order. That is a mind-expanding concept for transportation agencies, many of whom have this conflicting mission of being highway promoters on the one hand and air quality regulators on the other. They've always reconciled that conflict by forgetting about their Clean Air Act responsibilities and

mouthing a few ritual sentences every so often. In reality, they love highway projects. Since 1978 MTC has never seen a highway project that it
didn't like. The result in the Bay Area is that our air quality standard
remains below the standards set by the federal and state governments and
our vehicular end of the problem is out of control.

"I hope our case is regarded as a disaster scenario for what could happen
if you get caught. The idea that a federal judge may come in and enforce it,
and hold your projects hostage because you're not doing your air quality
homework, is a big deal. Transportation agencies have never had to live
within their air quality budget. They assume they have unlimited check
writing overdraft protection, and they have written check after check."

The Sierra Club's lawsuit did not win it any friends in the transportation
community. At the MTC offices in Oakland, MTC executive director
Lawrence Dahms told me, "I think the environmentalists should see us as
their friends, and instead they've got us positioned as their enemy. They're
bleeding me to death in court with this lawsuit. I don't have the kind of
budget to be able to sustain that sort of thing. I'm also having to divert a lot
of resources into the debate. My transportation modelers, the people I have
assigned to deal with air quality issues around here, are all chasing down
studies for the court case."

At first Dahms was defensive. He insisted that MTC was blameless. He
referred to the massive project of widening Interstate 680 and Highway 24
near Walnut Creek as "largely a product of history and the responsibility of
Caltrans. We did have to approve the funding for it, but it was a nonchoice.
It was: *approve* the funding for that project or *approve* the funding for that
project. The funds were already devoted by the state, and the project had an
incredible momentum."

Dahms didn't want to ruffle his relationship with federal and state
legislators. A generally reserved man, Dahms was beginning to get
steamed. "MTC's function essentially is mobility, with mass transit being
the preferred approach to mobility. OK? But had we decided, as the Sierra
Club has decided, that all highway development is bad, and yet had to deal
with a lot of people in Washington and Sacramento who don't agree with
that point of view, we could never be effective. So, you know, the Sierra
Club doesn't seem to make any bones about the fact that their suit has
nothing to do with air quality and has a lot to do with their desire to shut
down the highway program and try to slow growth."

Curtiss had no patience for MTC's political machinations. "Let's get real," he exclaimed. "The Sierra Club has never hidden its agenda about growth. Urban sprawl sucks. It consumes energy, it sucks up land, it drives away agriculture, it consumes more water, it consumes more of everything than other land-use practices. The thing that Larry won't concede is that air quality impacts what he's doing, with or without the land-use agenda. And it *isn't* just air quality that we're talking about. Larry's talking about a hidden agenda, but there's a broader agenda here. It not only includes land use but takes into account global warming, energy use, international and national energy policies. This freeway mentality and automobile-dependent growth is an ostrich with its head stuck in the sand of the past. All this talk about alternative fuels and alternative technologies to reduce air pollution is really a means to save the automobile and our relationship with the automobile. It's the Holy Grail of the highway-fixated planners that electric cars, or ultra-low-emitting cars, are going to save us. Technology is going to save us. It's the same old cry. Without any fundamental changes in transportation and land use, we're headed down a dead end at lightning speed."

Alas, Curtiss and company's freeway revolt failed. In May 1992, MTC convinced Judge Henderson that its planned transportation-control measures—such as more car pool lanes, van pool incentives, and better access to rail systems—constituted sufficient progress toward meeting the 1982 federal air standards. MTC's experts also produced studies to show that adding lanes to the disputed highway projects would increase mobility and thus reduce the emissions of cars otherwise idling in traffic. The environmentalists countered with their own transportation experts, who proved by iterating the equations over time that a reduction in emissions would soon be offset by the amount of cars, vehicle miles traveled, and growth that the highway projects would generate. But their arguments were to no avail. The judge lifted the ban, and Caltrans's tractors rolled back onto the job.

John Woodbury, former Oakland city planner, and now president of the board of directors of AC Transit, the public bus system that covers the East Bay, including Oakland and Berkeley, put the two-year dispute into perspective for me. "Ultimately, the case got into that area where the experts will debate each other so much that the court did what courts normally do, and that's say, 'We're outta here! This is beyond our expertise to question.'

The traffic engineers who argued MTC's side said there's no clear evidence on how much growth that highways induce, and because there's no clear evidence, we're going to assume there's none. Everyone agreed that highways fill up and trying to put a number on growth was difficult. But zero is clearly the wrong answer. Nevertheless, they got away with it legally. So now we have a court-approved methodology that proves that highway construction improves air quality. And MTC can continue to improve as many highway projects as they want."

We spoke in his home in Oakland, surrounded by maps of the Bay Area's topography and transit lines. Woodbury's friendly, casual manner almost belied his social conviction. He stressed that MTC's lack of power was indeed the flaw in the ISTEA panacea. In theory, he agreed that ISTEA's celebrated "flexibility" allowed more money to be spent on mass transit; but in reality, he said, "all the freeways still on the books have to be finished before new mass transit projects can go forward." Woodbury smiled when I told him that Congressman Mineta claimed that MTC could control land use by controlling transportation. "Historically, MTC has chosen, very clearly, not to get into land use. They have said, 'We're not a land-use-planning agency, we simply respond to what the local jurisdiction decides to do; we're not going to tell them they can't build in a certain area.' Just look at who's on MTC. The nineteen-member commission is composed primarily of people who are appointed—some are elected officials—by different elected officials, by mayors' offices, by the state legislature. So, by and large, MTC represents the status quo in how growth is occurring, and where it's occurring. I would argue that MTC is largely dominated by suburban interests. I'm sure MTC would disagree. But I look at where the money's going, and it's going primarily to the BART program, which to me is a suburban program: how to get people from the suburbs to downtown."

Practically before the ink on the document was dry, ISTEA awarded a large portion of the Bay Area's designated mass transit money—$568 million—to BART. The money will be employed to extend BART into the northeastern towns of Pittsburg and Antioch. Yet BART's route does not serve most Bay Area workers, who now commute from suburb to suburb. While San Francisco- and Oakland-bound commuters in far-flung Antioch may welcome the extension, Woodbury pointed out that the price of the extension—an annual capital expenditure of about $8,000 per rider—

outweighed the benefit. "That's a hell of a lot of money to spend to get someone in Antioch to take BART downtown." He added that the ISTEA funds granted to BART also shortchanged the inner city. "Eight thousand dollars a year is more than we give the typical welfare family—but then we consider capital expenditure to be good in our system of government, and welfare as bad. There's no recognition of social equity." Woodbury pointed out that inner-city bus companies like AC Transit would receive only a sliver of ISTEA funds for their operating budgets; in the case of AC Transit, that's not nearly enough to restore recently cut services into low-income areas in Oakland, where people don't own cars.

Woodbury admitted that ISTEA's mandate to channel funds past the highway-happy state transportation agency to MTC was indeed a step in the right direction. Yet, he explained, MTC's ability to affect land use and advocate mass transit was further undermined by a 1990 California law to allow county-appointed Congestion Management Planning Agencies (CMPAs) to oversee county transportation funding. These agencies screen all projects, then hand down the ones they deem sufficient for funding to MTC, whose members make the final call. The Sierra Club's Ken Ryan, who referred to MTC as a "toothless wonder," was worried that all this business of CMPAs, or federally mandated Metropolitan Planning Organizations (MPOs), would "empower a lot of local politicians" and be comprised of an area's respective public works departments carrying on in the only way they have ever known: building roads. Already Contra Costa County's CMPA was being sued by Greenbelt Alliance over the county's plan to expand highways. Ryan felt these regional planning trends might eventually prove beneficial. But for the present they weren't enough, and he and the Sierra Club would continue to wage their small battles with their "war chest of lawyers."

THE BOGEYMAN

My mind swimming with an endless swarm of vague political acronyms (VPAs), with this group taking on that group, I decided to cut to the quick and go visit the grand archvillains: the developers, especially those "brick sniffers" who were ripping up the East Bay's rolling hills and valleys. So over the Oakland Hills I ventured into sprawl-land, into the Tri-Valley area (whose population has more than doubled, its jobs tripled, in the last twenty years), to corner the president of the Northern California Building Industry Association, the man who maneuvered homebuilders through the maze of government laws and regulations. I figured that sprawl started at his doorstep—which, of course, was located in San Ramon, the absolute paradigm of a prefabricated community. San Ramon was home of the Bishop Ranch Business Park—office space of Toyota, Chevron, and Pacific Bell, among other Fortune 500 companies—and the most exclusive residences for sale in the Bay Area, the Blackhawk development. Carved out of the side of the hills, as if to mimic Pacific Heights in San Francisco, Blackhawk's extravagant houses stand behind manicured green lawns, flower beds, and baroque iron gates. If you've got an extra few million dollars lying around, you can buy a house in Blackhawk. And if you so desire, the developer will make sure the house is fully equipped: indoor and outdoor furniture, swimming pool toys, towels in the closet, food in the cupboards—even a pet of your choice. Just ask John Madden, former coach of the Oakland Raiders, media good guy, and now Blackhawk resident. Or Tom Selleck. Not that anybody who lives in Blackhawk actually cares about domestic amenities. A friend of mine who works for a Bay Area life-style magazine was sent to Blackhawk to ask residents how they would spend $100,000 to remodel their kitchens. The very first woman he interviewed laughed and said, "Oh, what a lovely idea. But I haven't been in my kitchen in two years!"

Strewn out beneath the Olympian Blackhawk are housing tracts of a hodgepodge of architectural styles, all located in neighborhoods with names like Echo Ridge and Bent Creek Estates. On Crow Canyon Road at the bottom of San Ramon Valley, past the postmodern office buildings with tinted windows, past the mall of pizza parlors, movie multiplexes, dry cleaning and auto parts stores, past the gas stations of every stripe, I found the Building Industry Association located in an A-frame office building shaded by trees. Inside I met recently appointed president and CEO Gary Hambly, previously the association's director of government affairs. Homebuilders face anywhere from three hundred to six hundred pieces of legislation each year, and it was Hambly's job to analyze the material, make recommendations to the homebuilders, and arm the association's lobbyists with information for their battles in Sacramento. Both direct and thoughtful, Hambly was well versed in Bay Area land-use skirmishes among politicians, developers, and environmentalists. Not that he sympathized with all sides, mind you.

"It's funny dealing with the environmental community and the policies they allegedly want," he said. "I think the building industry can pretty much live with a lot of them, but the problem is that by the year 2005, thirty-three percent of the workers for the nine Bay Area counties are going to be coming from outside the nine counties to work. It's an interesting problem that's caused by the property tax issues. Communities want to attract commercial developers because those types of land uses create a tax base and pay for themselves. Housing doesn't pay its way, and especially housing that is less than two hundred thousand dollars, doesn't pay its way. So you have situations like San Ramon attracting high-prestige, campus-style commercial development. At the same time you don't have enough land zoned to accommodate the workers. And the housing they do approve is housing that is not suitable for the workers because, again, for reasons of fiscal responsibility and prestige, the city tries to attract Blackhawk-type developments. So what you have are most of the people who work in commercial projects commuting from somewhere else. By the same token, the environmentalists talk about high-density, in-filled development. That is very difficult to get approved politically because communities don't want it—they look at the low property values. So we have this series of contradictions that don't lead to any solutions. It's amazingly frustrating.

"Basically, we need to build forty-eight thousand housing units in the nine Bay Area counties a year to meet demand. That's what the statistics say. We've only done that twice in the last ten years. So that's why housing prices are so high here, because there is always more demand chasing less supply. Bay Area prices are the third highest in the nation. It's also a function of incredibly expensive land-use fees. [On top of the cost of the "dirt," residential developers must pay a land-use fee to cover roads and other public services like street lamps. In San Ramon, the land-use fee is $30,000 per unit.] That's why you see so many expensive houses, and that's why we have this incredible jobs-housing imbalance. We have Hacienda Business Park near here, which created one hundred thousand job opportunities, but the city of Pleasanton capped their housing at forty thousand. They're not even creating enough houses for the graduating senior classes. So a lot of my builders are building up in Tracy, which is real dumb in terms of the commute and utilization of highways. There's this family that goes to bed at seven o'clock at night, wakes up at three in the morning, and both of them have to commute to the Santa Clara Valley and turn around and go back every day. That's their life. It's ludicrous.

"All cities are interested in attracting commercial development. Commercial is king. No one wants residential. The commercial guys come in and they don't have to pay land-use fees. So residential builders are asked to pay the fees to accommodate the commercial impacts. Each year, new houses add one percent to the housing stock of the state, and yet we are asked to pay for all the sins of the past, like traffic screwups. And most of the problems are streets and roads that were engineered to accommodate the planning of the sixties, not the realities of the nineties. In the fifties, when they did a lot of planning for these areas, there was one car per family. Now it's very common to have three cars per family. So if we didn't add another new home, another new resident to this area, we'd still have an increasingly inadequate transportation network. People are driving more. People have more cars. And it's frustrating as an industry that we're being asked to take care of that problem. We didn't create it to a degree. We shouldn't be held responsible for impacts that were created by the larger community."

"Yet all these housing tracts generate more sprawl," I said.

"A lot of builders will look you straight in the eye and say, 'Yeah, we're in the sprawl business.' They make money because they go out and find cheap land on urban fringes and buy it and hold it for five years. It appreciates in value because the growth comes to them. They put up a single-family subdivision and then go out and buy another piece of cheap land. So yeah, they want the car society, they depend on that society because that's what they do. They don't do commercial, they don't do retail, they do single-family. That's their niche. They're in the sprawl business; they need it to exist.

"We as an industry have a moral obligation to meet demand. So as long as cities continue to zone and approve job-creating projects, then we have the responsibility to create the housing for the people who take the jobs. By 2005 we'll have created 881,000 new jobs in this region, and if we looked at all the zoning maps in this entire region and built to the maximum—which never happens—you'll be lucky to build fifty percent of that maximum. So our challenge is: If you don't want us to build houses, don't create jobs. The interesting phenomenon is, so much of our growth, because it can't be accommodated here, is pushed out to the Central Valley, and the

Central Valley is the second worst air basin in the state. It's going to be just like L.A. It has the potential of having the same kind of inversion problem of L.A.—a lot of heat with cold air on top which keeps the pollution in. So we are creating the next L.A. in the Central Valley. We're going to spoil the most fertile farmland in the country, and the environmentalists are partly to blame.

"In his book *The Environmental Hustle*, Bernie Frieden alleges that environmentalists sat around and said, 'OK, how can we be most effective in obstructing the growth?' They realized that going after the job creators would be devastating because you have to fight the unions and the people who want jobs. So they went after housing, and it's come to pass in a lot of ways. I don't see where people can claim we have a high quality of life when we can't even house our people. In this region, even in this sluggish economy, only thirteen percent of the people can afford a medium-priced home. There's not enough houses. We've driven the price of housing outside of the reach of most people. If you could build a house in this area for a hundred and fifty thousand dollars you could sell it overnight. You show us where we can, and we'll build it. But no one can because land costs are so high. So basically what they're doing is forcing us farther and farther from the job center. That, indeed, is creating undue burdens on the transportation system and forcing people to take these ridiculous commutes. That's the facts.

"Whose fault is it? I guess it's all our faults. There's no bogeyman. The problem is piss-poor planning. We're just not planning well. It's a failure of government. Government was put in place to accommodate the citizens and they're not accommodating their needs in transportation. We drive too much. But it's not the homebuilders' fault that you can't get people out of their cars. We underutilize our resources. A lot of things could be done by the employers: staggered work hours, forced carpooling, company van pools, and charging for parking. It's funny, down in Silicon Valley, we tried to help institute a car pool or van pool service. Those companies don't want their employees carpooling with other employees because there are so many trade secret issues. They don't want Lockheed engineers talking to the HP engineers because something in conversation might transfer. So there are a lot of things that are working against us doing the right thing."

"Both you and the environmentalists are advocating affordable housing," I said. "So why the adversarial relationship?"

"Environmentalists have a vision that's more global than practical. Even among themselves they can't agree where housing's needed. And many people, many of the elitists and obstructionists, have co-opted the environmental rhetoric and are using it for very selfish needs. Like neighborhood groups, like my mom and dad, who sit in their house they bought for forty thousand dollars and now has an appraised value of three hundred and seventy-five thousand dollars. It's a single-family tract home, but the thing that makes it so much more expensive or valuable is they're paying no fees, no increased property taxes, and they've been successful in their own neighborhood in obstructing any growth happening around it. So they still have their view of Mount Diablo, they still have open space all around it. And they've done that to their benefit. But at whose expense?

"Environmental protection comes with a cost. If you want to have environmental protection, we as an industry are willing to accept growth control. But growth control can't be based on some hypothetical dream or hope or expectation. It has to be based on some hard realities. If you're going to create jobs you have to create housing. If you're going to create people you have to create jobs for those people. We're realists, real pragmatic people. As long as there is a demand for our product, we'll be here. OK, you don't want us to build on the ridges, then zone higher in the valleys. You don't want us to build in the valleys, put us on the ridges. You don't want us here at all, don't create jobs. There will be no demand for our product. There would be no growth. At least we in Northern California are different from our brothers in Southern California. What's happening in L.A. is a disaster. The way they do development is absolutely ludicrous. It's just willy-nilly go-for-it. We as Northern Californians, in our own organization, are always advocating a jobs-housing balance.

"Everywhere, the growth/no-growth issue has gotten out of control. We're talking about the need for a fundamental restructuring of our tax system, our government, our school system. That's all got to happen in this decade. There's never going to be enough money to throw down enough new pavement to catch up with growth in California and the use of the car. This next decade we're going to have to address the most fundamental issues."

At the end of our "formal" interview, Gary and I sat around making fun of Blackhawk and lamenting the insane increase of traffic on nearby I-680, traffic in which I was about to be enmeshed for my drive back to San

Francisco. Gary then turned reflective. "You know, when I talk to politicians off the record, they point to their constituents making the decisions that leaders used to make. We have no leaders anymore; we have followers, we have people who read too many polls.

"It's a frightening future if we leave it in the hands of the parochial, narrow self-interests. Somebody has to draw the line. It has to be done. What is the alternative? Are we winning? Hell, no. Housing prices are soaring, the state's congested. Are the environmentalists winning? I don't think so. All we're doing is moving around chairs on the *Titanic*."

RADICAL INDIVIDUALISM

There exists an obvious answer to this jigsaw puzzle of unconnected and dissatisfied pieces, one that Hambly himself strongly advocates, a cooperative effort that would not only work for the Bay Area but for other American urban areas as well. It's called regionalism. But no solution will work without first considering the individual, who, in our democratic society, reflects the larger scale of community or region. In fact, larger scale solutions, real solutions, originate in individual changes.

Most criticism leveled at the car is a variation on the theme of the car as a *vehicle of separation*. It separates us from each other and our surroundings; it paralyzes our sensory awareness of our communities and land. While we're driving, the environment becomes "mediated" as the world rushes past our windshields like another TV program. Just as our urban areas are fragmented into competing factions, our highways are often regarded as warring battalions of cars, each driver desperately trying to protect his or her individual patch of asphalt. Each driver sits in his or her own distinctively shaped and colored car cocoon, equipped with sofa-comfortable seats and rock concert sound. Each driver is separate from the next.

Beyond offering mobility and convenience and an expression of personality, the automobile (the "self-mover") facilitates a true psychological sense of autonomy and freedom. Our favorite machines have helped foster a strong sense of individualism in this country. They are, in fact, operating symbols of individualism. Every cowboy/cowgirl in America today has a "horse." Everybody in America today has a sense of who they are (at no other time in history have there been as many well-honed individual egos wandering about), and the central focus of our lives is to see the strengthening, promotion, and stimulation of self.

The problem, evidently, is the overemphasis on individualism. "For over a hundred years," state Robert Bellah and his sociologist colleagues in *Habits of the Heart*,

> a large part of the American people, the middle class, has imagined that the virtual meaning of life lies in the acquisition of ever-increasing status, income and authority, from which genuine freedom is supposed to come. Our achievements have been enormous. They permit us the aspirations to become a genuinely humane society in a genuinely decent world, and provide many of the means to attain that aspiration. Yet we seem to be hovering on the very brink of disaster, not only from international conflict but from the internal incoherence of our own society. . . . What has failed at every level—from the society of nations to the national society to the local community to the family—is integration: we have failed to remember "our community as members of the same body," as John Winthrop put it. We have committed what to the republican founders of our nation was the cardinal sin: we have put our own good, as individuals, as groups, as a nation, ahead of the common good.

Everybody is riding around in a vehicle of separation. While the automobile has contributed to individualism's bad press in recent times (from the "Me Decade" to the "Greed Decade"), seldom has individualism been viewed in an evolutionary context. We often assume that we have always perceived ourselves and the world in exactly the same way. Yet as psychologist and author James Hillman reminds us, the collective mind is continuously reorganizing itself in relation to its ecology. (How else to explain why yesterday's attractive bedroom communities appear to us as today's sprawling architectural nightmares.) Hillman calls the complex organizational faculties of mind "fantasies." In reference to the automobile, he talks about "the dominant fantasy of self-determination" and asserts that we cannot cure the transportation problem "without a deeper change in character structure, which means our view of ourselves in the universe. If we would move the transportation problem, we must also shift the fantasies in which it is embedded."

Further evolution of consciousness means shifting this fantasy. It means expanding our sense of self beyond the boundaries of individual ego. Terms such as *transpersonal* and *deep ecology* are used to describe this widening awareness, but old words such as *community* and *environment* will do just fine. When I was in Miami, Joe Podgor, of the Friends of the Everglades, told me that the goal of his public activities was to assure people that acting in their self-interest was also in the best interest of their communities. "The extent to which self-interest is exclusive from the rest of the world is the distance that has to be gapped," he said. "You've got to show people that survival of the planet is in their interest. People are going to have to stop looking at this question of environment as something external to their lives." Joe maintained that "harnessing this self-interest" was "the only energy we've got in the eighties and nineties. So we harness it and hope that there's going to be enlightenment and change. We have our self-interest, but our self-interest is so broad we feel it's a public interest. It's our neighborhood and our world."

Hillman would no doubt appreciate Joe's efforts. "I would rather define self as the *interiorization of community*," Hillman told Michael Ventura in their book *We've Had a Hundred Years of Psychotherapy and the World's Getting Worse*. "And if you make that little move, then you're going to feel very different about things. If the self were defined as the interiorization of community, then the boundaries between me and another would be less sure. I would be with myself when I'm with others. I would not be with myself when I'm walking alone or meditating or imagining or in my room working on my dreams. In fact, I would be less estranged from myself. And 'others' would not just include other people because community, as I see it, is something more ecological. . . . So it wouldn't be 'I am because I think.' It would be, as somebody said to me the other night—'I am because I party.' "

ECO-AWARENESS

Trying to follow the currents of consciousness is admittedly an odd job for a car biologist, but there appears to be evidence of a shift, the first flutterings of an evolving and expanding sense of self. Contemporary sociologists have been taking note. In *Lonely in America*, Suzanne Gordon writes, "After a virtual orgy of *individualism*, Americans may finally be rejecting the idea that the best things in life come from looking out for No. 1." After buzzing from this job to that city, from this to that intimate relationship, Americans—especially the baby boomers—want to settle down and be a part of something new. It's the making of a powerful social movement, claims Mark Satin in *New Options*, his newsletter, "an integration of individualism and community" that promises to form "a true grass-roots democracy." Gleaned from my own field notebooks, this shift is evinced by an unfolding eco-awareness.

Almost everyone I talked with across these vast United States was both concerned about the environmental impact of the automobile—checking in somewhere along the spectrum of pollution to sprawl to congestion to dependence on foreign oil—and willing to change his or her car-dependent life-style. Even dyed-in-the-wool car buffs like Scott Schuette in Florida said, "I'll have to change, that's all I can really say. I guess I don't really want to, but I do want to do my part for the environment. I'll go along with strict emission laws." Besides, he said, he could always soup up alternative-energy cars. Even the staunch conservatives I interviewed, loath to be labeled environmentalists of any kind, admitted they would choose less energy-draining modes of transportation such as light-rail trains and electric cars if they were available. Nearly everyone wanted government and industry leaders to rein in their profligate ways and take a more exemplary role in transportation. "I want to know that the people who are at the root of the economic system that's created this problem are willing to make the sacrifice," said Tracy Santa of New Orleans. "My criteria for my action is that if I'm going to make a sacrifice, I want it to have an impact. That's important. I do not want to rush the machine gunners by myself." Houston district attorney Terry O'Rourke claimed that the "collective wisdom" of the citizens was "way ahead of the politicians and cultural leaders." He believed that Americans were on the cusp of an environmental aquarian age, poised for change. Increasingly, he was witnessing juries willing to throw the book at polluters. "The juries are just tired of the bullshit," he said. "They are becoming more aware, especially in terms of their own health conscious-ness. . . . They are, even right here in Houston, healthier. So yes, it's a larger awareness."

My questionnaire also reflected this larger awareness. Over 80 percent of my respondents said they "would be willing to change [their] driving habits to improve the environment." Offered twelve ways to improve the environmentally precarious state of driving, my respondents revealed that they are no longer mad about large cars. The vast majority said they would "accept performance restrictions on cars' engines" and "drive a much smaller, lighter, and less powerful car." Sixty-one percent of respondents said they would ride mass transit if it was available in their area. I even devised a numerical scale to measure drivers' "environmental awareness." Given a scoring range of 0 to 73, the average was 45, suggesting that individuals were indeed concerned with driving's negative impact on the environment. Not a revolutionary discovery, but a significant indication of drivers' changing attitudes.

My survey held few surprises. All national polls point to an ever-increasing eco-awareness. Doug Wheeler, former executive director of the Sierra Club and now secretary of resources under the Pete Wilson regime in California, said: "It's gotten to the point now where eighty percent of people identify themselves as environmentalists." All barometric readings look good. "The challenge now," said Wheeler, "rather than simply pointing with alarm to all these problems, is to help find solutions." A survey conducted by the Roper Organization indicated that 78 percent of Americans believe that a "major national effort" is warranted to improve our environment. The rub is that of 1,413 people polled, less than one-fourth were currently active in preserving the ecology. Roper ranked respondents in a descending order of environmental commitment: "true-blue greens, greenback greens, sprouts, grousers, and basic browns," with only the first two groups "actively working toward solutions to the problems." These people sacrifice time, effort, and money, and "believe that individual actions can make a difference in protecting the environment." Access to information about environmental problems constituted the key difference among the five categories.

But whether you're a fully hooked-up true-blue green or merely a mixed-up grouser, attitudes are changing. Is it possible that the car, the great instrument of social change in this century, can become a symbol of an emerging sense of ecology? It may be crazy to imagine that the beast (*Tyrannus mobilitis*) that has nearly devastated its ecosystem can become a pivotal means of raising ecological consciousness, but that's how it's beginning to look. Strangely enough, our relationship with the car is changing to a point where driving is beginning to bring us into closer contact with nature, including *urban nature,* and providing an increased awareness of environment and community: things larger than our individual selves.

WELCOME TO THE MODERN WORLD

"Technology catalyzes changes not only in what we do but in how we think," writes Sherry Turkle in *The Second Self.* "It changes people's awareness of themselves, of one another, of their relationship with the world." Turkle is writing about the emergence of the computer in American life, but if there is any piece of technology that embodies a second self it is the automobile. Cars have forever shaped our sense of self and perception of the world, whether we're simply talking about a Corvette sending a person's self-esteem to the stars or a Geo Metro making a driver feel good about conserving oil. Yet many critics continue to disparage technology's role in modern life—and maintain, as author Kirkpatrick Sale points out, that the effect of scientific technology "has been to put a vast psychic distance between humans and nature." But such criticism fails to acknowledge the evolution of consciousness. Why shouldn't technology be viewed as part of nature? Maintaining the dichotomy only feeds the forces of fragmentation. Besides, people everywhere seem to have the same respect for a car or highway as they do for a tree or stream. By that I mean ecological respect: consideration for how cars and highways fit in with and relate to their lives and surroundings. Technology itself does not separate us from nature. The division is created by our own segmented beliefs and actions.

We're the products of a co-evolutionary process of mind and machine. Machines continually take on more mindlike qualities, while we continually become more dependent upon the fruits of technology. As we continue to merge with our machines, our relationship with the world cannot help but change. On the simple consumer level, as market researcher J. D. Power said, our kinship with the car has grown deeper and stronger: it's a relationship we expect to last longer, because cars are now better built and more dependable. But this kinship is not so one-dimensional. A sense of personness, of autonomy and personality, of freedom and mobility, has taken hold—but not in isolation. The car becomes a transparent extension of ourselves, feeling more self-assured motoring down the highway, and our awareness is expanded, not only to other drivers and the driving ecosystem but eventually to our entire ecological surroundings. We see the car in its environmental context and not only consider the car itself, but the community, the air, and the open land around us. Rather than a means of separation, the car becomes a *vehicle of integration*.

"The pleasure of driving is what I like," Tom Tompkins of the Bay Area said. "But it isn't just the act of driving. It's the world around you. You go through neighborhoods, you're feeling different parts of the city, you're interacting with people. You're seeing life as it exists—the daily trivialities of people going about their business. It's a mobile way of plugging into the world."

The car is a vehicle of integration in the sense that just as it feels good to own and drive a car, it feels good to experience the environment we're driving through. From behind the wheel there is a heightened awareness and sense of place that is very important. For to help change a troubled ecology (urban or otherwise) first we literally need to feel a part of it. We may take pride in how our car looks and is maintained, but our vision looking *out* of the car is just as important as our vision *of* the car. Driving through an environment that is crowded, smoggy, or just plain ugly—because of inner-city decay or haphazard sprawl and lack of open land—shatters our sense of integration. It's as though the car had all of a sudden malfunctioned and had become unpleasant to drive. Even if we're in a brand-new Lexus with the London Philharmonic Orchestra in the backseat, the comfort and music will not shield us from the uncomely muddle through which we're traveling.

When we truly feel a part of our environment, like the connection we feel with our car, with our family, with our house—when we realize we *are* the environment—then we will get stirred up enough for individual and political action. In any event, we will no longer be passive observers. We will no longer feel so separate from that high-energy, constantly fluctuating, self-organizing holomovement outside our windshield.

THE AUTOPOIETIC PARADOX

It's a stranger world out there than we sometimes know. The old models of reality that most of us learned in school are no longer appropriate. The old reductionist watchmaker view of the world has nearly vanished. It has given way to an understanding that all complex forms—a tree or automobile, a forest or city—are interwoven systems that require a holistic view. Describing a complex system in modern scientific terms requires taking a system's various factors, components, influences, and feedback loops and winding them into a nonlinear, unpredictable computer model. This "systems ecology" approach takes some odd twists and turns, one of which is known as the "autopoietic paradox." Basically, this paradox states that individuality is an illusion. Modern science, drawing on the disciplines of biology and physics, restates the essential Buddhist notion that the idea of separation or fragmentation is a delusion. Integration is the norm for complex systems, even for symbiotic human-machine forms such as the hucar.

The concept of autopoieses (Greek for "self-production") was developed by theoretical biologist Humberto Maturana. He stipulated that the internal organization of an organism (its structure) is maintained by a series of feedback loops that allow the organism to adjust to the fluctuating rigors of its environment. Maturana maintained that an organism derived its very identity from this continuous interchange. Gaining its autonomous identity from the environment, explain John Briggs and F. David Peat in *The Turbulent Mirror*, is what makes autopoietic systems "remarkable creatures of paradox." The authors continue:

> Because autopoietic structures [like you and me] are self-renewing, they are highly autonomous, each one having its separate identity, which it continually maintains. Yet, like other open systems, autopoietic structures are also inextricably embedded in and inextricably linked with their environment—which is necessarily a far-from-equilibrium environment of high-energy flows involving food, sunlight, available chemicals, and heat. To express the paradox another way: Each autopoietic structure has a unique history, but its history is tied to the history of the larger environment and other autopoietic structures: an interwovenness of time's arrow. Autopoietic structures have definite boundaries, such as a semipermeable membrane, but the boundaries are open and connect the system with almost unimaginable complexity to the world around it.

Other modern scientists have arrived at similar conclusions. Physicist David Bohm refers to each individual entity (organic or not) as a "relatively autonomous subtotality," a nifty term to blur the boundaries between the individual and environment. Ilya Prigogine calls each individual entity a "dissipative structure," and also maintains that each complex form maintains its shape as a result of constant and dynamic interchange with its environment, an interpenetration that exists on many levels. According to Prigogine, autonomous structures or organizations do not exist separately: their *independence* is literally based on *interdependence*. Again, the autopoietic paradox: the greater an entity's autonomy, the deeper its connection with the environment.

Briggs and Peat ask: "Could the discovery that individuality is at its root a cooperative venture be taking us toward a new kind of holism—a holism which will resolve the apparent conflict between individual freedom and collective need? . . . At this moment, immersed in a chaotic flux of our own making, we may come to realize that to continue as the individuals we have become we will have to couple on a worldwide scale with each other and with the environment." It's cooperate or perish, they point out.

The language of modern science may be the best way to describe today's predicament of cars and the environment. We can either resolve the conflict between our individual freedom as drivers and the collective health of our environment, or we can contribute to the ecosystem's perishment. Along the road the signs seem to be pointing toward resolution. Modern physics tells us we are both part of the environment and responsible for its evolution; psychologists find consciousness evolving beyond the bounds of the ego; sociologists see us understanding our role in the community; and pollsters and field biologists (like me) attest to an expanding ecological awareness in America.

A perception of systems ecology is definitely beginning to unfold. Even in Motor City. While I was there, David Cole agreed that resolving the country's transportation mess would mean adopting a systems approach to our urban areas. "It's absolutely a matter of survival of cities and nations that we look at things at the systems level," he said. "And ultimately, we're being driven more and more in that direction." By way of illustration, Cole pointed out that 80 percent of the cars they sell in Japan are white. "It used to be all white cars. And, you know, why did everybody buy white cars? Well, the reason is the individual Japanese did not want to stand apart from the group. They did not want to be viewed as the individual. What do we have in America? We want to stand out and be individual. I understand the Japanese pretty well. Win-win is a philosophy to them that has real meaning, because you need to work together and you need not to separate yourselves from the pack. You're working together for mutual benefit. They don't have many lawyers to speak of; the whole consensus process there operates very differently than ours.

"Here in our situation we have a culture that says, 'Sure, we love winners.' We talk win-win now, but we look at it more in a zero-sum way, which means if I win, you're going to have somebody else lose. And we're trying to shift that. But it is a hard cultural transition for us to make. A very difficult cultural shift."

What remains is the monumental task of translating a systems approach, a win-win consensus process, to effective public action. But then the task may not be so monumental if both public and individual efforts are coordinated on the proper scale.

THINK LOCALLY

The proper scale is our geographic regions. Although our houses or apartments are located in one small distinct neighborhood, we work, go to school, shop, recreate, visit friends and relatives over a fairly large urban region, which, for the most part, requires a car. My own region is the Bay Area, where my personal center is the San Francisco neighborhood called Duboce Triangle. I walk to the store, the café, the movies, some of my friends' houses, or to the underground Muni station to take me downtown in fifteen minutes. My experience of the region is easily widened by jumping in the van and driving to Muir Woods in Marin County, circling around to visit a friend in Oakland, dropping off some work in Redwood City, having dinner in the North Beach section of San Francisco, and heading to Berkeley to see a play. The people, culture, and biological terrain I encounter in the ordinary course of my life make up the community where I feel most at home.

The poet Gary Snyder said that "we North Americans are on the verge of discovering—for the first time—our place. . . . After two centuries of national history, people are beginning to wake up and notice that the United States is located on a landscape with a severe, spectacular, spacey, wildly demanding and ecstatic narrative to be learned." What's to be learned is that each regional system has a unique character that can be experienced directly and concretely, pleasures and problems and all. It's a "landscape connectedness" that provides a new appreciation, understanding, and excitement about the distinct places in which we actually live, whereby everything is included: topography, climate, watershed, airshed, highway corridors, wetlands, bird migration, wildlife, trees, sewer systems, buildings, culture, people, and so on. As Snyder put it: "a profound citizenship in both the natural and the social worlds."

Robert Yaro, former Boston city planner and director of a planning research institute at the University of Massachusetts, would agree with the emergence of this new form of citizenship. After conducting numerous personal interviews, Yaro told Tony Hiss in *The Experience of Place* that people today have become "very articulate and outspoken concerning the special qualities they care about in their communities." As a result, Yaro added, "there's a ferment in the country about land values that hasn't been seen since . . . the 1920s." I'm glad to attest, based on my own interviews, that people are concerned about the special qualities of their communities in places as diverse as Carson City, Nevada; Batavia, Illinois; Menno, South Dakota; Mechanicsburg, Pennsylvania; and New York City.

The importance of this growing sense of regional place cannot be undermined, as it forms the bedrock of social action. When we discover the personal and public value of a place, we become motivated to protect its integrity. As Yaro said, personal "stewardship springs from connectedness—it gives people back a sense of thinking responsibly on behalf of the whole community." At the same time, it's important to remember that each community is its own "relatively autonomous sub-totality," as the language of modern science would have it. Each community has an impact on its surrounding region; each region affects the state; each state affects the nation; and ultimately the nation depends on and affects the whole global environment. While that holistic view may indeed reflect social and scientific reality, seldom does effective action spring from such a weighty concept. "Think *locally*, act *locally*," urges a new generation of "bioregional" advocates, worried that environmental hazards are undermined if they're perceived as distant abstractions, worried that we're thinking about a hole in the ozone layer over Greenland rather than the toxics in the water coming out of our kitchen faucets. In *Dwellers in the Land: The Bioregional Vision*, author Kirkpatrick Sale relates how uncomfortable he once felt at a university symposium while being bombarded by a host of speakers demanding moral outrage over worldwide environmental problems such as endangered species, stratospheric pollution, and rapacious Japanese fishing methods. Finally Sale stood up and intervened:

> The issue is not one of morality, I said, but of *scale*. . . . The only way people will apply "right behavior" and behave in a responsible way is if they have been persuaded to see the problem concretely and to understand their own connections to it directly—and this can be done only at a limited scale. It can be done where the forces of government and society are still recognizable and comprehensible, where relations with other people are still intimate, and where the effects of individual actions are visible; where abstractions and intangibles give way to the here and now, the seen and felt, the real and known. Then people will do the environmentally "correct" thing not because it is thought to be the *moral*, but rather the *practical*, thing to do.

GRASS ROOTS

Again, the car is a vehicle of integration. If ever there was a means for us to realize the "effects of individual action" and feel ourselves planted in the here and now of environmental degradation, it's breathing dirty air while sitting alongside a strip of gas stations, motels, and fast-food stores in suburban traffic. It's a sad truth that we often feel most connected to a place when we see how we've stripped it of its natural integrity.

In fact, seeing and *feeling* what we're doing to our urban regions is spurring a new legion of citizens into public action. "In the last three years a strong group of activist leaders has shown up to delve into issues of urban development," asserted Ken Ryan, the Sierra Club's California transportation chair. "Up until now, especially among the Sierra Club's traditional leadership, the policy's been to draw a line around the city and protect what's outside of it. Now there's a solid body of us who are saying we've got to deal with what happens *inside* those boundaries. That's part of the environment, too. The air quality problems have really brought that to the fore." Ryan added that the largest group of volunteers in the Sierra Club's Bay Area chapter—eighty-five people—was working on transportation issues, from researching the travails of today's highway system to lobbying for alternatives like city bike paths. Furthermore, the transportation group had joined forces with the Sierra Club's urban-growth committee to begin shaping a transportation policy for the whole region. "What these issues are doing," said Ryan, "is bringing out a bunch of people who've never been activists before. It's a real interesting situation. We're empowering a grass roots movement to deal with transportation and urban growth through a forum such as the Sierra Club, which has leverage at the state and national level. I'm not sure what we're creating here, but it's coming."

The coming attraction is a grass roots movement, a participatory democracy, that is capable of upsetting hierarchical decision making and the us-versus-them models of doing things. "Our historical, adversarial method of conflict resolution tends to polarize personalities, cloud the commonalities of a problem, invite short-term (and shortsighted) solutions, and encourages heel-digging and saber-rattling rather than walking in step and sword-burying," wrote Richard Bangs in *Sierra* magazine. Only by bringing politicians, environmentalists, and developers together at the same table can our public representatives develop what Tony Hiss calls a "language of connectedness between social, environmental, and economic concerns." Once we view the urban ecosystem as an interrelated whole, we can begin creating regionwide solutions.

So far everyone agrees that traffic and pollution are bad for business; now the question is whether an appropriate plan can be drawn up using all hands. According to Building Industry Association president Gary Hambly, it's less a question than a dictate. "We absolutely need more ideal regional planning," he declared. "It's going to come from us all sitting down together and accepting the harsh realities and saying, 'OK, folks, this is it. How are we going to solve this?' Rather than duking it out in eleven jurisdictions using every rhetoric, excuse, and alibi possible, it's time to accept that if we're going to be a true society, and if we're going to meet society's needs, we have a responsibility to work in a more rational fashion. Leaders are going to have to emerge. Politicians are going to have to get their nose out of the polls because the civil rights movement would have never occurred if we were waiting for the polls to change.

"There has to be an overall plan that says, 'Here's where the transportation infrastructure is going to be, and here's how it can be best utilized. Here are the densities that make sense if you're going to take advantage of mass transit. Let's merge the twenty-eight bus districts in this region. Let's accept the fact that we're going to create this number of jobs that are going to create this amount of need for houses. Let's talk about parochialism, growth/no-growth, housing affordability, the job-housing balance.' All these fundamental issues can be discussed in this new forum of government regional planning. In fact, it's beginning to emerge, and that's really exciting."

REGIONAL VISION

Specifically, Hambly was referring to Bay Vision 2020, a citizen grass roots group formed in late 1989 to draft a plan to assure the Bay Area's "beauty, livability, economic strength, and the opportunities it affords those who live here." At best, the plan embodies an expanded sense of community while representing the Bay Area's paramount strategy for effective cooperative action.

Composed of thirty-one ethnically diverse professionals whose interests were based in city government, transportation, development, finance, education, and the environment, the Bay Vision group concluded after a year of public meetings that regional government was the only way to harness the Bay Area's dance toward environmental disaster. "We have no effective means for addressing the problems that cross city and county boundaries," said the panel's chair, Ira Michael Heyman, former UC Berkeley chancellor. He added that only a fundamental change in local government would allow the region to "tackle increasing traffic congestion, long commutes between home and job, shortages of affordable housing, loss of valued open space to urban sprawl, and deterioration of our economic base."

The first step would be the formation of a "Regional Commission." Rather than creating another dreaded level of government, the Regional Commission would consolidate existing single-purpose agencies. The first link would be the Bay Area Air Quality Management District, the Metropolitan Transportation Commission, and the Association of Bay Area Governments. Each agency would maintain its fundamental course of business. MTC would continue to corral funds for transportation projects from federal, state, and local coffers, but now it would have to consider how spending the funds would meet the commission's goal of maintaining ecological and economic vitality. The merger would also cause each agency to begin thinking how its particular actions would affect the other agencies, creating constant interaction and establishing a foundation of cooperation. As Bay Vision 2020 project manager Joe Bodovitz said, "The same group of people would have to think about air quality and transportation and land use—which are all parts of the same thing."

Ultimately, other single-purpose agencies such as the San Francisco Bay Regional Water Quality Board and Bay Conservation Development Commission would be incorporated into the Regional Commission. Policies could then be formulated to serve the entire region. Tax revenues from commercial and residential development could be funneled into a central account and evenly distributed to prevent the dominance of commercial development in one city. Affordable housing could be built inside urban limit lines and within walking distance of mass transit. Commercial developers could be made responsible for partially funding the roads, buses, and trains that surround their newfangled business parks. In sum, the merger of single-purpose agencies would assure that the Regional Commission's goals could be achieved on a wide political spectrum.

And who would be at the helm of this Regional Commission? A single governing board that, ideally, represents you and me—which is why regional government can be seen as a grass roots movement. According to the plan, the governing board must reflect "the racial, ethnic, social, and income diversity of the Bay Area." There would be fifty-seven commissioners, two-thirds of whom would be elected officials from the nine counties—mayors, city council members, county supervisors—and the rest would be drawn from the public. The public commissioners would be appointed by a ten-member panel consisting of regionally elected officials and two persons of "community stature and broad regional perspective," such as the president of Stanford University. Of course, under the specter of political appointees, it's easy to envision a city mayor choosing a sprawl-happy developer whose influence could deliver votes. But as long as the Regional Commission strives to uphold its goals of curbing sprawl, preserving air quality, revitalizing the inner city, and managing growth to ensure a high quality of life, perhaps politics as usual can be uprooted.

Furthermore, there is evidence from Minneapolis–St. Paul and Portland, Oregon, that regional governance can indeed be effective. The Metropolitan Council, which unites seven counties surrounding Minneapolis and St. Paul, has brought adversarial parties to the same table to consolidate social services, clean up pollution, and end lingering disputes over highway projects. The regional council that represents Portland's three counties has also succeeded in enhancing the quality of the life in the area. Marcia D. Lowe reports in *World Watch* that Portland has "successfully fended off sprawl and reclaimed valuable city space from the automobile. The city has increased its housing density by encouraging a blend of multi- and single-family homes in pleasant, compact patterns. Portland's vibrant downtown boasts such green spaces as a waterfront park, which was once an expressway, and Pioneer Courthouse Square, formerly a parking lot."

Bay Vision 2020 project manager Bodovitz, who is president of the California Environmental Trust, a nonprofit organization that fosters coop- eration among city and state agencies over growth and environmental protection, declared that the time was ripe for the Bay Area to set its own standard of regionalism. "We've got a lot of momentum worked up," he told me. "We've got a lot of support among a very impressive coalition of environmentalists, business leaders, and local government." Whether that momentum can be channeled into a state law mandating a Bay Area Regional Commission depends on four regional bills lingering in the legislature docket.

But even if the bills are defeated this time around—and they have plenty of opposition in Bay Area legislators fearful of losing control over their individual turfs—the seeds of regionalism have been planted from the individual to the federal level. Certainly Bay Area individuals favor region- alism. A 1991 poll revealed that 74 percent believed regional governance could deliver the area from daily traffic and ceaseless urban sprawl. At the state level, a group of transportation experts, government officials, and economic leaders have formed the California Transportation Directions Policy Committee. Led by former Caltrans director Robert Best, the com- mittee has drafted thirty-one state policies to encourage regional planning. The policies, according to the committee, are based on a holistic approach: "There is a recognition that the economy, energy and land-use policies, community values, and protection of the environment are all interwoven with transportation. A decision about one element affects all elements."

Holistic approaches are also emerging beyond California. In *The Expe- rience of Place*, Jim Riggert, director of operations for the American Farm- land Trust, offered an example of how Pennsylvania has begun to see the iniquity of single-mindedly paving the countryside. At a public meeting concerning a highway that would cut across Amish land, Riggert said, "more than a thousand Old Amish Order drove their buggies to the meeting hall and expressed their concern by simply sitting quietly in the audience in their black homespun suits." Their eloquent presence had such an effect on Pennsylvania's governor that he ordered work on the highway to be halted and a new route to be found. Riggert said the governor's act amounted to the first time that highway engineers considered their impact on the landscape and the first time that the "state transportation department has ever looked into the question of how a work of engineering will alter a way of life with the idea of actually protecting an ongoing, living culture."

At the federal end, holistic planning was bolstered by the 1991 passage of ISTEA, which turned over federal transportation funds to metropolitan planning organizations. In fact, ISTEA was designed distinctly to serve regional commissions in formulating comprehensive plans to meet air quality standards and relieve congestion. In the Bay Area, despite the political gamesmanship, it's nonetheless significant that environmental groups welcome the Transportation Act as a means of promoting regional planning and believe, as the Sierra Club's Ryan said, that it has "very good long-term benefits." It's promising that the Bay Area's Metropolitan Transportation Commission has also wasted no time in putting ISTEA funds to work. In early 1992 it inaugurated JUMP Start (Joint Urban Mobility Program), which unites forty transportation managers from federal, state, and local agencies. Among those represented are the Federal Highway Administration, Caltrans, the California Air Resources Board, the Bay Conservation and Development Commission, and RIDES for Bay Area Commuters. The partners have formulated congestion-relieving projects such as electronic toll collection on the Bay Bridge, a system that places sensors in both the toll plaza and cars, allowing commuters to zip across the bridge and receive a bill later in the mail; "intelligent highways" that relate changing road conditions to Bay Area commuters via road signs; roving tow trucks to clear away accidents faster; more call boxes; and improved traffic-signal coordination along frequently traveled city routes. By no stretch of the imagination does JUMP Start constitute a revolution in arresting traffic and smog. Yet it's a significant example of regional cooperation, and perhaps JUMP Start may one day symbolize the spark of grass roots regionalism that released the Bay Area from the clutches of political and highway gridlock.

DIVERSITY

Most every transportation and land-use expert I met agreed with Ken Ryan of the Sierra Club that regionalism "was coming." The experts also agreed that when urban planners brought a holistic vision and interagency policies to America's cities, there was no telling just how those cities would look and function. John Woodbury, AC Transit board director and former Oakland city planner, casually offered that the rise of regionalism was "just a maturation process." He stated that the look of our urban regions, their balance with wildlands and agricultural space, would have to pass through many more cycles of ownership and use before they settled into a mature, healthy form. Europe, he pointed out, has already fought its land-use battles. The pattern of European towns and countrysides was formed out of 150 generations, whereas the most "mature" lands in America have barely witnessed eleven generations, not counting Native Americans.

The European model was often mentioned in my travels. Nearly everyone praised the character of European cities and villages; their dependence on mass transit; their sensible gas tax; their adherence to strict urban-limit lines; and their preservation of agricultural space. Everything over there was so quaint and tidy and shaped and planned out. It was all very . . . European!

The maturation of America's urban regions will be quite different. Or let's hope so. When I was in Montana I talked with Cliff Martinka, the chief biologist for Glacier National Park. He had just returned from Germany. "A beautiful land," he said. "But on the other hand, the country has been simplified at the hand of man. They have *designed* that country precisely the way they want it to be." Every square yard of countryside and forest seemed groomed and ecologically manipulated toward a certain look. Such autocratic design runs counter to the American sensibility. Our mature regions will certainly reflect our bold American perspective, our love of innovation and technology, our ecological pride and vested interest in wildlife and wildlands. As our respect for the landscape continues to mature and deepen, our indefatigable American youth, our sense of the land as unpredictable and shifting, and our affinity for adventure and entrepreneurship are bound to be worked into the formula for managing and renewing our regions.

Our most difficult task in managing sustainable regions will be establishing urban-limit lines and controlling growth, which remains linked with economic plenitude. Yet that mentality can be conquered by shifting the emphasis from how an area can reap more profit to how it can become more livable. Harold Gilliam of the *San Francisco Chronicle*, one of the first environmental reporters in the nation, states that an area's growth should be decided upon by the people themselves, not urban planners wielding population forecasts. "Instead of accepting hard-and-fast population projections as a picture of an inevitable future," he writes, planners "might present the public with alternatives, saying, for example: 'Here's what we need year by year in the way of water, freeways, schools, roads, sewers, fire and police protection and taxes under conditions of unlimited growth, slow growth and no-growth. This is what it would be like to live here under the various growth scenarios.'" Given this holistic picture of the region, residents can make their own decisions on growth, decisions based on their own standards of livability and prosperity, not the standards of greed and power of many developers and politicians.

Most important, though, for our urban ecosystems to function at the height of utility and livability, they must return to citizens the most highly regarded American quality of all: choice. That is what our current car-and-road-dominant regions have robbed from us. The most frequent complaint I heard from frazzled commuters was that there was simply no other damn way to get to work. The car has gone from a symbol of freedom to a symbol of dread not because we have outgrown our need or love of the car—on the contrary, our relationship with technology is more entrenched than ever—but because our land-use practices have forced us to rely on the car as our sole means of transportation. Understandably, our enmity is going to be directed at the vehicle of our frustration. What is needed to save the car, to restore the pleasure of driving, and to revitalize our urban regions is the return of *diversity*.

The more mature an ecosystem, the more complex and diverse it becomes, making available a multitude of various niches, various roles for different organisms. It's also axiomatic in the science of ecology that complexity and diversity within a particular ecosystem guarantee stability. Writes leading bioregionalist advocate Kirkpatrick Sale: "A setback or calamity for one species in a fragile system of only ten is much more debilitating than in a system of several hundred—it could even lead to the system's overall collapse—which is why a temperate forest is likely to be more stable and recover from calamity more quickly than a subarctic tundra. In an ecosystem without centralization and hierarchy, where the natural tendencies to centrifugality and diffusion have full play, diversity and complexity of both animal and plant species are the inevitable consequences." The similarity to urban ecosystems is clear: with regional planning that diffuses centralized decisions and policies, diverse transportation and land-use practices are the inevitable consequences. The analogy is also clear to Michael Replogle, of the Institute for Transportation and Development Policy in Washington, D.C.: "Just as an ecological system is healthiest when it displays great diversity and differentiation, so too is a transportation system most healthy and robust when diverse modal options are available to those moving people or goods. A transportation system dependent on only one or two modes of transport is far more susceptible to disruption and system failure."

Professor William Garrison, the sagacious dean of UC Berkeley's transportation department, agreed that diversity was the key to deep change. Diversity, he believed, would restore "choices to the public." Garrison envisioned "renewing" the unitary highway system we have now by taking the present corridors and space and building segregated byways for different types of vehicles. "You've got to get the tear weight [engine weight] of the vehicle down relative to the load weight. We use a 3,000-pound car to haul 200 to 300 pounds of people. We use 35,000-pound trucks to haul 45,000 pounds of cargo when the average load capacity of a truck is more like 60,000. It's crazy.

"One of the more obvious things to do with trucks is to get them into special lanes. That begins to open up what you can do with automobiles because when you take the 80,000-pound truck away, you begin to worry less about bumping into them with your light vehicle. That's one thing— chisel away at getting the trucks in their own facility. That may seem like an expensive thing to do, but actually it's inexpensive because if you put the trucks on their own facilities then you can build the streets and structures and things that they need, and tailor those to the trucks. And we would stop building every lane in the street as if it had to accommodate a big, heavy truck.

"When you separate out the trucks then you can begin to think about entirely different classes of automobiles. There's one that I've been interested in which is a 500-pound car, a $5,000 vehicle that carries one-plus person. I'd like to see that as a commuter car. This is a car that exists in prototype. General Motors has it. It goes zero to sixty-eight in about eight seconds. It gets 115 miles per gallon. It's just for commuting. It's only three feet wide so you can put a stripe down the middle of the lane and you can have twice as many as you had before. Parking is no problem. But you can't worry about mixing that car in with 3,000-pound vehicles so you construct barriers. The thing is to provide a vehicle that is specialized for the job. As an extreme example, my mother-in-law is eighty-something and she can hardly see. She has terrible mobility problems, so she can't drive an ordinary automobile. What you need is maybe a 500-pound Nerf ball car that goes maybe fifteen miles per hour. Maybe just had a joystick that you point to where you want to go and pull back on when you want to stop. Begin to think about letting many flowers bloom."

Initiating the change was a relatively simple matter of "picking out little market niches where it seems like a good thing to do and just getting started. And there's some natural market niches around." For instance, he offered, retirement communities had no use for wide streets and 3,000-pound vehicles, and could easily adopt (no, not Nerf balls) "small, benign personal vehicles that were inexpensive and easy to use, like a golf cart."

Above all, Professor Garrison insisted that deep change must evolve from people's own real needs and desires. He didn't give a hoot about social awareness or what people *said* the world needed (he could look out his window and see all those Berkeley radicals running aimlessly around campus); his philosophy was, just give them something new to try out. "Let people vote for what they're willing to pay for, and let's put political effort behind that. Let's get feedback going so that the transportation system can be tuned to fit what they want." He believed that people's growing ecological awareness would serve as a corrective to stagnant policies and inventions. "There are enough people who are socially aware who affect policy. If a market niche opens up for a sixteen-cylinder commuter car that gets five miles to the gallon, there are enough people in the socially aware group to thwart that niche by saying that it's not socially acceptable. There's enough of them so that I don't think we're really in danger of inventing things that would be ecologically undesirable. I don't think society's at risk in that way."

POCKETS OF RENEWAL

Indeed, given the ecological and political fomentation, some innovative market niches are presently being filled by innovative planners and developers and economists. In the region I know best, the Bay Area, a significant market niche is opening up in that increasingly dreaded haven of traffic and pollution, Contra Costa Valley. The gorgeous rolling hills surrounding the junction of Interstate 580 and Interstate 680 near the city of San Ramon represent some of the most prime property for residential development in the country. Less than five miles away in either direction are the two major job centers, Bishop Ranch and Hacienda Business Park, soon to be home to 75,000 new jobs. What if a 2,300-acre residential community was built on those hills, a community that provided affordable housing, that didn't transgress the county's urban-limit line, and that provided a transit system that shuttled residents to either business park in less than ten minutes? Wouldn't such a development obviate the need for a large chunk of cars and reduce pollution in the area? Indeed it would, said Darryl Forman, president of just such a planned community, called Windermere. That and, of course, make a large chunk of money for the partners who own it.

I talked to Forman in his classy Windermere office located in Bishop Ranch. With his shoulder-length silver hair and wire-rim glasses, he was certainly not my idea of a wealthy developer. He reminded me of an elderly guy on the sidelines at a Grateful Dead concert, a sly grin on his face defining the very essence of "what a long strange trip it's been."

"Our generation has been very remiss," Forman began. "If you look at the history of the Bay Area, no major infrastructure pieces, with the exception of BART, have been placed here by our generation. All the bridges, highways, and all the major energy-production things were done before. We have literally lived off the investment of our forefathers, and where we did build some small thing, we bonded the sucker and gave the damn bill to our children. The essence of this YUP generation has been, I'm going to get it all now and I'm going to let my kids pay for it.

"I have a theory about what you need to drive all this planning and development stuff. In the end you have to have some kind of overall philosophy. Right now there's a tremendous concern about what's happening to the family. The family's really been torn apart, primarily because it takes at least two incomes to buy a house. In America, unlike other countries, housing is looked on as an investment and not a utility. So everybody struggles like hell to buy one. You got to jump on the log and go downstream with everybody else. Well, being so job-dependent means that you're spending far too much time away from home, which is made worse by an improper transportation system. You get an advancement in your position and they require you to move over here, or you lose your job and move over there. You're constantly looking for the centroid between where Spouse One works and Spouse Two works. Which means you don't have any stability for your family. Your children develop friends, and then one year later they're in another school. Or they have to be dropped off at day care on your way to work, which has no relationship to where they live and play, but where you work.

"So there are all of these things that tear and rip at this family structure and the end result—and I'm no sociologist, I guess I'm a pseudo-sociologist—is that in this valley you have a high incidence of wife beatings, major drug use, and a great divorce level. Even in this cranberry, double-neck community, there's lots of bashing and crashing and smashing. My sense is that we can change those things by building a community that has a lot of options for employment. When we are finished the housing will be diverse with respect to cost. Windermere would run the gamut of density, from twenty-unit lots to single-home, half-acre lots. You could start with a small place at a higher density, something like a three-story-type flat. Theoretically, you could move around in the community, depending on your income, and still relate to the same schools and the same open spaces. There's also a high probability—considering there are seventy thousand jobs that are eight minutes away by public transit—that you're going to find employment nearby. We figure thirty-five percent of residents will be employed locally. Then, the real critical thing is that if you have a transportation system which will access employment anywhere in the Bay Area, you've got it made. Both spouses could work locally, both spouses could work regionally, or they could change jobs. By having a good infrastructure system like that, married to diverse housing choices, you can introduce a kind of neighborhood stability that isn't available in your normal white-picket-fence community."

Windermere plans to feature a diverse transportation system revolving around light-rail trains and buses. There would be shuttles to the two major business parks, as well as foot and bike paths. Windermere would also be the terminus of a Sky Train system, similar to the one in Vancouver, that would connect to BART. Residents could commute to jobs in nearby Concord and Walnut Creek, or farther on to Oakland and San Francisco. Because Forman's proposed Sky Train system will cost about $800 million and cover two counties and five cities, he has been knee-deep in turf battles with politicians for five years. While attempting to raise money for the rail system through every avenue possible, from city revenues to federal matching funds, Forman has invariably locked horns with politicians courting their own agendas. Some are afraid their constituents will scream about rail lines running through their backyards; others are married to the idea of more roads; while others want no change at all. Yet Forman points out that his crusade has been longer than most politicians' stays in office, allowing him to "transcend various political viewpoints, be more idealistic, and really begin to deal with solving transportation problems for the whole region."

Forman has faith the project will succeed. In 1990 he helped lobby successfully for a sales tax increase for transportation in Contra Costa County, and firmly believes that regional cooperation among developers, environmentalists, and politicians is improving. In the end, of course, it all comes down to money. If Windermere succeeds in bringing a sense of community to residents and providing easy transit to jobs throughout the Bay Area, it can only increase the land value of the surrounding area. "The better the project is, the better conceived, and the better received it is, the higher price I can get for the land next door," Forman said. He smiled. "Yes, it's nice to have control."

While Windermere today is still a cow pasture, other integrated communities are nearing completion. In architectural circles, the best known is Laguna West, located in suburban Sacramento County. Designed by San Francisco architect Peter Calthorpe, Laguna West will eventually be home to 10,000 people and feature jobs (Apple Computer is building a 300-employee facility), stores, restaurants, and civic buildings all within walking distance of affordable town houses. Calthorpe calls his development model "pedestrian pockets." Located in the center of town is a public park—a pocket—that is also the hub for mass transit to carry people out of the community. That cars are regarded as second-class citizens in Laguna West is evidenced by the presence of narrow streets and wide sidewalks, and by the fact that garages are located in the back of the housing lots. Ultimately Calthorpe would like to see such pedestrian pocket communities spread across the county, linked by transit rather than highways. Calthorpe is certain people will not miss their cars "if you give them an environment they might want to walk around in."

Architects Andres Duany and Elizabeth Plater-Zyberk are also promoting communities that people will want to walk around in, what they call "Traditional Neighborhood Development." Their ideas are realized in Seaside, a resort community on Florida's panhandle that captures the look, feel, and pace of a small Southern town in the 1940s. The success of Seaside, for both residents and architects, has led a flock of developers to the doorstep of Duany and Plater-Zyberk, who have been hired to reconfigure a shopping mall in suburban Maryland as a traditional town square; convert a strip shopping center along Cape Cod into an old-fashioned Main Street; and apply their traditional principles to a whole cluster of towns and villages in Orlando, Florida. They are also key designers of two of the nation's most ambitious urban tracts to link housing, commerce, and mass transit—the 900-acre Playa Vista development in Los Angeles and the 4,500-acre Daniel Island development in Charleston, South Carolina. "The only permanent solution to the traffic problem is to bring housing, shopping, and workplaces within walking distance," Duany and Plater-Zyberk said in 1990. "Americans are ready for the return of the town. The signs of a revival of interest in community on a smaller scale are everywhere." And to keep the revival on course, "Americans need to be reacquainted with their small-town heritage and to be persuaded of the importance of protecting the human habitat every bit as rigorously as the natural habitat."

HERE AND NOW

Visionary developers like Forman and urban architects like Calthorpe and Duany and Plater-Zyberk represent a future of integrated urban regions. Working alongside the visionaries, though, is a new generation of economists determined to relieve traffic and pollution on today's streets and highways. These economists are striving to give a forceful nudge to Professor Garrison's market niche solutions by involving the drivers themselves. "People need to consider the impact of driving on others," said

Michael Cameron, an economist and air pollution expert for the Environmental Defense Fund. Cameron wants drivers to consider their environmental impact in terms of saving money. "If we are forced to pay for congestion, if we are forced to pay for pollution, when the price goes up, we will consume less as a society," he said. To make drivers pay for congestion and pollution, Cameron and other environmental economists are drafting plans with "market-based incentives."

A market plan is based on the notion that drivers do not pay a fair share for "consuming" the roads. In reality, roads are not free. We all "own" them by paying gasoline taxes and vehicle registration fees that in part fund their construction and maintenance. Ideally, then, everyone should receive the same benefit from the roads. But that's not the case. Some people use the roads more frequently, and that causes inequities. And it's not only distance, it's density. A driver who uses the highway at rush hour increases the congestion, causing everyone else to spend more money on wasted gasoline (most of which goes to feed an idling engine) and waste time and therefore work wages. Furthermore, since clustered, stop-and-go cars turn the skies a dirtier shade of brown, ultimately that pollution is going to rain down on us and lead to higher health-care bills.

According to Cameron, drivers who use the roads the most should be required to pay the most. "That is consistent with the principles of our economy," he said. "The price is a balance of supply and demand. We have a fixed supply of roadway, but it's underpriced and people are overconsuming it. It's what the economists are now calling 'demand management.' Raise the price to decrease the consumption of the roadway."

To encourage people to drive less during peak hours, share rides, and take mass transit (assuming, of course, it's available), economists are developing "incentives." These incentives include imposing a surcharge on existing toll roads, bridges, and main corridors of public highways during peak commute periods. Since a road increases in value when it's most in demand, commuters would have to pay a higher fee for traveling at seven A.M. than at nine. Perhaps the uproar would cause some businesses to stagger their work schedules, allowing employees to avoid driving during standard rush hours. Revenues raised during peak travel times would be spent to provide more car pool lanes and space for mass transit on frequently traveled corridors.

"What we're offering," said Cameron, "is something that's sort of a zero-capital outlay. The roads are already there, we use the same cars—so that all of a sudden has great appeal." Some of Cameron's futuristic ideas do, however, entail some slight modifications. One scheme would have a magnetic strip on the bottom of your car that records distances and locations and times of the day by running over sensors embedded in the highway. You would get a bill at the end of each month. Another technology would allocate, say, 650 miles per driver per month. You'd be issued a little plastic card. You'd stick your card in a meter in your car so that the car would run. But if you had more than 650 miles on your card the engine wouldn't start. You could buy more miles at various ATM-like machines; or, if you had a surplus, you could go to the same machine and get mileage credit or cash. Save up for that big trip to the Grand Canyon. Make money off habitual car users. You'd even have a slot in your car meter that would accept the cards of carpoolers or hitchhikers.

Throughout the country there are several (and more down-to-earth) market-incentive proposals before city, state, and federal governments. They include plans for businesses to provide preferred parking to employees who arrive in car pools, as well as provide a monthly allowance to employees who ride mass transit to work. Even more radical—and sensible— is the proposal by UCLA urban planning professor Martin Wachs to "cash out free parking." Instead of providing workers with free parking spaces, for which they have to pay property owners approximately $100 a month, employers should give the $100 directly to each employee, and then charge $100 a month for each parking space. That way, a person who arrived at work in a car pool of four people would only have to pay $25 every month. That's an extra $75 of pocket change. However, current federal tax laws allow employers to deduct free parking spaces from their yearly expenses, so their incentive to charge for parking is not exactly overwhelming. But like so many initiatives associated with reducing traffic and auto emissions, Wachs's parking proposal is currently gaining favor in Congress.

All these market niches and market incentives are exciting. They are tiny openings into a revitalized urban ecosystem, a sort of dabbling in the future. But like other fledgling efforts (such as those by the South Coast Air Quality Management District to clean up L.A.'s troubled skies) these maneuvers are, ultimately, dependent upon an integrated regional strategy. A region itself is one large market niche. And to fill a niche that size (say, the size of the greater Houston area) will require the coordinated effort of every conscious influence who lives there. Who else but Everybody Concerned is going to rebuild a major interstate so that it can separately accommodate large trucks, small commuter vehicles, and regular cars? Who's going to OK ripping up whole city blocks and rebuilding urban centers? Who's going to tell suburban developers that they need to have interconnected rail, pedestrian, and bicycle pathways? Who's going to provide fair-share housing? Who's going to decide how to share regionwide property revenues, set limit lines, manage growth, and set aside greenbelts? Who is going to decide that drivers start paying fees for miles traveled? Who but all of us together?

This is planning at the systems level. And for proof that such an approach works we can turn to the city of Curitiba in southeastern Brazil. As Deborah Bleviss and Peter Walzer report in *Scientific American*: "The city's transportation system revolves around five radial express lines reserved exclusively for buses. These arteries are connected by interdistrict lines, and the whole system is linked to neighborhoods by feeder lines. Land-use ordinances have encouraged the establishment of residences and businesses near bus stops. As a result, Curitiba enjoys one of the highest rates of motor vehicle ownership per capita and one of the lowest rates of fuel consumption per vehicle in Brazil."

Of course, no one who sits in traffic and ponders the massive cement sprawl would think that America's urban transportation ecosystem will be restored anytime soon. However, all the pieces are there, ready to be picked up by urban regions and assembled, abetted by an expanding ecological awareness, encouraged by new technologies, backed up by the new federal Transportation Act. There is just one last set of here-and-now solutions that should be added to the picture, and that is what you and I can do. We can get involved socially—put pressure on civic leaders, join a citizen-action group, and vote for people who have some sense of how (spiritually and scientifically) the modern world works. Individually, we can reduce traffic and pollution by driving sensibly and saving gas, which means avoiding unnecessary speeding and, conversely, unnecessary idling; by using public transit, riding a bike, and walking; by trying to live close to where we work; by buying a fuel-efficient car and keeping it properly maintained; and by taking an extra moment to consider what we need at the store to avoid unnecessary trips.

On the road I crossed paths with those inclined to say that such individual actions have no impact, those of the just-one-more-won't-make-no-nevermind school of thought. These are the ones driving down the freeway with their tinted windows rolled up, bad music blaring, blind to the cars and landscape surrounding them. Unaware of the environment, they are the ones who help keep us all stuck in terminal gridlock.

THE LAST PLEASURE DRIVE

"We affirm that the world's magnificence has been enriched by a new beauty," wrote the poet F. T. Marinetti in his manifesto for the Italian Futurist art movement in the early part of this century. The Futurists had adopted the automobile as the supreme emblem of beauty and a new era. It rejected the passivity of the past, tapped the underlying forces of nature— of speed, of dynamism!—and forged a new relationship between humans and their creation. "We want to hymn the man at the wheel, who hurls the lance of his spirit across the Earth, along the circle of its orbit."

"I think the car is the twentieth-century sculpture," renowned model-maker Gerald Wingrove said. "I think the artist of the twentieth century is the engineer, and to me this is the nearest man has ever got to nature, to produce something which is an extension of himself and to make it beautiful as well."

Today, heading into the twenty-first century, the car brings us into direct touch with nature, with both its fullness and its denigration. A casual drive across any urban region brings us into direct contact with the crucial problems of our time: overpopulation (congestion), pollution (smog), and lack of integrated planning (patches of green space and a proliferation of sprawl and urban decay). We actually feel the denigration as we drive; it settles into the pit of our stomach. Even several weeks after the Rodney King revolt in L.A., the effects could still be felt on the region's freeways. "Maybe it's just my perception," Steve Rauch, of the San Fernando Valley, told me, "but people are driving differently. I first noticed it on the San Diego Freeway. But it's all over. They're driving faster, and when it gets crowded you see people driving down the center divider or on the shoulder areas. They never did that before. It's a form of civil disobedience—the hell with the rules! L.A.'s not the same." But then no part of the country is the same.

That distant horizon where the road meets the sky is not so distant anymore. It's here now. We've hurled the motorized lance of our spirit across this land and extended ourselves into every developable nook and cranny of space. In our Wild West rush for the good life and progress we've forgotten the ecosystems where we live. We drive from inner cities that have been forsaken to edge cities that are without character or soul. We can drive from one side of the country to the other, but it's an identical story. We can drive in widening, twisting circles, but the only place left to go is right here where we're parked. It's high time to preserve and renew the region we inhabit. To make it a more harmonious place to live. And drive.

Selected Bibliography

Abrahamson, David. "A Storm of Protest." *Autoweek*, July 24, 1989.

Abrahamson, Eric. "A Fork in the Road." *Diablo*, January 1991.

Altshuler, Alan A. *The Future of the Automobile: The Report of MIT's International Automobile Program*. Cambridge: MIT Press, 1984.

Baker, Russell. "Slaves to Oil." *New York Times*, August 22, 1990.

Bay Area Council. *Roadmap to the Future: Solving the Bay Area's Transportation Mess*. Bay Area Council, October 1989.

Bay Area Economic Forum. *Market-Based Solutions to the Transportation Crisis*. Bay Area Economic Forum, May 1990.

Bellah, Robert, et al. *Habits of the Heart: Individualism and Commitment in American Life*. Berkeley: University of California Press, 1985.

Berman, Marshall. *All That Is Solid Melts into Air*. New York: Simon & Schuster, 1982.

Berry, Wendell. "Out of Your Car, Off Your Horse." *The Atlantic*, February 1991.

Bleviss, Deborah L., and Peter Walzer. "Energy for Motor Vehicles." *Scientific American*, September 1990.

Briggs, John, and F. David Peat. *The Turbulent Mirror: An Illustrated Guide to Chaos Theory and the Science of Wholeness*. New York: Harper & Row, 1989.

Brodsly, David. *L.A. Freeway: An Appreciative Essay.* Berkeley: University of California Press, 1981.

Brooke, Lindsay, et al. "40-MPG CAFE." *Automotive Industries*, May 1991.

Brown, Lester, et al. *State of the World 1992: A Worldwatch Institute Report on Progress Toward a Sustainable Society.* W. W. Norton, 1992.

_____. *State of the World 1991: A Worldwatch Institute Report on Progress Toward a Sustainable Society.* W. W. Norton, 1991.

Calthorpe, Peter. "The Post-Suburban Metropolis." *Whole Earth Review*, Winter 1991.

Caro, Robert. *The Power Broker: Robert Moses and the Fall of New York.* New York: Random House, 1974.

Center for Auto Safety. "The Safe Road to Fuel Economy." Washington, D.C.: Center for Auto Safety, 1991.

Cervero, Robert. *Suburban Gridlock.* New Brunswick, N.J.: Rutgers University Press, 1986.

Davis, Mike. *City of Quartz: Excavating the Future in Los Angeles.* New York: Verso, 1990.

Deen, Robert L., ed. *The Alternatives to Gridlock.* California Institute of Public Affairs, 1990.

Denny, Jeffrey. "King of the Road." *Common Cause Magazine*, May/June 1991.

Dettelbach, C. G. *In the Driver's Seat: A Study of the Automobile in American Literature and Popular Culture.* Westport, Conn.: Greenwood Press, 1976.

Difiglio, Carmen, K. G. Duleep, and David L. Greene. "Cost-Effectiveness of Future Fuel Economy Improvements." *The Energy Journal*, Winter 1990.

Duany, Andres, and Elizabeth Plater-Zyberk. "The Second Coming of the Small Town." *The Wilson Quarterly*, Winter 1992.

Dyer, Davis, Malcolm S. Salter, and Alan M. Webber. *Changing Alliances: The Harvard Business School Project on the Auto Industry and the American Economy.* Boston: Harvard Business School Press, 1987.

Ehrlich, Paul R. *The Machinery of Nature.* New York: Simon & Schuster, 1986.

Exline, Christopher, Gary L. Peters, and Robert Larkin. *The City: Patterns and Processes in the Urban Ecosystem.* Boulder, Colo.: Westview Press, 1982.

Flamsteed, Sam. "H$_2$ Oh!" *Discover*, February 1992.

Flavin, Christopher. "Blood and Oil." *Sierra Club Yodeler*, February 1991.

Flink, James. *The Automobile Age.* Cambridge: MIT Press, 1988.

Freedman, David H. "Batteries Included." *Discover*, March 1992.

Garreau, Joel. *Edge City: Life on the New Frontier.* New York: Doubleday, 1991.

_____. *The Nine Nations of North America.* Boston: Houghton Mifflin, 1981.

Gilliam, Harold. "Seven Arguments for the Elimination of the Automobile." *San Francisco Chronicle*, October 29, 1989.

Glenn, Jerome C. "Conscious Technology: The Co-Evolution of Mind and Machine." *The Futurist*, September–October 1989.

Halberstam, David. *The Reckoning*. New York: William Morrow, 1986.

_____. "An American Romance." *Popular Mechanics*, May 1989.

Hardin, Garrett, and John Baden, eds. *Managing the Commons*. W. H. Freeman, 1977.

Hillman, James. "Psychological Fantasies in Transportation Problems." Center for Civic Leadership, University of Dallas, December 1978.

Hillman, James, and Michael Ventura. *We've Had a Hundred Years of Psychotherapy and the World's Getting Worse*. San Francisco: Harper San Francisco, 1992.

Hiss, Tony. *The Experience of Place: A New Way of Looking at and Dealing with Our Radically Changing Cities and Countryside*. New York: Alfred A. Knopf, 1990.

Jacobs, James. *Drunk Driving*. Chicago: University of Chicago Press, 1989.

Jacobs, Jane. *The Death and Life of Great American Cities*. New York: Random House, 1961.

Jerome, John. *The Death of the Automobile: The Fatal Effect of the Golden Era, 1955–1970*. New York: W. W. Norton, 1972.

Kahn, Brenda, ed. *Transactions: Transportation News for the Nine-County San Francisco Bay Area*. Metropolitan Transportation Commission, August 1990–November 1992.

Kay, Jane Holtz. "Applying the Brakes." *The Nation*, September 17, 1990.

Keats, John. *The Insolent Chariots*. Philadelphia: J. B. Lippincott, 1958.

Keller, Maryann. *Rude Awakening: The Rise, Fall, and Struggle for Recovery of General Motors*. New York: William Morrow, 1989.

Kwitny, Jonathan. "The Great Transportation Conspiracy." *Harper's Magazine*, February 1981.

Lapham, Lewis. "Democracy in America?" *Harper's Magazine*, November 1990.

Lawrence, Jennifer. "How Volvo's Ad Collided with the Truth." *Advertising Age*, November 12, 1990.

Lauer, A. R. *The Psychology of Driving: Factors of Traffic Enforcement*. New York: Thomas, 1960.

Leavitt, Helen. *Superhighway—Super Hoax*. New York: Doubleday, 1970.

Lee, Patrick. "Addiction to Oil Still Drives U.S." *Los Angeles Times*, March 24, 1991.

————. "Bush Plan Leaves Alternative Energy Out in the Cold." *Los Angeles Times*, February 21, 1991.

Lewis, David L., and Laurence Goldstein, eds. *The Automobile and American Culture*. Ann Arbor: University of Michigan Press, 1980.

Lovins, Amory B., and L. Hunter Lovins. "Make Fuel Efficiency Our Gulf Strategy." *New York Times*, December 3, 1990.

Lowe, Marcia D. "Out of the Car, Into the Future." *World Watch*, November/December 1990.

Machalaba, Daniel. "States Try New Tactic to Curb Auto Traffic: Cut Highway Spending." *Wall Street Journal*, April 8, 1992.

Mandel, Leon. *Driven: The American Four-Wheeled Love Affair*. Briarcliff Manor, N.Y.: Stein & Day, 1977.

Marsh, Peter, and Peter Collett. *Driving Passion*. Winchester, Mass.: Faber & Faber, 1987.

Marshall, Jonathan. "Analysts Blame U.S. Recession on Auto Industry." *San Francisco Chronicle*, December 9, 1991.

Motor Vehicles Manufacturers Association. *Facts & Figures '90*. MVMA, 1990.

Novaco, Raymond W. "Aggression on Roadways," in *Targets of Violence and Aggression*, R. Baenninger, ed. New York: Elsevier Science Publications, 1989.

Pettifer, Julian. *Automania: Man and the Modern Car*. Boston: Little, Brown, 1984.

Postman, Neil. *Amusing Ourselves to Death: Public Discourse in the Age of Show Business*. New York: Viking Press, 1985.

Prigogine, Ilya, and Isabelle Stengers. *Order Out of Chaos: Man's New Dialogue with Nature*. New York: Bantam Books, 1984.

Range, Peter Ross. "Playboy Interview: Lee Iacocca." *Playboy*, January 1991.

Rapaport, Richard. "Gridlock." *San Francisco Focus*, January and February 1992.

Register, Richard. *Ecocity Berkeley*. Berkeley: North Atlantic Books, 1987.

Renner, Michael. "Rethinking the Role of the Automobile." Worldwatch Paper 84, June 1988.

Rifkin, Jeremy, ed. *The Green Lifestyle Handbook: 1001 Ways You Can Heal the Earth*. New York: Henry Holt, 1990.

Sale, Kirkpatrick. *Dwellers in the Land: The Bioregional Vision*. San Francisco: Sierra Club Books, 1985.

San Francisco Bay Guardian staff. "You Can't Get There from Here." *San Francisco Bay Guardian*, October 10, 1990.

Scharff, Virginia. *Taking the Wheel: Women and the Coming of the Motor Age*. New York: Free Press, 1991.

Schneider, Kenneth. *Autokind vs. Mankind: An Analysis of Tyranny, a Proposal for Rebellion, a Plan for Reconstruction*. W. W. Norton, 1971.

Schreiner, Tim. "Golden Gate Area Losing Its Glow." *San Francisco Chronicle*, May 18, 1992.

Schreiner, Tim, and Ramon G. McLeod. "Suburbs Big Winner in Census— Cities Continue to Decline." *San Francisco Chronicle*, January 25, 1991.

Sperling, Daniel. *New Transportation Fuels*. Berkeley: University of California Press, 1988.

Stern, Jane, and Michael Stern. *Auto Ads*. New York: Random House, 1978.

Tucker, William. "The Wreck of the Auto Industry." *Harper's Magazine*, November 1980.

Turkle, Sherry. *The Second Self: Computers and the Human Spirit*. New York: Simon & Schuster, 1984.

U.S. General Accounting Office. "Traffic Congestion: Trends, Measures and Effects." Washington, D.C.: Government Printing Office, November 1989.

Vale, V., and Andrea Juno, eds. *Re/Search #8/9: J. G. Ballard*. Re/Search Publications, 1984.

Wachs, Martin, and Margaret Crawford, eds. *The Car and the City: The Automobile, the Built Environment, and Daily Urban Life*. Ann Arbor: University of Michigan Press, 1992.

Waxman, Henry A. "The Environmental Pollution President." *New York Times*, April 29, 1992.

Wolfe, Tom. *The Kandy-Kolored Tangerine-Flake Streamline Baby*. New York: Farrar, Straus and Giroux, 1965.

Woutat, Donald. "Bold Designs, Exotic Fuels Seek to Curb Oil Appetite." *Los Angeles Times*, March 25, 1991.

Wright, Karen. "The Shape of Things to Go." *Scientific American*, May 1990.

Yergin, Daniel. *The Prize: The Epic Quest for Oil, Money and Power*. New York: Simon & Schuster, 1991.

Zuckerman, Wolfgang. *End of the Road: The World Car Crisis and How We Can Solve It*. Post Mills, Vt.: Chelsea Green Publishing Co., 1991.

Index

K. T. BERGER is brothers Kevin and Todd Berger. Kevin lives in San Francisco and works as an investigative reporter and editor. Todd is a psychotherapist living in Marin County, California. They both come from the automotive wilds of Los Angeles, and they collaborated on a previous book, *Zen Driving*.